The Philosophy Of Sex:

Contemporary Readings

Edited by

ALAN SOBLE

ROWMAN AND LITTLEFIELD
Totowa, New Jersey

Barnard
HQ
12
-P47
1980

Library edition first published in the United States of America, 1980, by Rowman and Littlefield, Totowa, New Jersey

Library of Congress Cataloging in Publication Data
Main entry under title:

The Philosophy of sex.

   Bibliography: p.
   1. Sex-- Addresses, essays, lectures. 2. Sexual ethics-- Addresses, essays, lectures. I. Soble, Alan.
HQ12.P47 1980   306.7   80-15302
ISBN 0-8476-6292-6

Acknowledgements

I wish to thank the authors of the essays included in this volume. They have been a helpful and patient bunch of people.

   Conversations and correspondence with a number of people contributed enormously to my introductory essay as well as to my continued interest in the philosophy of sex. These people include Richard Hull, Alison Jaggar and Lee C. Rice. Countless others, unfortunately, must go unnamed.

AGS
New Orleans, Louisiana

Printed in the United States of America

Contents

Alan Soble

An Introduction to the Philosophy of Sex

I

Joined together in this volume are some of the most interesting essays on the philosophy of sex written during the decade 1968–1978. Philosophers have only recently been concerned with human sexuality. In saying this I am not ignoring masterpieces such as Plato's *Symposium*, nor am I overlooking the fact that many of the major Western philosophers had something to say about human sexuality (see, for example, Donald Verene's *Sexual Love and Western Morality*). But much of the thinking of the great philosophers on sexuality has the appearance of an "aside" and is rarely central to their more general philosophical interests. In contrast, during the last few years philosophers of various persuasions and approaches have begun a self-conscious and systematic attack upon some of the philosophical problems that arise in attempting to understand human sexuality. Before this century it was perhaps safe to sidestep the apparently trivial question "What is sexual desire?" and to disregard the potentially revolutionary suggestions of the question "What sexual activities are normal, natural, or moral?" But in our time, after the work of Freud, the easy answers are no longer satisfying. In part, the interest that philosophers have been expressing quite recently in human sexuality has been elicited by the demand that they speak out on the issues that are important in daily life and that they do so in a way in which they can be readily understood. The philosophical discussion of sexuality, then, can be seen as part of the trend in philosophy to satisfy the need for relevance without obfuscation.

It is not difficult to be more specific about the reasons for the current attention that philosophers are paying to sexuality. In the 1970's there had been widespread criticism of sexual attitudes and sex-roles that emerged with the Women's Movement and the Gay Movement. Both these social movements have had unmistakable and dramatic effects on the routines of our daily lives and have compelled us to be serious about such questions as "What *is* sex?," "What is sex *for*?," and "What is *good* sex?." The Women's Movement has challenged the standard view of the connection between anatomical sex and social roles, and the Gay Movement has challenged the standard view of the connection between anatomical sex and sexual preferences and behavior. These challenges have not been taken lightly; the reaction against them has managed to stir up so much debate and controversy that it has become largely the responsibility of the philosopher to analyze the conflicting views and to find out what is philosophically pleasing and displeasing about the conflicting positions. The essays collected in this volume do not answer all or even most of the pressing questions, but they do establish a firm foundation for further thinking about sexuality.

Since Freud, the study of sexuality has been proceeding full-steam ahead in psychology, sociology, anthropology and medicine, and this scientific research has been impressively successful in unraveling the empirical side of this aspect of human behavior. It is appropriate that philosophers have come to realize that their special talents, techniques and knowledge can be brought to bear not only on the methodological and theoretical questions that are suggested by the research done within these other disciplines, but also on the specifically conceptual, social and political questions about human sexuality. This conclusion, however, does not come easily, for it is reasonable to complain that in this century there has been too much talk about sexuality. Once we consider the volumes that have been written on sexuality by the scientists, in which they dissect the finest features of the mechanical reactions of our organs and document with the most reliable statistics our patterns of behavior; once we remember the volumes published by the pornographers, who have provided the scientists with competition in the quest for an understanding of human sexuality and who claim that their approach and techniques are less detached and therefore yield more meaningful insight into this experience; and once we take stock of the outpouring of self-help sex manuals, the proliferation of sex-education courses and textbooks, and the superfluous availability of psychologists, those disguised Anns and Abbys, who are ever ready and willing to counsel us, with their *words*, on problems in marriage, love, and sex; do we really welcome the philosopher adding to this almost overwhelming symbolic confusion?[1] Fortunately, philosophy is immune from this sort of worry, in part because philosophy is the discipline which discusses, analyzes and clarifies the results of the scientist, the value of the pornographer, and the assumptions of the sex-educator, but also in part because philosophy is self-reflective and can ask whether the situation is so bad that philosophers should (or should not) add to all this talk about sexuality. In a moving passage, Engels wrote:

But what will there be new? That will be answered when a new generation has grown up: a generation of men who never in their lives have known what it is to buy a woman's surrender with money or with any other social instrument of power; a generation of women who have never known what it is to give themselves to a man from any other consideration than real love or to refuse to give themselves to their lover from fear of economic consequences. When these people are in the world, they will care precious little what anybody today thinks they ought to do; they will make their own practice . . . and that will be the end of it.[2]

And, I add, only that will be the appropriate end of the philosophy—or any other talk—of sex.

The reader of this book will discover that the essays have been divided into two Parts, one called "The Analysis of Sexual Concepts," the other called "Sexuality and Society." This division between, on the one hand, the conceptual and, on the other hand, the social and the political, is a common way of artificially categorizing differences in emphasis. Throughout the book the major questions that the authors deal with are "What is sex?," "What is sex for?," and "What is good sex?." The essays in Part I approach these questions from what might be loosely characterized as an analytic perspective. What the reader finds is bold conjecture of theories about the nature of human sexuality, the ushering of logical and semantic evidence, the presentation of striking behavioral and experiential counterexamples, the unwrapping of metaphysical niceties, and the clarification of our sexual linguistic machinery. This is not true, of course, of all the essays in Part I. Nor is it the case that the essays in Part II never engage in this type of analytic philosophy. The essays in "Sexuality and Society," however, do concentrate more on the interpretation of the causal connections that exist among human sexuality, politics, economics, and the "institution" of analytic philosophy itself. The essays are divided into these two Parts primarily because I have found it convenient and helpful to do so. When I inspect the essays they seem "naturally" to fall into a certain pattern that is captured by the organization I have selected. If my intuition is correct, then one *could* read only one (or the other) Part and one would not be missing much that is relevant to that Part; however, one *would* be missing a broader overview of this set of questions.

To a certain extent my forthcoming discussion of the content of the essays is simply a summation of the major points made by the authors and a catalogue or outline of the significant disagreements that arise among them. But the reader will notice that a number of themes (for example, masturbation, bisexuality, the family, feminism, political economy) arise repeatedly in my discussion of the essays; these are themes I have chosen to emphasize despite the fact (often, because of the fact) that they are not precisely the themes addressed directly by the authors. A good deal of the introductory essay is development of my thinking on several pet topics in the philosophy of sex. In thus expressing my own point of view I use the anthologized essays as tools, rather than allow the introduction to serve passively as a vehicle for the essays themselves. The views that I hold with respect to the themes mentioned above, views which will receive some support in what follows, can be presented as a set of theses. These are offered as a guide to the rest of this Introduction.

Thesis 1. Human sexuality is not naturally (in a strong sense of that word) heterosexual. It follows that the particular form taken by human sexual behavior will be determined primarily by social, historical and economic factors. Under the proper circumstances, persons could emerge into adulthood as practicing bisexuals; they would enjoy sexual relations regardless of the sexual anatomy of their partners.

Thesis 2. Despite the fact that we are living in a time of sexual "permissiveness," there persists a disparagement of masturbation (auto-erotic sexuality). During the last decade, of course, much has been written defending masturbation,[3] but that the practice requires such continual defense indicates to me that some very strange, hidden and powerful forces are at work in our society. I think these forces are simultaneously responsible for the disparagement of masturbation, the oppression of women, and the failure of liberal society to extend to homosexuals the full protection of its own notion of "rights."

Thesis 3. The family is one of the crucial elements, or forces, in the production of a consciousness that so far has lent support to a social system in which women and homosexuals are oppressed. My argument in favor of raising children in extended families depends on the promised ability of such a family (if one still wishes to use that term) to allow the development of bisexuality and to foster the psychological prerequisites for relating to other people in a noncompetitive, nonownership way.

Thesis 4. The other crucial force is our system of political economy: liberal capitalism. I find it plausible that the functional requirements of liberal capitalism include the maintenance of the family as we know it and the resulting predominant pattern of heterosexuality. I am less sure about the question of the appropriate, reliable or possible tactics to rely on in bringing about massive social change; it is not yet clear to me whether changes in the family will follow primary changes in political economy, or *vice versa*.

These claims emerge in my discussion of the essays included in Part II of this volume. However, the reader will note that in my discussion of the more analytic papers (Part I) some hint is already given of where I am going.

II

As far as I know, Roger Taylor's paper ("Sexual Experiences") is the first contemporary essay to deal with human sexuality from an analytic perspective. Taylor criticizes a thesis he attributes to Jean-Paul Sartre: that we can use the fact of the existence (or experience) of sexual desire to solve the philosophical problem of the existence of other persons. According to Taylor, Sartre claims that sexual desire is essentially intentional in that a person could not experience sexual desire unless there were other persons who are the object of the desire and who are the occasion for its being elicited. On the face of it, there seems to be nothing surprising in Sartre's view. If sexual desire is a desire to engage another person in a relation of some sort, and if I experience sexual desire, then I am assured that at least one other person exists. As a solution to the problem of the existence of other persons (which is the same problem as the problem of the existence of other minds), however, this argument has a flaw, for all that Sartre shows is only that *either* other persons exist *or* I never do truly experience sexual desire. (What I might be experiencing, and mistaking for sexual desire, are merely undirected stirrings.) But this is not the route taken by Taylor. Rather than denying, or raising doubts about, the existence of true sexual desire, Taylor argues that Sartre's analysis of sexual desire is incorrect. On Taylor's view, the existence of sexual desire entails only that we need acknowledge the existence of other *bodies* (fleshy items). Sexual desire, then, is a desire for contact with physical things and not necessarily for a relation with a conscious person. (Another way of stating Taylor's thesis is this: when saying what sexual desire is, we do not have to speak about any person beyond the person whose desire is being discussed.) Taylor, of course, is now not committed to saying that other persons do not exist, but only that some other argument is required to solve the problem of the existence of other persons.

It is interesting that Taylor's argument could be seen as a solution to a different philosophical problem, the problem of the existence of an "external" world (as G.E. Moore would put it) or of physical things. Even though Taylor speaks as if this were his argument (for example, he suggests that the experience of sexual desire can assure us that a tangible world exists), I think we ought to reject such an interpretation of his paper. The conclusion of such an argument would have to be: either other bodies do exist or I never truly experience sexual desire. But it seems odd to let the existence of physical things ride on whether I do, or do not, experience sexual desire; a more general argument for the existence of the material world seems to be required. (The argument, for example, falls into the type of solipsism that plagues Descartes' philosophical system. One who never experiences sexual desire— perhaps a rare, but not an impossible, person—would have no grounds for belief in an external world. The fact that my sexual desire assures me that an external world exists is no consolation to this rare person.) Furthermore, reading Taylor's argument in this way would undercut the philosophy of sexuality as a relatively autonomous area. For if we were to read the argument in this way, then the value of discussing sexuality would be primarily that it gave us insight not into sexuality *per se* but rather into more "important" questions of ontology. The philosophical discussion of sexuality would have only an indirect instrumental value; we would be affirming propositions about sexuality in the hunt for larger game. It is clearly wrongfooted, from the point of view of attempting to develop an autonomous philosophy of sexuality, to treat it as the hand-maiden of epistemology and ontology.

Taylor's essay, I submit, should be seen in this light. His conclusion is not an ontological one; rather, his thesis is that in explaining what sexual desire is, we need only refer to bodies which are the object of the desire, and not to other persons. The issue that is posed in this dispute between Taylor and Sartre can be stated using slightly different terminology. Is sexual desire a very narrow desire simply for the pleasure one has when having physical contact with the body of another person? Or, even it it does include (as a component) a desire for physical contact with a body and the pleasure thereby produced, is sexual desire a desire for something more than this that must, at least in the case of human sexuality, reflect the presence of mind, or spirit, or soul, or any of the things that minds are capable of (for example, intentions)? Taylor's view, not unjustly condensed, seems to be that sexuality is the pleasurable rubbing of skin against skin; there is nothing else that need be added to make an activity a sexual one. The opposing view is that human sexuality is more than just the rubbing of skin against skin; something is missing in an account of the *sexual* if it refers only to physical contact and pleasure. The conflict between these two views (the "reductionist" and the "expansionist") will be debated in several of the essays that follow Taylor's.

Thomas Nagel, in his "Sexual Perversion," proposes a Sartrean analysis of sexuality. Picking up on Sartre's notion of "double reciprocal incarnation" (from *Being and Nothingness*; see the essay "Sartre on Sex," in this volume, by L. Nathan Oaklander), Nagel argues that paradigmatic sexual activity involves not only desirings for another but also such elements as: desiring that the other recognize one's desire, the desire that the other be aroused by the other's recognition of one's desire, and (to achieve reciprocity) the recognition that the other also intends to arouse, in turn, by making one aware of the other's desire. In a paradigmatic sexual activity two persons enter into an ascent with one another, an ascent characterized by increasingly complex desires and recognitions of desires and intentions. (One simple way to capture what Nagel takes to be paradigmatic sexual activity is as follows: I am turned on because you are turned on because I am turned on because you are turned on because. . . . The pattern is more complex than this to the extent that not only am I turned on because you are turned on, but also I am turned on when I recognize that you intend to turn me on by getting me to notice that you are turned on. And so on.) What is unique about Nagel's account is that the brute, gut-level desire for sexual pleasure is modified in a typically human way; the expression of intentions, and their recognition, are necessary ingredients in the sexual experience. Nagel, therefore, clearly joins the camp of those who emphasize that sexual activity is essentially between persons rather than between bodies of persons. The difference between Nagel's view and Taylor's might be summarized: Nagel sees human sexuality as a highly complex phenomenon that occurs between persons who are capable of expressing intentions, while Taylor places the emphasis on a unidirectional desire for pleasurable contact with a physical thing.

Nagel's purpose in making this proposal was to be able to get a hold on the slippery notion of "sexual perversion." Having characterized the paradigm case of sexual activity, Nagel argues that the perversions are those sexual activities that deviate from this pattern of an ascent that occurs between two persons. Activities that do not involve the expression and recognition of intentions will be perverted, and will be more perverted the more they deviate from Nagel's "complete configuration." For example, the person who derives sexual pleasure from contact with a shoe performs a perverted activity because there is no possibility of a shoe recognizing an intention nor of a person expressing an intention to a shoe. Nagel's analysis of the perversions does divide the world of sexual activities into the perverted and the nonperverted roughly in the way in which we would ordinarily divide it up, simply because many of the standard perversions do not involve the reciprocal recognition of intentions (necrophilia, coprophilia, fetishism). But there are two major problems with his account. First, even though Nagel is successful in classifying such activities as bestiality and necrophilia as perversions, he is also "successful" in classifying the more mundane activity of autoerotic masturbation as a perversion. This counterintuitive consequence follows from the fact that in autoerotic masturbation there are no intentions expressed or recognized.[4] And second, if Nagel's analysis is an account of paradigmatic *sexual* activity, then activities which do not exhibit the complete configuration are not merely perverted but, more strongly, are not even *sexual* activities. (This point is made in the essays by Ketchum and Gray in this volume.) If it is true that for an activity to be sexual activity it must include the various stages in the ascent, then activities which lack the lower stages do not even qualify as sexual activities. These activities (shoe fetishism, necrophilia, and so forth) can still be called "perversions," but they cannot be called, more specifically, "sexual perversions." And so Nagel has not accomplished what he set out to accomplish. Another way of capturing this point is to say that Nagel has not provided an adequate analysis of the *sexual* itself. The reciprocal recognition of intentions is constitutive of many different human activities, and their presence or absence does not serve to pick out the sexual activities and only the sexual activities. This sort of criticism of Nagel can be found in Robert Solomon's "Sexual Paradigms."

Solomon agrees with Nagel that the *form* of sexuality is Sartrean, that sexuality is essentially a relation between persons and involves the reciprocal recognition of intentions. But Solomon argues that a specification of the form of sexuality alone does not distinguish sexuality from other human activities. What is needed in addition is a specification of the *content* of sexuality. The content of sexuality, according to Solomon, is the *goal* of the desire, or the reason why persons enter into an ascent of reciprocal recognition of intentions. Solomon claims that it is implicit in Nagel's account that the goal that persons have in mind is simply the experience of pleasure with each other. Now, this is not to say that Nagel's position is more like Taylor's than I have suggested; it is to say only that Nagel has a particularly narrow view of the content of the intentions expressed by persons in sexuality. Solomon believes that Nagel's specification of the content of sexuality is incorrect, that the intentions expressed in sexuality are not limited to intentions for or about pleasure. Rather, the goal of sexual activity is the interpersonal communication of the whole range of human emotions. On Nagel's view, what is expressed is the desire for physical sensation, whereas on Solomon's view persons express, in addition to this or as an alternative to it, such diverse emotions as love, hate, dominance, submissiveness, fear, disrespect, insecurity and indifference. What is *central* in sexuality is that some such emotion be expressed. Solomon's account, then, models sexuality along the lines of communication. And what might be communicated by persons in sexuality is not only the message that they want to experience pleasure, but a whole host of possible messages beyond this simple one.

The fascinating feature of Solomon's position is that he completes, in a sense, the "linguistic turn" in contemporary philosophy. The twentieth century is often characterized as the period in which philosophers turned their attention from questions about the world to questions about language. (It is often said that the Kantian question: "How is knowledge of the world possible?" has been replaced by the Wittgensteinian "How is communication by means of language possible?") But it is not that philosophers began to think that questions about language were more important or more challenging than questions about the world, but rather that answering questions about language provided one way (a new approach) to gain that knowledge of the world that had previously been sought "directly." Solomon's understanding of sexuality, as an example of this twist, is based on the assumption that revealing analogies can be established between linguistic communication and the communication that occurs, during sexual activity, through the medium of a *body* language. The messages that are communicated in sexual activity are not only or even very often expressed with *words*; rather, they are communicated by the gestures one makes with one's body. A very simple example: dislike or hatred can be communicated during sexual activity by causing the other to feel pain. Thus, if we do have a workable understanding of language and how we use it, we can draw conclusions about sexuality as long as the analogy holds up. In his paper "The Language of Sex and the Sex of Language," Hugh Wilder discusses the analogy between linguistic communication and sexual communication as well as the particular view of language that is presupposed by Solomon. Wilder is willing to grant that the analogy is a fruitful one; sexual activity is enough of a communicative activity for us to learn something about sexuality by focusing on the properties of language. But Wilder argues that the conception of language that Solomon relies on is not satisfactory. Solomon's mistake, he claims, is that he emphasizes spoken linguistic activity to the exclusion of written linguistic activity, and when conclusions are drawn by Solomon about sexuality, they are infected with this one-sided conception of the possibilities of language. For example, Solomon concluded that there is something suspicious about autoerotic masturbation, on the grounds that it does not involve the expression of emotions to another person—it is not a communicative activity. (That both Nagel and Solomon find fault with autoerotic masturbation follows from the fact that they embrace Sartre's view as to the form of sexuality. Communication and recognition of intentions quite clearly involve at least two per-

sons.) Wilder objects that by de-emphasizing the value and importance of written linguistic activity, which is characteristically
done alone and done *well* alone, Solomon has been unfair to masturbation as a worthwhile sexual activity. If Solomon had paid
more attention to written activity, he could have avoided the
counterintuitive conclusion that masturbation is a kind of second-
rate sexual activity (a sexist conclusion, says Wilder).

Janice Moulton, in her "Sexual Behavior: Another Position,"
replies to both Nagel and Solomon. Moulton argues that because
both Nagel and Solomon hold to a Sartrean view of the form of
sexuality, their analyses are better suited to an account of "flirtation and seduction" scenarios than to an account of the sexual
relations that occur between familiar partners involved in a long-
standing relationship. (Nagel's analysis of sexuality, importantly,
is derived from a description of, from his point of view, a *typical*
sexual exchange: two persons, strangers to each other, sit in a
cocktail lounge and look at each other through mirrors.) It is
quite likely, according to Moulton, that persons flirting with each
other upon first meeting engage in reciprocal recognition of intentions; and it is plausible that much seduction occurs when one
person attempts to get another person to recognize the expressed
desires and intentions. But Moulton claims that sexual activity between persons who are accustomed to each other, who have perhaps lived with each other for some period of time, cannot be
characterized in this way. What Moulton is pointing out, of
course, is that sexual activity between familiar partners is most often a rather straightforward affair, that it does not always or even
frequently involve the fancy items in the higher stages of Nagel's
complete configuration. On Nagel's account, we would have to
judge this sexual activity between familiar partners "perverted."
And so much the worse for Nagel's account. Nagel, however,
might want to respond, "Au contraire. So much the worse for sexual activity between familiar partners." By this he would mean
that sexual activity that involves his ascent is better sex, is more
satisfying sex, or is more exciting sex than sexual activity that occurs between familiar partners without the ascent. After all, married couples do report that after a length of time their sexual
interest in each other declines.[5]

Moulton has a response ready: sexual activity between strangers, even when it is preceded by Nagel's ascent, is often very miserable sex, while sexual activity between familiar partners is often
very satisfying, and can become more satisfying as the relation-

ship deepens. At this point her objection to Solomon's position is revealed. What makes sexual activity between familiar partners satisfying is just the fact that it *is* pleasurable. When two persons come to know each other well, and when they have had sufficient time to learn what it takes to "turn the other person on," then sexual relations between them have the potential for producing enormous pleasure. (In contrast, sexual activity between strangers can be dissatisfying because, not knowing each other, they fumble around.) Thus Moulton wants to re-emphasize the role of pleasure in sexuality, and to place a more narrow limit on the goal or content of sexual activity. As for Solomon's claim that sexual activity is not primarily employed to provide pleasure for the participants, but rather to provide a way of expressing emotions, Moulton says that it is sexual activity, more so than most other activities, that has the ability to provide this pleasure, and that the emotions can be expressed better by different, nonsexual human activities.[6] (As Alan Goldman suggests, love, for example, may be best expressed by getting out of bed on Sunday morning and doing the dishes left over from Saturday night.) Solomon is making sexuality carry too heavy a burden. Indeed, this seems to be a consequence of any position that argues that sexual activity is more than the rubbing of skin against skin. As soon as the "reductionist" position is rejected in favor of an "expansionist" account of sexuality, it follows that sexuality is elevated in status (it is not *merely* physical) because it performs some necessary and valuable human functions. These functions, we might note, can very easily serve as a justification (or: rationalization) of sexual activity. For suppose that unconsciously we thought that sexual activity was *prima facie* morally bad, or that performing an activity only for the sake of the pleasure to be gained was *prima facie* morally wrong. Yet we would still want to engage in sexual activity. We could retrieve or pardon sexual activity by saying that it essentially involves something more than mere physical desire, that it includes the expression and recognition of typically human intentions, or that it provides an extraordinary opportunity for relating with other persons on the truly important emotional level. Alan Goldman, in his "Plain Sex," develops this theme. Expansionist views of sexuality are infected, he claims, with our Platonic-Christian heritage which has always condemned the animalistic, pleasurable nature of human sexuality as morally questionable.

Goldman defends the narrow account of sexuality as the rubbing of skin against skin. In this dispute, then, he sides with Taylor against Nagel and Solomon, although his arguments are quite different from Taylor's. Like Taylor, Goldman sees sexual desire as "desire for contact with another person's body and for the pleasure which such contact produces," but Goldman does not advance this analysis in the context of a metaphysical discussion about the existence of other minds or persons. Rather, Goldman takes the path of trying to show that all other (expansionist) analyses of sexuality must be rejected because they yield either false or inconsistent views of sexual morality and sexual perversion. His narrow account of sexuality purports to capture the *core* of the notion of sexuality (hence, of course, his title).

Goldman objects to four analyses of sexuality which exemplify what he calls a "means-end" form. His choice of terms is misleading, for his criticism of these analyses is not that they portray sexual activity as a means, in the *causal* sense, for attaining specific ends, but rather that on these accounts sexual desire and activity have been linked *conceptually* to goals which Goldman thinks are extraneous to the essence (or core) of sexuality. The four accounts that he criticizes are those that conceptually link sexual desire to the goals of reproduction, love, communication, and interpersonal awareness. An analogy will help us to understand Goldman's criticism. Consider pie à la mode. The four accounts want to say that there is a conceptual connection between the pie and the ice cream; each analysis believes that a particular flavor of ice cream is an essential part of the pie. Goldman points out that pie is pie and ice cream is ice cream, and *if* there is a connection between the pie and ice cream, it is contingent and not necessary. Sometimes, according to Goldman, we can have the pie by itself (as in his plain sex) and sometimes the ice cream by itself (love or communication, for example), and when we mix the two, sometimes we cover the pie with vanilla and sometimes with butter almond. Thus for Goldman it *is* possible to use sexual activity as a means (causal) to attain something else, like love or babies, but that this is possible does not mean that any of these goals is necessary for an activity to be *sexual* activity. An analysis of sexuality should focus only on the pie. And as Goldman argues, this "least common denominator" is simply the desire to have pleasurable physical contact with the body of another person.

Goldman's complaint is not only that these analyses append something extraneous to sexuality, but also that when any of these goals is tied to the very meaning of sexual activity and desire, the result is a false concept of normal sexuality and a sexual morality that is either too restrictive or inconsistent, at least in practice. For example, the alternative analysis that claims that sexual desire is the desire to reproduce and that sexual activity is activity that tends to cause reproduction to happen, is too restrictive because (historically speaking) it has condemned, as immoral or as unnatural, activities which do not involve reproduction and yet which are significantly productive of pleasure and are widely practiced for that reason. Similarly, the account that claims that love is necessarily tied to sexuality yields a restrictive sexual ethic. If, says Goldman, it is the nature of love that it occurs in fairly infrequent and exclusive relationships, the view that ties together love and sex places too severe a limit on what actually *counts as* sexual activity. It also makes much behavior (that we *would* call sexual) inappropriate or even immoral. Goldman also suggests that this view of sexuality promotes the inability of persons to distinguish the basis of a sound marriage (a love relationship) from the basis of romance (a sexual relationship) and that this inability has disastrous consequences for those who marry for the wrong reason. (Note that Goldman's position does not entail that love and romance can never occur together. He means only that when they do occur together, it is a contingent fact about their occurrence. Also note that his position need not accept or reject the claim that people are happiest when love and romance occur together.) Finally, appending a goal such as communication or interpersonal awareness to sexual desire is also too restrictive, in part because such analyses tend to "overintellectualize" sexuality. Goldman wants an analysis that avoids these troubles and one that would not underestimate the purely animalistic features of human sexuality. He proposes, therefore, that sexual desire is a desire for pleasurable physical contact with the body of another person.[7]

But Goldman's account, as liberating and as down-to-earth as it seems, is not fully adequate, as can be seen by examining the connection he draws between sexual desire and sexual activity. Sexual activity, according to Goldman, is activity that "tends to fulfill" sexual desire. Because, on his view, sexual desire is the desire for physical contact with another body and for the pleasure thereby produced, sexual activity will be activity that tends to fulfill the desire for this pleasurable physical contact. This account of sexual activity, I want to argue, is at the same time both too broad and too narrow. It is too broad because it admits as sexual activities certain activities that clearly are not sexual, and it is too narrow because its excludes from the domain of sexual activity certain activities that are clearly sexual. To be more specific: the brute act of handing money to a prostitute would, on Goldman's account, be a sexual activity because it certainly does tend to fulfill the desire of the client to have physical contact with the prostitute. Without handing over the money before engaging in sexual activity with the prostitute, the client would not be able to satisfy his sexual desire. Thus, handing over the money is a necessary condition (in practice) and thereby "tends to fulfill" the desire. But surely we would want to say that handing over the money is not *itself* a sexual activity nor part of the sexual activity that the client is paying for. Of course, in some cases it might be true that the client does derive sexual pleasure from the mere act of handing over the money, but this fact does not help Goldman's account. First, it only applies to a small subset of all cases of a client handing money over to a prostitute, and for the cases in which there is no sexual pleasure derived from handing the money over, the act is still a sexual act on Goldman's account. Second, even if a person were to get sexual pleasure from handing over the money, this could count as a sexual activity but *not* on the grounds provided by Goldman. The act of handing money over does not satisfy the desire for physical contact with another person; more specifically, it satisfies the desire to hand money over to a prostitute and to experience the pleasure derived from doing so. Even when, therefore, sexual pleasure is derived from handing the money over, Goldman's analysis is incapable of describing this as a case of having a sexual desire. Goldman's theory has no way of explaining why the experience is a *sexual* one.

A somewhat more difficult example of how Goldman's analysis turns out to be too broad is the situation in which two persons are flirting with each other. Some flirting is meant to communicate signals which mean "if you are willing, I am willing" and is therefore an activity which tends to fulfill sexual desire if it initiates the appropriate causal chain. For that matter, merely *saying* to someone "Will you go to bed with me?" tends to fulfill sexual desire in the same way, if the answer is "Yes." On Goldman's account, then, this type of flirting, or simply asking that question, count as sexual activities. But I think we would rather say that flirting or asking questions are *preludes* to sexual activity and not sexual activities *per se*. If so, then Goldman's analysis is again too broad. (The root of the problem, apparently, is that the expression "tends to fulfill" is too weak to distinguish among preludes, ministrations, physical touchings intended to seduce, mountings, and so forth.) One rebuttal, however, does come to mind. If we were to say that some flirting is only a prelude to sexual activity and not sexual activity *per se*, then we *might* be forced to say that *foreplay* is not a sexual activity either—when compared, this time, to "actual" coitus. Thus, Goldman could try to defend his view by arguing that if we were to deny that some flirting is sexual activity we would also have to deny that foreplay is sexual activity. But to deny the latter is absurd. If correct, this rebuttal would allow Goldman's account to escape one objection. (I do not, however believe it is correct.)

An argument can also be given to the effect that Goldman's analysis is too narrow. Autoerotic masturbation does not count as a sexual activity on Goldman's account because it does not tend to fulfill the desire for physical contact with another body. Goldman does not find this a bothersome consequence of his theory, but he should have. Goldman, in this respect, is hoist by his own petard: his analysis succumbs to the same criticism that he levels at the other, expansionist accounts of sexuality. He had criticized the account, for example, that tied together sex and reproduction by pointing out that (1) the view entailed that some kissing was perverted (and it surely isn't), and (2) the view placed too severe a limit on acceptable sexual practices. But Goldman's view, in arriving at the conclusion that autoerotic masturbation is not a sexual activity at all, has the same effect; if autoerotic masturbation is not a full-fledged sexual activity, then (even if it is not exactly perverted) it is somehow highly questionable, and Goldman's analysis ends up disparaging a practice which is performed with a very high frequency. Goldman, however, is willing to say that autoerotic masturbation is a *borderline* case of a sexual activity when it involves fantasies about contact with another person's body. If this move were plausible, then perhaps we could accept Goldman's analysis of sexual desire and activity. But when we understand Goldman's account, it is clear that masturbation could never be a borderline case of a sexual activity. His position entails that masturbation is not a sexual activity, and we shall have to reject his analysis for yielding such a counterintuitive consequence. (Goldman's position entails that the expression "autoeroticism" is self-contradictory. It surely isn't.)[8]

How can Goldman suppose that the presence in the imagination of the bodies of other persons makes autoerotic masturbation at least a borderline case of sexual activity? Is it not true that one

who masturbates while thinking about physical contact with another person is no closer to tending to fulfill the desire for contact
with the particular body imagined or any other body, than one
who masturbates without such fantasies?[9] The person who masturbates while gazing on centerfolds is equally distant from satisfying sexual desire in Goldman's sense. If so, then the presence in
the imagination of "pictures" of bodies, or the presence before
one's eyes of a photograph, does not change an otherwise nonsexual activity into a borderline case. There is a connection, I think,
between Goldman's attempt to admit masturbation as a borderline case of sexual activity when it is accompanied by imaginings
and his saying that masturbation, like voyeurism, is a substitute
for "the real thing." (Goldman here unfortunately lapses into the
talk of the locker room and of television advertisements.) We
might want to say that the person who watches others engage in
sexual activity or walk about in the nude is relevantly similar to
the person who "watches" another person in a fantasy or in a
photograph ("through a fantasy" would be like "through a pair of
binoculars"). But it would make better sense to say that the voyeur's activity tends to fulfill the desire for contact with another
person's body more than does the activity of the fantasizing masturbator, either because sight (in contrast to imagining) is a kind
of contact in real space, or because the voyeur, unlike the person
gazing on centerfolds, has the opportunity to make his presence
known to the solidly existing persons being watched. On Goldman's account, then, there is some reason to claim that voyeurism
is a borderline case, but masturbation even with fantasies still does
not qualify. I have been assuming, of course, that with respect to
an account like Goldman's it even makes sense to speak of "borderline" cases. With respect to an account like Nagel's, "borderline" makes appreciable sense: those activities which fail to
achieve the complete configuration yet attain at least one stage of
the ascent can be seen as borderline cases, to be contrasted to activities which do not even involve the lowest rung. But the structure of Goldman's analysis does not permit such a discrimination.
If an activity tended to fulfill sexual desire even slightly, it would
not be a borderline case but a full-fledged sexual activity. We
could still say, of course, that it was not a very efficient sexual activity.

If the sexual is to be characterized as the rubbing of skin against
skin for the sake of the pleasurable sensations that are produced,
as in Goldman's account, then it seems to follow that the presence

of *another's* patch of skin is eliminable. For the pleasurable sensations that are produced by contact with another's patch of skin
can certainly be produced, and produced well, by rubbings that do
not rely on the presence of the other. A shoe, for example, might
do just as well. The problem that arises here appears clearly if we
examine an account of sexuality that has much in common with
Goldman's but which attempts to overcome the main drawback of
his theory—the fact that masturbation was excluded from the domain of sexual activity. This account would say that Goldman has
not really exposed the bare level or core of sexuality, that there is
a sexuality that is "plainer" than his plain sex. Sexual desire, on
this view, is the desire for certain pleasurable sensations (*period*;
no mention of contact with another body).[10] Now, if this is what
sexual desire is, then autoerotic masturbation very well counts as
a sexual activity as long as it does or can produce these pleasurable sensations. It qualifies because sexual desire is no longer necessarily connected with the existence of another body. In a sense
such a position tries to take Taylor and Goldman to their logical
extremes. It outreduces the reducers: it not only eliminates love or
communication, but it also eliminates another body. But the problem with this account is that it has a difficult time specifying
which pleasurable sensations are to count as the sexual ones.
Without such a specification there is no way to distinguish sexual
desire from other desires.

There are perhaps three ways of approaching this problem. One
might say that the sexual sensations are those sensations produced
by the manipulation of the sexual organs and those organs closely
related to the genitals. Sexual desire, then, would be the desire to
experience the pleasurable sensations associated with the workings of the sexual organs. This answer is not terribly satisfactory
because, for example, the rubbing of the backs of the knees or
slight pressure applied to the wrist can in some circumstances be
highly sexual, even when the genitals are left entirely unmanipu-
lated and there is no promise that they will be manipulated. Such
rubbing or pressure and the perception of sexual pleasure that accompany them are not always correlated with genital arousal and
genital pleasure. Furthermore, it is obvious that genital manipulation itself does not always correlate with the experience of sexual
pleasure.[11]

Another approach might say that *all* pleasurable sensations
produced by the manipulation of *any* part of the body count as
sexual (a Freudian kind of answer). The answer clearly handles

the difficulty we had previously with the pleasurable sensations produced in the wrist without genital arousal. But the cost of this victory is that this view must admit too many pleasurable sensations as the sexual ones. There is some point, after all, in distinguishing the pleasure felt in the mouth when drinking cool water on a warm and dry day, and the pleasure felt in the mouth when performing an oral sex act. And if the position retreats and says, instead, that all parts of the body are (simply) *capable* of producing sexual pleasure (which is undoubtedly true), we are still left with the problem of saying what makes the manipulation of part *x* sexual on one occasion but not sexual on another occasion, when on both occasions the physiological components are likely the same or at least overlapping.

A third answer would say that the sexual pleasures are those pleasures that we learn about by having contact with the body of another person, and it would add that once we learn how to produce sexual pleasure by such contact we can later produce them by ourselves. But, of course, not all contact with another person yields pleasurable sensations, not all pleasurable sensations we do get from contact with another person are sexual pleasures, not all the pleasurable sensations produced by contact with another person can be produced alone, and not all the pleasurable sensations one can have alone are copies of pleasures one has with another person.

In "The Good, the Bad and the Perverted," Sara Ann Ketchum discovers another major fault with the accounts of sexuality offered by Nagel and Solomon. Ketchum is not terribly concerned with the debate between the reductionists and the expansionists, nor with the question of the status of autoerotic masturbation. Instead, Ketchum is bothered by the fact that the theories of sexuality advanced by Nagel and Solomon entail that acts of rape may be examples of *good* sex. By this she does not mean that according to Nagel and Solomon rape is a *morally* good act; as a matter of fact, both theories say very little about the morality of sexual behavior. But if we can evaluate sexual acts as being either good sexual acts or as bad sexual acts—like we can evaluate cars, football teams and books as being either good or bad things of their kind—then it turns out that for Nagel and Solomon, rape could very well be a good sexual act. If a good football team is a football team that does well what football teams are supposed to do (such as winning most of its games and at least taking part in the play-offs), then a good sexual act is a sexual act that achieves what sexual acts are supposed to achieve. On Nagel's account, a good sexual act (in this nonmoral sense) is one that involves reciprocal recognition of intentions; but, as Ketchum points out, an act of rape may very well involve several stages of Nagel's ascent and therefore qualifies as good sex. (The rapist expresses his intention to rape and to frighten the victim; the victim recognizes this intention and, in turn, the victim's recognition is recognized by the rapist.) Similarly, on Solomon's account, good sexual acts are those that involve the successful communication of emotion; but many acts of rape will be successful in this sense and so qualify as good sex.[12] However, Ketchum does think that Nagel is at least partially correct in believing that the reciprocal recognition of intentions is an important ingredient in sexual activity. She therefore attempts to refine and improve Nagel's analysis by offering an analysis of "mutuality" that eliminates the possibility that rape is a case of good sex.

Robert Gray, in his "Sex and Sexual Perversion," begins by discussing some of the tangles that arise in ordinary attempts to give an account of "sexual perversion" that characterize it as *unnatural* sexual behavior. (The claim that unnatural sex is perverted sex can be found, for example, within the doctrines of Roman Catholicism.) Gray argues that a workable account is one that claims that a sexually perverted act is a sexual act that gives the actor sexual pleasure but one which is maladaptive or counterproductive from the point of view of the natural function of sexual activity. What is interesting about Gray's view is that (1) he dismisses the narrow view that *the* natural function of sexuality is reproduction, and yet he embraces the wider view that the natural function of sexuality is both the reproduction *and* raising of children, and (2) as a result, many of the standard perversions and many acts that others might want to classify as perverted (masturbation, homosexuality) turn out not to be perverted at all, given certain facts about the society in which they take place (in particular, whether practice of an act interferes with childraising). In advancing this account of the perverted *as* unnatural, Gray is at odds with Solomon and Goldman, who reject that connection. For Solomon and Nagel, perverted sexual acts are those acts that deviate from the patterns they propose are central to human sexuality, while for Goldman "perversion" is a simple satistical notion that picks out acts that are rarely or infrequently performed. Now, if it were true that the communication of emotions in sexual activity were done *naturally*, and if it were true that the reciprocal recognition of intentions were a *natural* feature of human sexual interactions, then there would be grounds for saying that even Nagel and Solomon connect "perversion" with "unnatural." But I take it that the communication of emotions and the recognition of intentions are "natural" only in that very broad and very unhelpful sense of "natural" in which anything done by anyone is natural. (See note 21.)

In "Perversion and the Unnatural as Moral Categories," Donald Levy sides with Gray and argues that perverted acts are unnatural in a nonvacuous sense of "natural." But Levy has two disagreements with Gray. In the first place, Levy argues that not only are the perversions unnatural, but also that they are *immoral*. In this regard Levy is advancing a position that divides him not only from Gray but also from Nagel, Solomon and Goldman, all of whom wish to deny the ordinary belief that the category "perversion" necessarily carries moral weight. Levy's second disagreement with Gray provides the grounds for his saying that perverted acts are immoral. Whereas for Gray unnatural acts are those acts which are contrary to the natural function of sexuality, for Levy the unnatural acts are those acts which deprive persons unnecessarily of basic human goods. If an act deprives a person unnecessarily of a basic human good and the act is done to secure sexual pleasure, then, for Levy, the act is sexually perverted. Levy sums up his view in the slogan "Perversion degrades is a necessary truth."

One of the interesting consequences of Levy's view is that rape turns out to be perverted. In discussing Nagel and Solomon, Ketchum criticized their views because they entailed that rape could qualify as good sex (in the nonmoral sense of "good"), and she suggested that because rape was *bad* sex (not mutual), at least from the point of view of the victim, it was less preferable than having no sex at all. Levy, however, wants to go further than this; rape, on his account, is not only bad (in the moral sense), but is also perverted, and it is perverted *because* it is morally bad. Ketchum, for one, would raise an objection to the conflation in Levy's position between the immoral and the perverted. She would argue that it makes plain sense to say that an act is immoral but not perverted (some cases of adultery with deception might fit this classification), and that an act could be perverted but not immoral (coprophilia, for example, is one of the standard perversions but hardly needs to be done immorally). Levy apparently would respond to this type of objection by saying that he is, in part, making a proposal for how we should use the concept "perversion." It is true, he admits, that we have not been in the habit of saying that to rape a person is to commit a perverted act, although we do normally say it is immoral. Levy would like for us to see the world of sexual activities in a new way, but what practical effects such a change in seeing would have is not clear. Certainly the problem of rape is an important one (and after Susan Brownmiller's *Against Our Will* it is impossible to turn one's back). In trying to understand the causes of rape behavior and to reduce its occurrence, which conceptual framework is the best one? On Nagel's and Solomon's view, rape may very well be good (nonmorally) sex; this conceptualization *could* undercut the move to eliminate rape. After all, if rape is good sex, then it does have some value, even if the value is not a moral value. And, as Ketchum suggests, if rape is good sex, then as a crime it is not as objectionable as it otherwise would be, for the victim stands to get something of value from it (e.g. having her recognition of intentions recognized?). Levy's conceptualization might have the same sort of consequence. We do ordinarily feel some degree of pity toward those who perform perverted acts (which pity may not, of course, be justified), and sometimes we even excuse the perverted because we tend to equate the perverted with the mentally ill. Thus, to say that rape is perverted is to offer the rapist a potential excuse for his behavior. Now, Levy might insist that we ought not to feel pity toward the perverted, nor should we look upon the perverted as somehow sick. (He might admonish us not to be so patronizing and paternalistic.) To prevent his conceptualization from undermining the move to eliminate rape, then, Levy might have to propose that we undergo yet another change, a substantial change in our emotions surrounding the perverted and the mentally ill. These changes may be commendable, but they cannot occur overnight. In the meantime we still have the problem of rape.

In the final essay of Part One, "Sartre on Sex," L. Nathan Oaklander speaks to a number of issues that arose in the preceding essays. His major concern is to lay out in some detail Sartre's position on sexuality: the phenomenon of double reciprocal incarnation, the situation in which the persons experiencing sexual desire are conscious of themselves as both subject and as object; the claim that during the experience of sexual desire (more precisely, during double reciprocal incarnation) we are able to overcome the essential conflict that exists between ourselves and other persons and that, therefore, the experience of sexual desire marks an ideal state; and the astonishing view that *all* sexual acitivity, because it undermines the ideal state of sexual desire (by satisfying and thereby terminating the desire), is perverted. The claim that all sexual activity is perverted is one that denies the approach taken in the preceding essays, in which it was assumed that some cases of sexual activity would be *clearly* nonperverted (for example, Nagel's "unadorned sexual intercourse") while other cases of sexual activity would be *clearly* perverted (for example, coprophilia). The task suggested by this approach is simply to find the criteria to be used in putting sexual activities into one class or the other. Sartre is arguing that there are no such criteria, for there are no clear cases of nonperverted sexual activity. As outrageous as the claim sounds, it does have an important connection with Gray's view of the perversions. Gray argued that the perversions ought to be understood as sexual activities that have effects contrary to the function of sexual activity (the debate, of course, is over how to characterize this function). Sartre's view can be seen as similar to Gray's: for Sartre, any (sexual) activity is perverted which runs counter to the *role* that sexual desire plays in the solution to the ontological conflict that exists between myself and the other. Even so, one might be thinking, it is absurd to argue that all sexual activity is perverted. To a certain extent Oaklander tries to defend Sartre by saying that the claim that all sexual activity is perverted is not evaluative but only "ontological." But it is not clear why *this* saves Sartre's account.

Despite the apparent implausibility of Sartre's position, his idea that the experience of sexual desire places persons in an ideal state in which they can conquer the essential tension that exists between themselves and others is a fascinating thought. It is common to report that during the experience of heightened sexual desire (and, especially, during the period of sexual arousal before the sexual desire can be satisfied), persons feel as if the barriers existing between them and other people crumble almost instantaneously. This break, commonly, is followed by a rapid reconstruction of the barriers when sexual desire has been satisfied (especially in *men*, after orgasmic release). Erich Fromm, for example, in his *The Art of Loving*, mentions that persons who experience a breakdown in barriers often make the mistake of confusing this breakdown with "love." This confusion is perhaps the same confusion that is lamented by Goldman, the incapacity to distinguish a romantic involvement (a sexual involvement) from a love relationship. But on the other side are those who maintain either that persons who have a good sexual relationship will tend to become closer in other, nonsexual ways, or (more strongly) that the good sexual relationship is just what a "love" relationship consists of (such a view can be found in Wilhelm Reich, for example). On this view, then, the confusion spoken of by Fromm and by Goldman is not a confusion at all, but rather a very accurate perception.

Whatever we might want to make of the fact that during sexual desire or sexual arousal the barriers between ourselves and others break down—where the choice seems to be between seeing the experience as a confusing illusion of love or as love itself—the observation that the barriers are reconstructed immediately afterwards remains. Because it is sexual activity that brings about the satisfaction and the termination of the desire and therefore destroys the ideal state in which we are "at one" with each other, perhaps we ought to take Sartre's classifying all sexual activity as perverted in an evaluative way. Then we might propose that we ought to aim only for those situations in which the barriers are broken down even if that means placing ourselves in a state of never-ending sexual arousal and abandoning sexual satisfaction (at least in the sense of "satisfaction" that makes the orgasm the satisfaction). Norman O. Brown, in his *Life Against Death*, talks about the Adamites, a sect that practices *coitus reservatus*: the Adamites engaged in continuous foreplay but did not attempt to achieve satisfaction through orgasmic release. These people, we might say, lived in a constant state of sexual desire and arousal without the resolution of that desire. But at the same time, the failure to terminate the desire means, according to Sartre, that they would be living ideally with each other, in that the existential barriers would remain forever broken down. Why is it, we might ask, that in our culture we place so much emphasis upon the achievement of the orgasm? (Is it because, living in a business culture, we tend to quantify experience? Only orgasms—like dollars—can be counted. The other pleasures of sexual activity cannot be quantified.) If we believe Sartre, there is much to be lost in this emphasis, and much to be gained from looking away from the orgasmic experience as the essential ingredient of sexual activity. Again, note the sharp contrast between this anti-orgasmic viewpoint and the overwhelming emphasis placed upon the achievement of *true* orgasm by the Reichians. Yet Reich offers the *same* reason for emphasizing the orgasm: it is during intense orgasm, rather than during arousal, that two persons can unite in a situation in which the self/other distinction collapses.

III

Irving Singer's *The Goals of Human Sexuality* is a gold mine for anyone seriously interested in the philosophy of sexuality and in the current research in the physiology of sexual excitement. Even if the reader does not always agree with some of the philosophical claims made by Singer, it will be found that this book is not only philosophically illuminating and suggestive, but also clear-headed in its reporting and summarizing of the recent results of physiological experimentation on human sexuality.

Singer's interesting distinction, between *sensuous* sexuality and *passionate* sexuality (explored in his chapter "The Sensuous and the Passionate") is not the same as Moulton's distinction between the sexuality of familiar partners and the sexuality of "seduction/flirtation" scenarios. It is true that the sexuality of familiar partners is very often a vehicle of sensuous pleasure for the participants (the death of passion in marriage does not entail the death of sensuality), and it is also true that seduction/flirtation scenarios often involve strong passion. But sex between familiar partners *may* be passionate, and the sex that results after the seduction has taken place *may* be purely sensual. Singer's distinction is one between a mode of sexuality in which pure sensory enjoyment is most important and a mode of sexuality in which strong but specifically sexual emotions are the most important ingredient. Singer traces the history of philosophical and theological thought about these two modes of sexuality from the Greeks to Freud. The distinction, however, assumes a new importance within today's social context; in particular, in relation to the research of Masters and Johnson and to the Women's Movement.

Consider what is known as the "transfer theory." According to this theory, the sexuality of females is originally clitoral; when the female is young, she derives sexual pleasure from the manipulation of the clitoris. If the female is to develop correctly, she must be able to transfer her sexual interest from her clitoris (the organ of her "infantile" sexuality) to her vagina (the organ of her "mature" sexuality). The complete sexual woman, the woman who has adequately resolved the Oedipus situation, the sexually adequate wife, is the female who has repudiated her clitoral sexuality and has achieved the ability to derive full sexual satisfaction from the insertion of the penis into her vagina.

There are a number of issues that can be explored at this point. One is the issue of what Freud (to whom the theory is attributed)

meant to do with the transfer theory. Part of Women's Movement
sees Freud as the supreme patriarch, in that he proliferated a theory that is antagonistic to the sexuality of women and was constructed to rationalize the male interest in penile insertion at the
cost of sexual satisfaction for women. But another part of the
Women's Movement interprets Freud in a different way (for example, Juliet Mitchell in *Psycho-Analysis and Feminism*).[13] This
group sees Freud sympathetically as a more-or-less neutral observer of the prevalent pattern of development of woman in a patriarchal society. Whereas the former reading of Freud makes him
out to be asserting what *he* thinks is an absolute truth about the
sexuality of women (but which is actually a false belief), the latter
reading claims that Freud meant only to describe what is true
about women (and unfortunately so) during a particular period of
social history. The first reading would place blame on Freud for
advancing a theory that is false about women and which is designed to keep women in a subservient position in society. The
second reading does not blame Freud; rather, it blames the society
that molds women in such a way that they are inhibited in the attempt to attain sexual satisfaction.

The agreement is that it is wrong to expect females to exchange
clitoral sexuality and sensitivity for vaginal sexuality. It is by now
well-known that many women do not experience orgasm (easily
or at all) through penile insertion into the vagina; and we also
know that the vagina is not endowed well with the kind of nerve
endings that are appropriate for a sexual response. These nerve
endings are found abundantly in the clitoris (the embryonic ana-
logue of the male's *glans*), and this anatomical fact correlates with
the finding that women can, as a rule, experience orgasm through
the direct stimulation of the clitoris. From the point of view of the
transfer theory, the fact that many women cannot experience the
"vaginal" orgasm, while many women can experience the "clitoral" orgasm, is to be explained by saying that many women have
not been able to transfer their sexuality correctly from clitoral to
vaginal, that many women are failing to attain a manner of sexuality that is proper for their sex. Many women, therefore, are to
be judged "immature." Rather than making this strong (and ob-
noxious) judgment about otherwise responsible women, the Wom-
en's Movement has challenged the idea that transference is
necessary (or even desirable) for the maturation of female sexuality. Males would like women to believe that women ought only to
have or to strive for vaginal orgasms, for the insertion of the penis

into the vagina (so men thought) was most satisfactory for the men. And convincing women that they should avoid clitoral sexuality, which is a manner of sexuality that can be carried out alone or with another woman, would help to perpetuate the female's dependence on the male (again, which males thought they wanted). Finally, keeping the clitoris in the closet might have been a way for males to avoid having to perform orally on their female lovers (which they thought they wanted to avoid, either for moral, religious or health reasons), for the clitoris is easier to stimulate orally than through the insertion of the penis into the vagina. Masters and Johnson provided scientific support for the Women's Movement by showing that the sexuality of women is primarily clitoral, even to the extent that when orgasm is reached during vaginal penetration by the penis, this is because the process of penetration indirectly stimulates the clitoris, not because of stimulation of the vaginal walls by the penis. Hence, there is no distinctive "vaginal" orgasm; all orgasms are derived, physiologically, from the manipulation (direct or indirect) of the clitoris; it is wrong, therefore, to expect women to transfer their sexual interest from the clitoris to the vagina. There is no way for a woman to forget her clitoris and yet remain sexually responsive; and there is nothing especially sexual about the vagina.

Singer begs to differ about a number of things, but most importantly about there being no distinctive orgasm achievable during the insertion of the penis. Singer proposes that we now ought to distinguish between a *vulvular* orgasm and a *uterine* orgasm (the physiological counterparts of sensuous and passionate sexuality, respectively), rather than between (and misleading so) a "clitoral" and a "vaginal" orgasm. In both the vulvular and the uterine orgasms, Singer claims, stimulation of the clitoris is involved (in agreement with Masters and Johnson); and both types of orgasm can be attained during the insertion of the penis. But Singer argues that the uterine orgasm can be attained only with penile insertion that is accompanied by deep thrusting against the cervix and uterus, a thrusting that causes the deep, internal tissues of the female to move in response. The uterine orgasm is clearly not a vaginal orgasm in the old sense; it is not an orgasm induced by the penis merely rubbing against the wall of the vagina. Rather, it is induced in part by the penis displacing the uterus, a displacement which yields a sexual feeling that is accompanied by passion rather than by the sensuousness that accompanies the direct stimulation of the clitoris orally (or manually) or the indirect stimulation of the clitoris that can occur during penile insertion. Whereas Masters and Johnson assert a "single-type" theory of the female orgasm (clitoral), Singer affirms that there are at least these two distinct types (as well as a third type, a "blended" orgasm).*

Singer supports his physiological claim by arguing that there are serious methodological problems with the research carried out by Masters and Johnson (see also Paul Robinson's *The Modernization of Sex*). In particular, he argues that the fact that Masters and Johnson found such a high degree of "clitoral" sexuality and such a low degree of "vaginal" sexuality among women is explained by the fact that Masters and Johnson studied only women who were able to achieve orgasm by masturbation (manual manipulation of the clitoris). This selection process may have resulted in Masters and Johnson studying women whose sexuality was already "committed" to only one manner of sexuality (clitoral, sensuous), while excluding from their research population women who may have been able to exhibit the uterine orgasm. After reviewing other research, Singer concludes that there is indeed a uterine orgasm that was overlooked by Masters and Johnson. On the philosophical side, Singer maintains that both the vulvular and the uterine orgasms are valuable, that women are capable of experiencing either kind (or both kinds) under suitable circumstances, and that, of course, penile insertion does have a role at least in the uterine orgasm. (Note that it does *not* follow that males are "indispensible.") Even though Singer advances a "two-type" theory of female sexuality (as does the transfer theory), he refrains from drawing any evaluative conclusions: the sensuous and the passionate remain equally legitimate modes of sexuality. As the title of his book suggests (*The Goals*), Singer embraces a thoroughly liberal approach to sexuality; in effect, whatever gets you off, whether it be sensuous sexuality resulting from vulvular manipulation, or passionate sexuality resulting from deep penile thrusting, is perfectly acceptable. The distinction between the sensuous and the passionate, or between vulvular and uterine orgasms, is not a distinction between "immature" and "mature" sexuality, and cannot be used to dictate to women how they should fashion their sexual lives.

The fact that the transfer theory, either as promulgated by professional psychologists or as held, implicity, by the public-at-large

---

*Singer's views on female orgasms can be found in a different chapter of *The Goals of Human Sexuality;* "Types of Female Orgasm," chapter 3, pp. 66–82.

in a patriarchal society, could have affected so many women, to the extent that many women feel guilt at not being able to achieve the "mature" vaginal sexuality of the sexually adequate wife or feel extreme frustration and loss of self-respect at not being able to transfer their sexual interest, shows that social norms and expectations can have a considerable effect upon psychosexuality. This observation leads us to ask how much of our sexual behavior and preferences are molded by social norms and how much can be attributed to "natural" causes or to "natural" dispositions. Singer, for example, says that males (but *not* females) have a *natural* sexual interest in *looking* upon the bodies of naked women (as in strip-tease shows). Thus, even though much other male sexual behavior may be socially conditioned, at least the fact that males are sexually arousable by the sight of a naked female body is to be explained by referring to the nature of males. Determining what part of our behavior is natural (biologically determined) and what part is not natural, but is rather socially produced, has always been a difficult task both for philosophers and psychologists. It is easy to imagine that the sexual interest males have in viewing naked bodies is not really natural, but rather is a manifestation of certain yet undiscovered social causes.

Ann Ferguson, in her paper "Androgyny as an Ideal for Human Development," argues, contrary to much writing on sexuality, that there are either no natural differences between the two sexes (no inherent differences in the psychology of males and females and, therefore, if only males but not females display an interest in nude bodies, this fact is due to social influences on the psychosexuality of males and females), or that the differences that do exist (the anatomical ones) should have no substantial effect on the role and treatment of the two sexes in society. For example, the characterization of males as the sexual aggressors and of females as sexually passive is culture-bound and not natural. Ferguson argues that persons would be ideal persons if they possessed the good sociopsychological features of each sex, and she suggests that true equality between the sexes and the possibility of satisfying sexual and love relationships between them will come only when persons are allowed to develop androgynously. I draw out of this the conclusion that persons should be bisexual as well as, psychologically speaking, aggressive and passive in the proper circumstances and in a balanced proportion. The claim that persons should develop bisexually (that is, that they should, as adults, be able to enjoy sexual relations with other persons regardless of the sexual anatomy of their partners) seems to fit very well with Ferguson's psychological thesis, although she is reluctant to draw that conclusion. She says that the changes in childrearing practices that would allow persons to develop androgynously in the psychological sense would also allow (indeed, make it likely) that children will become adult bisexuals, but she refuses to claim that "bisexuality is more desirable than homo- or heterosexuality."[14] On the contrary, I think asserting that bisexuality is desirable makes more sense given her position. First, if psychological androgyny is desirable (as she claims), and if (as she also claims) it is true that the conditions that generate androgyny also generate bisexuality, then it is *awkward* to refuse to say that bisexuality is desirable. Such a refusal leaves open the possibility that bisexuality is in fact *not* desirable; and if bisexuality is not desirable, then the conditions of childrearing that Ferguson so overwhelmingly advocates, those conditions that generate psychological androgyny, have the defect (at least this one) of yielding something possibly undesirable. Refusing to bless bisexuality, then, has the tactical imperfection of making her positive suggestions about the worth of altering childbearing practices less powerful. Second, because Ferguson is willing to assume that "there are no innate biological preferences in people for sexual objects of the same or opposite sex," she already has the machinery necessary for launching a full-scale argument to the effect that bisexuality is desirable. If there are no such innate, given preferences, then it is possible to claim about human sexuality (along with one possible reading of Freud) that humans are naturally bisexual (or polymorphously sexual). In this case, the claim that persons ought to be allowed to develop bisexually amounts to the claim that persons *should* be allowed to develop in a way consistent with the potentials of human sexuality. Clearly, there are profound problems with this formulation; I shall return to them below. But I do want to indicate here that there is a difference between the claim (Ferguson's) that persons should be allowed to develop psychologically androgynously and the claim (my appendage to Ferguson) that persons should be allowed to develop bisexually. Her major argument is not simply that under the proper circumstances persons could develop androgynously; rather, her claim is that persons who develop androgynously, who become adults in such a way that they have the good psychological characteristics of both men *and* women (as we know them now), will be *ideal* persons. This kind of normative position is quite different from the view that persons ought to be allowed to develop bisexually beause they are by nature bisexual. Only the latter view has to contend with the objection which says that if in fact persons *are by nature* such-and-such, then there is no logical room for the claim that persons *ought to be* such-and-such. Because Ferguson never claims that persons are naturally psychologically androgynous, she does not have to deal with this objection.

The opponent that Ferguson does have to worry about, however, is the one who does not find it convincing to see, for example, male aggression and female passivity as anything other than purely natural. In his *Human Aggression*, Anthony Storr argues that the mere anatomical fact (a biological given) that the male must penetrate the female in order to achieve a "complete" (i.e., conception-yielding) sexual act, has as a psychological correlate the fact that the male is aggressive and the female is passive.[15] But this argument from anatomy is not very plausible, as is well-known by anyone who has experienced (for example) sexual intercourse (penis in vagina) in the woman-above position. Speaking more generally, anatomical or sexual activity or passivity do not necessarily correspond with active or passive "egos"; when an active ego is matched with sexual and anatomical activity, this is a contingent fact that reflects socialization (at least on one reading of Freud). But even granting that the picture that Storr has in mind might have been true earlier in human history (the picture of men chasing women and forcefully penetrating them, perhaps against their will), this characterization of the relations between the sexes hardly holds today in contemporary society.[16] Storr does try to argue that the pattern still persists when he says "It is significant that there is a difference between the sexes in the type of phantasy which appeals to each. The idea of being seized and borne off by a ruthless male who will wreak his sexual will upon his helpless victim has a universal appeal to the female sex."[17] But the richness and variety of both male and female sexual fantasies is astounding. Depending on which poll one happens to be reading, the most popular fantasy can range from participating in an orgy in a swimming pool to having physical contact with animals. Males report having fantasies involving their submission to women. Not all, not even most, women report fantasies about being raped; they have, as a group, no difficulty entertaining fantasies much more exciting and creative than Storr's "Dominique" fantasy. But even to the extent that some women have fantasies about being carried off valiantly or ruthlessly by an aggressive male, there is a perfectly reasonable explanation that is based not on anatomically-generated psychological differences between the sexes, but rather on psychosexual conditioning. This response to Storr is the kind that would be offered by such writers as Suan Brownmiller (in *Against Our Will*) or by those feminists who interpret Freud as correctly describing the workings of patriarchal society. It boosts the egos of males, and thus serves male interests (so males thought), to convince women that what is appealing sexually is being carried off by an aggressive male. It is no coincidence, then, that apart from Ayn Rand and other nonfeminist women writers,[18] most literature and film depicting women as submissive and as liking to be submissive has been created by males.

In contemporary society, the pattern of male aggression and female passivity that Storr has in mind is incredible. It might be responded, on Storr's behalf, that the crude aggression/passivity of ancient humans has evolved into a more sophisticated or subtle kind of aggression and passivity. Thus, male aggression today consists of the man picking up the telephone and calling a woman for a date, making the decision as to where to go and what to do, driving the automobile, and, later in the evening, making sexual advances. But even this pattern is not so thoroughly universal as to count as firm evidence of continued (because innate) male aggression and female passivity. Women do often initiate sexual activity by verbally bringing up the subject before the man does. And even when it is the man who verbally proposes sexual activity, it often happens that he makes this outward advance only because the woman has already initiated the activity in nonverbal ways. When "aggression" and "passivity" become so highly sophisticated, and when the events that surround the commencement of sexual activity are so highly complex, we very quickly lose the stimulus for thinking of the behavior of the people involved in terms of aggression and passivity. It is true that our society has had a norm stipulating that the man must make the first move, but this norm has broken down to such an extent that not only is it safe to say that males no longer hold a monopoly on aggression, but also that it is no longer helpful or illuminating to think about sexual relations using those concepts.[19]

I want now to return to my claim, appended to Ferguson's, that persons should be allowed to develop bisexually *because* persons are by nature bisexual. This claim immediately runs up against what is apparently an indisputable brute fact: the predominant pattern of sexuality in our society, indeed in all human societies, is heterosexuality. This has suggested to many that heterosexuality is in fact the natural mode of human sexuality, and that homosexuality (as one deviation from this pattern) is unnatural. With respect to this "standard" view, there are two important counterclaims.

According to one counterclaim, homosexual behavior and preferences are just as natural as heterosexual behavior and preferences. This counterclaim does not deny that heterosexuality is natural; rather, it denies that heterosexuality is the only natural expression of human sexuality. Such a counterclaim can be made consistent with what we know about the genetic heritability of characteristics. For example, if heterosexuality is natural in the sense that it is heritable through a specific distribution of genetic material, it is also possible to say that homosexuality is natural in the same sense. One need only claim that the resulting pattern—heterosexuality predominating over homosexuality—is produced by the fact that homosexual genes (i.e., genes causally responsible for the homosexual phenotype) are recessive.[20]

The other important counterclaim to the thesis that heterosexuality (and only heterosexuality) is natural is the claim that heterosexuality is not natural at all. On this view, neither heterosexuality nor homosexuality are natural; rather, both modes of sexuality are largely determined by social factors. What *is* natural, according to this counterclaim, is just that persons have a sex drive; what is *not* natural is the particular way in which this drive is expressed. This counterclaim amounts to the idea, introduced above, that persons are naturally bisexual (or naturally polymorphously sexual). My inclination, obviously, is to side with this counterclaim. But there are two major problems with such a view. First, as I indicated above, if in fact persons are naturally bisexual, then it makes no sense to say that persons *should* be allowed to develop bisexually. In the significant sense of "natural,"[21] one cannot advocate (recommend on normative grounds) that persons should have a property (or exhibit a behavior) if that property is a natural property. (One cannot say, similarly, that the apple *should*, in a normative sense, fall on Newton's head.) Second, in this same sense of "natural" it is difficult to explain why, if a property (e.g., bisexuality) is a natural one, so many people apparently fail to possess it. Despite these two problems, I would still like to claim that persons are naturally bisexual and should be allowed to develop bisexually. Against the second objection, it can be argued that even though the behavior of people seems to indicate that most are heterosexual, in fact they *are* bisexual. What *looks* like a prevalent pattern of heterosexuality is, in fact, not that at all: the heterosexual behavior is a mask which conceals the deeper level of our bisexuality. The socialization I referred to above, then, does not disturb this deep core of bisexuality, but only induces variations in the content of the mask. [Part of the evidence that could be offered for this claim is the fact that both heterosexual men and women (behaviorally-speaking) have a good deal of homosexual fantasies. Other evidence, of a strictly Freudian kind, would be based on the interpretations of "projects"; a crude example would be the interpretation of the obsession men have with sports that use sticks and round objects (golf, baseball) as an expression of sublimated homosexuality.]

Now, if this is the sort of answer that is given to the second objection, how is it possible to overcome the first objection? If in fact persons *are* bisexual already, then how can it be claimed that persons ought to be allowed to develop bisexually? The "ought" here seems superfluous or already satisfied, and therefore lacks punch. If the claim that persons ought to be allowed to develop bisexually is to have any meaning, then, it must be rephrased as the claim that persons ought to be allowed to develop their bisexuality *behaviorally*. Thus, the claim amounts to saying that there should be no difference between the "core" of human sexuality and the "mask" of human sexuality, that there ought not to be any difference between the real and the apparent. It is interesting that when the claim is rephrased in this way, a normative question still intrudes. If persons are already bisexual, then the choice is between persons having a mask that conceals this bisexuality and persons not having such a mask. And what reasons can be given for preferring the latter situation to the former? The answer can only be: persons are happier, more satisfied, when there is no discrepancy between the real and the apparent; that actual bisexual behavior, in comparison with masked bisexuality, is more conducive to the good life. (We might say that the *direct* satisfaction of an innate bisexual drive, which would occur if there were no mask, yields more pleasure than the *indirect* satisfaction of the bisexual drive, which occurs when persons behave heterosexually and engage in projects or fantasies to satisfy the repressed homosexuality.) But if so, one might respond, why does society bother to interfere with the actual manifestation of bisexuality? How is it that socialization induces the construction and maintenance of the heterosexual mask?

Some of these social factors are presented and discussed by Singer near the end of his paper, by Bernard Gendron (in "Sexual Alienation," in this volume), and by Lee C. Rice in his paper "Homosexuality and the Social Order" (which is concerned with a number of other issues as well). The place to start is with Freud's discussion, in *Civilization and Its Discontents*, of the incompatability between the maintenance of higher civilization and the sexual satisfaction of the persons who comprise such a society. Freud argued that the demands made on persons by advanced society, demands made in the interest of maintaining the products, both economic and cultural, of such a society, could be satisfied only if the persons "sacrificed" energy that otherwise could be used in the satisfaction of the sex drive.[22] Freud's evaluation of the situation was pessimistic (in comparison with the reserved optimism of *Future of an Illusion*). He believed that there was no way in which the incompatibility could be overcome in order to achieve both full sexual satisfaction and the maintenance of higher civilization. Freud seemed to resign himself to accepting some degree of sexual dissatisfaction (we are all discontent) for the apparently greater good of the benefits that come with advanced culture and technology. Herbert Marcuse, however, has argued (in *Eros and Civilization*) that one of the current causes of much sexual dissatisfaction is more specific: it is not civilization *per se* but rather how some higher civilizations are internally organized that is incompatible with sexual satisfaction. The thrust of Marcuse's argument is that capitalistic patriarchy, in particular, is antagonistic to sexual satisfaction. According to Marcuse, it is in the interest of the established order of domination that the polymorphous sex drive of persons be directed into purely heterosexual channels, that persons be conditioned in such a way that they will become adult heterosexuals.

There are many details to be filled in. How does the capitalist mode of production require or make it useful that persons be conditioned to behave heterosexually? How does capitalism benefit from social interference with the expression of polymorphous sexuality? Here is a Marcusian hint: capitalist mass production is made more efficient by (1) eliminating the possibility of (homosexual) sexual attraction among the workers, (2) destroying the possibility of affectional (nonsexual) ties among workers that would help bind them together, and (3) releasing energy that can be used to perform functions that are purely mechanical and not libidinally gratifying (for more of this, see Horowitz's *Repression*).

John McMurtry[23] has dissected the institution of monogamous heterosexual marriage and has concluded that it "is a linchpin of our present social structure," and he has provided quite a number of reasons for this. (I have space only for one example. The system of monogamous heterosexual marriage develops a "complex of suppressed sexual desires to which sales techniques may be effectively applied in creating those new consumer wants that provide indispensible outlets for ever increasing capital funds.") Ferguson also suggests that the perpetuation of sex-roles, the division of labor into a male role and a female role within a pattern of heterosexuality, helps maintain the correlative division of power, both social and economic, that exists between men and women in this society. More thinking, however, must be done in order to construct a complete explanation. (Again, see Horowitz's *Repression*, especially Chapter 4; and Paul Robinson's *The Freudian Left*.)[24]

Bernard Gendron, in his essay "Sexual Alienation," is worried that the widespread presence of technology in our society has appreciable and unpleasant effects upon human personality. For example, if the kind of work that people generally are engaged in doing is technical, cold, detached, mechanical and repetitious, then persons will tend to behave in a similar manner in their other activities, including sexual activity. (Persons *are* what they do, or persons *become* what they do, or persons are molded in part by themselves in carrying out their chosen or assigned tasks. Persons create themselves in practice.[25]) One of our current social problems, then, is that in living and working in a technological society, persons will tend to view sexual activity in a technological way. They would approach the body of another person as if they were approaching a machine; the process of arousing another person sexually will be seen simply as the process of manipulating buttons and knobs and, as a result, sexual activity will be not a relation between two full-fledged persons but rather one between a person and a complicated machine that can be turned on by pressing the correct levers. (It is funny that the Cartesian metaphysics, the dualism of mind and body, also suggests that the process of sexually arousing a person is just the technical manipulation of the body that happens to be attached to a particular mind.) This possibility connects up nicely with an issue that was raised earlier. On Solomon's view, it is incorrect to conceptualize sexuality as primarily a vehicle of pleasure. One of the faults with the pleasure model is that it leads, perhaps not logically but at least psychologically, to a view of sexuality as a basically mechanical activity. For if pleasure is the primary goal, then what we need to learn is how to produce this pleasure, and this means that we have to be concerned with what buttons to press and how exactly to press them, in order to maximize the pleasure. (Think about Moulton's familiar partners, who know exactly what to do to turn the other person on.) Solomon's emphasizing the function of sexuality in the expression of emotion and his de-emphasizing the potential pleasure of sexual activity, then, is a way of attempting to draw us away from a mechanized approach to sexual interaction. This mechanized approach to sexuality is illustrated nicely by books like *The Joy of Sex*, a *technical* treatise on sexuality that implicity urges us to take a more manipulative view toward the workings of our bodies. From Solomon's perspective, such a view seems at odds not merely with the spontaneous pleasure that is attainable with sexual activity, but also (and more importantly) at odds with our viewing sexual activity as something greater than the rubbing of skin against skin, as something shot through and through with the depth of human experience. (It is perhaps ironic that Solomon's view lends itself so readily to this interpretation. For his own view is that sexual activity is a form of communication, where this communication is accomplished using the "sentences" of a body language. It is not too far-fetched to say that the supreme technician is the one who has mastered the grammar and vocabulary of a language. This point is made by Alan Goldman and by Jacqueline Fortunata in this volume.) Gendron's interest in this issue is broader. He would like to know whether the technological threat to human sexual satisfaction is the result of the advance of technology *per se* or is, instead, the result of deeper social, political and economic causes. There is reason to believe, according to Gendron, that our sexual lives are not as fulfilling as they could be. At the same time, our society has become more and more technological. Is there a simple causal connection from the latter to the former? Or is the relationship more complex and devious? One important question is whether we could maintain our advanced state of technology and yet overcome these sexual problems. This would be possible, of course, if our sexual discontent were the result of other factors. And here we are led to consider, once again, the claim that the demand made on persons by the capitalist mode of production is the crucial cause of our current sexual dissatisfaction. The culprit may not be technology itself, but how technology is used within a particular social system.

Richard Sennett's contribution, "Destructive Gemeinschaft," is a historical treatment of the sexuality of the West during the last two hundred years. His major argument is that there have been two major trends: first, a continuing decrease in the willingness of persons to take significant part in the political process; and second, a "retreat" of persons into the realm of personal psychological experience and the glorification of psychological self-exposure. (The popularity of sensitivity groups, psychological counseling, and self-help psychology books is a recent manifestation of the delving into the self. The increase in the use of hallucinogenic drugs is another manifestation of the retreat to personal experience and from political activity.) It is possible to see the second trend as partially responsible for the first; the increase in viewing the exploration of the self as crucially important results in a decrease in participation in politics in which the individual's psychology takes a back seat to the interests of a larger group. Sennett laments these trends.[26] What is interesting about Sennett's remarks on 20th-century sexuality is that it is easy to make him out to be a stern critic of the conceptualization of sexuality offered by Solomon. In Solomon's model, the psychological self-exposure that comes with successful communication in sexual activity is seen as something of extraordinary value, and so valuable that not only does it give meaning to sexuality, but it also is an essential feature of human personality. Sennett, however, does not seem to think that psychological self-exposure is a terribly important feature of human personality. The obsession with knowing the self, with coming to grips with one's own particular character, interferes with the development of community, with the integration of the self within the community, and with understanding oneself as a member of the community. In the twentieth century the notion of a solid community based on shared tangible interests has been shelved in favor of a shallow notion of a community of psychological identity.

I have not been very specific when talking about the existence of sexual dissatisfaction in modern society. There are problems not only in saying what sexual dissatisfaction consists of, but also in pointing to signs or manifestations of an underlying sexual dissatisfaction. It is generally assumed, however, that two major social phenomena can be taken as evidence that a good deal of sexual dissatisfaction exists. These phenomena are the production and distribution of pornography, and the continuation, if not the intensification, of prostitution. One standard view is that pornography sells because some people do not find satisfaction in the sexual experiences they have either alone or with other people, or because some people have no other sexual activity available to them.[27] Similarly, one standard view about prostitution is that prostitutes are in demand because married men, for example, desire a type of sexual activity they cannot obtain from their wives, or because some men do not have wives or other outlets for their sex drive. These standard ways of looking at pornography and prostitution undoubtedly have some truth, but they cannot be the whole story. For example, if pornography sells because some persons lack sexual partners, then why is it that wealthy persons, who do not obviously lack partners, also enjoy pornography as part of their sexual repertoires? (And why is it that we look with pity upon the *old* fellow—very nicely described by the young Alexander Portnoy—who sits on the first row in a pornographic movie theatre with his hat in his lap, yet we tend to excuse the *middle-aged* man, the collector of pornographic photographs, who is the center of John Hawkes' *Death, Sleep, and the Traveler*? Is it because the first resorts to masturbating in a public place while the second man can relax with his pornography at home? Is it because the first is pitiably lonely and old and the second is married to a lovely wife and in good health? Or is it because the first is decidedly poor and the second is rather well-off? It is worth thinking about exactly what we react to.) And if pornography sells because some do not find satisfaction in the sexual experiences they have with other people, then why is it that some who are apparently sexually satisfied with the partners they have, claim to find, nevertheless, some sexual benefit in pornography? With respect to prostitution, does the institution flourish simply because it enables persons to buy a type of sexual activity they cannot obtain elsewhere, or does it allow males a way of expressing their dominance over women? Does the institution serve purposes other than sexual ones? There are further conceptual and empirical questions that are generated by the observation that pornography and prostitution are not merely effects or signs of an underlying sexual discontent. Rather than seeing them as symptoms of a sexual ailment, both can be seen either as causes of sexual ailments or even as constitutive of the ailment itself. When we do begin to realize that pornography and prostitution can be causes, effects and definitive of sexual discontent (or seen even as perfectly unobjectionable), we begin to realize how complicated the relationship is between sexuality and society.

Fred Berger ("Pornography, Sex, and Censorship") is con-

cerned with the question of whether pornography ought to be prohibited. He is not, however, concerned with the Constitutional
debate about the censorship of pornography. Berger wants to go
deeper than this and analyze the question of censorship from a
sex-theoretical point of view. This means that Berger is interested
in the harms and benefits of pornography in relation to human
sexuality. What Berger does is to show that our views as to whether pornography has any value, what value it does have if any, and
whether it may be harmful to persons who read it or harmful to
others who do not read it, will depend on our antecedent views of
the nature, purpose and value of sexuality itself. Berger argues
that much of the recent attack on pornography is a disguised attack on sexuality, a way of, for example, condemning masturbation without saying so directly, and that it amounts to a reaction
against the loosening of sexual morality which has occurred during the last twenty years or so. Berger concludes that it is not possible to demonstrate convincingly that pornography (its
publication, distribution and its use by adults) has any harmful effects, and there can be, therefore, no case for its censorship apart
from First Amendment considerations.

Alison Jaggar, in "Prostitution," discusses a second major social institution. Jaggar analyzes the problem of prostitution from
three political perspectives: the liberal, the socialist and the feminist. Each political philosophy is shown to have its own specific
conception of the nature of sexuality, its own characterization of
sexual relations between persons, and its own view of the role of
government in the regulation of these relations. The liberal view is
contrasted with both the socialist and the feminist views in its theoretical permission of prostitution, at least when it can be guaran-
teed that both the prostitute and the client enter the relation
voluntarily. The liberal view, then, plays down the incidence of
prostitution as being a sign that something is wrong with the state
of society's sexuality, as being definitive of that which is wrong,
and as being a possible cause of sexual or other psychosocial ailments. The liberal is committed to saying that prostitution, if
done voluntarily, cannot *be* an ailment; and this means that even
if it were a cause of some ailment, the liberal cannot handle this
ailment by prohibiting prostitution but must seek other methods.
To the extent that the liberal can view prostitution as a sign that
something is wrong, it cannot be viewed as a sign that something
is *sexually* wrong in society, but only that something may be
wrong *economically* such that some women are induced by cir-

cumstances to take on an activity they would rather not take on. For this reason the modern liberal can appeal to redistribution (fiscal or monetary manipulations), but this can be a part only of a much larger program to salvage some semblance of equality in a competitive society, and not a method to deal with prostitution directly and specifically. Here the liberal must not go too far, for the extent of permissible redistribution is limited by the necessities of the economy, and this means that prostitution that remains after redistribution is prostitution that cannot be dealt with at all from the liberal point of view.

The socialist emphasizes more than the liberal the economic causes of prostitution and claims that prostitution (and its prohibition) will cease to be a problem when these economic causes are removed. But the socialist program differs substantially from the liberal's, in that the socialist (1) does not see that there are insuperable obstacles in the way of carrying out an effective and far-reaching redistribution, and (2) is not fearful of making strong judgments about the threat to human personality posed by the practice of prostitution. Similarly, the feminist does not shy away from making strong value judgments about the worth of prostitution, but, in contrast to the socialist, the feminist does not believe that economic causes (in particular, the mode of production) are ultimately responsible for the current existence of the institution. To the extent that economic inequality is itself an effect of the social dominance of men, the existence of prostitution, for the feminist, when it is caused by economic factors, is ultimately due to that dominance and not simply to the economic inequality. But one need not refer to economic factors even as the mediating cause of prostitution. When women live and develop in a patriarchy, it is often difficult for them to think of themselves as persons with multiple talents or as being able to develop their potential talents, and one of the results of this loss of self-esteem is the willingness to take on work such as prostitution, even when there are no compelling economic reasons for doing so.[28]

Elizabeth Rapaport, in her "On the Future of Love," discusses in more detail the various views on sexuality that are held by feminists. In particular, she concentrates on Shulamith Firestone (the author of *The Dialectic of Sex*) and on Ti-Grace Atkinson. Atkinson believes that sexual relationships between men and women in today's society are plagued by undesirable characteristics such as dependency, inequality and manipulation. She also believes that the dependency resulting from the ties of sexual love are always destructive of human autonomy. For these reasons, Atkinson attacks the practice of sexual intercourse itself, and envisions a society of the future in which this practice is eliminated (reproduction would take place, perhaps, as in *Brave New World*). Atkinson does allow, however, that certain practices would remain. These seem to have much in common with what Singer calls "sensuous sexuality"; but on Atkinson's account there will be no passionate sexuality. Firestone's position bears some resemblance to Atkinson's: she agrees that heterosexual relations today are plagued with various evils, and although she argues that reproduction should be done artificially in order to free women of that burden and to thereby promote their social equality, she disagrees about the persistence of sexual love between the two sexes. Firestone maintains that in the future relationships can thrive, for she does not equate the dependency of such a relationship with a destructive loss of autonomy. Indeed, Firestone argues that in several ways close relationships can have the effect of increasing a person's freedom, in that they provide an extra window on the world. The issues of dependency and autonomy are explored again in the final essay, Jacqueline Fortunata's "Masturbation and Women's Sexuality." Fortunata argues that most contemporary discussions of sexuality express a male bias and do not accord masturbation a sufficiently high status. Her major argument is that philosophical emphasis upon genital sexuality and intercourse in the analysis of concepts treats women's sexuality both inadequately and unfairly, and that analyses of sexuality that condemn or impugn masturbation are both too restrictive of human variability and overlook the fact that masturbation in women often has beneficial effects in helping them to overcome nonorgasmic tendencies. The relevance of masturbation to the question of dependency is this: there is a pressure on persons in society to match themselves up with other persons. The pressure to get married is the most common form this pressure takes. The message that is communicated by this pressure has been that there is something wrong with a person who lives alone, or who is unmarried, or who is not involved in a relationship with another person. (We might want to call this prejudice "coupleism.") The single person—and especially the single woman—is seen by society as deficient; she is deficient in that she does not have a partner, or she is deficient in other ways and so cannot find a partner. The general disparagement of masturbation is another aspect of this pressure. The message that is communicated by the pressure against masturbation is that there is something wrong with a person who lacks a sexual partner, or who enjoys sexual pleasure alone. Deficiency is overcome, completeness occurs, only when a single person finally does manage to secure a partner in a sexual relationship. A defense of masturbation, then, is a direct challenge to this view that single persons must complete themselves by entering a relationship in which ties of dependency are created. The defense can be seen as a re-emphasizing of the value of autonomy, of being self-dependent, in sexual matters.[29] And because the defense of masturbation is at the same time a criticism of the prevailing pattern of persons coming together in the traditional way of forming couples, it is no wonder that masturbation is continually condemned and continually requires defense. The continual disparagement of masturbation, therefore, is not only an attack on women's sexuality but is, at the same time, a defense of the nuclear family household that is the "linchpin" in the current political-economic order.

If it is true that "couple-ism" is a central feature of capitalistic patriarchy, then the denial in practice of that feature may serve to undermine both the patriarchy and the economic domination. Fortunata's defense of masturbation, falling within radical feminist thinking, promises primarily to challenge the patriarchy but not the economic domination. On the other hand, socialist programs have usually been aimed primarily (or only) at undermining economic domination but not sexism. The two movements, many believe, must be joined together to form a coherent philosophical position that promises to outline the proper tactics and strategy for overcoming both sexism and economic domination. Now, there are two logical denials of couple-ism. One denial asserts the autonomy of the individual and re-emphasizes the value of masturbation. The problem with this denial is that even though it has the potential for undermining sexism by re-establishing women's sexuality, it also supports economic domination by encouraging the individualistic philosophy of liberal-capitalist theory. A defense of masturbation, that is, may produce a more extreme form of the atomization of society that occurs within capitalism (an atomization which is likely to serve the established order by increasing consumer demand).[30] The second denial encourages persons to repudiate confining couple relationships by entering into extended "families." Extended families, for one, fail to support the consumer economy by making duplicate purchases unnecessary. Extended families also make it possible to raise children such that they have a better chance to emerge into adulthood with the sense of *communitas* that is so crucial to a nonoppressive economic order.[31] But it may be difficult to find philosophical room for a defense of masturbation within the theory of extended families. This is not necessarily because in the context of an extended family the private space required for serious masturbation is not available. Proponents of extended families (and socialists in general) have usually been sensitive to the real need of persons for privacy and for time to be alone with one's thoughts and body. Yet there is the possibility that the pressure on persons within capitalistic patriarchy to merge into couples (where being single is a deficiency) may be reproduced in a slightly different form within extended families. Here I don't mean *only* that extended families have a tendency to divide up into more-or-less permanent couples within the family, for that tendency can be fought by the family and can, to a certain extent, be prevented by forming the family out of previously single individuals rather than out of couples. Even when these precautions are taken there may remain within the family the pressure not to masturbate and not to spend time alone because such behavior would be seen as a sign of withdrawal from the community, a sign that in some way the family is failing the individual and the individual is failing the family. However, there is also the possibility that extended families may very well have a positive outlook on masturbation. Socialist feminists have argued that in the socialization of children by extended families, not only are children given the important sense of *communitas* but also they are *not* given strictly defined gender roles. The extended family, that is, is the medium for producing our earlier ideal: the androgynous and bisexual (or, polymorphously sexual) person. If an extended family is made up of adults who seriously attempt to attain androgyny and bisexuality for themselves and who socialize their children in that way, it is very unlikely that there will be pressure in that family for persons not to masturbate and for persons to form more-or-less permanent couples. It is this androgynous/bisexual extended family, then, that should receive our attention as a primary strategy for undermining both sexism and economic domination.

NOTES

1. See Robert D'Amico's review of Michael Foucault's *The History of Sexuality, Volume 1,* in *Telos* 36 (Summer, 1978), pp. 169–183. It is

possible to find it amusing that Foucault, who laments the obsession he claims we have with talking about sex, plans to write six volumes on the subject. However, we should take seriously Foucault's implicit idea that the freedom to talk so openly about sex may very well be another illustration of "repressive tolerance" (see later in the essay).

2. Friedrich Engels, *The Origin of the Family, Private Property, and the State* (New York: International Publishers, 1942), p. 73.

3. See, for example: Lonnie Garfield Barbach, *For Yourself: The Fulfillment of Female Sexuality* (New York: Signet, 1975), pp. 87–93 (Chapter 7, "Why Masturbation?"); Vern and Bonnie Bullough, *Sin, Sickness, and Sanity* (New York: Meridian, 1977), pp. 55–73 (Chapter 5, "The Secret Sin"); Manfred DeMartino (ed.), *Human Erotic Practices* (New York: Human Sciences Press, 1979); Shere Hite, *The Hite Report* (New York: Dell Publishing Company, 1976), pp. 61–126; Irwin Marcus and John Francis (eds.), *Masturbation. From Infancy to Senescence* (New York: International Universities Press, 1975); Thomas Szasz, *The Manufacture of Madness* (New York: Harper and Row, 1970), pp. 180–206 (Chapter 11, "The New Product—Masturbatory Insanity"); and Bernie Zilbergeld, *Male Sexuality* (New York: Bantam Books, 1978), pp. 160–176 (Chapter 10, "Masturbation: From Self-Abuse to Pleasure and Self-Help").

4. It might be argued that Nagel's position does not entail that autoerotic masturbation is a perversion, because Nagel also claims that the perversions must be "sexual *inclinations* rather than . . . practices adopted not from inclination but for other reasons." One significant "other reason" that would enable Nagel to avoid speaking of mundane masturbation as a perversion is sexual frustration. If one *preferred* to have sexual relations with another person, and one tried but could not find a partner, then if one masturbated, one would not be performing a perverted act. The possession of this preference means that the person was not inclined to masturbate. But this adjustment to Nagel's theory of perversion is inadequate. For example, on Nagel's account a woman who prefers to masturbate because it is more enjoyable for her than sleeping with men is perverted (here her other reason creates the inclination to masturbate). Women with inconsiderate husbands, or women who have already had enough bad sex with men "jumping on and jumping in" and who do not feel inclinced to repeat that experience, are perverted. It is insufficient to argue on Nagel's behalf that these women (probably) prefer that the world be different, that it contain more considerate and competent male lovers than it actually does, and that, therefore, these women "really" prefer sexual relations with men and do not have a "real" inclination for masturbation. For Nagel's sense of "inclination" is not this esoteric idealist sense. The response also allows the shoe fetishist to escape the charge of perversion too easily, contrary to Nagel's intention, by similarly arguing that because he prefers that whatever

happened that eventually lead to his strange behavior had not happened, he really has no inclination or preference for sexual activity with patent-leather heels. In rejecting Nagel's account, I am at the same time rejecting a popular psychoanalytic account: "Masturbation is certainly pathological ... whenever it is preferred by adult persons to sexual intercourse" [Otto Fenichel, *The Psychoanalytic Theory of Neurosis* (New York: Norton, 1945), p. 76].

5. Three theories of the source and maintenance of sexual desire and attraction entail different explanations for the fact that sexual interest in one's partner declines as marriage or a relationship continues in time. The *obstacle theory* claims that sexual desire and attraction are direct functions of the presence of obstacles (physical or mental) which impede the satisfaction of the desire. In marriage, then, the constant availability of the object of one's desire reduces that desire. According to this theory, sexual interest during marriage can be maintained by artificially creating obstacles: sleeping in separate bedrooms, picking fights over trivial matters, taking trips away from home, etc. (One problem for the obstacle theory: when it is realized that an obstacle impeding satisfaction has been only artificially created, how can that "obstacle" be efficacious? "Playing hard to get" may work when I am not aware that you are doing so, but it may not succeed if I see through your scheme.) The *complementarity thesis* claims that sexual desire and attraction are direct functions of the "fitness" of two persons for each other (see Aristophane's speech in the *Symposium*). If two persons are perfectly suited for each other, sexual interest should not decline with time. The decrease in sexual activity between married persons indicates that these persons have not (contrary to what they may have believed) found their perfect mates. A third theory, the *variety theory,* claims that sexual desire is a function of the variety of sexual situations and partners that are available. In a marriage in which sexual interest in one's mate is declining, sexual desire can be rekindled for *that* partner by imaginative changes in the sexual routine: wearing different clothing before and during sexual relations, having sexual relations at different times or in different places, and so forth. (If these methods fail, the variety theory, of course, suggests that the married persons seek sexual relations outside of marriage.)

A curious presentation of the variety theory can be found in "Sexual Renewal," by Marcia Lasswell and Norman Lobsenz (*McCall's,* October 1978, pp. 88, 90, 95 and 170). The authors cautiously support trying to renew sexual interest in one's spouse by introducing variety. One reservation they have concerns the technique of flirting with people with whom one is not married, and then relying on this stimulation at a later time to increase sexual pleasure with one's spouse. The authors worry that in this situation "there may be a nagging guilt in the thought that the excitement was triggered by another person" (p. 88); the implication is that this particular technique, which borders on infidelity, is likely to be counterproductive. Yet the authors argue that relying on the excitement produced by reading pornographic literature is a "practical and legitimate" technique for introducing variety (p. 170). However, they do not apparently realize (1) that to the extent that guilt is produced by imagining another person while having sex with one's spouse, there may not be very much difference between imagining the person with whom one has recently flirted and imagining the person one has recently "seen" in a pornographic magazine or movie, and (2) that pornography generates, in many people, guilt and anxiety that are *unrelated* to the suggestion of infidelity, but are rather caused by our social sexual norms. For discussion, see Fred Berger's "Pornography, Sex and Censorship," in this volume. (My opinion is that Lasswell and Lobsenz would do well to reasses their claim of the disutility of flirting with persons with whom one is not married.)

6. In another article ["Sex and Perversion," in Robert Baker and Frederick Ellison, eds., *Philosophy and Sex* (Buffalo: Prometheus, 1975), p. 276], Solomon argues against a "pleasure" view of sexuality by claiming that if persons were really motivated sexually by considerations of pleasure, they would prefer autoerotic masturbation to coupled sexual intercourse, because the former activity provides the most pleasure (in that the strongest orgasms are produced autoerotically). Persons, however, do *not* generally prefer autoerotic masturbation to intercourse (according to Solomon); therefore, the pleasure model must be incorrect. There are a number of ways to respond to Solomon's argument. (1) One could say that perhaps *because* of the prohibition—both medical and religious—of masturbation, persons have not appreciably learned that their pleasure can be maximized by masturbating rather than by having coupled sexual relations. Once they learn this fact about their sexual physiology, they will come to prefer masturbation more and more, and the fact that Solomon's argument depends on will no longer be a fact. (2) Another response would reject the equivalence between maximal sexual pleasure and the orgasm (see Jacqueline Fortunata's "Masturbation and Women's Sexuality," in this volume.) Even if it is true that autoerotic masturbation produces the strongest orgasm, it does not follow that autoerotic masturbation produces the most pleasure in a broader sense of "pleasure." There are some sexual pleasures (for example, the smells of another person) that cannot be obtained during autoerotic masturbation. Thus, a pleasure model is still capable of handling the fact that most persons prefer coupled sexual relations to autoerotic masturbation. (3) Janice Moulton's approach is to argue that "interpersonal sexual activity is more enjoyable [than masturbation] . . . in the 'pure physical' sense," perhaps because "moderate discrepancies from predicted sensation [are] more pleasurable than sensations that

are completely expected. Sensations produced by a sexual partner are not as adequately predicted as autoerotic stimulation." But Moulton's response is inadequate. First, her "discrepancy" argument undermines her appraisal of the quite satisfactory quality of coupled sexual relations between familiar partners, in which "sexual satisfaction involves sexual feelings which are increased by the other person's *knowledge* of one's preferences and sensitivities, the *familiarity* of their touch and smell or way of moving, and *not* by the novelty of their sexual interest." The quality of sexual relations with familiar partners, that is, depends on the ability of the partners to know what to do exactly when it should be done, and this leaves little or no room for discrepancies. The "discrepancy" argument fails also because autoerotic masturbation, contrary to what Moulton implies, is not plagued by the boredom of completely expected sensations. Both males and females are thoroughly ingenious in devising new methods for masturbating.

7. There is something quite obviously true in Goldman's analysis. For a great many people, sexual desire is just the desire to have physical contact with the body of another person and to obtain pleasure in this way. But this fact is "so" true that Goldman's analysis is trivial. His analysis, that is, is simply a *description* of so-called "normal" adult sexuality. Goldman is not doing philosophy in any interesting sense; he is only capturing, in a concise expression, the facts of our behavior. In particular, Goldman is not doing philosophy because he takes as unproblematic precisely this mysterious connection between our desires and the bodies of other persons, and because he has reified one possible manifestation of sexuality as the essence of sexuality. This consequence will not appear troublesome for Goldman, who writes "We all know what sex is, at least in obvious cases, and do not need philosophers to tell us." It is also understandable that Goldman is one of the few who think that "perversion" marks a deviation from a *statistical* norm. Freud, by the way, displayed his philosophical inquisitiveness when he wrote that, for him, heterosexual behavior was just as much a mystery and just as much in need of explanation as homosexual behavior. See James Strachey, ed. and trans., *Three Essays on the Theory of Sexuality* (New York: Basic Books, 1962), p. 10, fn. 1, section added in 1915.

8. Professor Alison Jaggar pointed this out to me. Note that any "binary" account of sexuality will entail that the phrase "autoerotic" is self-contradictory. A "binary" account of sexuality is an account which claims that sexual desire is necessarily connected with another person or another (person's) body. Nagel's and Solomon's accounts are also binary in this sense. A "unitary" account is discussed below in the text and in fn. 10.

9. Recall Wittgenstein: (1)" . . . if water boils in a pot, steam comes out of the pot and also pictured steam comes out of the pictured pot. But

what if one insisted on saying that there must also be something boiling in the picture of the pot?" (*Philosophical Investigations,* para. 297); and (2) "Looking up a table in the imagination is no more looking up a table than the image of the result of an imagined experiment is the result of an experiment" (*PI,* para. 265). Goldman seems to commit the same mistake as Descartes when the latter claimed that the cause of an idea must have as much formal reality as the content of the idea has so-called "objective" reality (3rd *Meditation*).

10. This account of sexual desire is a "unitary" account. In saying what sexual desire is, it does not refer to another person or to another body. Whether one embraces a binary account (see fn. 8) or a unitary account of sexual desire will influence how one sees the sexual world. For example, Nagel's use of the word "intercourse" (in the phrase "intercourse with . . . inanimate objects") to talk about autoerotic masturbation (of the shoe fetishist) illustrates how his employment of the binary framework has colored his view of the sexual. If we take genital intercourse as logically primary or paradigmatic, then even the rubbing of the penis on a shoe will be seen as intercourse. On the other side, employing a unitary framework might lead us to see coupled intercourse as masturbation. If the rubbing of skin for the sake of the pleasure it produces is paradigmatic of the sexual, then even the ordinary insertion of the penis into the vagina will be seen as simply another instance of the rubbing of skin for pleasure. For both types of theory, what is picked out as an important property of the nonparadigmatic case will have its source in the properties of the paradigmatic case.

11. For an account of sexual desire that relies heavily on genital arousal see Jerome Shaffer, "Sexual Desire," *Journal of Philosophy 75* (1978), pp. 175–189.

12. Also note that the obstacle theory (see fn. 5) seems to imply that rape is the paradigm of good sex. Playing hard to get, on this view, is a mild form of the resistance overcome by the rapist. Pamela Foa ["What's Wrong With Rape," in Vetterling-Braggin, *et al.,* eds., *Feminism and Philosophy* (Totowa, N.J.: Littlefield, Adams and Co., 1977), pp. 347–359] argues that our society lives according to the obstacle theory in that we conceptualize sexual relations as instances of rape. She claims that because we conceptualize sex as rape, Nagel's and Solomon's analyses, which stress a "mutual desire for communication," have only "the most tangential relation to reality." Ketchum would find irony in Foa's analysis and would respond, I imagine, by saying that both Nagel and Solomon were trying to outline "ideal" sex and that on their models rape is ideal. The fact that they accidentally correctly described the current sexual model as rape is beside the point.

13. See also Juliet Mitchell's essay "On Freud and the Distinction Between the Sexes," in Jean Strouse (ed.), *Women and Analysis* (New

York: Grossman Publishers, 1974), pp. 27–36. She concludes by writing that Freud "is a key to the understanding of the oppression of women under patriarchy" (p. 36). A more balanced view of Freud can be found in Nancy Chodorow, *The Reproduction of Mothering* (Berkeley: University of California Press, 1978), pp. 141–158.

14. Ferguson's reluctance is expressed in her footnote 22. Despite this reluctance, Ferguson *ends* her paper apparently praising the possibility that persons could transcend sexual gender and have sex-love relationships with others regardless of their biological sex.

15. Anthony Storr, *Human Aggression* (New York: Atheneum Publishers, 1968), pp. 69–72.

16. I feel that I should exert some caution here. It might very well have been true that eons ago the predominent pattern of human sexuality was rape. But even though it may be illuminating to claim that current sexual behavior is infected with a consciousness that conceptualizes sex as rape, the predominant pattern, at least in our society, is not one of forceful rape. This is not to deny that rape occurs. It is simply to deny that when rape occurs we should frame an explanation in terms of residual natural male aggressiveness; it is just not very plausible to claim that men "naturally" rape women because this characteristic has been selected by evolutionary forces. At the same time, however, I think the feminist claim, that many instances of sexual intercourse between males and females in today's society are instances of rape, should be acknowledged to possess an important insight—where the term "rape" in this claim is to be understood in a broad sense, such that if a particular male has more social prestige than a particular female (money, status, power), then it is likely that sexual interaction between them is tainted by coercion that originates in their social inequality.

17. Storr, pp. 69–72.

18. Philosophical Feminism has the problem of explaining why so many women are antagonistic to what feminists take to be the interests of women. Marxists have the analogous problem of explaining why so many workers are antagonistic to socialism. Both explanations start by referring to the power of the respective dominant classes (men, capitalists) to instill their ideologies into the minds of the members of the oppressed classes (women, workers).

19. In his short paper "Vs. Ms.," Michael Levin writes that "In the human species Man is the aggressor and Woman the accepter" [in Jane English (ed.), *Sex Equality* (Englewood Cliffs, N.J.: Prentice-Hall, 1977), p. 218]. Levin provides not one iota of evidence for this claim, and apparently believes that mere capitalization of the appropriate words suffices to make the point. Later in the paper Levin appeals to "each person's experience of trying to do things over the long haul in any other than what Bill Cosby once called 'the regular way' " (p. 219). Although there is some room for doubt, what Levin means is

that persons are bound to be frustrated if they attempt to ignore the standard characterization of males as aggressors and females as passive recipients. To a certain extent Levin is correct; the prevailing ideology has sunk deeply into the brains of many persons, and it is quite difficult to unlearn behavior that has been reinforced over and over again. But at the same time Levin is terribly incorrect. Many persons report being able to repudiate the prevailing pattern. About this Levin seems somewhat naive (was he simply observing the behavior of his male colleagues?), and why he thinks that he ends the debate by citing a stand-up comic is beyond me. Levin's homogenization of persons ("Man," "Woman") is symptomatic of his tendency to make sweeping generalizations.

20. Other explanations for the occurrence of homosexuality, explanations which make it out to be natural in the sense of being genetically heritable, can be found in Michael Ruse, "Sociobiology and Homosexuality," paper read at a meeting of The Society for the Philosophy of Sex and Love, New York, December 28, 1979.

21. Christine Pierce, in her "Natural Law Language and Women" [in Jane English (ed.), *Sex Equality* (Englewood Cliffs, N.J.: Prentice-Hall, 1977), pp. 131–142], finds that the term "natural" can have at least five different meanings: (1) untouched by human invention; in this sense a broken bone may happen naturally but to mend it would be unnatural; (2) everything that human beings do; this is the vacuous sense of "natural" I spoke of in the text on p. 21; (3) whatever human beings have in common with all other animals; (4) whatever distinguishes human beings from all other animals; and (5) unalterable properties of human beings. The "significant" sense of "natural" that I speak of at this stage is Pierce's fifth sense. Note that it is entirely consistent with bisexuality being an "unalterable property of human beings" that the true bisexuality of persons be masked, or covered, by a pattern of behavior that is predominantly heterosexual.

22. My account of Freud's argument is terribly oversimplified. I have not said enough about repression (basic and surplus), the workings of the "unconscious," or about the way in which sublimation is responsible for social products.

23. See his "Monogamy: A Critique," *The Monist 56,* No. 4 (1972), pp. 587–599.

24. If capitalism is supposed to be a prime cause of sexual dissatisfaction, then how can we explain a large number of phenomena that appear to involve sexual liberation? For example, during the last twenty years or so more people have been able to lead gay lifestyles openly, heterosexual activity without fear of pregnancy is more-or-less a reality, the older sexual morality has been breaking down, and so forth. The first move one might want to make is to view these developments as falsifications of the hypothesis that capitalism and sexual dissatisfaction are causally related (the Popperian move), and to assert the

optimism that, after all, capitalism can be a good egg to us all. I think that a more reasonable, less hasty move would be to suggest that what appears to be sexual liberation may not, on closer analysis, turn out to be real liberation (the Lakatosian move). And by this I do not simply mean that there has been recently a heavy attack on the gay lifestyle, or that the pill, for example, benefits males at the expense of the health of females, or that teenage sexual morality is still strictly governed by the wisdom of Ann Landers. All of this is true, but we have to go further and keep our eyes open to what Marcuse has called "repressive desublimation." Being able to have sex whenever and wherever we want may be deceptive, for it may lead us to over-look the quality of the sex that we are having. Better we should, with perhaps a trace of paranoia, ask: what long-term interests are being secured by the apparent sexual liberation? Orwell and Vonnegut showed us that a repressive regime can rule by curtailing sexual free-dom. But Huxley showed us that a repressive regime can control by allowing more sexual "freedom" than anyone could imagine.

25. A word about "persons create themselves in practice." Having ob-served that persons working in a technological society perform me-chanical tasks, and that these persons could or might approach sexual partners as if they were machines, we could say (1) that per-sons create themselves in practice, that persons treat other persons as machines because their major life activity is a relationship with a ma-chine; this effect can be both vertical (the person creates *himself* or *herself* through practice) and horizontal or longitudinal (the person fosters the creation of *others* in the same pattern); or (2) that the psy-chology of persons is antecedently such that they can both efficiently work with machines and have the capability to treat others as ma-chines, where there is no causal relationship between treating a ma-chine as a machine and treating a person as a machine. A similar problem arises within the context of the "psychological" justification of capitalism. Is capitalism justified because it gives free reign to antecedent human nature—where this nature happens to be egocen-tric, acquisitive and competitive? Or does capitalism require and thereby create that aspect of human personality—does living and working within a capitalistic society foster the development of per-sons who are egocentric, etc.? For a lively discussion, see Richard Schmitt, "The Desire for Private Gain. Capitalism and the Theory of Motives," *Inquiry* 16 (1973), pp. 149–167; T. S. Torrance, "Capital-ism and the Desire for Private Gain," *Inquiry* 17 (1974), pp. 241–245; and Schmitt, "Reply to Torrance," *Ibid.*, pp. 245–248.

26. Here it is important to recall a similar point made by Marx in the *Economic and Philosophical Manuscripts of 1844* and in *On the Jew-ish Question.* In bourgeois society, people repudiate their species-be-ing by treating the political process simply as a means to ensure the achievement of their personal, private ends in civil life, rather than treating the political realm as an end in itself. Similarly, in bourgeois

society, workers are compelled to repudiate their species-being by treating laboring (producing) only as a means to achieve relaxation during leisure time, rather than treating work as a valuable process, as an end in itself. ("The animal becomes human and the human becomes animal.") Christopher Lasch, in his recent *The Culture of Narcissism*, also presents a critique of the psychological patterns emerging in advanced capitalism.

27. There is an analogous view that says that some homosexuality and much masturbation are merely responses to lacking a heterosexual partner. On this view, then, homosexuality and masturbation would also be signs of sexual dissatisfaction. This position nicely raises the question of "what is homosexuality?" Does the person who prefers heterosexual activity but settles on homosexual activity for lack of a suitable partner thereby count as a homosexual? Rice discusses this issue at the beginning of his paper; see also the chapter on Kinsey in Paul Robinson's *The Modernization of Sex*.

28. Sara Ann Ketchum has pointed out to me another function of prostitution in maintaining the patriarchy. ("Function" here, I imagine, should be taken in the sense of Herbert Gans, as in his *More Equality*.) The presence of the institution of prostitution, because it involves an extraordinarily disparaging view of women ("whore," for example), provides women with a strong motive to enter the comparatively "respectable" institution of monogamous heterosexual marriage. To the extent that the latter institution is detrimental to the self-respect, self-development and power of women, the dual prostitution/marriage institution puts women in a very awkward catch-22 situation. Furthermore, the radical feminist (as reported by Jaggar in her paper) makes the stronger claim that what we have is not two institutions but only one: prostitution. In the words of Emma Goldman, "it is merely a question of degree whether she sells herself to one man, in or out of marriage, or to many men."

29. Joseph E. Barnhart and Mary Ann Barnhart ["The Myth of the Complete Person," in Vetterling-Braggin, *et al.*, eds., *Feminism and Philosophy* (Totowa, N.J.: Littlefield, Adams and Co., 1977), pp. 277–290] agree that it is wrong to call a single person "deficient" merely on the grounds that persons can become complete only by pairing together. But the Barnharts do not defend either masturbation or living as a single on the converse grounds that only these practices allow autonomy and completeness. The Barnharts, at times, seem to claim that there is no way for people to be "complete" (neither through marriage nor living as a single); at other times they appear to argue that the concept of "completeness" is either vacuous or unhelpful.

30. What should be feared, that is, is the "repressive desublimation" of masturbation. See my footnote 24 and Rice's "Homosexuality and the Social Order," in this volume.

31. For a stimulating account of why childrearing must be done equally

by women and men from the very moment of birth, see Dorothy Dinnerstein, *The Mermaid and the Minotaur* (New York: Harper and
Row, 1976). A psychoanalytic account (which is compatible with
both Marxism and feminism) of the importance of equalizing pre-Oedipal childcare between women and men can be found in Chodorow's
The Reproduction of Mothering.

Bibliography

Baker, Robert and Frederick Elliston (eds.). *Philosophy and Sex.* Buffalo,
N.Y.: Prometheus Books, 1975.

Barbach, Lonnie Garfield. *For Yourself: The Fulfillment of Female Sexuality.* New York: Signet, 1975.

Barnhart, Joseph E. and Mary Ann Barnhart, "The Myth of the Complete Person," in Vetterling-Braggin, *et al.* (eds.), *Feminism and Philosophy.* Totowa N.J.: Littlefield, Adams and Co., 1977.

Brown, Norman O. *Life Against Death.* Middletown, Connecticut: Wes-
leyan University Press, 1959.

Brownmiller, Susan. *Against Our Will. Men, Women and Rape.* New
York: Simon and Schuster, 1975.

Bullough, Vern and Bonnie Bullough. *Sin, Sickness, and Sanity.* New
York: Meridian, 1977.

Chodorow, Nancy. *The Reproduction of Mothering.* Berkeley: University
of California Press, 1978.

Comfort, Alex. *The Joy of Sex.* New York: Crown Publishers, 1972.

D'Amico, Robert, "Review," *Telos* 36 (Summer, 1978), pp. 169–183.

DeMartino, Manfred (ed.). *Human Erotic Practices.* New York: Human
Sciences Press, 1979.

Descartes, René. *Meditations on First Philosophy* (ed. Laurence J. La-
fleur). Indianapolis: Bobbs-Merrill Company, 1960.

Dinnerstein, Dorothy. *The Mermaid and the Minotaur. Sexual Arrangements and Human Malaise.* New York: Harper and Row, 1976.

Engels, Friedrich. *The Origin of the Family, Private Property, and the
State.* New York: International Publishers, 1974.

English, Jane (ed.). *Sex Equality.* Englewood Cliffs, N.J.: Prentice-Hall,
1977.

Fenichel, Otto. *The Psychoanalytic Theory of Neurosis.* New York: Norton, 1945.

Firestone, Shulamith. *The Dialectic of Sex. The Case for Feminist Revolution.* New York: William Morrow and Company, 1970.

Foa, Pamela, "What's Wrong with Rape," in Vetterling-Baggin, *et al.*
(eds.), *Feminism and Philosophy.*

Freud, Sigmund. *Civilization and Its Discontents. Standard Edition.* London: Hogarth Press, Vol. 21 (1961).

————. *The Future of an Illusion* (ed. James Strachey). Garden City, N.Y.: Anchor Books, 1964.

————. *Three Essays on the Theory of Sexuality* (ed. and trans. James Strachey). New York: Basic Books, 1962.

Fromm, Erich. *The Art of Loving.* New York: Harper and Row, 1956.

Gans, Herbert. *More Equality.* New York: Pantheon, 1968.

Hawkes, John. *Death, Sleep and the Traveler.* New York: New Directions, 1974.

Hite, Shere. *The Hite Report.* New York: Dell Publishing Company, 1976.

Horowitz, Gad. *Repression. Basic and Surplus Repression in Psychoanalytic Theory: Freud, Reich, and Marcuse.* Toronto: University of Toronto Press, 1977.

Huxley, Aldous. *Brave New World.* New York: Harper and Row, 1969.

Lasch, Christopher. *The Culture of Narcissism.* New York: W.W. Norton, 1979.

Lasswell, Marcia and Norman Lobsenz, "Sexual Renewal," *McCall's* (October, 1978), pp. 88, 90, 95, 170.

Levin, Michael, "Vs. Ms.," in Jane English (ed.), *Sex Equality.*

Marcus, Irwin and John Francis (eds.). *Masturbation. From Infancy to Senescence.* New York: International Universities Press, 1975.

Marcuse, Herbert. *Eros and Civilization.* New York: Vintage, 1962.

Masters, William H. and Virginia E. Johnson. *Human Sexual Response.* Boston: Little, Brown and Company, 1966.

Marx, Karl. *Early Writings* (trans. R. Livingstone and G. Benton). New York: Vintage, 1975.

McMurtry, John, "Monogamy: A Critique," *The Monist* 56, No. 4 (1972), pp. 587–599 (also included in Baker and Elliston (eds.), *Philosophy and Sex*).

Mitchell, Juliet, "On Freud and the Distinction between the Sexes," in Jean Strouse (ed.), *Women and Analysis.* New York: Grossman Publishers, 1974.

————. *Psychoanalysis and Feminism.* New York: Vintage, 1975.

Pierce, Christine, "Natural Law, Language and Women," in Jane English (ed.), *Sex Equality.*

Plato. *The Symposium* (trans. M. Joyce), in *The Collected Dialogues* (ed. Edith Hamilton and Huntington Cairns), Princeton: Princeton University Press, 1961.

Robinson, Paul. *The Freudian Left.* New York: Harper and Row, 1969.

————. *The Modernization of Sex.* New York: Harper and Row, 1976.

Roth, Philip. *Portnoy's Complaint.* New York: Random House, 1969.

Sartre, Jean-Paul. *Being and Nothingness.* New York: Philosophical Library, 1956.

Schmitt, Richard, "The Desire for Private Gain. Capitalism and the Theory of Motives," *Inquiry* 16 (1973), pp. 149–167.

————. "Reply to Torrance," *Inquiry* 17 (1974), pp. 245–248.

Shaffer, Jerome, "Sexual Desire," *The Journal of Philosophy* 75 (1978), pp. 175–189.

Solomon, Robert, "Sex and Perversion," in Baker and Elliston (eds.), *Philosophy and Sex.*

Storr, Anthony. *Human Aggression.* New York: Atheneum Publishers, 1968.

Strouse, Jean (ed.). *Women and Analysis.* New York: Grossman, 1974.

Szasz, Thomas S. *The Manufacture of Madness.* New York: Harper and Row, 1970.

Torrance, T. S., "Capitalism and the Desire for Private Gain," *Inquiry* 17 (1974), pp. 241–245.

Verene, Donald (ed.). *Sexual Love and Western Morality.* New York: Harper and Row, 1972.

Vetterling-Braggin, Mary, Frederick Elliston and Jane English (eds.), *Feminism and Philosophy.* Totowa, N.J.: Littlefield, Adams and Company, 1977.

Wittgenstein, Ludwig. *Philosophical Investigations* (trans. G. E. M. Anscombe). New York: The Macmillan Company, 1968.

Zilbergeld, Bernie. *Male Sexuality. A Guide to Sexual Fulfillment.* New York: Bantam Books, 1978.

Part I

The Analysis of Sexual Concepts

Roger Taylor

Sexual Experiences

In Manser's book on Sartre,[1] he points out both that English philosophers have not attended to our sex concepts, and that Sartre
wishes to show through his analysis of 'sexual desire', that in sexual desiring, we affirm there are other persons. If my aims, in
what follows, are open to general description, I suppose they are
(i) to give some attention to our sex concepts, and (ii) to cast
doubts on the view, that the fact of sexual desire allows us to solve
the problem of other persons.

This paper has two sections. Firstly, I shall look at concepts
like and including 'love' and 'sexual desire', which in themselves
indicate the territory with which I shall concern myself. Secondly,
I shall examine Sartre's explanations of the principal sectors of
this territory, and I shall assess how viable are certain contrasting
explanations. The issues of the second section are in part conveyed by saying that basically, Sartre wishes to explain the territory in terms of relationships between persons, whereas the
contrasting explanations point to the sufficiency of relationships
between persons and things lacking consciousness.

Reprinted by permission from *Proceedings of the Aristotelian Society* 68
(1967–8), pp. 87–104.

I

If the notions to be examined in this section have any technical senses they are not meant as such.

To begin with, 'being in love' and 'sexual love'. To tread a road already trodden to excess by preachers, though not to much philosophical profit, there is a mother's love for her child, Christ's love for men and a man's love for a woman. Not all instances of *a* loving *b* are instances of *a being in love*. The mother and Christ, in virtue of their loving, are not deemed *in love*, whereas the standard interpretation of a man's love for a woman leads to this conclusion. One can love without *being in love*, but not *be in love* without loving. It is arguable that the fact of maternal love does not lead us to say the mother is in love with her child, though clearly a person can both love and be in love with a book. Such a person however is not *in love*. To know a man is in love with a woman is to know he is *in love*. The same would not follow if we only knew that he loved the woman. In this connection consider the relationship between Arthur and Mrs. Poulter in P. White's novel 'The Solid Mandala'. Now, is *being in love*, loving or being in love with *someone*, as one can love or be in love with a book? There are similarities between loving a person and loving a book, for instance, in a normal case, one would not want to be deprived of either. However, well-rounded experience teaches that it would be frivolous to equate the love in these two cases. If it is not the object of one's love (*i.e.* what or whom one loves) which explains what it is *to be in love*, then does the answer lie in the nature of the love itself? We might think this was so if we held that the love of a man *in love* was a sexual love. Certainly in the case of maternal love, the love for a book, Christ's love, the love involved is not sexual.

But is it really the case that if *in love*, one's love must be sexual?

It might be allowed that *being in love* normally coincides with sexual love, but not allowed that the latter notion exhausts the former. To some extent, it goes against this view, to construct a case in which a man is fond of, feels affection for, likes the company of a woman, but is not in love, though he loves her. The relationship between Arthur and Mrs. Poulter is of this kind. In White's novel the point about Arthur, is his love for all living things. If a case of this sort fails to show the two notions to be separate, what sort of case will do so?

Can we not imagine a case in which *a* has no sexual relations with b, experiences no sexual sensations or bodily feelings[2] in the presence of or with the appearance of b, yet craves glimpses of b, is constantly thinking of b and is enraptured at the sight of b? This is the case of the adoring fan, or the poet who worships from afar. Surely, it might be urged, this is the case of a person *in love*, whose love is not a sexual love. A sensitive reply to this would be that it was a severely limited view of our sexual interests which saw it as conclusive, that they were not involved if no sexual sensations or bodily feelings were experienced. Less securely, we might add, to look at and to be interested in b's person for itself is, in the context given, a guarantee of sexual interest. This latter move will not do, given that a's interest in b's appearance for itself, is compatible with a's interest being wholly aesthetic. However, a wholly aesthetic interest in something, even when accompanied by cravings and rapture, is not a relevant reason for thinking the observer *in love*. If the observer's interest is wholly aesthetic, then it is not in part sexual. If the interest is not in part sexual, then the observer does not find the object of his interest sexually attractive. Certainly one can judge that something is sexually attractive, without being sexually aroused (*i.e.*, without experiencing sexual sensations). If one finds something sexually attractive, one shows a sexual interest in it. To show a sexual interest in something must be to do more than pass judgment on its sexual attractiveness. To show a sexual interest in something is to find it sexually interesting. Here 'sexual interest' contrasts quite sharply with, for example, 'medical interest'. If a doctor shows a medical interest in one, it, of course, does not follow that he finds one medically interesting. What we might be asked to accept then, is that a does not find b sexually attractive, shows no sexual interest in b, yet craves to look at, constantly is thinking of and swoons at the sight of b, and in virtue of this would be said to *be in love*. Where b is a person, quite apart from the conclusion drawn, this case is odd if the interest which explains the reaction is wholly aesthetic. With the conclusion, the oddity becomes logical, as a is said to *be in love*, because the object of his interest is a person as opposed to a picture or landscape. If we neglect this oddity we are saying that we mark the difference between two persons, where one is aesthetically interested in a person and the other in a picture, by saying the one is *in love* whereas the other is not. The way in which the difference would be marked here is just like marking the difference between actor and confidence trickster by saying the one acts while the other pretends. Our notion of *being in love* always points to more than the area of our aesthetic interest and the excesses to which it leads us.

Concentration on aesthetic interest and behaviour to which it may lead provides a more favourable case than many in trying to divorce 'being in love' from 'sexual love'. The case just constructed and rejected is more favourable than, for instance, a case we might construct out of a woman's rapture at the sight of children. It might be thought though, that exclusive concentration on aesthetic interest and possible associated behaviour makes for a case which immediately appears artificial, and that to pay attention to a blend of interests would be more relevant. For instance, consider the plausibility of *a* being *in love*, but his love not being a sexual love, because it was only grounded on a strong, personal admiration for *b*, bordering on worship, plus an intense, aesthetic and pleasing response to *b*'s appearance, the two together going to explain *a*'s cravings and rapture. However, this blend of interests, though not clearly a weak choice among those available, is unsatisfactory. In the eventuality of *a* and *b* being male, the fact that *a* is *in love* and is in love with *b* entails that *a* is homosexual, but no such consequence follows if we reflect on those facts, which it has just been alleged, would give rise to the proposition '*a* is *in love*'. Amongst people who intensely admire and are aesthetically intrigued by others, we find the admirers of aristocracies and monarchies, but such people are not therefore *in love*, and some of them homosexual at that.

Another case we might point to in trying to find an effective wedge, is that of a person *in love* though the sexual characteristics of the loved one are not known to the person. Pen-friends might be a case in point. Here the claim might be, sexual love for another must presuppose sexual awareness of, or, at least belief in sexual awareness of, the one loved. If one thinks one remains ignorant of the other's sexual characteristics, and one is, then how could one have a sexual love for the other? A possible countermove would be to point to the activity of framing pictures of others, which may not correspond with the facts; perhaps one only has a groundless hope that it will be so. This move is beset with something like the difficulties which arise when we ask if a man can be in love with Ophelia (*i.e.*, the character in the play). A more solid objection concerns how we interpret the alleged ignorance of the loved one's sexual characteristic. If the one who loves is heterosexual he cannot love, such that he is *in love*, in the belief that in this instance his love may be homosexual. If the ignorance here is interpreted as ignorance of the sex of the loved one, then the case cannot be allowed. If ignorance of the loved one's sex cannot be allowed, then what else but sexual love could explain the necessity of its being presupposed? The remaining difficulty is to explain the presence of sexual love when one's knowledge of the other, in sexual terms, is confined to the other's sex. Sense can be made of this however. To know the other's sex is to know a good number of facts relevant to one's sexual appetites. To be in some kind of contact with the other, as is the pen-friend, is possibly to find sustenance for one's fantasies, and to feel close to someone possessing sexual attributes of a kind attractive to one. With the realisation of these possibilities the presence of sexual love is explicable. This sexual love may cease when the particularities of the other's sexual attributes are disclosed, but then one would expect the love of the person *in love* to be open to influence by these disclosures.

To close the argument, I conclude that one's love, when *in love*, is a sexual love, though descriptions of the love of a man *in love* may go beyond descriptions of sexual love. Even if we hold the popular view that a person *in love*, is in a state compounded of love and sexual desire, we need not resist the equation. Thus we do not speak of a person's sexual love for another in virtue of his sexual desire for the other.

I shall next say something general about 'sexual arousal', 'sexual excitement' and 'feeling sexy'.

To be sexually aroused is to be sexually excited and to feel sexy. The three notions are tied tightly to the experience of sexual sensations and bodily feelings. Of sexual sensations we can at least say they are thrilling. They are thrilling sensations in contrast to sensations which accompany thrills (*e.g.*, a shiver). A sexual sensation thrills one. It is difficult to conceive how a thrilling sensation in the penis, or emanating from the penis, could be other than sexual. It is though a contingent fact that in the male the penis is the centre of sexual sensations. The philosophical point must be then, that it is difficult to see how a thrilling sensation could be other than sexual. In this connexion, urolagnia, for instance, does not provide a clear counter-example. Authorities here find it difficult to decide whether or not the pleasure involved is sexual.[3] In the light of the point being made these doubts may be explained by difficulties in deciding whether or not the sensations involved are thrilling. No doubt we can distinguish between different kinds of sensations, all of which are thrilling, but to do so is to detail the picture of our sexual experiences. Given this characterisation of sexual sensations, something more can be concluded. The occurrence of sexual sensations must fit into a framework of behavior or desires, which seek their continuation or intensification. Thus, a person who thought it wrong to satisfy sexual appetites could not, with the occurrence of sexual sensations, bring them to a conclusion as one might an itch; his problem would be one of resisting their allied desires. This is a consequence of describing a sensation as thrilling. The conclusion being drawn here could only be resisted if it made sense to say one was sexually aroused but the sensations involved were rather nasty and certainly not thrilling. Given such an account we could be forced to conclude that the person involved was sexually cold. In this case we can believe the person has sensations associated with the genital organs, and that the mechanism for their production is similar to that of a sexually normal individual, but must we go further? May we not say that the person who claims to have sexual sensations which are not at all thrilling makes the same kind of mistake as the person who claims he experiences pains which do not hurt at all? Even the masochist cannot say the latter, nor the sexually frigid the former.

If 'sexual arousal', 'sexual excitement' and 'feeling sexy' are tied to sexual sensations and bodily feelings, the same is not true of 'sexual desire' and 'sexual interest'. It has been allowed that one can show a sexual interest in someone without being sexually aroused (e.g., one does so in finding a person sexually interesting), and it is clear one's desire is a sexual desire if one desires stimulation to sexual sensations. There is a tie between this latter instance of sexual desire and sexual sensations, but obviously it is not the same kind as that between sexual sensations and sexual arousal.

Sexual desire, like criminal desire or creative desire, can be a desire for one of a multiplicity of things. For instance, the desire for sexual sensations is a sexual desire, so is the desire for the continuation or intensification of these sensations when present, and so is the desire to go on looking at her because she is sexually attractive. To be general, to sexually desire is to desire to engage in sexual activities and practices or just to be in a sexual state; to sexually desire is to desire these things for their own sake. There is a slight difficulty, however, in seeing how this generalisation applies to sexually desiring someone. To be sexually stimulated, or, to look up her skirt, is the desire, but in sexually desiring someone, the person cannot be the desire. The immediate temptation is to equate this deviation with wanting a cake in the hunger situation; in this situation wanting a cake means no more and no less than wanting to eat a cake. How we translate 'I sexually desire a' is not so easy. The translation will not be 'I desire sexual intercourse with a', nor, because of necromancy, 'I desire to enter into sexual practices with a' nor, because of self-stimulation where a's appearance acts as stimulant, 'I desire to enter into sexual practices which include a'. The translation which is adequate has two aspects to it. First, to sexually desire someone is to desire to enter into physical contact with that person. Thus, the man whose desire really is limited to peeping at her and masturbating does not sexually desire her. The significance of the other aspect is seen by noting the similarity between sexually desiring a person and sexually desiring a donkey, and by noting the inappropriateness of saying one sexually desires a shoe. This second aspect is that, in this case, the object of the sexual desire be fleshy, or, if not, importantly resemble a fleshy thing. Where in specifying what we sexually desire we do not specify the desire itself, then it is a fact about how we use the words 'sexual desire' that we do not say we sexually desire non-fleshy objects. We might say 'I sexually desire her breasts', but not 'I sexually desire her hair'. This is not to say non-fleshy things must fail to sexually excite and interest us. The translation of 'sexually desiring a' is 'to sexually desire to enter into physical contact with a particular fleshy object.'

I conclude this section with a consideration of sexual interest. The question I select here is, 'What is it to look at something out of sexual interest, where the looking at it, is sexually interesting?' This question is clarified by another, though not equivalent question, namely, 'What is it to attend to another's sex-appeal?'

It might be supposed that the kind of answer required by these questions would be found in looking for some feature common to those objects we perceive, where the perceiving is sexually interesting. However, as a list of objects looked at in this way is extended, this idea loses its attraction. The list would certainly have to contain things as different as her breasts and her underclothes. A possible move to accommodate this difference would be that in looking at her, our interest becomes more intense the closer we get to looking at certain parts of her body, and that our interest in her other parts is an interest in clues. It would be in accordance with this suggestion to explain an interest in looking at underwear as an interest in clues. This suggestion does not take us very far. What is it that makes looking at certain parts of the body the looking at crucial parts, or what is it that makes the looking at these parts sexually interesting? Further, room must be allowed for being sexually interested in her face, her fingers, her ankles *etc.*, without it being supposed the observer uses these items as indicators, or merely as starting points. According to Kinsey the kind of looking which eventually involves a fixation on certain parts of the body is more normal in the male than in the female, but it would be rash to conclude from this that the female never finds looking at someone sexually interesting.[4]

If something about the object looked at will not help us, and as it is clear an appeal to sexual arousal is of no avail, then perhaps a characterisation of the perceiving of the object will provide the answer. But first let it be supposed it is the object which explains our coming to look at it sexually, but not supposed there is some feature of the object, common to all objects looked at in this way. We may then hold whatever object it is, it makes one look at it sexually. This allows for the possibility that 'I found looking at it sexually interesting' can be partially analysed as 'it made me look at it in a certain way'. If this is so what is this way of looking? To begin with it is characteristic of this looking, that if gaining only a partial view of an object or part of an object to which one responds, then one wants a total view of it. Secondly, if one takes in the whole object in a glance, then one's eyes become riveted to it; one finds some difficulty in looking away, and if one looks away, one wants to return to it. In this situation one's eyes are sluggish;[5] they lack the quickness and agility relevant to, for example, the study of a work of art. In other words, in this situation one's gaze becomes fixed, and one becomes trance-like. But one does not enter into a trance. One continues to assimilate and explore. It is not like undergoing hypnosis. These features are necessary features of prolonged sexual perception, and perceptions of a shorter duration begin to show these features. The fixed stare involved is not what one chooses to adopt; the fixed stare is demanded in giving the object our sexual attention. One may choose to give the object sexual attention, but when the choice is made the object makes us look at it in the manner described. It is a necessary truth that prolonged sexual attention to *a* involves a fixed stare, whereas it is a contingent truth that *a* occasions the fixed stare, but typically *a* only occasions the fixed stare in so far as we allow it to. Here I have concentrated on 'looking at', to cover other cases (*e.g.*, sexual attention in the blind), different, though similar, descriptions are required.

II

In this section I shall first briefly outline Sartre's views on 'being in love' and 'sexual desire' as put forward in *Being and Nothing-*

ness, and then offer some criticisms of them, which will rest very much on points already argued for. The criticisms will be at two levels indicated by sub-sections.

Sartre attempts to explain what it is we seek in the situation of being in love. He indicates he regards love as involving desires, or even being a desire. If it is a desire, it is not purely the desire for physical possession. If it was this it would be satisfied easily. Love is not easily satisfied, it is doomed to failure. To love is to make an impossible demand, it is to want to possess or capture a consciousness. That this is so ensures that love is aimed at persons as persons, and thus is not just concerned with the body. It may be that by capture of a consciousness, Sartre means no more than capture of the will, but if this is the aim of the lover, it will have the consequence that the loved one is sought out as a person. The lover desires the love of the loved one. He demands it be freely given, but at the same time he demands the other's will be chained to him. He demands of himself that he freely loves her, but also that his will be tied to her. This, for Sartre, is the impossible demand made by love. However, love, when it brings joy, makes us feel that existence is justified. One's body, which before, one may have regarded simply as a protuberance, becomes something good in one's eyes, in so far as it is the object of the other's tireless desire. The essence of the project in being in love is making oneself be loved. To love is to want to be loved. That this is so shows up another of the contradictions of love, for love involves us in the situation of 'indefinite reference'. Another of its regrettable aspects is, that at any moment, the loved one can turn one into an object in one's own eyes by a withdrawal of love. A final contradiction of love, as mentioned by Sartre, is that it is destroyed by the awareness of a third person, and inevitably we find ourselves in a world of more than two persons.

There is a contrast between Sartre's account of sexual desire and his views on being in love, but there is also an important resemblance between the two accounts.

For Sartre the sex-life is not simply an addition to the human condition, something we could fully explain by reference to the sex-organs. The sex-organs are not fundamental to sexual experiences. The eunuch still feels desire, and the child has sexual experiences long before physical maturation. Further, the erection of the penis, or any other physiological phenomenon, can never explain or provoke sexual desire, any more than dilation of the pupils can explain fear. Sexual desire is a desire for another human being. This is not offered as a contingent feature of sexual desire. The argument for this, provided by Sartre, runs as follows. In specifying the object of sexual desire, it is clear it will not be for the pleasure of ejaculation; inevitably it will be the body which is the object of this desire. The mature with their knowledge of ejaculation may be tempted to forget this. However, it is not the body as a purely material object which is desired, but rather the body 'in situation', that is, the body exhibiting an appropriate kind of consciousness. It is true one can desire a person who sleeps, but this is only possible in so far as the person's sleeping suggests his being conscious. In sexual desire one aims at reducing oneself to a physical thing, to pure flesh; further, it is this aim one has with regard to the object of one's desire. What one is after in sexually desiring is the reduction of another to pure flesh. One wishes to imprison the other in his flesh.

To generalise, for Sartre, it seems that to be in love and to sexually desire is to assault other persons as persons, or to seek to. In being in love one seeks to chain the other's will to one, in sexually desiring one seeks to reduce a person's consciousness of himself to a consciousness of himself as pure flesh. In these two situations one also makes this demand of oneself. We cannot conceive then of love and sexual desire, without at the same time conceiving of others. To live as persons is then, as a matter of fact, to live with the idea of others firmly in mind.

(a) This account has many weaknesses.

To begin with there is the claim that love involves, or is, a desire, though the desire involved cannot be satisfied. To be in love is to be in a state of mind. To say 'I love you' is to say one has been put in, and is sustained in, a certain state of mind by the other, but over and above this state of mind in which one finds oneself is in some way directed at the other. In this respect being in love is not unlike being drugged. One way, although there would be others, of explaining how this state of mind comes to be aimed at the other, would be to say that being in love could be a state of mind, which was really the state of having a number of desires, desires which concerned the beloved. The combinations of particular desires, which would in this respect be explanatory, could be various, although there would be certain desires or certain kinds of desires which would be crucial. Thus, if the state was to be wholly explained by a combination of desires, some would need to be sexual. Further, the desire to be in range or not to be deprived of the loved one would in all cases be central and necessary. Now,

unless we specify that in this context, the desire to capture another's consciousness is crucial, which of course Sartre does, then
it would seem unwarranted to hold that all of the combinations
could not be satisfied. It will be shown in a moment that the desire just specified is not crucial. However one thing Sartre clearly
gets right here is that being in love is not simply the desire to possess a body.

What is to be made of this claim that in being in love one wants
to capture the beloved's will? The explanation of this claim is supposed to be that in being in love one demands the other's love. It
is true, Sartre thinks, one wants the love to be freely given, but
once given, one demands it remains; one vainly tries to chain the
other's will to one. The temptation here to become involved with
Sartre's views on free-will can be resisted, in so far as what Sartre
maintains rests on a premiss which is itself at most a contingent
truth. The premiss is that in being in love, one demands the love
of the other. It is feasible that a necessary condition of a's being in
love with b, is that b remains imperial and untouchable; if b was
to grovel before a or anyone, a might find himself unable to love
b. It is true that often the lover does demand the love of the beloved, but just why this is and whether or not Sartre adequately
deals with it is something I for the moment postpone. At another
level of criticism I shall re-examine the question.

Sartre's three remaining points about being in love are ineffec-
tual. To begin with even if he were right in holding that to love is
to want to be loved, the fact that this leads to what he calls 'indefinite reference' (*i.e.*, in so far as a wants b to want him to love b,
would entail a wants b to want him to want b to love him) is not
to show that love is doomed in some logical incoherence. Similarly, there is no inner inconsistency in the notion 'being in the position to be of the opinion that', because from the fact that a was in
the position to be of the opinion that he was of the opinion that p,
it follows that he was in the position to be of the opinion that he
was in the position to be of the opinion that he was of the opinion
that p. Secondly, that the withdrawal of love has regrettable aspects is not of itself enough to show that loving is absurd. The fact
that the withdrawal of love brings the lover to view himself purely
as an object is a perceptive insight which will be expanded in a
moment. The last of these remaining points, which concerns the
influence of the third person on the lovers, is much too exaggerated. Undoubtedly lovers seek seclusion, and if in the presence of
others, try to cut them off. Why lovers behave in this way is an in-

teresting question, but it is not a question requiring an answer as strong as Sartre gives. One cannot move from the fact that *a* was upset when he caught a third person watching him making love to *b*, to conclude that *a* lives in a world populated by more than himself and *b* and thus in loving *b* is doomed to failure.

From arguments already provided a number of Sartre's claims about sexual desire can be accepted. What has been said about looking with sexual interest and the range of sexual desires shows that an account can be given of these aspects of the sex-life without it being in some way incomplete, because no reference is made to sensations in the genital organs. Further, in empirical terms Sartre appears to be correct. Sartre's additional claim that we cannot relate the sex-life in purely physiological terms also must be conceded. It is not just the erection of the penis, which puts this event into the sexual sphere, it is only when coincidental with sensations of a certain kind that this classification is applicable. There is only one other claim Sartre makes about sexual desire to which I shall give direct attention. This is the claim that sexual desire is aimed at the body and that our knowledge of ejaculation may tend to conceal this fact from us. There are difficulties in knowing how this claim is to be interpreted. Does it mean that we first come to experience sexual desire in attending to the attractions of the body, or a body, but thereafter may proceed by other routes? Or, does it mean that whenever I experience sexual desire, that among a number of possible desires I may have in this state will be the sexual desire for a body? From a certain point of view the primacy of sexual desire for the body can be admitted. The sex-life of our society would be vastly different if this particular sexual desire did not arise. However, I cannot see that more life than this may be wrung from Sartre's point. It is conceivable, and more than this in general true, that a person may come upon sexual desire, or upon a sexual desire by an absent-minded manipulation of himself. From the evidence available it is not the case that a person begins his sexual education with the experience of sexual desire for a particular body. Further, the same evidence points to the intelligibility of autoerotic experiences which do not involve either the desire for one's own body (*i.e.*, one may not even desire to come into fleshy contact with certain parts of oneself, one can manipulate oneself by means of instruments) or the desire for the body of another whether real or fantasy. These are empirical assertions but it is far from clear how they fail to meet the challenge Sartre offers.

(b) The criticisms above are of a piecemeal nature. If we view

Sartre's accounts very generally these criticisms do little to impair its conclusions. At most the conclusions of this account tell us why we fall in love and why we sexually desire, *i.e.*, at most they point to there being ultimate projects involved in these experiences, and to the nature of these projects. At least they tell us what it is we choose or what it is we must seek in falling in love and sexually desiring. Whichever interpretation we allow, we are left with the consequence that in the sexual sphere we must choose or want to have relations with other persons. To be in the sexual sphere is to aim at other persons as persons. Already some doubts have been cast on some of the arguments leading to these conclusions, and some factors provided which call into question the necessity of these conclusions in explaining all instances of sexual activity and the giving of sexual attention. However, the explanatory value of these conclusions may stand, if they can be seen as applying to at least the central cases of sexual activity. One way of denying them this significance would be to erect an opposing theory. A theory which tried to explain the territory by reference to the demands that persons made of things, which incidentally might be person's bodies, would be an opposing theory.

Before giving a description of a theory of this kind there is a prior question which needs attention, namely, a question concerning the status of such a theory. I tentatively suggest it is not an irrational demand that we make our concern with sex self-explanatory. This demand is, for instance, a demand that sexual wants be explained. Behind this demand lies a larger problem, of just how fundamental an explanation of human interests and desires we may have. Certainly there must be some areas where our explanation becomes basic when we point to contingently inescapable relationships between men and their physical environment. The structure of other kinds of explanations, and the extent to which they may be revealed through *a priori* investigations must, in this context, be evaded. What may be done though, and what it is relevant to do, is to indicate the non-explanatory character, with reference to our sexual concerns, of our involvement with persons, and the general adequacy of a theory about certain relations between a person and his physical environment. There may be a number of distinct ways in which we might try to explain sexual concern by reference to what persons seek of other persons, but what is clear is that Sartre's conclusions here fail to convince that these are our reasons for sexual concern. For Sartre, it could hardly be that the reasons he offers are our reasons, although we cannot avow that they are. Would anyone really avow that he fell in love in order to capture another's will, or that his falling in love was attempting to capture another's will, or that he sexually desired in order to reduce another's consciousness to a consciousness of himself as flesh only, or this was what he attempted in sexually desiring? What other things persons may ask of others, or find in others which might appear to explain our sexual concern, I shall try to undermine in describing an opposing theory. In my reluctance to accept an explanation which concerns relations between persons, I do not deny that sexual concerns, as a matter of fact, involve us with others as persons. To describe these relations is really to describe our means to an end.

An opposing theory does not have to point to the primacy of a particular relationship between a person and a thing either lacking or only incidentally possessing consciousness, to explain all of our sexual concerns. In auto-erotic experiences the intrusion of the body may only concern one's thoughts about one's sensations, in other cases of sexual experience its intrusion will be very different. All that is required is a theory which explains those instances of sexual experience where it might appear that another was fundamentally required to be involved as a person. Roughly we might explain these experiences by saying they were occasioned by, sustained by, directed at, some body. This explanation is rough, because one can enter the sexual arena at the sound of a voice, with the glimpse of underclothes, with another's written confession of sexual interest in oneself. One's sexual involvement because of these factors will be explained either by pointing to some depersonalised aspect of the occasioning factor, or by pointing to it as a sign of, or as giving an indication of, a sexually interesting situation. The fact that someone tells me sexual experiences await me around the corner may be enough to excite me, but this is not enough to show that my sexual experiences must involve me in thinking of others as persons. Now as soon as we begin to construct an account of this sort the pressure to distinguish between being in love with someone, and simply feeling sexual desire for someone, is felt. The possibility of some sort of distinction is provided by the earlier account. Thus the desire to have fleshy contact is not necessarily bound up with being in love. However, the one who is in love can feel sexual desire for the beloved, and it is this case that presses us to make a clear distinction. This distinction can be made in specifying the nature of the attachment to the other's body. If a man's love is to be explained wholly by his sexual desire for someone, then it must be that his sexual desire is more constant and demanding than that of the man who just sexually desires. Surely we would have no hesitation in affirming that the person who constantly sexually craves, and is sexually concerned with another, is in love with the other. If a theory of this kind provides basic explanations, then the early claim that being in love was not to be explained by the notion of a love for a person, is justified. That being in love is being in love with someone, is then a coincidence of no mystery.

To this point the theory has been very thinly argued for, but certain things can be done immediately which make it more substantial. To do this we must take up some questions which were left undisturbed a little earlier. Namely the questions 'Why is it that the lover does demand the love of the beloved?', and 'Why is it that the withdrawal of love by the beloved makes the lover conceive of himself purely as an object?' If the theory, with modifications or extensions, can accommodate these questions it will be much stronger. In looking at the first of these questions we get quickly to its centre, if we allow the lover's context to be one in which he has no problems concerning physical appropriation of the beloved. Let it be allowed that the lover can do whatever he likes with the beloved, and that her body is animated in accordance with all his wants, thus she moves her body for him. Further let it be allowed that he is sure of her fidelity. Thus he has no fears about losing this physical object, nor of it being contaminated by its contact with some other physical object. In this situation to learn that the beloved does not love him might matter, but in terms of the theory being offered how could this be? In feeling dissatisfaction with any alleged self-explanatory character of the lover's concern here, we might hold that his concern stems from feeling the force of his physical limitations. Thus if typically sexual love is fully explained as a relationship between a person and a body, then to know the beloved is not in love with one is to know one's body fails to bring her into this relationship with it. According to the theory being offered, to bring about changes in one's body would be to be in a position to induce the required state in the beloved. That this cannot be done, that the beloved does not love one, underlines one's physical limitations. What will matter here will be one's sense of inadequacy, which is fully explained by the contingent limitations governing one's relationship with oneself as a physical thing. One demands the love of the other to assure oneself of the adequacy of one's physical self. Thus, if these suggestions are correct, we may account for the whole situation by pointing out that the lover loves because of the physical presence of the other, and that in this state he may (though there is no necessity that he should) seek the love of his beloved, but that he only makes this demand of the other as a person because he seeks assurance about his immediate physical environment. There is no suggestion in any of this that the lover's fundamental project is to enter into relations with other persons. That one demands love of the other to assure oneself of one's physical adequacy helps to explain why the withdrawal of love makes one regard oneself as an object, as an inert and clumsy impediment. In this connexion we might profitably compare the lover's perception of himself as a body with the athlete's. Both may find their feelings about their bodies change as they discover their capacities. The failing athlete finds his eyes resting on the bones of his feet, his knees seemingly out of control beneath him and his muscles seemingly thinner and more frail. The lover whose body fails to intoxicate the beloved cannot regard himself physically as limp and smooth; instead his skin appears coarse to him and fails to conceal awkward bones.

What I have provided is a bare sketch of a theory. Possibly in its construction it is less adequate than Sartre's. Certainly it shares with Sartre's account the feature of appearing to run against common sense. Thus the account I have been detailing allows that sexual love for objects is plausible, and Sartre's account insists that in sexual desire we aim at persons as persons. In conclusion I shall do no more than make two new points in support of the theory I have been constructing.

First, in taking on persons as persons, how they are, may of course make it impossible for us to be sexually concerned with them, but this is not the same as in being sexually concerned with persons, one's ultimate project is to take them on as persons.

Secondly, that our descriptions of how persons do things involve us in considering them as persons, and that we may be sexually attracted when we see them doing things in certain ways, does not guarantee that as the peculiar agents they are, they sexually involve us. Thus, is it at all clear, that it is the movement as a deft movement which sexually excites us, as opposed to the movement's being of a certain physical character (*e.g.*, light, airy, delicate)?

NOTES

1. A. Manser, *Sartre: A Philosophic Study*, ch. vi (London: Althone Press, 1966).

2. For the point of this distinction see D. M. Armstrong, *Bodily Sensations* ch. viii (London: Routledge, 1962).

3. Read I. and S. Hegeler, *An ABZ of Love*, (London: Neville Spearman, 1963), p. 281.

4. Kinsey, Pomeroy, Martin and Gebhard, *Sexual Behaviour in the Human Female* (Philadelphia: Saunders 1953).

5. Compare J. P. Sartre, *Being and Nothingness*, translated by H. E. Barnes (London: Methuen, 1957), p. 388.

Thomas Nagel

Sexual Perversion

There is something to be learned about sex from the fact that we possess a concept of sexual perversion. I wish to examine the concept, defending it against the charge of unintelligibility and trying to say exactly what about human sexuality qualifies it to admit of perversions. Let me make some preliminary comments about the problem before embarking on its solution.

Some people do not believe that the notion of sexual perversion makes sense, and even those who do disagree over its application. Nevertheless I think it will be widely conceded that, if the concept is viable at all, it must meet certain general conditions. First, if there are any sexual perversions, they will have to be sexual desires or practices that can be plausibly described as in some sense unnatural, though the explanation of this natural/unnatural distinction is of course the main problem. Second, certain practices will be perversions if anything is, such as shoe fetishism, bestiality, and sadism; other practices, such as unadorned sexual intercourse, will not be; about still others there is controversy. Third, if there are perversions, they will be unnatural sexual *inclinations* rather than merely unnatural practices adopted not from inclination but for other reasons. I realize that this is at variance with the veiw, maintained by some Roman Catholics, that contraception is

Reprinted by permission from *The Journal of Philosophy 66,* No. 1 (1969), pp. 5–17. My research was supported in part by the National Science Foundation.

a sexual perversion. But although contraception may qualify as a deliberate perversion of the sexual and reproductive functions, it cannot be significantly described as a *sexual* perversion. A sexual perversion must reveal itself in conduct that expresses an unnatural *sexual* preference. And although there might be a form of fetishism focused on the employment of contraceptive devices, that is not the usual explanation for their use.

I wish to declare at the outset my belief that the connection between sex and reproduction has no bearing on sexual perversion. The latter is a concept of psychological, not physiological interest, and it is a concept that we do not apply to the lower animals, let alone to plants, all of which have reproductive functions that can go astray in various ways. (Think of seedless oranges.) Insofar as we are prepared to regard higher animals as perverted, it is because of their psychological, not their anatomical similarity to humans. Furthermore, we do not regard as a perversion every deviation from the reproductive function of sex in humans: sterility, miscarriage, contraception, abortion.

Another matter that I believe has no bearing on the concept of sexual perversion is social disapprobation or custom. Anyone inclined to think that in each society the perversions are those sexual practices of which the community disapproves, should consider all the societies that have frowned upon adultery and fornication. These have not been regarded as unnatural practices, but have been thought objectionable in other ways. What is regarded as unnatural admittedly varies from culture to culture, but the classification is not a pure expression of disapproval or distaste. In fact it is often regarded as a *ground* for disapproval, and that suggests that the classification has an independent content.

I am going to attempt a psychological account of sexual perversion, which will depend on a specific psychological theory of sexual desire and human sexual interactions. To approach this solution I wish first to consider a contrary position, one which provides a basis for skepticism about the existence of any sexual perversions at all, and perhaps about the very significance of the term. The skeptical argument runs as follows:

"Sexual desire is simply one of the appetites, like hunger and thirst. As such it may have various objects, some more common than others perhaps, but none in any sense 'natural'. An appetite is identified as sexual by means of the organs and erogenous zones in which its satisfaction can be to some extent localized, and the special sensory pleasures which form the core of that satisfaction.

This enables us to recognize widely divergent goals, activities, and desires as sexual, since it is conceivable in principle that anything should produce sexual pleasure and that a nondeliberate, sexually charged desire for it should arise (as a result of conditioning, if nothing else). We may fail to empathize with some of these desires, and some of them, like sadism, may be objectionable on extraneous grounds, but once we have observed that they meet the criteria for being sexual, there is nothing more to be said on *that* score. Either they are sexual or they are not: sexuality does not admit of imperfection, or perversion, or any other such qualification—it is not that sort of affection."

This is probably the received radical position. It suggests that the cost of defending a psychological account may be to deny that sexual desire is an appetite. But insofar as that line of defense is plausible, it should make us suspicious of the simple picture of appetites on which the skepticism depends. Perhaps the standard appetites, like hunger, cannot be classed as pure appetites in that sense either, at least in their human versions.

Let us approach the matter by asking whether we can imagine anything that would qualify as a gastronomical perversion. Hunger and eating are importantly like sex in that they serve a biological function and also play a significant role in our inner lives. It is noteworthy that there is little temptation to describe as perverted an appetite for substances that are not nourishing. We should probably not consider someone's appetites as *perverted* if he liked to eat paper, sand, wood, or cotton. Those are merely rather odd and very unhealthy tastes: they lack the psychological complexity that we expect of perversions. (Coprophilia, being already a sexual perversion, may be disregarded.) If on the other hand someone liked to eat cookbooks, or magazines with pictures of food in them, and preferred these to ordinary food—or if when hungry he sought satisfaction by fondling a napkin or ashtray from his favorite restaurant—then the concept of perversion might seem appropriate (in fact it would be natural to describe this as a case of gastronomical fetishism). It would be natural to describe as gastronomically perverted someone who could eat only by having food forced down his throat through a funnel, or only if the meal were a living animal. What helps in such cases is the peculiarity of the desire itself, rather than the inappropriateness of its object to the biological function that the desire serves. Even an appetite, it would seem, can have perversions if in addition to its biological function it has a significant psychological structure.

In the case of hunger, psychological complexity is provided by the activities that give it expression. Hunger is not merely a disturbing sensation that can be quelled by eating; it is an attitude toward edible portions of the external world, a desire to relate to them in rather special ways. The method of ingestion: chewing, savoring, swallowing, appreciating the texture and smell, all are important components of the relation, as is the passivity and controllability of the food (the only animals we eat live are helpless mollusks). Our relation to food depends also on our size: we do not live upon it or burrow into it like aphids or worms. Some of these features are more central than others, but any adequate phenomenology of eating would have to treat it as a relation to the external world and a way of appropriating bits of that world, with characteristic affection. Displacements or serious restrictions of the desire to eat could then be described as perversions, if they undermined that direct relation between man and food which is the natural expression of hunger. This explains why it is easy to imagine gastronomical fetishism, voyeurism, exhibitionism, or even gastronomical sadism and masochism. Indeed some of these perversions are fairly common.

If we can imagine perversions of an appetite like hunger, it should be possible to make sense of the concept of sexual perversion. I do not wish to imply that sexual desire is an appetite—only that being an appetite is no bar to admitting of perversions. Like hunger, sexual desire has as its characteristic object a certain relation with something in the external world; only in this case it is usually a person rather than an omelet, and the relation is considerably more complicated. This added complication allows scope for correspondingly complicated perversions.

The fact that sexual desire is a feeling about other persons may tempt us to take a pious view of its psychological content. There are those who believe that sexual desire is properly the expression of some other attitude, like love, and that when it occurs by itself it is incomplete and unhealthy—or at any rate subhuman. (The extreme Platonic version of such a view is that sexual practices are all vain attempts to express something they cannot in principle achieve: this makes them all perversions, in a sense.) I do not believe that any such view is correct. Sexual desire is complicated enough without having to be linked to anything else as a condition for phenomenological analysis. It cannot be denied that sex may serve various functions—economic, social, altruistic—but it also has its own content as a relation between persons, and it is only by analyzing that relation that we can understand the conditions of sexual perversion.

I believe it is very important that the object of sexual attraction is a particular individual, who transcends the properties that make him attractive. When different persons are attracted to a single person for different reasons: eyes, hair, figure, laugh, intelligence—we feel that the object of their desire is nevertheless the same, namely that person. There is even an inclination to feel that this is so if the lovers have different sexual aims, if they include both men and women, for example. Different specific attractive characteristics seem to provide enabling conditions for the operation of a single basic feeling, and the different aims all provide expressions of it. We approach the sexual attitude toward the person through the features that we find attractive, but these features are not the objects of that attitude.

This is very different from the case of an omelet. Various people may desire it for different reasons, one for its fluffiness, another for its mushrooms, another for its unique combination of aroma and visual aspect; yet we do not enshrine the transcendental omelet as the true common object of their affections. Instead we might say that several desires have accidentally converged on the same object: any omelet with the crucial characteristics would do as well. It is not similarly true that any person with the same flesh distribution and way of smoking can be substituted as object for a particular sexual desire that has been elicited by those characteristics. It may be that they will arouse attraction whenever they recur, but it will be a new sexual attraction with a new particular object, not merely a transfer of the old desire to someone else. (I believe this is true even in cases where the new object is unconsciously identified with a former one.)

The importance of this point will emerge when we see how complex a psychological interchange constitutes the natural development of sexual attraction. This would be incomprehensible if its object were not a particular person, but rather a person of a certain *kind*. Attraction is only the beginning, and fulfillment does not consist merely of behavior and contact expressing this attraction, but involves much more.

The best discussion of these matters that I have seen appears in part III of Sartre's *Being and Nothingness*.[1] Since it has influenced my own views, I shall say a few things about it now. Sartre's treatment of sexual desire and of love, hate, sadism, masochism, and further attitudes toward others, depends on a general theory of consciousness and the body which we can neither expound nor assume here. He does not discuss perversion, and this is partly because he regards sexual desire as one form of the perpetual attempt of an embodied consciousness to come to terms with the existence of others, an attempt that is as doomed to fail in this form as it is in any of the others, which include sadism and masochism (if not certain of the more impersonal deviations) as well as several nonsexual attitudes. According to Sartre, all attempts to incorporate the other into my world as another subject, i.e., to apprehend him at once as an object for me and as a subject for whom I am an object, are unstable and doomed to collapse into one or other of the two aspects. Either I reduce him entirely to an object, in which case his subjectivity escapes the possession or appropriation I can extend to that object: or I become merely an object for him, in which case I am no longer in a position to appropriate his subjectivity. Moreover, neither of these aspects is stable; each is continually in danger of giving way to the other. This has the consequence that there can be no such thing as a *successful* sexual relation, since the deep aim of sexual desire cannot in principle be accomplished. It seems likely, therefore, that the view will not permit a basic distinction between successful or complete and unsuccessful or incomplete sex, and therefore cannot admit the concept of perversion.

I do not adopt this aspect of the theory, nor many of its metaphysical underpinnings. What interests me is Sartre's picture of the attempt. He says that the type of possession that is the object of sexual desire is carried out by "a double reciprocal incarnation" and that this is accomplished, typically in the form of a caress, in the following way: "I make myself flesh in order to impel the Other to realize *for herself* and *for me* her own flesh, and my caresses cause my flesh to be born for me in so far as it is for the Other *flesh causing her to be born as flesh*" (391; italics Sartre's). The incarnation in question is described variously as a clogging or troubling of consciousness, which is inundated by the flesh in which it is embodied.

The view I am going to suggest, I hope in less obscure language, is related to this one, but it differs from Sartre's in allowing sexuality to achieve its goal on occasion and thus in providing the concept of perversion with a foothold.

Sexual desire involves a kind of perception, but not merely a single perception of its object, for in the paradigm case of mutual desire there is a complex system of superimposed mutual perceptions—not only perceptions of the sexual object, but perceptions of oneself. Moreover, sexual awareness of another involves considerable self-awareness to begin with—more than is involved in ordinary sensory perception. The experience is felt as an assault on oneself by the view (or touch, or whatever) of the sexual object.

Let us consider a case in which the elements can be separated. For clarity we will restrict ourselves initially to the somewhat artificial case of desire at a distance. Suppose a man and a woman, whom we may call Romeo and Juliet, are at opposite ends of a cocktail lounge, with many mirrors on the walls which permit unobserved observation, and even mutual unobserved observation. Each of them is sipping a martini and studying other people in the mirrors. At some point Romeo notices Juliet. He is moved, somehow, by the softness of her hair and the diffidence with which she sips her martini, and this arouses him sexually. Let us say that X senses Y whenever X regards Y with sexual desire. (Y need not be a person, and X's apprehension of Y can be visual, tactile, olfactory, etc., or purely imaginary; in the present example we shall concentrate on vision.) So Romeo senses Juliet, rather than merely noticing her. At this stage he is aroused by an unaroused object, so he is more in the sexual grip of his body than she of hers.

Let us suppose, however, that Juliet now senses Romeo in another mirror on the opposite wall, though neither of them yet knows that he is seen by the other (the mirror angles provide three-quarter views). Romeo then begins to notice in Juliet the subtle signs of sexual arousal: heavy-lidded stare, dilating pupils, faint flush, et cetera. This of course renders her much more bodily, and he not only notices but senses this as well. His arousal is nevertheless still solitary. But now, cleverly calculating the line of her stare without actually looking her in the eyes, he realizes that it is directed at him through the mirror on the opposite wall. That is, he notices, and moreover senses, Juliet sensing him. This is definitely a new development, for it gives him a sense of embodiment not only through his own reactions but through the eyes and reactions of another. Moreover, it is separable from the initial sensing of Juliet; for sexual arousal might begin with a person's sensing that he is sensed and being assailed by the perception of the other person's desire rather than merely by the perception of the person.

But there is a further step. Let us suppose that Juliet, who is a little slower than Romeo, now senses that he senses her. This puts Romeo in a position to notice, and be aroused by, her arousal at being sensed by him. He senses that she senses that he senses her. This is still another level of arousal, for he becomes conscious of his sexuality through his awareness of its effect on her and of her awareness that this effect is due to him. Once she takes the same step and senses that he senses her sensing him, it becomes difficult to state, let alone imagine, further iterations, though they may be logically distinct. If both are alone, they will presumably turn to look at each other directly, and the proceedings will continue on another plane. Physical contact and intercourse are perfectly natural extensions of this complicated visual exchange, and mutual touch can involve all the complexities of awareness present in the visual case, but with a far greater range of subtlety and acuteness.

Ordinarily, of course, things happen in a less orderly fashion—sometimes in a great rush—but I believe that some version of this overlapping system of distinct sexual perceptions and interactions is the basic framework of any full-fledged sexual relation and that relations involving only part of the complex are significantly incomplete. The account is only schematic, as it must be to achieve generality. Every real sexual act will be psychologically far more specific and detailed, in ways that depend not only on the physical techniques employed and on anatomical details, but also on countless features of the participants' conceptions of themselves and of each other, which become embodied in the act. (It is a familiar enough fact, for example, that people often take their social roles and the social roles of their partners to bed with them.)

The general schema is important, however, and the proliferation of levels of mutual awareness it involves is an example of a type of complexity that typifies human interactions. Consider aggression, for example. If I am angry with someone, I want to make him feel it, either to produce self-reproach by getting him to see himself through the eyes of my anger, and to dislike what he sees—or else to produce reciprocal anger or fear, by getting him to perceive my anger as a threat or attack. What I want will depend on the details of my anger, but in either case it will involve a desire that the object of that anger be aroused. This accomplishment constitutes the fulfillment of my emotion, through domination of the object's feelings.

Another example of such reflexive mutual recognition is to be found in the phenomenon of meaning, which appears to involve an intention to produce a belief or other effect in another by bringing about his recognition of one's intention to produce the effect. (That result is due to H. P. Grice,[2] whose position I shall not attempt to reproduce in detail.) Sex has a related structure: it involves a desire that one's partner be aroused by the recognition of one's desire that he or she be aroused.

It is not easy to define the basic types of awareness and arousal of which these complexes are composed, and that remains a lacuna in this discussion. I believe that the object of awareness is the same in one's own case as it is in one's sexual awareness of another, although the two awarenesses will not be the same, the difference being as great as that between feeling angry and experiencing the anger of another. All stages of sexual perception are varieties of identification of a person with his body. What is perceived is one's own or another's *subjection* to or *immersion* in his body, a phenomenon which has been recognized with loathing by St. Paul and St. Augustine, both of whom regarded "the law of sin which is in my members" as a grave threat to the dominion of the holy will.[3] In sexual desire and its expression the blending of involuntary response with deliberate control is extremely important. For Augustine, the revolution launched against him by his body is symbolized by erection and the other involuntary physical components of arousal. Sartre too stresses the fact that the penis is not a prehensile organ. But mere involuntariness characterizes other bodily processes as well. In sexual desire the involuntary responses are combined with submission to spontaneous impulses: not only one's pulse and secretions but one's actions are taken over by the body; ideally, deliberate control is needed only to guide the expression of those impulses. This is to some extent also true of an appetite like hunger, but the takeover there is more localized, less pervasive, less extreme. One's whole body does not become saturated with hunger as it can with desire. But the most characteristic feature of a specifically sexual immersion in the body is its ability to fit into the complex of mutual perceptions that we have described. Hunger leads to spontaneous interactions with food; sexual desire leads to spontaneous interactions with other persons, whose bodies are asserting their sovereignty in the same way, producing involuntary reactions and spontaneous impulses in *them*. These reactions are perceived, and the perception of them is perceived, and that perception is in turn perceived; at each step the domination of the person by his body is reinforced, and the sexual partner becomes more possessible by physical contact, penetration, and envelopment.

Desire is therefore not merely the perception of a preexisting embodiment of the other, but ideally a contribution to his further embodiment which in turn enhances the original subject's sense of himself. This explains why it is important that the partner be aroused, and not merely aroused, but aroused by the awareness of one's desire. It also explains the sense in which desire has unity and possession as its object: physical possession must eventuate in creation of the sexual object in the image of one's desire, and not merely in the object's recognition of that desire, or in his or her own private arousal. (This may reveal a male bias: I shall say something about that later.)

To return, finally, to the topic of perversion: I believe that various familiar deviations constitute truncated or incomplete versions of the complete configuration, and may therefore be regarded as perversions of the central impulse.

In particular, narcissistic practices and intercourse with animals, infants, and inanimate objects seem to be stuck at some primitive version of the first stage. If the object is not alive, the experience is reduced entirely to an awareness of one's own sexual embodiment. Small children and animals permit awareness of the embodiment of the other, but present obstacles to reciprocity, to the recognition by the sexual object of the subject's desire as the source of his (the object's) sexual self-awareness.

Sadism concentrates on the evocation of passive self-awareness in others, but the sadist's engagement is itself active and requires a retention of deliberate control which impedes awareness of himself as a bodily subject of passion in the required sense. The victim must recognize him as the source of his own sexual passivity, but only as the active source. De Sade claimed that the object of sexual desire was to evoke involuntary responses from one's partner, especially audible ones. The infliction of pain is no doubt the most efficient way to accomplish this, but it requires a certain abrogation of one's own exposed spontaneity. All this, incidentally, helps to explain why it is tempting to regard as sadistic an excessive preoccupation with sexual technique, which does not permit one to abandon the role of agent at any stage of the sexual act. Ideally one should be able to surmount one's technique at some point.

A masochist on the other hand imposes the same disability on his partner as the sadist imposes on himself. The masochist cannot find a satisfactory embodiment as the object of another's sexual desire, but only as the object of his control. He is passive not in relation to his partner's passion but in relation to his nonpassive agency. In addition, the subjection to one's body characteristic of pain and physical restraint is of a very different kind from that of sexual excitement: pain causes people to contract rather than dissolve.

Both of these disorders have to do with the second stage, which involves the awareness of oneself as an object of desire. In straightforward sadism and masochism other attentions are substituted for desire as a source of the object's self-awareness. But it is also possible for nothing of that sort to be substituted, as in the case of a masochist who is satisfied with self-inflicted pain or of a sadist who does not insist on playing a role in the suffering that arouses him. Greater difficulties of classification are presented by three other categories of sexual activity: elaborations of the sexual act; intercourse of more than two persons; and homosexuality.

If we apply our model to the various forms that may be taken by two-party heterosexual intercourse, none of them seem clearly to qualify as perversions. Hardly anyone can be found these days to inveigh against oral-genital contact, and the merits of buggery are urged by such respectable figures as D. H. Lawrence and Norman Mailer. There may be something vaguely sadistic about the latter technique (in Mailer's writings it seems to be a method of introducing an element of rape), but it is not obvious that this has to be so. In general, it would appear that any bodily contact between a man and a woman that gives them sexual pleasure, is a possible vehicle for the system of multi-level interpersonal awareness that I have claimed is the basic psychological content of sexual interaction. Thus a liberal platitude about sex is upheld.

About multiple combinations, the least that can be said is that they are bound to be complicated. If one considers how difficult it is to carry on two conversations simultaneously, one may appreciate the problems of multiple simultaneous interpersonal perception that can arise in even a small-scale orgy. It may be inevitable that some of the component relations should degenerate into mutual epidermal stimulation by participants otherwise isolated from each other. There may also be a tendency toward voyeurism and exhibitionism, both of which are incomplete relations. The exhibitionist wishes to display his desire without needing to be desired in return; he may even fear the sexual attentions of others. A voyeur, on the other hand, need not require any recognition by his object at all: certainly not a recognition of the voyeur's arousal.

It is not clear whether homosexuality is a perversion if that is measured by the standard of the described configuration, but it seems unlikely. For such a classification would have to depend on the possibility of extracting from the system a distinction between male and female sexuality; and much that has been said so far applies equally to men and women. Moreover, it would have to be maintained that there was a natural tie between the type of sexuality and the sex of the body, and also that two sexualities of the same type could not interact properly.

Certainly there is much support for an aggressive-passive distinction between male and female sexuality. In our culture the male's arousal tends to initiate the perceptual exchange, he usually makes the sexual approach, largely controls the course of the act, and of course penetrates whereas the woman receives. When two men or two women engage in intercourse they cannot both adhere to these sexual roles. The question is how essential the roles are to an adequate sexual relation. One relevant observation is that a good deal of deviation from the roles occurs in heterosexual intercourse. Women can be sexually aggressive and men passive, and temporary reversals of role are not uncommon in heterosexual exchanges of reasonable length. If such conditions are set aside, it may be urged that there is something irreducibly perverted in attraction to a body anatomically like one's own. But alarming as some people in our culture may find such attraction, it remains psychologically unilluminating to class it as perverted. Certainly if homosexuality is a perversion, it is so in a very different sense from that in which shoe-fetishism is a perversion, for some version of the full range of interpersonal perceptions seems perfectly possible between two persons of the same sex.

In any case, even if the proposed model is correct, it remains implausible to describe as perverted every deviation from it. For example, if the partners in heterosexual intercourse indulge in private heterosexual fantasies, that obscures the recognition of the real partner and so, on the theory, constitutes a defective sexual relation. It is not, however, generally regarded as a perversion. Such examples suggest that a simple dichotomy between perverted and unperverted sex is too crude to organize the phenomena adequately.

I should like to close with some remarks about the relation of perversion to good, bad, and morality. The concept of perversion can hardly fail to be evaluative in some sense, for it appears to involve the notion of an ideal or at least adequate sexuality which the perversions in some way fail to achieve. So, if the concept is viable, the judgment that a person or practice or desire is perverted will constitute a sexual evaluation, implying that better sex, or a better specimen of sex, is possible. This in itself is a very weak claim, since the evaluation might be in a dimension that is of little interest to us. (Though, if my account is correct, that will not be true.)

Whether it is a moral evaluation, however, is another question entirely—one whose answer would require more understanding of both morality and perversion that can be deployed here. Moral evaluation of acts and of persons is a rather special and very complicated matter, and by no means all our evaluations of persons and their activities are moral evaluations. We make judgments about people's beauty or health or intelligence which are evaluative without being moral. Assessments of their sexuality may be similar in that respect.

Furthermore, moral issues aside, it is not clear that unperverted sex is necessarily *preferable* to the perversions. It may be that sex which receives the highest marks for perfection *as sex* is less enjoyable than certain perversions; and if enjoyment is considered very important, that might outweigh considerations of sexual perfection in determining rational preference.

That raises the question of the relation between the evaluative content of judgments of perversion and the rather common *general* distinction between good and bad sex. The latter distinction is usually confined to sexual acts, and it would seem, within limits, to cut across the other: even someone who believed, for example, that homosexuality was a perversion could admit a distinction between better and worse homosexual sex, and might even allow that good homosexual sex could be better *sex* than not very good unperverted sex. If this is correct, it supports the position that, if judgments of perversion are viable at all, they represent only one aspect of the possible evaluation of sex, even *qua sex*. Moreover it is not the only important aspect: certainly sexual deficiencies that evidently do not constitute perversions can be the object of great concern.

Finally, even if perverted sex is to that extent not so good as it might be, bad sex is generally better than none at all. This should not be controversial: it seems to hold for other important matters, like food, music, literature, and society. In the end, one must choose from among the available alternatives, whether their availability depends on the environment or on one's own constitution. And the alternatives have to be fairly grim before it becomes rational to opt for nothing.

NOTES

1. Translated by Hazel E. Barnes (New York: Philosophical Library, 1956).
2. "Meaning," *Philosophical Review*, LXVI, 3 (July 1957), pp. 377–388.
3. See Romans, VII, 23; and the *Confessions*, Book 8, v.

Robert Solomon

Sexual Paradigms

It is a cocktail lounge, well-lit and mirrored, not a bar, martinis and not beer, two strangers—a furtive glance from him, shy recognition from her. It is 1950's American high comedy; boy arouses girl, both are led through ninety minutes of misunderstandings of identity and intention, and, finally, by the end of the popcorn, boy kisses girl with a clean-cut fade-out or panned clip of a postcard horizon. It is one of the dangers of conceptual analysis that the philosopher's choice of paradigms betrays a personal bias, but it is an exceptional danger of sexual conceptual analysis that one's choice of paradigms also betrays one's private fantasies and personal obsessions.[1] No doubt that is why, despite their extraprofessional interest in the subject, most philosophers would rather write about indirect discourse than intercourse, the philosophy of mind rather than the philosophy of body.

In Tom Nagel's pioneering effort[2] there are too many recognizable symptoms of liberal American sexual mythology. His analysis is cautious and competent, but absolutely sexless. His Romeo and Juliet exemplify at most a romanticized version of the initial phases of (hetero-)sexual attraction in a casual and innocent pickup. They "arouse" each other, but there is no indication to what end. They "incarnate each other as flesh," in Sartre's awkward but precise terminology, but Nagel gives us no clue as to why they

Reprinted by permission from *The Journal of Philosophy* 71, No. 11 (1974), pp. 336–345.

should indulge in such a peculiar activity. Presumably a pair of dermatologists or fashion models might have a similar effect on each other, but without the slightest hint of sexual intention. What makes this situation paradigmatically sexual? We may assume, as we would in a Doris Day comedy, that the object of this protracted arousal is sexual intercourse, but we are not told this. Sexuality without content. Liberal sexual mythology takes this Hollywood element of "leave it to the imagination" as its starting point and adds the equally inexplicit suggestion that whatever activities two consenting adults choose as the object of their arousal and its gratification is "their business." In a society with such secrets, pornography is bound to serve a radical end as a vulgar valve of reality. In a philosophical analysis that stops short of the very matter investigated, a bit of perverseness may be necessary just in order to refocus the question.

Sexual desire is distinguished, like all desires, by its aims and objects. What are these peculiarly sexual aims and objects? Notice that Nagel employs a fairly standard "paradigm case argument" in his analysis; he begins,

. . . certain practices will be perversions if anything is, such as shoe fetishism, bestiality and sadism; other practices, such as unadorned sexual intercourse will not be (76).

So we can assume that the end of Romeo and Juliet's tryst will be intercourse—we do not know whether "adorned" or not. But what is it that makes intercourse the paradigm of sexual activity—its biological role in conception, its heterosexuality, its convenience for mutual orgasm? Would Nagel's drama still serve as a sexual paradigm if Juliet turns out to be a virgin, or if Romeo and Juliet find that they are complementarily sado-masochistic, if Romeo is in drag, if they are both knee-fetishists? Why does Nagel choose two *strangers?* Why not, as in the days of sexual moralism, a happily married couple enjoying their seventh anniversary? Or is not the essence of sex, as Sartre so brutally argues, Romeo and Juliet's mutual attempts to possess each other, with each's own enjoyment only a secondary and essentially distracting effect? Are we expected to presume the most prominent paradigm, at least since Freud, the lusty ejaculation of Romeo into the submissive, if not passive, Juliet? Suppose Juliet is in fact a prostitute, skillfully mocking the signs of innocent arousal: is this a breach of the paradigm, or might not such subsequent "unadorned" intercourse be just the model that Nagel claims to defend?

To what end does Romeo arouse Juliet? And to what end does Juliet become affected and in turn excite Romeo? In this exemplary instance, I would think that "unadorned" intercourse would be perverse, or at least distasteful, in the extreme. It would be different, however, if the paradigm were our seven-year married couple, for in such cases "adorned" intercourse might well be something of a rarity. In homosexual encounters, in the frenzy of adolescent virginal petting, in cases in which intercourse is restricted for temporary medical or political reasons, arousal may be no different, even though intercourse cannot be the end. And it is only in the crudest cases of physiological need that the desire for intercourse is the sole or even the leading component in the convoluted motivation of sexuality. A nineteen-year-old sailor back after having discussed nothing but sex on a three-month cruise may be so aroused, but that surely is not the nature of Juliet's arousal. Romeo may remind her of her father, or of her favorite philosophy professor, and he may inspire respect, or fear, or curiosity. He may simply arouse self-consciousness or embarrassment. Any of these attitudes may be dominant, but none is particularly sexual.

Sexuality has an essential bodily dimension, and this might well be described as the "incarnation" or "submersion" of a person into his body. The end of this desire is interpersonal communication; but where Sartre gives a complex theory of the nature of this communication, Nagel gives us only an empty notion of "multi-level interpersonal awareness." Presumably the mutual arousal that is the means to this awareness is enjoyable in itself. But it is important that Nagel resists the current (W.) Reichian-American fetish for the wonders of the genital orgasm, for he does not leap to the facile conclusion that the aim of sexual activity is mutual or at least personal orgasm. It is here that Nagel opens a breach with liberal sexual mythology, one that might at first appear absurd because of his total neglect of the role of the genitalia and orgasm in sexuality. But we have an overgenitalized conception of sexuality, and, if sexual satisfaction involves and even requires orgasm, it does not follow that orgasm is the goal of the convoluted sexual games we play with each other. Orgasm is the "end" of sexual activity, perhaps, but only in the sense that swallowing is the "end" of tasting a Viennese torte.

There was a time, and it was not long ago and may come soon again, when sexuality required defending. It had to be argued that we had a right to sex, not for any purpose other than our personal enjoyment. But that defense has turned stale, and sexual deprivation is no longer our problem. The "swollen bladder" model of repressed sexuality may have been convincing in sex-scared bourgeois Vienna of 1905, but not today, where the problem is not sexual deprivation but sexual dissatisfaction. The fetishism of the orgasm, now shared by women as well as men, threatens our sex lives with becoming antipersonal and mechanical, anxiety-filled athletic arenas with mutual multiple orgasm its goal. Behind much of this unhappiness and anxiety, ironically, stands the liberal defense of sexuality as enjoyment. It is one of the virtues of Nagel's essay that he begins to overcome this oppressive liberal mythology. But at the same time he relies upon it for his support and becomes trapped in it, and the result is an account which displays the emptiness we have pointed out and the final note of despair with which he ends his essay.

Liberal sexual mythology appears to stand upon a tripod of mutually supporting platitudes: (1) and foremost, that the essential aim (and even the sole aim) of sex is enjoyment; (2) that sexual activity is and ought to be essentially private activity, and (3) that any sexual activity is as valid as any other. The first platitude was once a radical proposition, a reaction to the conservative and pious belief that sexual activity was activity whose end was reproduction, the serving of God's will or natural law. Kant, for example, always good for a shocking opinion in the realm of normative ethics, suggests that sexual lust is an appetite with an end intended by nature, and that any sexual activity contrary to that end is "unnatural and revolting," by which one "makes himself an object of abomination and stands bereft of all reverence of any kind."[3] It was Sigmund Freud who destroyed this long-standing paradigm, in identifying sexuality as "discharge of tension" (physical and psychological), which he simply equated with "pleasure," regardless of the areas of the body or what activities or how many people happened to be involved. Sex was thus defined as self-serving, activity for its own sake, with pleasure as its only principle. If Freud is now accused of sexual conservatism, it is necessary to remind ourselves that he introduced the radical paradigm that is now used against him. Since Freud's classic efforts, the conception of sexuality as a means to other ends, whether procreation or pious love, has become bankrupt in terms of the currency of opinion. Even radical sexual ideology has confined its critique to the social and political *abuses* of this liberal platitude without openly rejecting it.

The second platitude is a hold-over from more conservative

days, in which sexual activity, like defecation, menstruation, and the bodily reactions to illness, was considered distasteful, if not shameful and to be hidden from view. Yet this conservative platitude is as essential as the first, for the typically utilitarian argument in defense of sexuality as enjoyment is based on the idea that sex is private activity and, when confined to "consenting adults," should be left as a matter of taste. And sex is, we are reminded by liberals, a natural appetite, and therefore a matter of taste.

The platitude of privacy also bolsters the third principle, still considered a radical principle by many, that any sexual activity is as valid as any other. Again, the utilitarian argument prevails, that private and mutually consented activity between adults, no matter how distasteful it might be to others and no matter how we may think its enthusiasts to be depraved, is "their own business."

Nagel's analysis calls this tri-part ideology to his side, although he clearly attempts to go beyond it as well. The platitude of enjoyment functions only loosely in his essay, and at one point he makes it clear that sexuality need not aim at enjoyment. ["It may be that . . . perfection *as sex* is less enjoyable than certain perversions; and if enjoyment is considered very important, that might outweigh considerations of sexual perfection in determining rational preference" (88).] His central notion of "arousal," however, is equivocal. On the one hand, arousal is itself not necessarily enjoyable, particularly if it fails to be accompanied with expectations of release. But on the other hand, Nagel's "arousal" plays precisely the same role in his analysis that "tension" (or "cathexis") plays in Freud, and though the arousal itself is not enjoyable, its release is, and the impression we get from Nagel, which Freud makes explicit, is that sexual activity is the intentional arousal both of self and other in order to enjoy its release. On this interpretation, Nagel's analysis is perfectly in line with post-Freudian liberal theory.

Regarding the second platitude, Nagel's analysis does not mention it, but rather it appears to be presupposed throughout that sexuality is a private affair. One might repeat that the notion of privacy is more symptomatic of his analysis itself. One cannot imagine J. L. Austin spending a dozen pages describing the intentions and inclinations involved in a public performance of making a promise or christening a ship without mentioning the performance itself. Yet Nagel spends that much space giving us the preliminaries of sexuality without ever quite breaching the private sector in which sexual activity is to be found.

The third platitude emerges only slowly in Nagel's essay. He begins by chastising an approach to that same conclusion by a radical "skeptic," who argues of sexual desires, as "appetites,"

Either they are sexual or they are not; sexuality does not admit of imperfection, or perversion, or any other such qualification (78).

Nagel's analysis goes beyond this "skepticism" in important ways, yet he does conclude that "any bodily contact between a man and a woman that gives them sexual *pleasure* [italics mine], is a possible vehicle for the system of multi-level interpersonal awareness that I have claimed is the basic psychological content of sexual interaction" (86). Here the first platitude is partially employed to support the third, presumably with the second implied. Notice again that Nagel has given us no indication what distinguishes "sexual pleasure" from other pleasures, whether bodily pleasures or the enjoyment of conquest or domination, seduction or submission, sleeping with the president's daughter or earning thirty dollars.

To knock down a tripod, one need kick out only one of its supporting legs. I for one would not wish to advocate, along with several recent sexual pundits, an increased display of fornication and fellatio in public places, nor would I view the return of "sexual morality" as a desirable state of affairs. Surprisingly, it is the essential enjoyment of sex that is the least palatable of the liberal myths.

No one would deny that sex is enjoyable, but it does not follow that sexuality is the activity of "pure enjoyment" and that "gratification," or "pure physical pleasure," that is, orgasm, is its end. Sex is indeed pleasurable, but, as Aristotle argued against the hedonists of his day, this enjoyment accompanies sexual activity and its ends, but is not that activity or these ends. We enjoy being sexually satisfied; we are not satisfied by our enjoyment. In fact, one might reasonably hypothesize that the performance of any activity, pleasurable or not, which is as intensely promoted and obsessively pursued as sex in America would provide tremendous gratification. [One might further speculate on the fact that recent American politics shows that "every (white, male Christian) American boy's dream of becoming President" seems to encourage the exploitation of all three sexual platitudes of enjoyment, privacy, and "anything goes." (Cf. H. Kissinger, "Power is the ultimate aphrodisiac.")]

If sexuality does not essentially aim at pleasure, does it have any purpose? Jean-Paul Sartre has given us an alternative to the liberal theory in his *Being and Nothingness*, in which he argues that our sexual relations with others, like all our various relationships with others, are to be construed as *conflicts,* modeled after Hegel's parable of master and slave. Sexual desire is not desire for pleasure, and pleasure is more likely to distract us from sexuality than to deepen our involvement. For Sartre, sexual desire is the desire to possess, to gain recognition of one's own freedom at the expense of the other. By "incarnating" and degrading him/her in flesh, one reduces him/her to an object. Sadism is but an extension of this domination over the other. Or one allows himself to be "incarnated" as a devious route to the same end, making the other his/her sexual slave. Sexual activity concentrates its attention on the least personal, most inert parts of the body—breasts, thighs, stomach, and emphasizes awkward and immobile postures and activities. On this model, degradation is the central activity of sex, to convince the other that he/she is a slave, to persuade the other of one's own power, whether it be through the skills of sexual technique or through the passive demands of being sexually served. Intercourse has no privileged position in this model, except that intercourse, particularly in these liberated times in which it has become a contest, is ideal for this competition for power and recognition. And no doubt Sartre, who, like Freud, adopts a paradigmatically male perspective, senses that intercourse is more likely to be degrading to the woman, who thus begins at a disadvantage.

Sartre's notion of sexuality, taken seriously, would be enough to keep us out of bed for a month. Surely, we must object, something has been left out of account, for example, the two-person *Mitsein* that Sartre himself suggests in the same book. It is impossible for us to delve into the complex ontology that leads Sartre into this pessimistic model, but its essential structure is precisely what we need to carry us beyond the liberal mythology. According to Sartre, sexuality is interpersonal communication with the body as its medium. Sartre's mistake, if we may be brief, is his narrow constriction of the message of that communication to mutual degradation and conflict. Nagel, who accepts Sartre's communication model but, in line with the liberal mythology, seeks to reject its pessimistic conclusions, makes a mistake in the opposite direction. He accepts the communication model, but leaves it utterly without content. What is communicated, he suggests, is arousal. But, as we have seen, arousal is too broad a notion; we must know arousal of what, for what, to what end. Nagel's notion of "arousal" and "interpersonal awareness" gives us an outline of the grammar of the communication model, but no semantics. One might add that sexual activity in which what is aroused and intended are pleasurable sensations alone is a limiting and rare case. A sensation is only pleasurable or enjoyable, not in itself, but in the context of the meaning of the activity in which it is embedded. This is as true of orgasm as it is of a hard passion-bite on the shoulder.

This view of sexuality answers some strong questions which the liberal model leaves a mystery. If sex is pure physical enjoyment, why is sexual activity between persons far more satisfying than masturbation, where, if we accept recent physiological studies, orgasm is at its highest intensity and the post-coital period is cleansed of its interpersonal hassles and arguments? On the Freudian model, sex with other people ("objects") becomes a matter of "secondary process," with masturbation primary. On the communication model, masturbation is like talking to yourself; possible, even enjoyable, but clearly secondary to sexuality in its broader interpersonal context. (It is significant that even this carnal solipsism is typically accompanied by imaginings and pictures; "No masturbation without representation," perhaps.) If sex is physical pleasure, then the fetish of the genital orgasm is no doubt justifiable, but then why in our orgasm-cluttered sex lives are we so dissatisfied? Because orgasm is not the "end" of sex but its resolution, and obsessive concentration on reaching climax effectively overwhelms or distorts whatever else is being said sexually. It is this focus on orgasm that has made Sartre's model more persuasive; for the battle over the orgasm, whether in selfish or altruistic guise ("my orgasm first" or "I'll *give* you the best ever") has become an unavoidable medium for conflict and control. "Unadorned sexual intercourse," on this model, becomes the ultimate perversion, since it is the sexual equivalent of hanging up the telephone without saying anything. Even an obscene telephone caller has a message to convey.

Sexual activity consists in speaking what we might call "body language." It has its own grammar, delineated by the body, and its own phonetics of touch and movement. Its unit of meaningfulness, the bodily equivalent of a sentence, is the *gesture*. No doubt one could add considerably to its vocabulary, and perhaps it could be possible to discuss world politics or the mind-body problem by an appropriate set of invented gestures. But body language is essentially expressive, and its content is limited to interpersonal attitudes and feelings—shyness, domination, fear, submissiveness and dependence, love or hatred or indifference, lack of confidence and embarrassment, shame, jealousy, possessiveness. There is little value in stressing the overworked point that such expressions are "natural" expressions, as opposed to verbal expressions of the same attitudes and feelings. In our highly verbal society, it may well be that verbal expression, whether it be poetry or clumsy blurting, feels more natural than the use of our bodies. Yet it does seem true that some attitudes, e.g., tenderness and trust, domination and passivity, are best expressed sexually. Love, it seems, is not best expressed sexually, for its sexual expression is indistinguishable from the expressions of a number of other attitudes. Possessiveness, mutual recognition, "being-with," and conflict are expressed by body language almost essentially, virtually as its deep structure, and here Sartre's model obtains its plausibility.

According to Nagel, "perversion" is "truncated or incomplete versions of the complete configuration" (85). But again, his emphasis is entirely on the form of "interpersonal awareness" rather than its content. For example, he analyzes sadism as "the concentration on the evocation of passive self-awareness in others . . . which impedes awareness of himself as a bodily subject of passion in the required sense." But surely sadism is not so much a breakdown in communication (any more than the domination of a conversation by one speaker, with the agreement of his listener, is a breach of language) as an excessive expression of a particular content, namely the attitude of domination, perhaps mixed with hatred, fear, and other negative attitudes. Similarly, masochism is not simply the relinquishing of one's activity (an inability to speak, in a sense), for the masochist may well be active in inviting punishment from his sadistic partner. Masochism is excessive expression of an attitude of victimization, shame, or inferiority. Moreover, it is clear that there is not the slightest taint of "perversion" in homosexuality, which need differ from heterosexuality only in its mode of resolution. Fetishism and bestiality certainly do constitute perversions, since the first is the same as, for example, talking to someone else's shoes, and the second is like discussing Spinoza with a moderately intelligent sheep.

This model also makes it evident why Nagel chose as his example a couple of strangers; one has far more to say, for one can freely express one's fantasies as well as the truth, to a stranger. A husband and wife of seven years have probably been repeating the same messages for years, and their sexual activity now is probably no more than an abbreviated ritual incantation of the lengthy conversations they had years before. One can imagine Romeo and Juliet climbing into bed together each with a spectacular set of expectations and fantasies, trying to overwhelm each other with extravagant expressions and experiments. But it may be, accordingly, that they won't understand each other, or, as the weekend plods on, sex, like any extended conversation, tends to become either more truthful or more incoherent.

Qua body language, sex admits of at least two forms of perversion: one deviance of form, the other deviance in content. There are the techniques of sexuality, overly celebrated in our society, and there are the attitudes that these techniques allegedly express. Nagel and most theorists have concentrated on perversions in technique, deviations in the forms of sexual activity. But it seems to me that the more problematic perversions are the semantic deviations, of which the most serious are those involving insincerity, the bodily equivalent of the lie. Entertaining private fantasies and neglecting one's real sexual partner is thus an innocent semantic perversion, while pretended tenderness and affection that reverses itself soon after orgasm is a potentially vicious perversion. However, again joining Nagel, I would argue that perverse sex is not necessarily bad or immoral sex. Pretense is the premise of imagination as well as of falsehood, and sexual fantasies may enrich our lives far more than sexual realities alone. Perhaps it is an unfortunate comment on the poverty of contemporary life that our fantasies have become so confined, that our sexuality has been forced to serve needs which far exceed its expressive capacity. That is why the liberal mythology has been so disastrous, for it has rendered unconscious the expressive functions of sex in its stress on enjoyment and, in its platitude of privacy, has reduced sexuality to each man's/woman's private language, first spoken clumsily and barely articulately on wedding nights and in the back seats of Fords. It is thus understandable why sex is so utterly important in our lives, and why it is typically so unsatisfactory.

NOTES

1. I confess, for example, that certain male biases infiltrate my own analysis. I thank Janice Moulton for pointing this out to me.
2. "Sexual Perversion," *The Journal of Philosophy* 66, No. 1 (1969), pp. 5–17. (This volume, pp. 76–88).
3. *Metaphysics of Ethics*, trans. Semple (Edinburgh: Clark, 1971) IV, pt. I, ch. 1, sec. 7.

Hugh T. Wilder

The Language of Sex and the Sex of Language

It has long been popular to compare sex with language. The comparison is plausible and suggestive: sexual activity and linguistic activity both seem to be intentionally communicative, both foster interpersonal intimacy and understanding, both have a grammar of sorts, and so on. Robert Solomon has recently given a philosophical defense of this comparison,[1] to the detriment, I believe, of both sex and language. Both deserve better treatment, which I hope to provide in this paper. I will explore the comparison between sex and language through a close reading of Solomon's texts on sex. Solomon defends a particular instrumentalist and phonocentric view of language, which results, I will argue, in a repressive and sexist view of sex. This view of sex is clear in two claims made by Solomon which we will look at closely: that heterosexual intercourse is the "paradigm of sexual activity,"[2] and that masturbation is a "deviation."[3] Through this study of Solomon's treatment of sex and language, I will be offering what

A slightly different version of this paper was read at a meeting of the Society for the Philosophy of Sex and Love, Pacific Division of the American Philosophical Association, San Diego, March, 1979.

seems to be a richer understanding of the comparison between sex and language.

I

In his writing on sexuality, Solomon is attempting to develop a theory of "natural" or "paradigmatic" sex. He says that his

starting point will be that human sexuality has its own 'natural purpose,' its own 'nature,' apart from any *further* purposes attributed to our creator, and apart from any biological function of increasing the numbers of an already too numerous natural kind.[4]

Natural or paradigmatic sex is sex which serves this natural purpose; perverted sex is sex which does not.

The natural purpose of sex is, according to Solomon, interpersonal communication. Interpersonal communication is also the essential purpose of language. Therefore, he claims, sex is a language: communication is the aim, the body is the medium.[5] Sex which does not serve the purpose of interpersonal communication is deviant sex, just as language not serving the same purpose is deviant language. Communication essentially involves more than one person; therefore, natural sexual activities essentially involve more than one person. Masturbation is not interpersonal communication; therefore, Solomon argues, masturbation is "borderline" sex, a deviation, sex misfired.

II

Granting Solomon's major thesis, that sex is a language, we may learn about the nature of sex by studying the nature of language. More immediately, we may learn about Solomon's conception of sex by studying his conception of language. Solomon gives an instrumentalist analysis of language: language is an instrument serving the end of interpersonal communication, and it has succeeded in serving this end when mutual understanding is produced. Since sex is language, it is not surprising that Solomon also endorses an instrumentalist analysis of sex.

But, the essential purpose of language is *not* interpersonal communication. Claims about the essential purposes of language may be interpreted in either of two ways: according to the stronger interpretation, language not serving the putative essential purpose is not even language; according to the weaker, language not serving the putative essential purpose is deviant or abnormal language. While it is not clear which interpretation Solomon intends, this is relatively unimportant; the thesis, that the essential purpose of language is communication, is false on both readings. If it were true, many perfectly good, non-deviant uses of language would be marked as deviant or even non-linguistic, as not serving the putative essential purpose of language. The issue here is two-fold: does language have an essential purpose, and, if it does, what is it? Although the issues obviously cannot be resolved here, I will argue that, especially in the context of comparing language with sex, language is best understood as having *no essential* purpose.

Those who believe that language does have an essential purpose fall roughly into two traditions: the instrumentalist and the formalist. The instrumentalists (Solomon, Searle, Austin, and many other post-Wittgensteinians) claim that language is an instrument, essentially used for communication. The formalists (Descartes, Humboldt, Chomsky, etc.) claim that language is essentially a means of thought and self-expression.[6] As Chomsky points out, when the instrumentalists limit normal, non-deviant communication to *interpersonal* communication, as Solomon does, they are surely wrong. To say that soliloquies are non-linguistic or deviant is absurd; thinking out loud, talking to express and clarify one's thoughts, whether or not anything is communicated, are normal linguistic activities.

A second argument against the instrumentalist view is that even if the concept of communication is extended to include communication with one's self—i.e., thinking in words—still, the intent of normal language is not always to communicate.[7] Sometimes we use language to deceive, sometimes to fill embarrassing silences, sometimes to play a part in a ritual (to use Chomsky's examples);[8] in these and countless other normal, non-deviant cases, language is being used, while nothing is communicated and there is not even an intention to communicate anything.

The last argument may be used—although it is not by those I have called linguistic "formalists"—to support the view that language has no inherent purpose. Our uses of language have as wide a variety of purposes as humans may have, and none of these purposes is inherent in language; none is more normal, in either a normative or statistical sense, than any other. The linguistic formalists are just as wrong as the instrumentalists. To cite just a few examples, to speak a part in a verbal ritual, to read aloud, to transcribe, summarize, and even write a text are all perfectly good "uses of language," but are hardly ever expressions of one's thoughts, as the formalists might have us believe. We have many different reasons for saying and writing what we do; sometimes our reasons are so vague and amorphous as to be non-existent. Language has no one purpose to the exclusion of others, unless one so general could be found that it was utterly trivial.

The rubric "sex is language" takes on new significance in this non-instrumentalist and non-essentialist view of language. One traditional support of the phallocentric view of sex is knocked out. On the phallocentric view, sexuality in general is understood as "normal" (Freudian) male sexuality: i.e., sex with a direction, a point, a central thrust, a purpose; sex which has results, sex with a clear criterion of success and completion; sex modeled on male ejaculation.[9] This theme will be further developed in the next few pages; the way has already been opened, however, for a non-sexist, non-phallocentric conception of sex. Sex is still language, but perhaps aimless language. The concepts of directionality, thrust, goal, success, and completion drop out, or at least lose potency. Sex is no longer necessarily productive: perhaps, to be extreme, not even productive of male ejaculate.

The language of sex—as any language—can have any number of different purposes, but it has no essential purpose. Therefore no one sexual activity can be said to serve the putative purpose of sex/language, and no activity can be said to be deviant because it does not serve the putative purpose.[10] In particular, conceiving sex as language no longer provides support to those, including Solomon, who elevate heterosexual intercourse to paradigmatic sex while derogating masturbation as a "borderline case" of sexual activity.

III

The second main problem with Solomon's conception of language is that language is assumed to be entirely spoken and never written. This "phonocentrism" leads to a narrow, repressive conception of the language of sex; and to a sexist conception, because, as Derrida has shown, linguistic phonocentrism is one aspect of philosophical phallocentrism which becomes apparent once philosophy has made the linguistic turn.

Solomon is not alone among philosophers in valuing speech over writing, and in conceiving of language exclusively in terms of speech; as Jacques Derrida has shown, Western philosophers from Plato to Austin[11] have, with very few exceptions, shared this bias.

The bias in favor of speech is traced by Derrida to "the doctrine of presence," the pervasive search for Being, which has animated Western philosophy from the beginning. Being is truth, beauty and goodness; the closer we are to it and the clearer we are about it, the better. Intuition, immediacy, and clarity are valued in the search; opacity, indirection, and inference are risky; aimlessness is anathema.

The doctrine of presence is hierarchical. Being is at the top: the really real, the object of all inquiry. Thought is (better or worse) representation of Being, speech is representation of thought, and writing is representation of speech. If proximity to Being is good, writing is very bad. This hierarchy is explicit in Aristotle:

Spoken words are the symbols of mental experience and written words are the symbols of spoken words. Just as all men have not the same writing, so all men have not the same speech sounds, but the mental experiences, which these directly symbolize, are the same for all, as also are those things of which our experiences are the images.[12]

The doctrine of presence dictates a program for scientific and philosophical writing. Science is the attempt to correctly represent Being, and philosophy is the meta-scientific attempt to correctly represent representation. Both scientific and philosophical writing aspire to the lucidity of speech, and to proximity with Being. Such writing-as-speech is self-destructive, in the sense that good scientific and philosophical writing is clear, invisible, transparent; it denies its existence as writing in its attempt to let Being shine through.

Normal scientific language is phallocentric.[13] Such language— whether speech or writing-as-speech—is used as an instrument, to get something or somewhere else. It is not important or pleasurable in itself; it is important as a means to the end of mirroring Being. It is language with a point. It is a way of "getting off"— getting off itself, onto or closer to Being. The language which has the best chance of getting off is spoken language. If one's goal is Being, to begin with writing is risky and dangerous; the path through representations of representations of representations is too easy to miss.

If normal scientific language is phallocentric, writing-as-writing—writing without aspirations to speech—is masturbatory. It is not non-sexy masturbation for quick orgasm, but rather masturbation as aimless self-pleasuring.[14] Writing-as-writing is opaque and dense rather than transparent; it is non-self-destructive; it is writing content with its status as writing; it is playful and indirect rather than serious and direct; aimless and pointless, never finished, infinitely readable and interpretable rather than definitively communicative.

If this discussion—invited by Solomon—of the sex of language seems extravagant, one only need read for justification the phallocentric writers on language cited by Derrida. The terms of their elevation of speech and derogation of writing are the same as philosophers' elevation of heterosexual intercourse (which is described, all too often, as male evacuation lust coupled with female submissiveness) and derogation of masturbation. Plato: writing is a drug. Levi-Strauss: writing is perfidy. Saussure: writing is to speech as a photograph is to reality (compare Sartre's "masturbation counterfeits intercourse"[15]). Rousseau: "languages are made to be spoken, writing serves only as a supplement to speech"; writing is "dangerous," "scandalous," "perverse," even "a sin."[16] Writing is a cheat: writing-as-writing makes no pretense of representing Being. (Compare Sartre's "dishonest masturbator": the masturbator by choice, the one who can get away—"off"—without the real thing, i.e., without intersubjectivity.) Speech carries the burden of purpose; writing-as-writing is light and free. It is therefore too easy, seductive, and dangerous.

IV

With this Derridean understanding of the sex of language, we may return to Solomon. For him, sex is language, language is speech, good—"natural"—sex is speech, and masturbation as far from "natural" sex as writing is from speech. Solomon's probably unwitting censure of writing parallels his censure of masturbation.

Solomon assumes that language is essentially spoken language, and that sexual language is the sexual equivalent of speech. He writes this, explicitly: "sexuality is primarily a means of communicating with other people, a way of *talking* to them."[17] The language of sex has its own "phonetics," but no alphabet.[18] The language of sex is "*essentially* an activity performed with other people."[19] It is plausible (but false, I believe) to think that *spoken* language is essentially interpersonal; it is obviously false that *written* language is essentially interpersonal. In fact, an argument could be given showing that writing is best understood as a private activity, not surprisingly, on the model of masturbation: both are done by oneself for oneself, and are perhaps shared and observed by others but usually not.

Solomon's treatments of sexual perversions and aberrations, as well as of refined and offensive sex, provide further illustration of his phonocentric view of the language of sex. Consider, first, masturbation: a "borderline case" of sex, for Solomon. Solomon explains masturbation mostly in terms of verbal analysis: masturbation "is essentially speaking to oneself," "muttering to oneself," the sexual equivalent of a soliloquy, "an inability or a refusal to say what one wants to say."[20] No wonder masturbation is not quite sex: neither is refusal to say what one wants to say speech. Solomon does use one writing metaphor: masturbation is like writing a letter and not mailing it. This metaphor is intended to support the claim that masturbation is a borderline case of sexual language. But in this the metaphor fails; writing a letter and not mailing it—not even intending to mail it—is a fine case of *written* language.

Consider also Solomon's treatment of sexual aberrations. Fetishism is "talking to someone else's shoes," bestiality is "like discussing Spinoza with a moderately intelligent sheep;"[21] a voyeur is "someone with nothing to say;" in sexual promiscuity "one risks carrying over from one conversation gestures that are appropriate to another," and group sex "creates the serious danger of simultaneous incoherent polylogues," but "offers the rare possibility of linguistic forms unavailable with fewer voices."[22] Sexual aberrations are *verbal* aberrations.

Further, refined sex—i.e., communicative, "non-animalistic"[23] sex—is always compared to verbal language; one of the few times Solomon switches to sex-as-written language is when he is describing offensive sex. Thus,

blatant sexual propositions and subway exhibitionism are offensive . . . because they are vulgar, the equivalent of an antipoetry poet who writes an entire poem consisting of a single vulgar word, or a comedian who, unable to handle condensation and understatement, has to spell out his obscene jokes explicitly.[24]

To admittedly lift a line out of context, Solomon also writes: "The cry of perversion with regard to body language is very much like that of censorship with regard to the written word."[25] This is precisely my complaint: Solomon's probably unwitting censorship of the written word from his conception of language has as its sexual analog his own censorship of masturbation from the realm of the sexual.

Solomon also equates what he thinks are the genuine sexual perversions with the Austinian verbal "infelicities" of lying and insincerity.[26] Perversions *are* sexual, and they need not be vulgar or bad in any sense;[27] hence they receive treatment as *verbal* infelicities. For example, on Solomon's view it is a perversion to entertain private fantasies while having sex with another, because this is a form of insincerity in the language of sex.

But surely fantasizing while having sex—whether fantasizing other partners, other situations, other kinds of sex, etc.—is not a perversion, especially not the central case of perversion it turns out to be on Solomon's view. The problem is, again, that Solomon's phonocentric view of language is too narrow: in this case, it leads him to classify as perverse something which is not. Lying and insincerity are fairly straightforward notions in spoken language; not so in written language, however. As Derrida has written in response to Austin,[28] the very idea that lying and insincerity are infelicities in written language is nonsense; most literature depends essentially on what would be lying and insincerity in verbal contexts. Had Solomon compared sex with *language*—spoken and written—instead of speech, he might have been able to develop a less repressive and non-sexist view of sex and its aberrations.

V

Solomon's instrumentalist and phonocentric conception of the language of sex leads to a conception of sex which is peculiarly non-sexy. Sex is a language with communication as its aim; further, normal sex is restricted to communication with others, and some communications are evidently taboo. Solomon writes: sexual communication "is *essentially* an activity performed with other people;"[29] the messages communicated in sexual language are "*limited to* interpersonal attitudes and feelings."[30] These limitations on sex and on language generally only make sense on the assumption that Solomon has some sort of grudge against diaries, journals, any manner of self-expression of personal (as opposed to interpersonal) feelings, as well as against masturbation. It may seem extravagant to be defending the writing of diaries as genuine linguistic activity—as extravagant, as I hope it seems, to be defending masturbation as genuine sex. After reading Solomon, both seem to be necessary.

Solomon begins his paper on "Sexual Paradigms" with the announcement that heterosexual intercourse is "the paradigm of sexual activity"; toward the end of the paper he offers his "linguistic" derogation of masturbation. The point of sex, for Solomon, is to communicate messages. While refinement is good, anything which inhibits communication is bad. As with male sexuality, success in Solomon's verbal sexual encounters is well defined and easily recognizable: reception and comprehension of the message is all that counts. Incomprehension is sex misfired; deliberate obfuscation of the message is perverse.

Not only is sex not important in itself, or at least not as important as the messages communicated; Solomon even argues that it is tasteless to think that the aim of sex is enjoyment.[31] It may well be misleading to think that the aim of sex is enjoyment; but when this view is combined with Solomon's instrumentalist view of sexual language, one is left with a repressive, stereotypically male view of sex: straight heterosexual intercourse, little dallying around, finished when the man comes, and if the proceedings are pleasurable at all, the pleasure is in the coming. If one insists that sex is language, then sex must be seen as including non-instrumental written language—Derrida's writing-as-writing—if one is to allow oneself to see the sexiness of dalliance, indirection, softness, pointlessness, density, playfulness, and endless incompletion. Masturbation, among other things, happily turns out to be real sex.

Solomon's instrumentalist analysis of sexuality is repressive: any activity not serving the interests of interpersonal communication is stigmatized as deviant. For some unexplained reason, heterosexual intercourse is claimed to be a paradigm case of interpersonal communication. Obviously, cases of heterosexual intercourse are not always cases of interpersonal communication. And, other actions and practices—forms of dyadic homosexual lovemaking, for example—are often perfectly good cases of interpersonal communication.

Further, in denying the validity of masturbation as sex, Solomon is denying to both men and women a primary source of sexual self-discovery and independence. This denial weighs most heavily on women: in celebrating heterosexual intercourse at the expense of masturbation, Solomon is defending exclusively a kind of sex in which traditionally the shots are called by the man.

Notice that from the instrumentalist point of view heterosexual intercourse and masturbation are equally effective *for men*: both virtually always result in male ejaculation. Masturbation is often a reliable source of orgasms *for women*; a much more reliable source, at least in our culture, than heterosexual intercourse. Further, male masturbation is also perceived by men as dangerous *for men*: it is linked in most men's thoughts with castration fears.

And, most importantly, female masturbation is also perceived by men as dangerous *for men*, for a different reason: it restores sexual power and independence to women. To glorify heterosexual intercourse while derogating masturbation turns out to be a subtle kind of sexism.

To give up instrumentalist analyses of language and sex is not to deny all similarities between the two. Sex is still comparable to language in many ways. For example, language can be used to communicate, to express ideas and feelings, to produce ideas and feelings, to fill silences, to start conversations, to end conversations, to inform, to entertain, to deceive; it can be an instrument of pleasure, of pain, of goodness, of vice; it can be refined and offensive, boring and exciting, pointed and pointless. So can sex. To limit sex to one kind of thing serving one kind of purpose degrades sex and degrades the language with which it is being compared.

NOTES

1. Robert Solomon, "Sexual Paradigms, *Journal of Philosophy* 71 (1974), pp. 336–345 (pp. 89–98 in this volume). See also Robert Solomon, "Sex and Perversion", Robert Baker and Frederick Elliston, eds., *Philosophy and Sex* (Buffalo: Prometheus Books, 1975), pp. 268–287.
2. *Ibid.*, (1974), p. 90 (in this volume).
3. *Ibid.*, (1975), p. 283.
4. *Ibid.*, (1975), p. 271.
5. *Ibid.*, (1975), p. 279 ff. and (1974), p. 96 (in this volume).
6. Noam Chomsky, *Cartesian Linguistics* (New York: Harper and Row, 1966). See also Noam Chomsky, *Reflections on Language* (New York: Random House, 1975), p. 55ff, and Noam Chomsky, *Problems of Knowledge and Freedom* (New York: Random House, 1971), p. 19.
7. Moulton makes this same point against Solomon without herself giving up the instrumentalist analysis of language and sex. She writes: "Solomon's comparison of sexual behavior with linguistic behavior is handicapped by the limited view he has about their purposes. Language has more purposes than transmitting information . . . [It] has a phatic function to evoke feelings and attitudes. Language is often used to produce a shared experience . . ." (See Janice Moulton, "Sexual Behavior: Another Position" in this volume, pp. 110–118.
8. Chomsky, *op. cit.*, (1971), p. 19.
9. Richard Rorty, "Derrida on Language, Being and Abnormal Philos-

ophy," *Journal of Philosophy* 74 (1977), pp. 673–681. My understanding of "the sex of language" is borrowed from Jacques Derrida; Rorty's article is an excellent introduction to this aspect of Derrida's writing.

10. However, charges of deviance might be sustained on other, non-teleological grounds.

11. Jacques Derrida, "Signature Event Context," *Glyph I* (Baltimore: Johns Hopkins University Press, 1977), pp. 172–197.

12. Aristotle, *De Interpretatione*, in E.M. Edgehill, trans. *The Basic Works of Aristotle* (New York: Random House, 1941): I, 16a, 3. See also Jacques Derrida, *Of Grammatology*, Gayatri Chakravorty Spivak, trans. (Baltimore: Johns Hopkins University Press, 1974), p. 11.

13. Rorty, *op. cit.*, p. 681.

14. This important distinction is developed by several contemporary writers on masturbation. See, for example, Bernie Zilbergeld, *Male Sexuality: A Guide to Sexual Fulfillment* (Boston: Little, Brown and Co., 1978), p. 139, and Barry McCarthy, *What You (Still) Don't Know About Male Sexuality* (New York: Crowell Press, 1977), Chapter 3.

15. See R.D. Laing, *Self and Others* 2nd ed. (Middlesex: Penguin Books, 1969), p. 59.

16. Examples cited are from Michael Wood, "Deconstructing Derrida," *New York Review of Books* 24 (March 3, 1977), pp. 27–30 and Derrida, *op. cit.*, (1974), pp. 141–164.

17. Solomon, *op. cit.*, (1975), p. 279. My Emphasis.

18. Solomon, *op. cit.*, (1974), p. 96 (in this volume).

19. Solomon, *op. cit.*, (1975), p. 279. My Emphasis.

20. *Ibid.*, p. 283.

21. Solomon, *op. cit.*, (1974), p. 97 (in this volume).

22. Solomon, *op. cit.*, (1975), pp. 285–286.

23. *Ibid.*, p. 285.

24. *Ibid.*

25. *Ibid.*, p. 284.

26. Solomon, *op. cit.*, (1975), p. 286 and (1974), p. 98 (in this volume).

27. Solomon, *op. cit.*, (1974), p. 98 (in this volume).

28. Derrida, *op. cit.*, (1977), p. 191.

29. Solomon, *op. cit.*, (1975), p. 279. Solomon's emphasis.

30. Solomon, *op. cit.*, (1974), p. 96 (in this volume). My emphasis.

31. *Ibid.*, p. 94 (in this volume).

Janice Moulton

Sexual Behavior: Another Position

We can often distinguish behavior that is sexual from behavior
that is not. Sexual intercourse may be one clear example of the
former, but other sexual behaviors are not so clearly defined.
Some kissing is sexual; some is not. Sometimes looking is sexual;
sometimes *not* looking is sexual. Is it possible, then, to *characterize* sexual behavior?

Thomas Nagel in "Sexual Perversion"[1] and Robert Solomon in
"Sexual Paradigms"[2] each offer an answer to this question. Nagel
analyzes sexual desire as a "complex system of superimposed mutual perceptions" (81–82). He claims that sexual relations that do
not fit his account are incomplete and, consequently, perversions.

Solomon claims that sexual behavior should be analyzed in
terms of goals rather than feelings. He maintains that "the end of
desire is interpersonal communication" (91) and not enjoyment.
According to Solomon, the sexual relations between regular partners will be inferior to novel encounters because there is less remaining to communicate sexually.

I believe that sexual behavior will not fit any single character-

Reprinted by permission from *The Journal of Philosophy* 73, No. 16 (1976), pp.
537–546. This paper has been greatly improved by the discussions and careful
criticisms of G.M. Robinson and Helen Heise, the suggestions of Tim Binkley and
Jay Rosenberg that it be expanded, and the comments from audiences of the Society for Women in Philosophy and the American Philosophical Association.

ization; that there are at least two sorts of sexual behavior to characterize. Both Nagel and Solomon have interesting things to say about one sort of sexual behavior. However, both have assumed that a model of flirtation and seduction constitutes an adequate model of sexual behavior in general. Although a characterization of flirtation and seduction can continue to apply to a relationship that is secret, forbidden, or in which there is some reason to remain unsure of one's sexual acceptability, I shall argue that most sexual behavior does not involve flirtation and seduction, and that what characterizes flirtation and seduction is not what characterizes the sexual behavior of regular partners. Nagel takes the development of what I shall call "sexual anticipation" to be characteristic of all sexual behavior and gives no account of sexual satisfaction.[3] Solomon believes that flirtation and seduction are different from regular sexual relationships. However, he too considers only characteristics of sexual anticipation in his analysis and concludes that regular sexual relationships are inferior to novel ones because they lack some of those characteristics.

Flirtation, seduction, and traditional courtship involve sexual feelings that are quite independent of physical contact. These feelings are increased by anticipation of success, winning, or conquest. Because what is anticipated is the opportunity for sexual intimacy and satisfaction, the feelings of sexual satisfaction are usually not distinguished from those of sexual anticipation. Sexual satisfaction involves sexual feelings which are increased by the other person's knowledge of one's preferences and sensitivities, the familiarity of their touch or smell or way of moving, and not by the novelty of their sexual interest.

It is easy to think that the more excitement and enthusiasm involved in the anticipation of an event, the more enjoyable and exciting the event itself is likely to be. However, anticipation and satisfaction are often divorced. Many experiences with no associated build-up of anticipation are very satisfying, and others, awaited and begun with great eagerness, produce no feelings of satisfaction at all. In sexual activity this dissociation is likely to be frequent. A strong feeling of sexual anticipation is produced by the uncertainty, challenge, or secrecy of novel sexual experiences, but the tension and excitement that increase anticipation often interfere with sexual satisfaction. The comfort and trust and experience with familiar partners may increase sexual satisfaction, but decrease the uncertainty and challenge that heighten sexual anticipation. Given the distinction between anticipation and satisfaction, there is no reason to believe that an increase of trust and love ought to increase feelings of sexual anticipation nor that sexual anticipation should be a prerequisite for any long-term sexual relationship.

For some people the processes that create sexual anticipation, the exchange of indirect signals, the awareness of the other person's sexual interest, and the accompanying sexual anticipation may be *all* that is valued in sexual behavior. Satisfaction is equated with release, the end of a good time, and is not considered a process in its own right. But although flirtation and seduction are the main objects of sexual fantasy and fiction, most people, even those whose sexual relations are frequently casual, seek to continue some sexual relationships after the flirtation and seduction are over, when the uncertainty and challenge are gone. And the motives, goals, and feelings of sexual satisfaction that characterize these continued sexual relations are not the same as the motives, goals, and feelings of sexual anticipation that characterize the novel sexual relations Nagel and Solomon have tried to analyze. Let us consider their accounts.

Nagel's account is illustrated by a tale of a Romeo and a Juliet who are sexually aroused by each other, notice each other's arousal and become further aroused by that:

He senses that she senses that he senses her. This is still another level of arousal, for he becomes conscious of his sexuality through his awareness of its effect on her and of her awareness that this effect is due to him. Once she takes the same step and senses that he senses her sensing him, it becomes difficult to state, let alone imagine, further iterations, though they may be logically distinct. If both are alone, they will presumably turn to look at each other directly, and the proceedings will continue on another plane. Physical contact and intercourse are perfectly natural extensions of this complicated visual exchange, and mutual touch can involve all the complexities of awareness present in the visual case, but with a far greater range of subtlety and acuteness.

Ordinarily, of course, things happen in a less orderly fashion—sometimes in a great rush—but I believe that some version of this overlapping system of distinct sexual perceptions and interactions is the basic framework of any full-fledged sexual relation and that relations involving only part of the complex are significantly incomplete (83).

Nagel then characterizes sexual perversion as a "truncated or incomplete version" (85) of sexual *arousal*, rather than as some deviation from a standard of subsequent physical interaction.

Nagel's account applies only to the development of sexual anticipation. He says that "the proliferation of levels of mutual awareness . . . is a type of complexity that typifies human interactions" (83), so he might argue that his account will cover Romeo and Juliet's later relationship as well. Granted that levels of mutual awareness exist in any close human relationship. But it does not follow that the development of levels of awareness *characterize* all human relationships, particularly sexual relationships between familiar partners. In particular, the sort of awareness Nagel emphasizes—"a desire that one's partner be aroused by the recognition of one's desire that he or she be aroused" (85)—does not seem essential to regular sexual relationships. If we accept Nagel's account for sexual behavior in general, then we must classify as a perversion the behavior of an intimate and satisfying sexual relation begun without any preliminary exchange of multi-level arousals.[4]

Sexual desire can be generated by many different things—a smell, a phrase in a book, a familiar voice. The sexual interest of another person is only on occasion novel enough to be the main cause or focus of sexual arousal. A characterization of sexual behavior on other occasions should describe the development and sharing of sexual pleasure—the creation of sexual satisfaction. Nagel's contribution lies in directing our attention to the analysis of sexual behavior in terms of its perceptions and feelings. However, he characterizes only a limited sort of sexual behavior, flirtation and seduction.

Solomon characterizes sexual behavior by analogy with linguistic behavior, emphasizing that the goals are the same. He says:

Sexual activity consists in speaking what we might call "body language." It has its own grammar, delineated by the body, and its own phonetics of touch and movement. Its unit of meaningfulness, the bodily equivalent of a sentence, is the *gesture* . . . body language is essentially expressive, and its content is limited to interpersonal attitudes and feelings (96).

The analogy with language can be valuable for understanding sexual behavior. However, Solomon construes the goals of both activities too narrowly and hence draws the wrong conclusions.

He argues that the aim of sexual behavior is to communicate ones attitudes and feelings, to express oneself, and further, that such self-expression is made less effective by aiming at enjoyment:

That is why the liberal mythology has been so disastrous, for it has rendered unconscious the expressive functions of sex in its stress on enjoyment . . . It is thus understandable why sex is so utterly important in our lives, and why it is typically so unsatisfactory (98).

Does stress on enjoyment hinder self-expression? Trying to do one thing, X, may interfere with trying to do another, Y, for some Xs and Ys. For example, trying to eat peanut butter or swim under water may interfere with vocal self-expression. But enjoyment is a different sort of goal. One isn't trying to do both Y and something else when aiming at Y and enjoyment, but to do one sort of thing, Y, a certain way. Far from interfering, one is more likely to be successful at a venture if one can manage to enjoy oneself during the process.

Solomon claims to refute that enjoyment is the essential aim of sexual activity, but he erroneously identifies enjoyment with orgasm:[5]

No one would deny that sex is enjoyable, but it does not follow that sexuality is the activity of "pure enjoyment" and that "gratification," or "pure physical pleasure," that is, orgasm, is its end (94).

and consequently he shows merely that orgasm is not the only aim of sexual activity. His main argument is:

If sex is pure physical enjoyment, why is sexual activity between persons far more satisfying than masturbation, where, if we accept recent physiological studies, orgasm is at its highest intensity and the post-coital period is cleansed of its interpersonal hassles and arguments? (96).

One obvious answer is that, even for people who have hassles and arguments, interpersonal sexual activity is more enjoyable, even in the "pure physical" sense.[6] Solomon's argument does not show that enjoyment is not the appropriate aim of sexual activity, only that maximum-intensity orgasm is not. As those recent physiological studies pointed out, participants report interpersonal sexual activity as more enjoyable and satisfying even though their orgasms are less intense.[7] Only someone who mistakenly equated enjoyment with orgasm would find this paradoxical.

One need not claim that orgasm is always desired or desirable in sexual activity. That might be like supposing that in all conversations the participants do, or should, express their deepest thoughts. In sexual, as in linguistic, behavior, there is great variety and subtlety of purpose. But this is not to say that the desire for orgasm should be ignored. The disappointment and physical discomfort of expected but unachieved orgasm is only faintly parallel to the frustration of not being able to "get a word in edgewise" after being moved to express an important thought. It is usually rude or boorish to use language with indifference to the interests and cares of one's listeners. Sexual behavior with such indifference can be no better.

Solomon does not need these arguments to claim that enjoyment is not the only or the essential goal of sexual behavior. His comparison of sexual behavior with linguistic (or other social) behavior could have been used to do the job. The same social and moral distinctions and evaluations can be applied to both behaviors: hurting and humiliating people is bad; making people happy is good; loyalty, kindness, intelligence, and wit are valued; stupidity, clumsiness, and insincerity are not. The purpose of contact, sexual or otherwise, with other people is not just to produce or receive enjoyment—there are times of sadness, solace, and anguish that are important and meaningful to share, but not enjoyable.

Is self-expression, then, the essential goal of sexual behavior? Solomon lists a number of feelings and attitudes that can be expressed sexually:

—love, tenderness and trust, "being-with," mutual recognition
—hatred, indifference, jealousy, conflict
—shyness, fear, lack of confidence, embarrassment, shame
—domination, submissiveness, dependence, possessiveness, passivity

He claims "some attitudes, e.g., tenderness and trust, domination and passivity are best expressed sexually" (97), and says his account:

. . . makes it evident why Nagel chose as his example a couple of strangers; one has far more to say, for one can freely express one's fantasies as well as the truth to a stranger. A husband and wife of seven years have probably been repeating the same messages for years, and their sexual activity now is probably no more than an abbreviated ritual incantation of the lengthy conversations they had years before (97).

A glance at the list of feelings and attitudes above will show that its items are not independent. Shame, for example, may include components of embarrassment, lack of confidence, fear, and probably mutual recognition and submissiveness. To the extent that they can be conveyed by sexual body language,[8] a mere grunt or whimper would be able to express the whole range of the attitudes and feelings as well, if not better, than sexual gestures. Moreover, it is not clear that some attitudes are best expressed sexually. Tenderness and trust are often expressed between people who are not sexual partners. The tenderness and trust that may exist between an adult and a child is not best expressed sexually. Even if we take Solomon's claim to apply only to sexual partners, a joint checking account may be a better expression of trust than sexual activity. And domination, which in sado-masochistic sexual activity is expressed most elaborately with the cooperation of the partner, is an attitude much better expressed by nonsexual activities[9] such as beating an opponent, firing an employee, or mugging a passerby, where the domination is real, and does not require the cooperation of the other person. Even if some attitudes and feelings (for example, prurience, wantonness, lust) are best expressed sexually, it would be questionable whether the primary aim of sexual activity should be to express them.

The usual conversation of strangers is "small talk": cautious, shallow, and predictable because there has not been time for the participants to assess the extent and nature of common interests they share. So too with sexual behavior; first sexual encounters may be charged with novelty and anticipation, but are usually characterized by stereotypic physical interactions. If the physical interaction is seen as "body language," the analogy with linguistic behavior suggests that first encounters are likely to consist of sexual small talk.

Solomon's comparison of sexual behavior with linguistic behavior is handicapped by the limited view he has about their purposes. Language has more purposes than transmitting information. If all there were to sexual behavior was the development of the sexual anticipation prominent in flirtation and seduction, then Solomon's conclusions might be correct. The fact that people will continue sexual relations with the same partners even after the appropriate attitudes and feelings from Solomon's list have been expressed indicates that sexual behavior, like linguistic behavior, has other functions that are important. Solomon's analogy with linguistic behavior is valuable not because communication is the main goal of sexual behavior but because he directs attention to the social nature of sexual behavior. Solomon's analogy can be made to take on new importance by considering that sexual behavior not only transmits information about feelings and attitudes—something any activity can do—but also, like language, it has a *phatic* function to evoke feelings and attitudes.

Language is often used to produce a shared experience, a feeling of togetherness or unity. Duets, greetings, and many religious services use language with little information content to establish or reaffirm a relation among the participants. Long-term sexual relationships, like regular musical ensembles, may be valued more for the feelings produced than the feelings communicated. With both sexual and linguistic behavior, an interaction with a stranger might be an enjoyable novelty, but the pleasures of linguistic and sexual activity with good friends are probably much more frequent and more reliable.

Solomon's conclusion that sexually one should have more to "say" to a stranger and will find oneself "repeating the same messages for years" to old acquaintances,[10] violates the analogy. With natural language, one usually has more to say to old friends than to strangers.

Both Nagel and Solomon give incomplete accounts because they assume that a characterization of flirtation and seduction should apply to sexual behavior in general. I have argued that this is not so. Whether we analyze sexual behavior in terms of characteristic perceptions and feelings, as Nagel does, or by a comparison with other complex social behavior, as Solomon does, the characteristics of novel sexual encounters differ from those of sexual relationships between familiar and recognized partners.

What about the philosophical enterprise of characterizing sexual behavior? A characterization of something will tell what is unique about it and how to identify a standard or paradigm case of it. Criteria for a standard or paradigm case of sexual behavior unavoidably have normative implications. It is my position that normative judgments about sexual behavior should not be unrelated to the social and moral standards that apply to other social behavior. Many people, in reaction to old standards, avoid disapproving of sexual behavior that involves deceit or humiliation to another, but will condemn or ridicule sexual behavior that hurts no one yet fails to conform to a sexual standard. Both Nagel and Solomon classify sexual behavior that does not fit their characterizations as perversion, extending this strong negative judgment to behavior that is neither morally nor socially condemned (i.e., sex without multilevel awareness of arousal; sex without communication of attitudes and feelings). Yet perversion can be more accurately accounted for as whatever makes people frightened or uncomfortable by its bizarreness.[11]

Sexual behavior differs from other behavior by virtue of its unique feelings and emotions and its unique ability to create shared intimacy. These unique features of sexual behavior may influence particular normative judgments, but they do not justify applying *different* normative principles to sexual behavior.

NOTES

1. *The Journal of Philosophy* 66, No. 1 (1969), pp. 5–17. (In this volume, pp. 76–88. All references are to this volume.)
2. *The Journal of Philosophy* 71, No. 11 (1974), pp. 336–345. (In this volume, pp. 89–98. All references are to this volume.)
3. Satisfaction includes the good feelings of intimacy, warm friendship, the pleasure of being appreciated and of giving pleasure. 'Satisfaction' is not intended as a euphemism for orgasm, although the physical and social discomforts of the absence of orgasm often make a feeling of satisfaction impossible.
4. This was first pointed out to me by Sara Ketchum.
5. Solomon also claims that aiming at *orgasm* "overwhelms or distorts whatever else is being said sexually" (96). In this case there might be interference. However, if one is trying to express feelings and attitudes through the giving or having of an orgasm, then "aiming at self-expression" and "aiming at orgasm" will describe the same activity and there will be no interference. It should be pointed out that whatever else is being said sexually should have been said before orgasm is imminent or should be postponed because one will not do a very good job of transmitting or receiving any other communication during orgasm. Instead of an objection to aiming at orgasm, the potential interference raises an objection to aiming at self-expression during the time that orgasm is the goal.
6. Several theories of motivation in psychology (e.g., McClelland's) easily incorporate this fact: Creatures find moderate discrepancies from predicted sensation more pleasurable than sensations that are completely expected. Sensations produced by a sexual partner are not as adequately predicted as autoerotic stimulation.
7. William Masters and Virginia Johnson, *Human Sexual Response* (Boston: Little, Brown, 1966), p. 113.
8. More than gestures must be employed to communicate such feelings as love, trust, hatred, shame, dependence, and possessiveness. I doubt that jealousy or a distinction between "one's fantasies [and] the truth" (97–98) can be communicated by sexual body language at all.
9. In her comments on a relative of this paper at the 1976 Pacific Division APA meetings, Sara Ketchum pointed out that I have completely overlooked one sort of sexual activity in which the domination *is* real and the cooperation of the other person is not required: rape.
10. Repeated messages about one's feelings are not merely redundant; they convey new information: the continuation, renewal, or salience of those feelings.
11. See Mary Douglas, *Purity and Danger* (London: Routledge & Kegan Paul, 1966).

Alan Goldman

Plain Sex

I

Several recent articles on sex herald its acceptance as a legitimate topic for analytic philosophers (although it has been a topic in philosophy since Plato). One might have thought conceptual analysis unnecessary in this area; despite the notorious struggles of judges and legislators to define pornography suitably, we all might be expected to know what sex is and to be able to identify at least paradigm sexual desires and activities without much difficulty. Philosophy is nevertheless of relevance here if for no other reason than that the concept of sex remains at the center of moral and social consciousness in our, and perhaps any, society. Before we can get a sensible view of the relation of sex to morality, perversion, social regulation, and marriage, we require a sensible analysis of the concept itself; one which neither understates its animal pleasure nor overstates its importance within a theory or system of value. I say "before," but the order is not quite so clear, for questions in this area, as elsewhere in moral philosophy, are both conceptual and normative at the same time. Our concept of sex will partially determine our moral view of it, but as philosophers we should formulate a concept that will accord with its proper moral status. What we require here, as elsewhere, is "reflective equilibri-

Reprinted by permission from *Philosophy and Public Affairs* 6, No. 3 (Spring 1977), pp. 267–287. © 1977 by Princeton University Press.

um," a goal not achieved by traditional and recent analysis together with their moral implications. Because sexual activity, like other natural functions such as eating or exercising, has become imbedded in layers of cultural, moral, and superstitious superstructure, it is hard to conceive it in its simplest terms. But partially for this reason, it is only by thinking about plain sex that we can begin to achieve this conceptual equilibrium.

I shall suggest here that sex continues to be misrepresented in recent writings, at least in philosophical writings, and I shall criticize the predominant form of analysis which I term "means-end analysis." Such conceptions attribute a necessary external goal or purpose to sexual activity, whether it be reproduction, the expression of love, simple communication, or interpersonal awareness. They analyze sexual activity as a means to one of these ends, implying that sexual desire is a desire to reproduce, to love or be loved, or to communicate with others. All definitions of this type suggest false views of the relation of sex to perversion and morality by implying that sex which does not fit one of these models or fulfill one of these functions is in some way deviant or incomplete.

The alternative, simpler analysis with which I will begin is that sexual desire is desire for contact with another person's body and for the pleasure which such contact produces; sexual activity is activity which tends to fulfill such desire of the agent. Whereas Aristotle and Butler were correct in holding that pleasure is normally a byproduct rather than a goal of purposeful action, in the case of sex this is not so clear. The desire for another's body is, principally among other things, the desire for the pleasure that physical contact brings. On the other hand, it is not a desire for a particular sensation detachable from its causal context, a sensation which can be derived in other ways. This definition in terms of the general goal of sexual desire appears preferable to an attempt to more explicitly list or define specific sexual activities, for many activities such as kissing, embracing, massaging, or holding hands may or may not be sexual, depending upon the context and more specifically upon the purposes, needs, or desires into which such activities fit. The generality of the definition also represents a refusal (common in recent psychological texts) to overemphasize orgasm as the goal of sexual desire or genital sex as the only norm of sexual activity (this will be hedged slightly in the discussion of perversion below).

Central to the definition is the fact that the goal of sexual desire and activity is the physical contact itself, rather than something else which this contact might express. By contrast, what I term "means-end analyses" posit ends which I take to be extraneous to plain sex, and they view sex as a means to these ends. Their fault lies not in defining sex in terms of its general goal, but in seeing plain sex as merely a means to other separable ends. I term these "means-end analyses" for convenience, although "means-separable-end analyses," while too cumbersome, might be more fully explanatory. The desire for physical contact with another person is a minimal criterion for (normal) sexual desire, but is both necessary and sufficient to qualify normal desire as sexual. Of course, we may want to express other feelings through sexual acts in various contexts; but without the desire for the physical contact in and for itself, or when it is sought for other reasons, activities in which contact is involved are not predominantly sexual. Furthermore, the desire for physical contact in itself, without the wish to express affection or other feelings through it, is sufficient to render sexual the activity of the agent which fulfills it. Various activities with this goal alone, such as kissing and caressing in certain contexts, qualify as sexual even without the presence of genital symptoms of sexual excitement. The latter are not therefore necessary criteria for sexual activity.

This initial analysis may seem to some either over- or underinclusive. It might seem too broad in leading us to interpret physical contact as sexual desire in activities such as football and other contact sports. In these cases, however, the desire is not for contact with another body per se, it is not directed toward a particular person for that purpose, and it is not the goal of the activity—the goal is winning or exercising or knocking someone down or displaying one's prowess. If the desire is purely for contact with another specific person's body, then to interpret it as sexual does not seem an exaggeration. A slightly more difficult case is that of a baby's desire to be cuddled and our natural response in wanting to cuddle it. In the case of the baby, the desire may be simply for the physical contact, for the pleasure of the caresses. If so, we may characterize this desire, especially in keeping with Freudian theory, as sexual or protosexual. It will differ nevertheless from full-fledged sexual desire in being more amorphous, not directed outward toward another specific person's body It may also be that what the infant unconsciously desires is not physical contact per se but signs of affection, tenderness, or security, in which case we have further reason for hesitating to characterize its wants as clearly sexual. The intent of our response to the baby is often the showing of affection, not the pure physical contact, so that our definition in terms of action which fulfills sexual desire *on the part of the agent* does not capture such actions, whatever we say of the baby. (If it is intuitive to characterize our response as sexual as well, there is clearly no problem here for my analysis.) The same can be said of signs of affection (or in some cultures polite greeting) among men or women: these certainly need not be homosexual when the intent is only to show friendship, something extrinsic to plain sex although valuable when added to it.

Our definition of sex in terms of the desire for physical contact may appear too narrow in that a person's personality, not merely her or his body, may be sexually attractive to another, and in that looking or conversing in a certain way can be sexual in a given context without bodily contact. Nevertheless, it is not the contents of one's thoughts per se that are sexually appealing, but one's personality as embodied in certain manners of behavior. Furthermore, if a person is sexually attracted by another's personality, he or she will desire not just further conversation, but actual sexual contact. While looking at or conversing with someone can be interpreted as sexual in given contexts it is so when intended as preliminary to, and hence parasitic upon, elemental sexual interest. Voyeurism or viewing a pornographic movie qualifies as a sexual activity, but only as an imaginative substitute for the real thing (otherwise a deviation from the norm as expressed in our definition). The same is true of masturbation as a sexual activity without a partner.

That the initial definition indicates at least an ingredient of sexual desire and activity is too obvious to argue. We all know what sex is, at least in obvious cases, and do not need philosophers to tell us. My preliminary analysis is meant to serve as a contrast to what sex is not, at least, not necessarily. I concentrate upon the physically manifested desire for another's body, and I take as central the immersion in the physical aspect of one's own existence and attention to the physical embodiment of the other. One may derive pleasure in a sex act from expressing certain feelings to one's partner or from awareness of the attitude of one's partner, but sexual desire is essentially desire for physical contact itself: it is a bodily desire for the body of another that dominates our mental life for more or less brief periods. Traditional writings were correct to emphasize the purely physical or animal aspect of sex; they were wrong only in condemning it. This characterization of sex as an intensely pleasurable physical activity and acute physical desire may seem to some to capture only its barest level. But it is worth distinguishing and focusing upon this least common denominator in order to avoid the false views of sexual morality and perversion which emerge from thinking that sex is essentially something else.

II

We may turn then to what sex is not, to the arguments regarding supposed conceptual connections between sex and other activities which it is necessary to conceptually distinguish. The most comprehensible attempt to build an extraneous purpose into the sex act identifies that purpose as reproduction, its primary biological function. While this may be "nature's" purpose, it certainly need not be ours (the analogy with eating, while sometimes overworked, is pertinent here). While this identification may once have had a rational basis which also grounded the identification of the value and morality of sex with that applicable to reproduction and childrearing, the development of contraception rendered the connection weak. Methods of contraception are by now so familiar and so widely used that it is not necessary to dwell upon the changes wrought by these developments in the concept of sex itself and in a rational sexual ethic dependent upon that concept. In the past, the ever present possibility of children rendered the concepts of sex and sexual morality different from those required at present. There may be good reasons, if the presence and care of both mother and father are beneficial to children, for restricting reproduction to marriage. Insofar as society has a legitimate role in protecting children's interests, it may be justified in giving marriage a legal status, although this question is complicated by the fact (among others) that children born to single mothers deserve no penalties. In any case, the point here is simply that these questions are irrelevant at the present time to those regarding the morality of sex and its potential social regulation. (Further connections with marriage will be discussed below.)

It is obvious that the desire for sex is not necessarily a desire to reproduce, that the psychological manifestation has become, if it were not always, distinct from its biological roots. There are many parallels, as previously mentioned, with other natural functions. The pleasures of eating and exercising are to a large extent independent of their roles in nourishment or health (as the junk-food industry discovered with a vengeance). Despite the obvious parallel with sex, there is still a tendency for many to think that sex acts which can be reproductive are, if not more moral or less immoral, at least more natural. These categories of morality and "naturalness," or normality, are not to be identified with each other, as will be argued below, and neither is applicable to sex by virtue of its connection to reproduction. The tendency to identify reproduction as the conceptually connected end of sex is most prevalent now in the pronouncements of the Catholic church. There the assumed analysis is clearly tied to a restrictive sexual morality according to which acts become immoral and unnatural when they are not oriented towards reproduction, a morality which has independent roots in the Christian sexual ethic as it derives from Paul. However, the means-end analysis fails to generate a consistent sexual ethic: homosexual and oral-genital sex is condemned while kissing or caressing, acts equally unlikely to lead in themselves to fertilization, even when properly characterized as sexual according to our definition, are not.

III

Before discussing further relations of means-end analyses to false or inconsistent sexual ethics and concepts of perversion, I turn to other examples of these analyses. One common position views sex as essentially an expression of love or affection between the partners. It is generally recognized that there are other types of love besides sexual, but sex itself is taken as an expression of one type, sometimes termed "romantic" love.[1] Various factors again ought to weaken this identification. First, there are other types of love besides that which it is appropriate to express sexually, and "romantic" love itself can be expressed in many other ways. I am not denying that sex can take on heightened value and meaning when it becomes a vehicle for the expression of feelings of love or tenderness, but so can many other usually mundane activities such as getting up early to make breakfast on Sunday, cleaning the house, and so on. Second, sex itself can be used to communicate many other emotions besides love, and, as I will argue below, can communicate nothing in particular and still be good sex.

On a deeper level, an internal tension is bound to result from an identification of sex, which I have described as a physical-psychological desire, with love as a long-term, deep emotional relationship between two individuals. As this type of relationship, love is permanent, at least in intent, and more or less exclusive. A normal person cannot deeply love more than a few individuals even in a lifetime. We may be suspicious that those who attempt or claim to love many love them weakly if at all. Yet, fleeting sexual desire can arise in relation to a variety of other individuals one finds sexually attractive. It may even be, as some have claimed, that sexual desire in humans naturally seeks variety, while this is obviously false of love. For this reason, monogamous sex, even if justified, almost always represents a sacrifice or the exercise of self-control on the part of the spouses, while monogamous love generally does not. There is no such thing as casual love in the sense in which I intend the term "love." It may occasionally happen that a spouse falls deeply in love with someone else (especially when sex is conceived in terms of love), but this is relatively rare in comparison to passing sexual desires for others; and while the former often indicates a weakness or fault in the marriage relation, the latter does not.

If love is indeed more exclusive in its objects than is sexual desire, this explains why those who view sex as essentially an expression of love would again tend to hold a repressive or restrictive sexual ethic. As in the case of reproduction, there may be good reasons for reserving the total commitment of deep love to the context of marriage and family—the normal personality may not withstand additional divisions of ultimate commitment and allegiance. There is no question that marriage itself is best sustained by a deep relation of love and affection; and even if love is not naturally monogamous, the benefits of family units to children provide additonal reason to avoid serious commitments elsewhere which weaken family ties. It can be argued similarly that monogamous sex strengthens families by restricting and at the same time guaranteeing an outlet for sexual desire in marriage. But there is more force to the argument that recognition of a clear distinction between sex and love in society would help avoid disastrous marriages which result from adolescent confusion of the two when sexual desire is mistaken for permanent love, and would weaken damaging jealousies which arise in marriages in relation to passing sexual desires. The love and affection of a sound marriage certainly differs from the adolescent romantic variety, which is often a mere substitute for sex in the context of a repressive sexual ethic.

In fact, the restrictive sexual ethic tied to the means-end analysis in terms of love again has failed to be consistent. At least, it has not been applied consistently, but forms part of the double standard which has curtailed the freedom of women. It is predict-able in light of this history that some women would now advocate using sex as another kind of means, as a political weapon or as a way to increase unjustly denied power and freedom. The inconsistency in the sexual ethic typically attached to the sex-love analy-sis, according to which it has generally been taken with a grain of salt when applied to men, is simply another example of the impos-sibility of tailoring a plausible moral theory in this area to a con-ception of sex which builds in conceptually extraneous factors.

I am not suggesting here that sex ought never to be connected with love or that it is not a more significant and valuable activity when it is. Nor am I denying that individuals need love as much as sex and perhaps emotionally need at least one complete rela-tionship which encompasses both. Just as sex can express love and take on heightened significance when it does, so love is often natu-rally accompanied by an intermittent desire for sex. But again love is accompanied appropriately by desires for other shared ac-tivities as well. What makes the desire for sex seem more intimate-ly connected with love is the intimacy which is seen to be a natural feature of mutual sex acts. Like love, sex is held to lay one bare psychologically as well as physically. Sex is unquestionably intimate, but beyond that the psychological toll often attached may be a function of the restrictive sexual ethic itself, rather than a legitimate apology for it. The intimacy involved in love is psy-chologically consuming in a generally healthy way, while the psy-chological tolls of sexual relations, often including embarrassment as a correlate of intimacy, are too often the result of artificial sex-ual ethics and taboos. The intimacy involved in both love and sex is insufficient in any case in light of previous points to render a means-end analysis in these terms appropriate.

IV

In recent articles, Thomas Nagel and Robert Solomon, who rec-ognize that sex is not merely a means to communicate love, never-theless retain the form of this analysis while broadening it. For Solomon, sex remains a means of communicating (he explicitly uses the metaphor of body language), although the feelings that can be communicated now include, in addition to love and tender-ness, domination, dependence, anger, trust, and so on.[2] Nagel does not refer explicitly to communication, but his analysis is similar in that he views sex as a complex form of interpersonal awareness in which desire itself is consciously communicated on several different levels. In sex, according to his analysis, two people are aroused by each other, aware of the other's arousal, and further aroused by this awareness.[3] Such multileveled conscious awareness of one's own and the other's desire is taken as the norm of a sexual relation, and this model is therefore close to that which views sex as a means of interpersonal communication.

Solomon's analysis is beset by the same difficulties as those pointed out in relation to the narrower sex-love concept. Just as love can be communicated by many activities other than sex, which do not therefore become properly analyzed as essentially vehicles of communication (making breakfast, cleaning the house, and so on), the same is true of the other feelings mentioned by Solomon. Domination can be communicated through economic manipulation, trust by a joint savings account. Driving a car can be simultaneously expressing anger, pride, joy, and so on. We may, in fact, communicate or express feelings in anything we do, but this does not make everything we do into language. Driving a car is not to be defined as an automotive means of communication, although with a little ingenuity we might work out an automotive vocabulary (tailgating as an expression of aggression or impatience; beating another car away from a stoplight as expressing domination) to match the vocabulary of "body language." That one can communicate various feelings during sex acts does not make these acts merely or primarily a means of communicating.

More importantly, to analyze sex as a means of communication is to overlook the intrinsic nature and value of the act itself. Sex is not a gesture or series of gestures, in fact not necessarily a means to any other end, but a physical activity intensely pleasurable in itself. When a language is used, the symbols normally have no importance in themselves; they function merely as vehicles for what can be communicated by them. Furthermore skill in the use of language is a technical achievement that must be carefully learned; if better sex is more successful communication by means of a more skillful use of body language, then we had all better be well schooled in the vocabulary and grammar. Solomon's analysis, which uses the language metaphor, suggests the appropriateness of a sex-manual approach, the substitution of a bit of technological prowess for the natural pleasure of the unforced surrender to feeling and desire.

It may be that Solomon's position could be improved by using the analogy of music rather than that of language, as an aesthetic form of communication. Music might be thought of as a form of aesthetic communicating, in which the experience of the "phonemes" themselves is generally pleasing. And listening to music is perhaps more of a sexual experience than having someone talk to you. Yet, it seems to me that insofar as music is aesthetic and pleasing in itself, it is not best conceived as primarily a means for communicating specific feelings. Such an analysis does injustice to aesthetic experience in much the same way as the sex-communication analysis debases sexual experience itself.[4]

For Solomon, sex that is not a totally self-conscious communicative art tends toward vulgarity,[5] whereas I would have thought it the other way around. This is another illustration of the tendency of means-end analyses to condemn what appears perfectly natural or normal sex on my account. Both Solomon and Nagel use their definitions, however, not primarily to stipulate moral norms for sex, as we saw in earlier analyses, but to define norms against which to measure perversion. Once again, neither is capable of generating consistency or reflective equilibrium with our firm intuitions as to what counts as subnormal sex, the problem being that both build factors into their norms which are extraneous to an unromanticized view of normal sexual desire and activity. If perversion represents a breakdown in communication, as Solomon maintains, then any unsuccessful or misunderstood advance should count as perverted. Furthermore, sex between husband and wife married for several years, or between any partners already familiar with each other, would be, if not perverted, nevertheless subnormal or trite and dull, in that the communicative content would be minimal in lacking all novelty. In fact the pleasures of sex need not wear off with familiarity, as they would if dependent upon the communicative content of the feelings. Finally, rather than a release or relief from physical desire through a substitute imaginative outlet, masturbation would become a way of practicing or rehearsing one's technique or vocabulary on oneself, or simply a way of talking to oneself, as Solomon himself says.[6]

Nagel fares no better in the implications of his overintellectualized norm. Spontaneous and heated sex between two familiar partners may well lack the complex conscious multileveled interpersonal awareness of which he speaks without being in the least perverted. The egotistical desire that one's partner be aroused by one's own desire does not seem a primary element of the sexual urge, and during sex acts one may like one's partner to be sometimes active and aroused, sometimes more passive. Just as sex can

be more significant when love is communicated, so it can sometimes be heightened by an awareness of the other's desire. But at
other times this awareness of an avid desire of one's partner can
be merely distracting. The conscious awareness to which Nagel
refers may actually impede the immersion in the physical of
which I spoke above, just as may concentration upon one's "vocabulary" or technique. Sex is a way of relating to another, but
primarily a physical rather than intellectual way. For Nagel, the
ultimate in degeneration or perversion would have to be what he
calls "mutual epidermal stimulation"[7] without mutual awareness
of each other's state of mind. But this sounds like normal, if not
ideal, sex to me (perhaps only a minimal description of it). His
model certainly seems more appropriate to a sophisticated seduction scene than to the sex act itself,[8] which according to the model
would often have to count as a subnormal anticlimax to the intellectual foreplay. While Nagel's account resembles Solomon's
means-end analysis of sex, here the sex act itself does not even
qualify as a preferred or central means to the end of interpersonal
communication.

V

I have now criticized various types of analysis sharing or suggesting a common means-end form. I have suggested that analyses of
this form relate to attempts to limit moral or natural sex to that
which fulfills some purpose or function extraneous to basic sexual
desire. The attempts to brand forms of sex outside the idealized
models as immoral or perverted fail to achieve consistency with
intuitions that they themselves do not directly question. The reproductive model brands oral-genital sex a deviation, but cannot
account for kissing or holding hands; the communication account
holds voyeurism to be perverted but cannot accommodate sex acts
without much conscious thought or seductive nonphysical foreplay; the sex-love model makes most sexual desire seem degrading
or base. The first and last condemn extra-marital sex on the sound
but irrelevant grounds that reproduction and deep commitment
are best confined to family contexts. The romanticization of sex
and the confusion of sexual desire with love operate in both directions: sex outside the context of romantic love is repressed; once it
is repressed, partners become more difficult to find and sex becomes romanticized further, out of proportion to its real value for
the individual.

What all these analyses share in addition to a common form is accordance with and perhaps derivation from the Platonic-Christian moral tradition, according to which the animal or purely physical element of humans is the source of immorality, and plain sex in the sense I defined it is an expression of this element, hence in itself to be condemned. All the analyses examined seem to seek a distance from sexual desire itself in attempting to extend it conceptually beyond the physical. The love and communication analyses seek refinement or intellectualization of the desire; plain physical sex becomes vulgar, and too straightforward sexual encounters without an aura of respectable cerebral communicative content are to be avoided. Solomon explicitly argues that sex cannot be a "mere" appetite, his argument being that if it were, subway exhibitionism and other vulgar forms would be pleasing.[9] This fails to recognize that sexual desire can be focused or selective at the same time as being physical. Lower animals are not attracted by every other member of their species, either. Rancid food forced down one's throat is not pleasing, but that certainly fails to show that hunger is not a physical appetite. Sexual desire lets us know that we are physical beings and, indeed, animals; this is why traditional Platonic morality is so thorough in its condemnation. Means-end analyses continue to reflect this tradition, sometimes unwittingly. They show that in conceptualizing sex it is still difficult, despite years of so-called revolution in this area, to free ourselves from the lingering suspicion that plain sex as physical desire is an expression of our "lower selves," that yielding to our animal natures is subhuman or vulgar.

VI

Having criticized these analyses for the sexual ethics and concepts of perversion they imply, it remains to contrast my account along these lines. To the question of what morality might be implied by my analysis, the answer is that there are no moral implications whatever. Any analysis of sex which imputes a moral character to sex acts in themselves is wrong for that reason. There is no morality intrinsic to sex, although general moral rules apply to the treatment of others in sex acts as they apply to all human relations. We can speak of a sexual ethic as we can speak of a business ethic, without implying that business in itself is either moral or immoral or that special rules are required to judge business practices which are not derived from rules that apply elsewhere as well. Sex is not in itself a moral category, although like business it invariably places us into relations with others in which moral rules apply. It gives us opportunity to do what is otherwise recognized as wrong, to harm others, deceive them or manipulate them against their wills. Just as the fact that an act is sexual in itself never renders it wrong or adds to its wrongness if it is wrong on other grounds (sexual acts towards minors are wrong on other grounds, as will be argued below), so no wrong act is to be excused because done from a sexual motive. If a "crime of passion" is to be excused, it would have to be on grounds of temporary insanity rather than sexual context (whether insanity does constitute a legitimate excuse for certain actions is too big a topic to argue here). Sexual motives are among others which may become deranged, and the fact that they are sexual has no bearing in itself on the moral character, whether negative or exculpatory, of the actions deriving from them. Whatever might be true of war, it is certainly not the case that all's fair in love or sex.

Our first conclusion regarding morality and sex is therefore that no conduct otherwise immoral should be excused because it is sexual conduct, and nothing in sex is immoral unless condemned by rules which apply elsewhere as well. The last clause requires further clarification. Sexual conduct can be governed by particular rules relating only to sex itself. But these precepts must be implied by general moral rules when these are applied to specific sexual relations or types of conduct. The same is true of rules of fair business, ethical medicine, or courtesy in driving a car. In the latter case, particular acts on the road may be reprehensible, such as tailgating or passing on the right, which seem to bear no resemblance as actions to any outside the context of highway safety. Nevertheless their immorality derives from the fact that they place others in danger, a circumstance which, when avoidable, is to be condemned in any context. This structure of general and specifically applicable rules describes a reasonable sexual ethic as well. To take an extreme case, rape is always a sexual act and it is always immoral. A rule against rape can therefore be considered an obvious part of sexual morality which has no bearing on nonsexual conduct. But the immorality of rape derives from its being an extreme violation of a person's body, of the right not to be humiliated, and of the general moral prohibition against using other persons against their wills, not from the fact that it is a sexual act.

The application elsewhere of general moral rules to sexual conduct is further complicated by the fact that it will be relative to the particular desires and preferences of one's partner (these may be influenced by and hence in some sense include misguided beliefs about sexual morality itself). This means that there will be fewer specific rules in the area of sexual ethics than in other areas of conduct, such as driving cars, where the relativity of preference is irrelevant to the prohibition of objectively dangerous conduct. More reliance will have to be placed upon the general moral rule, which in this area holds simply that the preferences, desires, and interests of one's partner or potential partner ought to be taken into account. This rule is certainly not specifically formulated to govern sexual relations; it is a form of the central principle of morality itself. But when applied to sex, it prohibits certain actions, such as molestation of children, which cannot be categorized as violations of the rule without at the same time being classified as sexual. I believe this last case is the closest we can come to an action which is wrong *because* it is sexual, but even here its wrongness is better characterized as deriving from the detrimental effects such behavior can have on the future emotional and sexual life of the naive victims, and from the fact that such behavior therefore involves manipulation of innocent persons without regard for their interests. Hence, this case also involves violation of a general moral rule which applies elsewhere as well.

Aside from faulty conceptual analyses of sex and the influence of the Platonic moral tradition, there are two more plausible reasons for thinking that there are moral dimensions intrinsic to sex acts per se. The first is that such acts are normally intensely pleasurable. According to a hedonistic, utilitarian moral theory they therefore should be at least prima facie morally right, rather than morally neutral in themselves. To me this seems incorrect and reflects unfavorably on the ethical theory in question. The pleasure intrinsic to sex acts is a good, but not, it seems to me, a good with much positive moral significance. Certainly I can have no duty to pursue such pleasure myself, and while it may be nice to give pleasure of any form to others, there is no ethical requirement to do so, given my right over my own body. The exception relates to the context of sex acts themselves, when one partner derives pleasure from the other and ought to return the favor. This duty to reciprocate takes us out of the domain of hedonistic utilitarianism, however, and into a Kantian moral framework, the central principles of which call for such reciprocity in human relations. Since independent moral judgments regarding sexual activities constitute one area in which ethical theories are to be tested, these observations indicate here, as I believe others indicate elsewhere, the fertility of the Kantian, as opposed to the utilitarian, principle in reconstructing reasoned moral consciousness.

It may appear from this alternative Kantian viewpoint that sexual acts must be at least prima facie wrong in themselves. This is because they invariably involve at different stages the manipulation of one's partner for one's own pleasure, which might appear to be prohibited on the formulation of Kant's principle which holds that one ought not to treat another as a means to such private ends. A more realistic rendering of this formulation, however, one which recognizes its intended equivalence to the first universalizability principle, admits no such absolute prohibition. Many human relations, most economic transactions for example, involve using other individuals for personal benefit. These relations are immoral only when they are one-sided, when the benefits are not mutual, or when the transactions are not freely and rationally endorsed by all parties. The same holds true of sexual acts. The central principle governing them is the Kantian demand for reciprocity in sexual relations. In order to comply with the second formulation of the categorical imperative, one must recognize the subjectivity of one's partner (not merely by being aroused by her or his desire, as Nagel describes). Even in an act which by its nature "objectifies" the other, one recognizes a partner as a subject with demands and desires by yielding to those desires, by allowing oneself to be a sexual object as well, by giving pleasure or ensuring that the pleasures of the acts are mutual. It is this kind of reciprocity which forms the basis for morality in sex, which distinguishes right acts from wrong in this area as in others. (Of course, prior to sex acts one must gauge their effects upon potential partners and take these longer range interests into account.)

VII

I suggested earlier that in addition to generating confusion regarding the rightness or wrongness of sex acts, false conceptual analyses of the means-end form cause confusion about the value of sex to the individual. My account recognizes the satisfaction of desire and the pleasure this brings as the central psychological function of the sex act for the individual. Sex affords us a paradigm of pleasure, but not a cornerstone of value. For most of us it is not only a needed outlet for desire but also the most enjoyable form of recreation we know. Its value is nevertheless easily mistaken by being confused with that of love, when it is taken as essentially an expression of that emotion. Although intense, the pleasures of sex are brief and repetitive rather than cumulative. They give value to the specific acts which generate them, but not the lasting kind of value which enhances one's whole life. The briefness of these pleasures contributes to their intensity (or perhaps their intensity makes them necessarily brief), but it also relegates them to the periphery of most rational plans for the good life.

By contrast, love typically develops over a long term relation; while its pleasures may be less intense and physical, they are of more cumulative value. The importance of love to the individual may well be central in a rational system of value. And it has perhaps an even deeper moral significance relating to the identification with the interests of another person, which broadens one's possible relationships with others as well. Marriage is again important in preserving this relation between adults and children, which seems as important to the adults as it is to the children in broadening concerns which have a tendency to become selfish. Sexual desire, by contrast, is desire for another which is nevertheless essentially self-regarding. Sexual pleasure is certainly a good for the individual, and for many it may be necessary in order for them to function in a reasonably cheerful way. But it bears little relation to those other values just discussed, to which some analyses falsely suggest a conceptual connection.

VIII

While my initial analysis lacks moral implications in itself, as it should, it does suggest by contrast a concept of sexual perversion. Since the concept of perversion is itself a sexual concept, it will always be defined relative to some definition of normal sex; and any conception of the norm will imply a contrary notion of perverse forms. The concept suggested by my account again differs sharply from those implied by the means-end analyses examined above. Perversion does not represent a deviation from the reproductive function (or kissing would be perverted), from a loving relationship (or most sexual desire and many heterosexual acts would be perverted), or from efficiency in communicating (or unsuccessful seduction attempts would be perverted). It is a deviation from a norm, but the norm in question is merely statistical. Of course, not all sexual acts that are statistically unusual are perverted—a three-hour continuous sexual act would be unusual but not necessarily abnormal in the requisite sense. The abnormality in question must relate to the *form of the desire* itself in order to constitute sexual perversion; for example, desire, not for contact with another, but for merely looking, for harming or being harmed, for contact with items of clothing. This concept of sexual abnormality is that suggested by my definition of normal sex in terms of its typical desire. However not all unusual desires qualify either, only those with the typical physical sexual effects upon the individual who satisfies them. These effects, such as erection in males, were not built into the original definition of sex in terms of sexual desire, for they do not always occur in activities that are properly characterized as sexual, say, kissing for the pleasure of it. But they do seem to bear a closer relation to the definition of activities as perverted. (For those who consider only genital sex sexual, we could build such symptoms into a narrower definition, then speaking of sex in a broad sense as well as "proper" sex.)

Solomon and Nagel disagree with this statistical notion of perversion. For them the concept is evaluative rather than statistical. I do not deny that the term "perverted" is often used evaluatively (and purely emotively for that matter), or that it has a negative connotation for the average speaker. I do deny that we can find a norm, other than that of statistically usual desire, against which all and only activities that properly count as sexual perversions can be contrasted. Perverted sex is simply abnormal sex, and if the norm is not to be an idealized or romanticized extraneous end or purpose, it must express the way human sexual desires usually manifest themselves. Of course not all norms in other areas of discourse need be statistical in this way. Physical health is an example of a relatively clear norm which does not seem to depend upon the numbers of healthy people. But the concept in this case achieves its clarity through the connection of physical health with other clearly desirable physical functions and characteristics, for example, living longer. In the case of sex, that which is statistically abnormal is not necessarily incapacitating in other ways, and yet these abnormal desires with sexual effects upon their subject do count as perverted to the degree to which their objects deviate from usual ones. The connotations of the concept of perversion beyond those connected with abnormality or statistical deviation derive more from the attitudes of those likely to call certain acts perverted than from specifiable features of the acts themselves. These connotations add to the concept of abnormality that of *sub*-normality, but there is no norm against which the latter can be measured intelligibly in accord with all and only acts intuitively called perverted.

The only proper evaluative norms relating to sex involve degrees of pleasure in the acts and moral norms, but neither of these scales coincides with statistical degrees of abnormality, according to which perversion is to be measured. The three parameters operate independently (this was implied for the first two when it was held above that the pleasure of sex is a good, but not necessarily a moral good). Perverted sex may be more or less enjoyable to particular individuals than normal sex, and more or less moral, depending upon the particular relations involved. Raping a sheep may be more perverted than raping a woman, but certainly not more condemnable morally.[10] It is nevertheless true that the evaluative connotations attaching to the term "perverted" derive partly from the fact that most people consider perverted sex highly immoral. Many such acts are forbidden by long standing taboos, and it is sometimes difficult to distinguish what is forbidden from what is immoral. Others, such as sadistic acts, are genuinely immoral, but again not at all because of their connection with sex or abnormality. The principles which condemn these acts would condemn them equally if they were common and nonsexual. It is not true that we properly could continue to consider acts perverted which were found to be very common practice across societies. Such acts, if harmful, might continue to be condemned properly as immoral, but it was just shown that the immorality of an act does not vary with its degree of perversion. If not harmful, common acts previously considered abnormal might continue to be called perverted for a time by the moralistic minority; but the term when applied to such cases would retain only its emotive negative connotation without consistent logical criteria for application. It would represent merely prejudiced moral judgments.

To adequately explain why there is a tendency to so deeply condemn perverted acts would require a treatise in psychology beyond the scope of this paper. Part of the reason undoubtedly relates to the tradition of repressive sexual ethics and false conceptions of sex; another part to the fact that all abnormality seems to disturb and fascinate us at the same time. The former explains why sexual perversion is more abhorrent to many than other forms of abnormality; the latter indicates why we tend to have an emotive and evaluative reaction to perversion in the first place. It may be, as has been suggested according to a Freudian line,[11] that our uneasiness derives from latent desires we are loathe to admit, but this thesis takes us into psychological issues I am not competent to judge. Whatever the psychological explanation, it suffices to point out here that the conceptual connection between perversion and genuine or consistent moral evaluation is spurious and again suggested by misleading means-end idealizations of the concept of sex.

The position I have taken in this paper against those concepts is not totally new. Something similar to it is found in Freud's view of sex, which of course was genuinely revolutionary, and in the body of writings deriving from Freud to the present time. But in his revolt against romanticized and repressive conceptions, Freud went too far—from a refusal to view sex as merely a means to a view of it as the end of all human behavior, although sometimes an elaborately disguised end. This pansexualism led to the thesis (among others) that repression was indeed an inevitable and necessary part of social regulation of any form, a strange consequence of a position that began by opposing the repressive aspects of the means-end view. Perhaps the time finally has arrived when we can achieve a reasonable middle ground in this area, at least in philosophy if not in society.

NOTES

1. Even Bertrand Russell, whose writing in this area was a model of rationality, at least for its period, tends to make this identification and to condemn plain sex in the absence of love: "sex intercourse apart from love has little value, and is to be regarded primarily as experimentation with a view to love." *Marriage and Morals* (New York: Bantam, 1959), p. 87.
2. Robert Solomon, "Sex and Perversion," *Philosophy and Sex,* ed. R. Baker and F. Elliston (Buffalo: Prometheus, 1975).
3. Thomas Nagel, "Sexual Perversion," *The Journal of Philosophy* 66, No. 1 (1969), pp. 5–17. (This volume, pp. 76–88.)
4. Sex might be considered (at least partially) as communication in a very broad sense in the same way as performing ensemble music, in the sense that there is in both ideally a communion or perfectly shared experience with another. This is, however, one possible ideal view whose central feature is not necessary to sexual acts or desire per se. And in emphasizing the communication of specific feelings by means of body language, the analysis under consideration narrows the end to one clearly extrinsic to plain and even good sex.
5. Solomon, pp. 284–285.
6. *Ibid.*, p. 283. One is reminded of Woody Allen's rejoinder to praise of his technique: "I practice a lot when I'm alone."
7. Nagel, p. 15. (This volume, p. 86.)

8. Janice Moulton made the same point in a paper at the Pacific APA meeting, March 1976. (This volume, pp. 110–118.)

9. Solomon, p. 285.

10. The example is like one from Sara Ruddick, "Better Sex," *Philosophy and Sex*, p. 96.

11. See Michael Slote, "Inapplicable Concepts and Sexual Perversion," *Philosophy and Sex*.

Sara Ann Ketchum

The Good, the Bad and the Perverted: Sexual Paradigms Revisited

That rape is morally wrong is a reasonably uncontroversial assertion and the principles underlying it have been given serious attention in recent philosophical literature.[1] A question which has not
been asked and which may be more controversial is whether rape
is good or bad sex. The recent attempts by Thomas Nagel[2] and
Robert Solomon[3] to provide a normative (although non-moral)
account of the concept of sexual perversion are notably silent on
the topic of rape, presumably on the assumption that the only
normative issues related to rape have to do with its moral wrongness and that it is not a relevant example in either a characterization of sex or a theory of the good-making characteristics of sex.[4] I
will argue that the omission of rape as an example is more problematic for the theories of both Nagel and Solomon than such an
assumption would indicate, that Nagel's theory of sexual perversion leaves open the possibility that some rapes are good sex and
that Solomon's account has the consequence that rape is typically
very good sex indeed.

© 1980 by Sara Ann Ketchum. Research on this topic was funded by the State
University of New York Research Foundation. An earlier version of the discussion, in part I, of Solomon's theory was read at the Pacific Division Meetings of
the American Philosophical Association in 1976.

139

At first glance, the question of whether or not rape is good sex may seem fairly trivial in comparison to questions related to the moral wrongness of rape. However, as I will argue, the assumption that rape is good sex or that "bad sex is generally better than none at all,"[5] undermines the assertion that rape is a serious moral offense. Moreover, the failure of Nagel's and Solomon's accounts to deal with the problem of the goodness or badness of rape is only an instance of the more general failure to deal with the possibility that there is genuinely bad sex. I will argue that an adequate normative account of sex must allow for the possibility that there is genuinely bad sex and will propose a theory of sexual perversion according to which perverted sexual relations are genuinely bad and are an evil to be rationally avoided.

At the outset, I wish to make clear which aspects of Nagel's and Solomon's discussions I will not be concerned with. Much of the criticism of Nagel and Solomon has dealt with their theories as attempts to characterize the sexual.[6] I will instead be concerned with the normative implications of their theories—that is, with their attempts to distinguish good sex from bad sex, and perverted sexual relations from non-perverted sexual relations. In particular, I do not intend to get into the controversy over whether sex should be characterized as private or as interpersonal. The account I propose is intended as an account of the goodness and badness of sexual *relations* and of what constitutes a perverted sexual relation; it leaves open the question of whether or not masturbation could be good sex (it is neither a good nor a bad sexual relation because it is not a relation).

I

The traditional concept of perversion is complex. To call a sexual act perverted commits one to some notion of normal, natural or ideal sex and implies that the act in question is not good sex *qua* sex or that it is immoral. Although it has consistently been recognized that "perversion" is an evaluative, rather than a purely descriptive, concept, the two distinct normative questions involved in the concept have not been sufficiently distinguished. For a given sexual act might be good sex but morally wrong, bad sex and morally indifferent, and so on. To make the distinction clearer, consider the principle that adultery is immoral. Someone who assents to this principle is not thereby committed to the claim that adultery is bad sex. Thus, many people quite consistently (although not necessarily correctly) believe that the adulterer is both blameworthy and enviable with respect to his adultery.

With the traditional Judeo-Christian notion of perversion, the connection between perversion and the goodness or badness of sex is muddled, perhaps because of its connection with the assumption that sex is, as such, bad. However, whether considered as a theory of good and bad sex or as a theory of right or wrong sex, the notion that reproductive acts constitute the paradigm of sexuality and that any deviations (and only deviations) from this paradigm are perverted has various peculiar consequences, as evidenced by the following quotation:

Fornication, rape, adultery, incest, respect nature's order in the performance of the sexual act. . . . The worst form of luxury is bestiality, and after it, sodomy, irregularities in the sexual act and onanism.[7]

The confusion of sexuality with reproduction has the consequence that consensual sodomy and masturbation are perversions and, hence, either morally worse or at least not as good *qua* sex as vaginal rape. This seemingly counterintuitive ranking is produced by tying the notion of perversion to mechanistic biological functioning rather than to the relationship between the persons involved. On the reproductive view, consent or lack of it, violence and coercion are all irrelevant to the quality of sex *qua* sex or of sexual relations *qua* sexual relations.

Although both Nagel and Solomon avoid any connection between perversion and moral wrongness, on the question of whether or not rape is good sex, their theories may not be much improvement over the traditional natural law position. In an attempt to provide an analysis of sex such that sex is not morally wrong *qua* sex, they end up being committed to the position that there is no genuinely bad sex and no genuinely bad sexual relation. Both theories define perversion as sexual acts, attitudes or dispositions which deviate from an ideal or paradigm. But, surely, 'perversion' is too strong a term to use for all but the ideal. Their definitions of 'perversion' leave us with a normative range from ideal sex to sex which deviates from the ideal, with no room left for genuinely bad sex.

That this poverty of evaluative terms is intentional on Nagel's part is evident in his conclusion that bad sex is generally better than no sex at all.[8] If we can accept masturbation as an appropriate paradigm of bad sex, as Nagel suggests, this claim may be plausible. However, it is only if there is no genuinely bad sex that it would be reasonable to appropriate the term 'bad sex' for sex that is simply not good. But there is sex that is worse than no sex at all. It is clearly preferable to have no sex at all than to be raped, and it is at least not obvious that a consensual sexual act which involves a determination to humiliate and degrade the other person is better than no sex at all for the person who is being humiliated and degraded; nor is the sex which the prostitute engages in for pay better for her than no sex at all. It seems plausible to assume that many of the sexual acts which are undertaken for nonsexual and nonaffectional reasons are not better than no sex at all and some may be positive evils which would be rightly and rationally avoided if one of the participants had available alternative means to the same nonsexual end—such as making a living or avoiding being killed. It would be insensitive to assume that the average street prostitute has an enviable job because she is paid for sex, which is, after all, even when it is bad a good thing. Nor do we need to revert to the puritanical assumption that sex is in itself bad to find a rational defense for an aversion to the job of prostitution.

Both Solomon's and Nagel's analyses of sex and perversion leave open the possibility that at least some acts of rape are not only not bad, but are actually good, sex. Nagel's lack of specificity in developing the criteria of his ideal leads to the possibility of this conclusion, even though he does not commit himself to any examples which are relevantly rape-like. On the other hand, the very specificity of Solomon's examples and criteria seems to commit him to the position that the standard case of rape, and, perhaps, most rapes are very good and, perhaps, even ideal, sex.

The sexual paradigm that Solomon proposes is that of communication. He claims that communicating feelings is the primary function of sexual activity. Thus, perversion and bad sex result when there is a breakdown in communication or when the communication is not successful. Presumably, good sex occurs when the communication is effective and successful. As to the content of the communication, Solomon suggests that it should be varied; for example, he claims that sex between strangers might be better than sex between long-standing partners because the strangers would, so to speak, have more to say to each other.[9] Among the feelings which Solomon lists as being those which one should aim at expressing in sexual activity are: hatred, shame, fear, submissiveness and possessiveness. In particular, he cites domination and passivity as feelings which are "best expressed sexually."[10] Thus, it would seem that, with respect to deciding whether or not some-thing is good sex, the appropriate questions to ask are: 1) Are feel-ings successfully communicated in this act? 2) Are the feelings which are communicated ones which are best communicated sex-ually? and, 3) How much feeling is communicated, and how new—that is, non-repetitive—is it? The more communication there is and the more successful it is, the better the sex.

The feeling of domination is certainly one we would expect on the part of the rapist and probably also hatred, or at least, hostil-ity, and possessiveness. Fear, shame, and submissiveness are part of the lot of the rapee (or person being raped). The communica-tion in rape is almost invariably successful—indeed, the rapee of-ten cannot forget the message and lives in fear long after the rape. The rapist effectively communicates to the rapee his feelings and his domination; the rapist understands that the rapee is afraid and he either does not care or finds the fear exciting. There would seem to be no more effective or appropriate means of communi-cating dominance than to force someone to submit to something she does not want.[11] And, whether it is a result of cultural condi-tioning or not, perhaps the most successful means of communicat-ing contempt, hostility and domination is through a sexual violation.

Solomon does go beyond the effectiveness of communication to what he calls "semantic deviations"[12]—that is, he claims that sex could be perverted in the same way that lying and insincerity are perverted. But this will not get us any further with rape, since the intention on the part of the rapist to dominate and the fear on the part of the rapee are usually perfectly sincere. Moreover, if we in-clude his mention of the value of variety as part of his theory of good sex, rape might well be recommended as providing intensity and variety of emotional expression. The feelings in rape are in-tense, and they are not feelings which would be typically ex-pressed in consensual sex. On the other hand, if repeated too often, rape would get repetitive and boring, since it is most appro-priate to a narrow range of feelings.

Solomon makes no mention of consent or coercion in his paper "Sexual Paradigms," but in a later paper on the same topic, he claims that cases where domination or sadism is not met with a complementary dependence or masochism "can only be interpret-ed as a breakdown in communication."[13] From this, one might as-sume that he thinks that consent—or at least mutual desire—is built into his sex-as-communication model on the grounds that lack of consent is a breakdown of communication. But this is simply false. In linguistic communication, lack of consent is neither logically nor causally inconsistent with successful communication. Of course, there are people who do not "hear" what they do not want to hear and, in these cases, their lack of consent will have a causal effect on the effectiveness of the communication, but this is not the standard case, and it certainly is not necessarily the case. He may be assuming that the communication he is talking about includes an intention to persuade someone into cooperation since, if consent is the object of the persuasive act, lack of consent would indicate its failure. But the rapist may have no intention of inducing willing cooperation, so that lack of consent is in no way inconsistent with the attitudes he is expressing. Lack of consent is perfectly appropriate to domination, since a paradigm case of domination is the ability and willingness to do things to others without their consent. Since Solomon includes attitudes such as hatred, domination, and fear in his list of feelings that are appropriate to express sexually, he is clearly not limiting sexual expression to those attitudes which would include a desire for willing cooperation as a necessary component. Thus, to the extent that Solomon claims lack of consent to be a deviation, he is, himself, deviating from his model of sex-as-communication.

Nagel's analysis of sexuality and sexual perversion runs into problems with rape because of its lack of specificity. The paradigm he uses is one of mutual arousal, but, as he admits, he is unspecific about what that arousal is.[14] The rapee's fear may arouse in the rapist both excitement and sexual desire and the arousal of the rapist may in turn arouse more fear in the rapee, and so on. It is not clear that Nagel's analysis will rule out such cases. If it does not, then the analysis will have the consequence that a rapist who is aroused by his victim's fear is less perverted than one who is not so aroused—surely a peculiar consequence.

It appears, from Nagel's discussion of sadism and masochism, that he intends to rule out such cases, but the vagueness of his criteria make it unlikely that he will succeed without adding further qualifications. I will argue later for a set of such qualifications which would rule out such cases.

Nagel does give one specification of how a sexual attitude might be different from a non-sexual attitude:

All stages of sexual perception are varieties of identification of a person with his body. What is perceived is one's own or another's *subjection* or immersion in his body . . .[15]

As with Solomon's choice of communication, it might be argued that here Nagel has singled out a characteristic according to which rape is perhaps the most successful kind of sex. Rape is an attempt to identify the victim with her body as an object. The rapee may become excruciatingly aware of her body as a body—as an object to be used by someone else—and, consequently, of herself as the object which her body is perceived as. The rapist becomes incarnated into his body as a weapon, as a dominating presence, as power, as an incarnation of masculinity, dominance and freedom. Thus, again, Nagel's vagueness leads him to overlook the fact that his theory may commit him to recommending rape as a paradigm of good sex.

Nagel's discussion of sexual desire as a desire for the other may enable us to rule out cases which are not only against a person's will, but are also against all of a person's sexual desires, on the grounds that, for example, the fear felt on the part of the rapee cannot be part of the appropriate reciprocity, since it does not include a desire for the other. However, it would still not rule out coercion. Juliet may be sexually aroused by Romeo, but unwilling to have sexual relations with him because of some other factor—for example, she may wish to remain faithful to a steady lover or husband, or to maintain a friendship with Rosalyn who is in love with Romeo. Even if we assume, then, that the criterion of arousal is specifically tied to mutual arousal of desire, Nagel's analysis would not rule out Romeo's raping Juliet under these circumstances. Nagel's failure to go beyond an analysis of the flirtation leaves a point at which coercion is likely to be used out of the analysis altogether.

II

If we claim that there is no bad sex such that it is worse than no sex at all, then, unless we deny that rape is a sexual act,[16] it follows that the rape victim is better off being raped than she would be if she had no sex at all. Moreover, to the extent that we are claiming that rape is better than either bad sex or no sex at all, we are committed to saying that a person who is rational and who has no reason for avoiding sex should—moral considerations aside—prefer either raping or being raped to no sex or to not very good sex. At the very least, this claim commits us to saying that the rapee has gotten some good out of the experience. On Solomon's analysis, then, a woman should prefer being raped to having sex with her husband of ten years since, according to Solomon, she and her husband probably do not have that much left to say to each other. Being raped would usually be an improvement in the rapee's sex life; and why should anyone be punished for improving someone's sex life? This is exactly the kind of argument used by jurors who refuse to convict rapists.[17]

Of course, even if rape is good sex, it is still an instance of coercion. However, if rape were good sex and, therefore, good for the rapee, it would be benevolent coercion rather than malevolent coercion. And benevolent coercion is much less morally objectionable than malevolent coercion. Indeed, many people find some instances of benevolent coercion unobjectionable or even praiseworthy—for example, a physician coercing a patient into undergoing medical treatment. The claim either that rape is good sex or that the worst sex is better than no sex at all would commit us to classifying rape, as such, as benevolent rather than as malevolent coercion.

It would be a mistake to assume that, in order to support a claim that rape is, as such, malevolent coercion rather than benevolent coercion we must be committed to the position that sex is bad. It is tempting, but not necessary, to fall prey to the following argument: a) rape is the act of forcing someone to engage in sexual relations; b) sex is good, therefore, c) rape is benevolent coercion. The plausibility of this argument rests on the quantificational ambiguity of premise b. The argument is only valid if we assume that b is a universal statement, but that is not a very plausible interpretation. The statement that sex is good, if not interpreted universally, may entail that good sex is good, but it does not entail that bad sex is good.

A more plausible approach would be to develop a theory of good and bad sex which provides an account of genuinely bad sex which is worse than no sex at all. In the next section, I will suggest how Nagel's theory could be modified to provide such an account.

III

Nagel's theory of sexual perversion could be developed to provide a strong analysis of bad sex. Solomon's theory seems less likely to provide such an analysis, for two reasons: 1) Solomon's ready acceptance of non-symmetrical and aversive feelings as appropriate to good sex seems to be a consequence of his basic premise that sex is communication. If so, it will not be a simple matter to build in such constraints as willingness and consent or mutuality and equality. 2) It is not at all clear that good communication is a good. The delivery of a threat might be very good communication, but it is not the case that it adds a good to each of the participants. On the other hand, a good interpersonal relationship does seem to be a good.

Nagel's theory is, basically, that good sex is interpersonal. And it is interpersonal not only in the sense that it is a relation between two persons, but also in the stronger sense that it entails reciprocal states of awareness between persons.

One restriction on what counts as a paradigm case under this theory would allow us to avoid the consequence that rape and sex undertaken for prostitution are good sex. In order to explain this restriction, I will need the following distinction:

A *reciprocal* relation is one in which both (or all) parties have as objects of their awareness or consciousness the other person's consciousness or state of awareness. Reciprocal arousal, then, would occur when this reciprocal awareness arouses new feelings or intensifies existing feelings in each of the participants.

A *mutual* relation is a reciprocal relation in which the reciprocal states of awareness are symmetrical.

All mutual relations are reciprocal, but not all reciprocal relations are mutual.

To illustrate this distinction, let us go back to compare Nagel's Romeo and Juliet example to the rape example. In the Romeo and Juliet example, the states of awareness are symmetrical and the relation is mutual—Romeo is attracted to Juliet, Juliet is attracted to Romeo, Romeo is aroused by his awareness that Juliet is attracted to him, and so on. On the other hand, in the example of the sadistic rapist, the states of awareness are not symmetrical. The rapist desires to rape and humiliate the rapee; the rapee perceives his intention and is aroused to fear by it; the rapist perceives the fear and is further excited and aroused in his intention; the rapee perceives this further excitement and becomes more afraid, and so on. In this example, the relation is reciprocal—each of the participants is aware of the other's awareness and that awareness arouses or intensifies feelings in each—but the feelings and the states of awareness are not symmetrical, and, thus, the relation is not mutual.

If we add to Nagel's requirement of reciprocal states of consciousness the requirement that these reciprocal states be mutual, the theory affords us coherent and plausible grounds for denying that rape is good sex. However, we still seem to be committed to the position that a relation of mutual hatred is good sex. If we add the further requirement that there be a mutually desired common state of affairs which is realized in the relation, we can deal with this problem. Let us compare Romeo and Juliet to (with apologies to Shakespeare) Iago and Desdemona.

Suppose that Iago and Desdemona hate each other equally. Their hatred is reciprocal and mutual and they intend to act it out sexually. Each hates the other and wishes to humiliate, degrade and injure the other, and each is aroused to greater hatred by their awareness of the other's hatred. It might seem that they desire the same thing: the humiliation of the other. But, on closer inspection, they desire opposite states of affairs: Desdemona desires that Iago be humiliated, degraded and injured and that Desdemona emerge triumphant and unscathed; Iago, on the other hand, desires that Desdemona be humiliated, degraded and injured, but that Iago emerge triumphant and unscathed.

At first glance, it might seem that Romeo and Juliet have different objects of desire: Romeo's object of desire is Juliet and Juliet's object of desire is Romeo; Romeo does not desire Romeo and Juliet does not desire Juliet. However, the seeming difference rests on the ambiguity of "X desires Y." In this context "Juliet desires Romeo" does not mean that she wants, for example, to hang him up among her objects of art, but rather that she desires a specific state of affairs: that is, that Romeo and Juliet engage in a physical, sexual and interpersonal relationship. And this is the same state of affairs that Romeo desires—assuming that their desires are interpersonal, reciprocal and mutual.

This restriction also makes it clear that the requirement of reciprocal sexual arousal is too vague, since the state of affairs which is the object of sexual desire is variable. Take the case of a reciprocal arousal of desire between a foot-fetishist and a person who has a sexual aversion to foot fondling. In this example, if we remain at the level of abstractness of describing the relation as a mutual arousal of sexual desire, it would appear to be fully mutual, whereas, if the state of affairs which is the object of each person's desire is specified, it becomes clear that the reciprocal desires are, by their nature, incapable of mutual fulfillment. In this example, the flirtation may be ideal on Nagel's analysis even though the desires aroused are inconsistent. Whereas, the criterion of a state of affairs as a common object of desire guarantees that the reciprocal desires are, in principle, capable of mutual fulfillment.

Moreover, on this analysis, love is more appropriate to sexual relations than hatred, not because love is, for some unspecified reason, a better emotion, but because it lends itself to mutuality, while reciprocal hatred is not capable of mutual fulfillment. The value of love, liking, friendship and sexual attraction to sexual relationships is based on their universalizability; the inappropriateness of hatred, dominance, and sadism is based on their non-universalizability. This analysis also shows why fetishism, although not a perversion, would be a disadvantage: a fetish places an unnecessary limitation on the situations in which mutuality is possible. Unlike a preference for hatred, however, a foot fetish does not preclude, *a priori*, the possibility of mutuality (two foot fetishists might have a fully mutual foot-fondling relationship).

This analysis of good-making characteristics of sexual relations also builds in the requirements of consent and communication. Communication is an element of reciprocity and, hence, a precondition of mutuality. And, if we require that the mutuality be sustained throughout the relation, and that the reciprocal desires be mutually fulfilled, then the relation must be one which both partners desire and consent to.

It follows from the requirements of mutuality and common objects of desire that to the degree that a sexual relation is a good sexual relation, each of the partners is getting good sex, since the relation is symmetrical. Of course, the restrictions delineate an ideal, and even close approximations to that ideal will probably be asymmetrical to some degree or other, and, to the extent that the reciprocity is asymmetrical, the good will also be asymmetrical.

These restrictions allow us to avoid the possible consequences that some acts of rape are good sex, but it does not yet provide us with a concept of bad sex. The paradigms of bad sex which Nagel presents are cases of noninterpersonal sex, for example, masturbation or shoe fetishism. If we use Nagel's analysis as an analysis of the goodness or badness of sexual relations, however, it is clear that such examples are neither good sexual relations nor bad sexual relations; they are not sexual relations at all. Moreover, the assumption that masturbation is the worst that could happen to one sexually indicates a remarkable poverty of imagination and, since rape victims and prostitutes tend to be female, a rather serious male bias. If the best sex is a particular kind of interpersonal relation (I think it is clear that both Nagel and Solomon are committed to this claim) then it would be plausible to assume that bad sex is another kind of interpersonal relation.

From the foregoing analysis of good sex, it seems reasonable to conclude that some forms of asymmetrical reciprocity would be bad-making characteristics of sex with respect to interpersonal values. Thus, a relation of mutual hatred would be bad sex because it is intrinsically incapable of mutual fulfillment. However, this example is not only asymmetrical but also nonuniversalizable: that is, the desires of Iago and Desdemona are not only not matching, but their objects are contraries and the desires are such that they are incapable of mutuality. On the other hand, relations which are simply non-matching may be indifferent rather than bad. For example, if the foot-fetishist relates to someone who neither desires foot-fondling nor is averse to it, the relation is one in which at least some aspects of the objects of desire are nonmutual but also not contrary. Such a relation would be indifferent with respect to interpersonal values and may or may not be better than no sex at all, depending on other aspects of the relation.

IV

Perverted sex, on my analysis, is a subset of bad sex. I will argue that the concept of sexual perversion is appropriately analyzed in terms of a concept of perversion which is universalizable to nonsexual cases. Such an approach to the concept of sexual perversion is contrary both to the analysis of sexual perversion in terms of the unnatural, which is standard to the approach of traditional theology and of natural law theory, and to the analysis of sexual perversion in terms of abnormality, an approach standard to contemporary psychology.

Sara Ruddick, in "On Sexual Morality," proposes a definition of "sexual perversion" according to which "natural" is the antonym of "perverted" and natural sex is necessarily connected to reproduction:

The final characteristic of better sex is that it is 'natural' rather than perverted. The *ground* for classifying sexual acts into the natural and the unnatural is that the former serve or could serve the evolutionary and biological function of sexuality—viz., reproduction. . . . The connection of sexual desire with reproduction is not sufficient to yield the concept of perversion but it is surely necessary.[18]

Ruddick assumes that the concept of sexual perversion, presumably unlike other normative concepts and unlike the concept of nonsexual perversion, is only coherent in the context of natural law theory or, at least, of a concept of "natural" sex. Admittedly, both our popular culture and our habits of language have clung to the notions of natural sex and natural sex roles long after abandoning the notion of a natural class structure or a natural form of government. But there is no reason why philosophers who have abandoned natural law theory and the concept of natural function must revert to such conceptual props when discussing either sex or perversion. If we can coherently talk about, for example, a perverted sense of humor, without committing ourselves to a notion of natural humor, it seems unlikely that we should need a notion of the natural for other perversions, including sexual ones. Moreover, the assumption that reproduction is the natural (and, therefore, right or good) function of sexuality evaluates sexual acts and relations in ways inimical to women. On such a theory, the rapist (particularly if part of his motive is to impregnate as many unwilling women as possible) is perfectly sexually natural, while the man who chooses nonreproductive sexual acts because he does not want to burden his sexually willing partner with an unwanted pregnancy is a pervert. Moreover, the identification of sex with reproduction ignores the existence of female sexual organs (the clitoris has no direct reproductive function)[19] and the process of pregnancy, which is not sexual. On this view, the male reproductive function (impregnation) is elevated to the status of the paradigm of sexuality and reproduction.[20]

Alan Goldman, in "Plain Sex," proposes a similar claim about what kind of theory or concept a definition of perversion *must* rest on:

Since the concept of perversion is itself a sexual concept, it will always be defined relative to some definition of *normal* sex; and any conception of the norm will imply a contrary notion of perverse forms. . . . I do deny that we can find a norm, other than that of statistically usual desire, against which all and only activities that properly count as sexual perversions can be contrasted.[21]

Elsewhere in the same paper, Goldman argues that what is morally wrong in sexual behavior is what is morally wrong in other behavior, that sexual ethics is simply an instance of more general moral considerations.[22] Unfortunately, he does not see fit to extend this principle to the concept of perversion. He makes specificity to sexual perversion a criterion of adequacy of any analysis of perversion and insists on giving sexual 'perversion' a meaning quite different from the use of the term in nonsexual cases.[23]

My describing someone's taste in food as perverted does commit me to some culinary standard but not necessarily to any standard of naturalness or normality. For example, one might consider perverted the taste of someone who prefers chocolate sauce on mashed potatoes and gravy on peppermint ice-cream. Such a preference is not contrary to the natural function of food—this combination would have exactly the same nutritional value as the reverse combination recommended by American cuisine. Nor is the combination perverted because it is unusual—rather it is unusual because most of us follow the standards of eating and cooking of the cuisine of our culture. Quite simply, such a preference is perverted because it runs directly counter to culinary standards and rules which specify what foods and seasonings go with what. It is perfectly coherent to claim that standards of this type can be violated in a way that represents a perversion of the rules. There is no *a priori* reason to believe that perversion, unlike good or right, can only find a firm foundation in natural law theory or social science.

The concept of perversion should be stronger than the concept of the merely bad. A perversion of x is not simply something which does not match up to the ideal, but, rather, a preference in which the ideal is reversed. In the nonsexual use of "perversion," a perverted attitude is one which, for example, takes delight in another's discomfort and pain simply because it is the other's discomfort and pain ("a perverted sense of humor," "He took a perverse delight in watching the candidate's embarrassment," etc.). Or, to use a nonmoral example, a perverse style of writing might be one which is deliberately and studiedly awkward, ungrammatical or difficult to understand.

The analysis of good and bad sex that I have offered does allow us to distinguish between perverted sex and merely bad sex and between a perverted sexual preference and a merely unfortunate one. If mutuality is a criterion of good sex, then universalizability will be a criterion of nonperverted sex. A person with sexual desires which are, in principle, nonuniversalizable—in particular, a sexual desire such that the lack of reciprocity or mutuality on the part of the other is part of the object of the desire—has a perverted sexual attitude or preference.

On this theory, then, there are three levels of less-than-good sexual preferences or attitudes: the perverted, the bad, and the merely unfortunate. To illustrate the first two, let me make a distinction between two types of rapists. The contingent rapist is a man who simply desires sexual intercourse and is indifferent as to whether or not the relationship is mutual. If he desires to engage in intercourse with Jane, he does not care whether or not she reciprocates the emotion. If she does not reciprocate, he will simply coerce her into submitting. For the essential or sadistic rapist, the sexual act's being a case of rape is an essential element of the object of desire. The contingent rapist is like the egoist: he does not desire the bad, but is indifferent to the good (of others, at least). One can conceive of a world in which the contingent rapist fulfills his desires and does no harm—that is, a world in which his interests happen not to collide with those of other persons. The essential rapist, on the other hand, desires asymmetry and desires that his sexual acts be bad sex (for the other, at least). He cannot fulfill his desires without bringing about the bad. Thus, his sexual attitude or preference is genuinely twisted, perverted, contrary to the ideal, while the attitude of the contingent rapist is merely bad.

Some other kinds of sexual preference might be merely unfortunate, and even that only under the appropriate conditions. For example, a foot-fetishist has desires such that the likelihood of mutuality with respect to those desires is lessened. But, there is nothing in foot-fetishism as such which constitutes either a desire for asymmetry and lack of mutuality or an indifference to it.

V

This account of good, bad and perverted sexual relations has the advantage of providing an account of genuinely bad sex. Thus, it preserves the meaning of 'perversion' as used in nonsexual contexts. It does not, and is not intended to, provide a framework for evaluating noninterpersonal sexual acts such as masturbation. Sexual perversion, like sexual immorality, is dependent on ideals and principles which can apply in nonsexual cases. Moreover, a specific instance of bad sex or sexual perversion may or may not make essential reference to sexual states or desires. Sexual infidelity, for example, falls under sexual morality because the problem is created by the sexual relationship. However, if it is wrong, it would seem to be so because of the nonsexual feelings of one's partner (jealousy, fear of loss of love, etc.), rather than because of the sexual feelings of the persons involved. Similarly, sexual perversion may be such that the relevant elements of the object of desire is sexual (for example, desiring to have sexual relations only with those who do not reciprocate the sexual feeling) or such that the relevant element is nonsexual (for example, desiring to have sexual relations only with those whom one can professionally or economically humiliate).

Like the accounts of Nagel and Solomon, and unlike the sex as reproduction theory, this account avoids the implication that the gender of one's sexual partner is, in itself, sufficient to make a sexual act perverted—neither homosexuality nor heterosexuality as such is a perversion. On the other hand, it provides sufficient grounds for classifying sadism and a preference for children as perversions, which the other analyses do not. Sadism is not perverted (or even bad sex) on Solomon's sex-as-communication model or on the sex-as-reproduction model offered by Ruddick for the same reasons that rape is, in itself, neither bad nor perverted on those accounts. A sadistic sexual act may be very effective communication and may be perfectly suitable for reproduction.[24]

The sadist whose desire is to humiliate and cause pain to the other against the other's will has a desire which is incapable of mutuality. A sadist who desires consent on the part of the partner still desires that the responses be asymmetrical—one feeling pain, humiliation and submission and the other feeling mastery and dominance. The case of the person with a sexual preference for children is somewhat more complicated. If the child-preferer desires sexual relations with children because children are incapable of full sexual reciprocity and because he can dominate them, then an essential element of his desire is lack of mutuality. If, on the other hand, his desire is for someone who has a six-year-old child's body with the sexual and mental capacities of an adult, his desires will be irrational, but not perverted, although his actions are likely to be perverted.

I have argued that theories of sexual perversion that do not deal with the badness of aversive sexual relations, such as rape and prostitution, are inadequate and distorted. At best, they leave us with no explanation of what is rational about an aversion to rape; at worst, they degrade women by their acceptance of the conclusion that rape is a good and desirable sexual relation. The theory I have offered avoids these problems. Moreover, in connecting the goodness, badness and perversion of sexual relations to the ideal of universalizable emotions, my theory may illuminate the tradition of illustrating the social perversion of human relations with sexual examples, as in the often quoted passage in Marx's *Manuscripts*:

In the relationship with *woman*, as the prey and handmaiden of communal lust, is expressed the infinite degradation in which man [sic] exists for himself ... It [the sexual relation between men and women] also shows how far man's [sic] needs have become *human* needs, and consequently how far the other person, as a person, has become one of his needs.[25]

Despite Marx's sexist assumption of maleness as the normative condition of humanity (for women, the heterosexual relation is not a relation with woman), this passage reveals an important and generalizable point: the perversion of sexual relations is an index of the corruption of society as a whole, and the ideal of sexual relations may serve as a model of the ideal of social relations. My account of sexual perversion should offer some insight into what is degrading about those relations (most notably rape and prostitution) that are sexual indices of a corrupt (in this case sexist) society.[26]

NOTES

1. See, for example, Carolyn Shafer and Marilyn Frye, "Rape and Respect" and Pamela Foa, "What's Wrong With Rape," both in Mary Vetterling-Braggin, Frederick Elliston and Jane English, eds. *Feminism and Philosophy* (Totowa, N.J.: Littlefield, Adams and Co., 1977), pp. 333–359.
2. Thomas Nagel, "Sexual Perversion," *The Journal of Philosophy* 66, No. 1 (January 16, 1969), pp. 1–17 (in this volume, pp. 76–88).
3. Robert Solomon, "Sexual Paradigms," *The Journal of Philosophy* 71, No. 11 (June 13, 1974), pp. 336–345 (in this volume, pp. 89–98). See also his "Sex and Perversion," in Robert Baker and Frederick Elliston, eds. *Philosophy and Sex* (Buffalo: Prometheus, 1975), pp. 286–287.
4. Alan Goldman does briefly discuss rape, but only under the heading of sexual ethics, not in his discussion of perversion or of good or bad sex. See his "Plain Sex," *Philosophy and Public Affairs* 6, No. 3 (Spring, 1977), p. 281 (in this volume, pp. 119–138; p. 131).
5. Nagel, *op. cit.,* p. 88 (in this volume).
6. See, for example: Goldman, *op. cit.,* pp. 119–138 in this volume; Janice Moulton, "Sexual Behavior: Another Position," *The Journal of Philosophy* 73, No. 16 (September 16, 1976), pp. 537–546 (in this volume, pp. 110–118); Jerome Shafer, "Sexual Desire," *The Journal of Philosophy* 75, No. 4 (April, 1978), pp. 175–189; and Robert Gray,

"Sex and Sexual Perversion," *The Journal of Philosophy* 75, No. 4 (April, 1978), pp. 189–199 (in this volume, pp. 158–168).

7. Etienne Gilson, *The Christian Philosophy of St. Thomas Aquinas*, L.K. Shook, trans. (New York: Random House, 1956), pp. 298. For further discussion, see Christine Pierce, "Natural Law Language and Women," in Jane English, ed. *Sex Equality* (Englewood Cliffs, N.J.: Prentice-Hall, 1977), pp. 130–142.

8. Nagel further concludes that "the alternatives have to be fairly grim before it becomes rational to opt for nothing" (p. 88 in this volume), which indicates that he is at least leaving open the possibility that there is some sex that is worse than no sex at all. However, his *paradigm* case of bad sex (masturbation) is such that he considers it better than no sex at all, and his theory does not provide an account of how any sex could be worse than no sex at all.

9. Solomon, *op. cit.,* (1974), p. 97 (in this volume).

10. *Ibid.*, p. 97 (in this volume).

11. I will follow the practice (by this time, the standard practice) of referring to the rape victim as "she" and the rapist as "he." Not only are rape victims statistically overwhemingly female and rapists overwhelmingly male, but also, in those situations in which males are raped (male prisons, in particular), being raped is perceived by both the victim and the perpetrator as a mode of feminization; the (biologically male) rapee becomes, socially speaking, a woman. It is evident that the femaleness of the victim is part of the social and cultural significance of rape.

12. Solomon, *op. cit.,* p. 98 (in this volume).

13. Solomon, *op. cit.* (1975), pp. 283–284.

14. Nagel, *op. cit.,* p. 84 (in this volume). Solomon, in "Sexual Paradigms," criticizes Nagel for leaving the communication model "utterly without content" (p. 95 in this volume).

15. Nagel, *op. cit.*, p. 84 (in this volume).

16. Gray (see footnote 6) suggests that we modify the use of the phrase "sexual activity" in such a way that the rape victim will not be said to have engaged in sexual activity because "from her point of view, the activity may not have been sexual at all" (p. 162 in this volume). The problem he points out is very important, but if we follow his linguistic suggestion, we are left with no language for describing rape. For what is the rape victim being coerced into if not participating in (someone else's) sexual act?

17. For example, Samuel Rhone, juror in the Inez Garica trial, told reporter Nan Blitman that a woman could not plead self-defense if she killed a man during a rape attack because "the guy's not trying to kill her. He's just trying to give her a good time." *Mother Jones* 1, No.1 (February/March, 1976), pp. 67.

18. Sara Ruddick, "On Sexual Morality," in James Rachels, ed. *Moral Problems*, 2nd edition (New York: Harper and Row, 1975), p. 23. A

revised version of this article ("Better Sex") is reprinted in Baker and Elliston, eds. *Philosophy and Sex, op. cit.* In that version, "allegedly better sex acts" is substituted for "better sex" (p. 91). However, the analysis of perversion remains the same.

19. For a discussion of the sexual asymmetry of the concept of sexual intercourse, see Janice Moulton, "Sex and Reference," in Robert Baker and Frederick Elliston, eds. *Philosophy and Sex, op. cit.,* pp. 34–44.

20. Contrary to the arguments I have offered here, Ruddick claims that Nagel's view of reproduction (Nagel rejects the sex-as-reproduction theory) is "the clearest instance of male bias in Nagel's paper," *op. cit.,* p. 24. She, in particular, criticizes Nagel for claiming that reproduction is purely physiological rather than psychological. But, if this is a fault, it is one that she has not corrected in her own account of the connection between reproduction and perversion.

21. Goldman, *op. cit.,* p. 134 (in this volume).

22. *Ibid.,* p. 130 (in this volume).

23. If we take dictionary definitions as any guide at all, Goldman is proposing a radical change of meaning for 'perversion.' Not only does he propose restricting the concept of perversion to sex, but he proposes that perversion should be stripped of evaluative meaning. If we remove evaluative terms from the definition "turned from the right way, from the proper use, from truth to error" (*Oxford English Dictionary*) or from the definition "deviating from what is considered right, natural, or true" (*Webster's New Twentieth Century,* Unabridged), it is not clear what we have left of the meaning of 'perverted.' Nor is it clear why it should be so desirable to abandon the old meaning so completely.

24. I criticize one of Solomon's attempts to bring sadism under the category of perversion in Section I. In "Sexual Paradigms," *op. cit.,* pp. 97 (in this volume), he suggests that sadism is "an excessive expression of a particular content." This would suggest that there is nothing even mildly perverted about moderate and occasional sadism and that an excessive expression of a universalizable emotion—for example, affection—would have the same problems as sadism. Ruddick assumes that sadism is a perversion without offering any explanation as to why it might be so. See her "On Sexual Morality," *op. cit.,* p. 28 and "Better Sex," *op. cit.,* p. 96.

25. *Karl Marx: Early Writings,* T. B. Bottomore, ed. and trans. (New York: McGraw-Hill, 1964), p. 154.

26. See, in addition: Sara Ann Ketchum and Christine Pierce, "Separatism and Sexual Relationships," in *Philosophy and Women,* Sharon Bishop and Marjorie Weinzweig, eds. (Belmont, Calif.: Wadsworth, 1979), pp. 166–171, which includes a discussion of the importance of power to human relationships.

Robert Gray

Sex and Sexual Perversion

Sara Ruddick has suggested, what seems probable, that intrinsic to the notion of perversion is that of unnaturalness.[1] That and only that sexual activity which is unnatural is perverted. There are, of course, difficulties with the notion of naturalness itself. 'Natural' may be used synonomously with 'usual' or 'ordinary', in which case perversion would appear to be entirely culturally relative. (We should have, perhaps, to except such things as adultery, which seem to be common to virtually all human societies.) On the other hand, 'natural' may be used to describe particular activities as the outcomes of naturally occurring processes. Ignoring the circularity in this, such a definition would have as a consequence that all perversions are natural, since the fetishes of the coprophiliac are as much the outcome of his natural desires and propensities as those of the "normal" heterosexual. Even if it were argued that there has been some sort of breakdown in the control mechanisms governing the behavior of the coprophiliac, still that breakdown itself could be accounted for ultimately only by an appeal to naturally occurring events, in this case, perhaps, biological laws. There is, however, a sense of 'natural' which may allow an argument such as Ruddick's to get off the ground.

Typically, by 'unnatural' we mean not just "unusual," but something more like "contrary to nature." The question is, in

Reprinted by permission from *The Journal of Philosophy* 75, No. 4 (1978), pp. 189–199.

what sense anything may be regarded as contrary to nature. To this, the best answer would appear to be that something is contrary to (its own) nature if it is counterproductive. What this requires, of course, is that there be some end or function of a given kind of behavior in terms of which we may say that a particular behavior is counterproductive or contrary to its nature as an instance of behavior of that kind, and the question is, "How do we fix that end or function in a noncircular way?" The way Ruddick would seem to favor, and the only way I see if we are to avoid cultural relativism, is in terms of evolutionary theory. If, then, we are able to show that there is some adaptive function or end that sexual activity evolved to fulfill, we may speak of sexual activity that departs from that function and, more clearly, of sexual activity that, by departing from that function, is maladaptive, as counterproductive and, in that sense, contrary to nature or unnatural. Thus, if reproduction is the adaptive function of sexual activity, those forms of sexual activity which are nonreproductive and, more clearly, those which are inimical to successful reproduction (for example, any nonreproductive sexual obsession) would be unnatural and perverted; they would constitute, as it were, a twisting of sexual activity away from its "natural" object or function. Put more simply, those forms of sexual activity would be perverted which, in evolutionary terms, are dysfunctional.

This would, in fact, seem to be Ruddick's position. On her view, the adaptive function or, if one prefers, the natural end of sexual activity is reproduction, and she concludes that all and only those forms of sexual activity which may, under normal conditions, be expected to fulfill this end are natural (24). All others are unnatural and perverted. However, this view raises some problems.

In the first place, one might ask how sexual activities are to be identified. If, for example, the natural function of sexual activity is reproduction, an end to which coprophilia has no relation at all, would that not by itself be ground for suggesting that the activities of the coprophiliac are not *sexual* activities at all, and so, of course, not sexual perversions? The problem may not be one whose solution is difficult, but for our question it is important, for in order to elucidate the notion of sexual perversion it would seem crucial that we be able to specify just what it is about an activity that makes it an instance of sexual activity. The coprophiliac's activities might well be perverted, but there need be nothing about them in virtue of which they are sexually perverted. I might, for example, have developed some sort of penchant for eating cow dung, doubtless disgusting, doubtless nonnutritive, almost certainly perverted, but what has this to do with sex? Clearly, if I regard the eating of manure simply as the only means of fulfilling my appetite for food, if in other words, I eat it because I am hungry and because it tastes good or better than the available alternatives, or, if it tastes worse, because it leaves me feeling less hungry, my perversion is not sexual. Sexually, I might be entirely normal. Now the only thing I can see in this example that would constitute it as a nonsexual form of coprophilia and the only thing whose change could conceivably make it an example of coprophilia in the sexual sense, is the motive assigned. Hunger is a fairly distinct, clearly recognizable form of displeasure; as such, it gives rise, circumstances permitting, to activities that will remove or assuage it. In the same way, sexual desire (although, unlike hunger, it may be in itself pleasant or partially so) is a distinct, recognizable appetite, typically unpleasant if unfulfilled, which gives rise to activities that will remove or assuage it.

What is to be noted here is that neither hunger nor sexual desire is in itself a desire for a particular (kind of) object. In itself, each is a feeling which, all things considered, it would, at the time, be better not to have, or, better, which one would, when circumstances permit, so act as to remove. Hunger seems to be a desire for food because, typically, it is food that relieves it, and it is therefore food that the hungry person seeks. But it is entirely possible that someone should develop a food fetish for the coprolites of cattle; that is to say, it is entirely possible that, for whatever reason, someone's feeling of hunger might be relieved only by the ingestion of manure. Such a person we might well call a food pervert. But we would not call him a sexual pervert. The difference lies in his motive. His motive is hunger, not sex. On the other hand, if what he had eaten gave him sexual pleasure, his perversion, and therefore his activity, would have been sexual. Since the activities I have described here are otherwise identical (need the coprophiliac who is sexually perverted display any overt signs of sexual excitement?), I see no other way by which the one might be classed as sexual and the other not. Those activities, accordingly, are sexual which serve to relieve sexual feeling or, alternatively put, which give rise to sexual pleasure.

Of course, it might well be objected that sexual activity does not, in fact, serve so much to relieve, as to heighten sexual feeling (which, for purposes of this discussion, we may take to refer, at least initially, to a physiological state, although many emotional and cognitive states may, and typically do, come to be intimately associated with it). The objection has some force; however, I believe it may be fairly easily answered, for, in much the same way, food, which typically serves to relieve hunger, may also serve to heighten it. There is, of course, a point at which the analogy between hunger and sexual feeling breaks down, for sexual feeling is typically relieved by intensifying it. Whereas a little food may, in some cases, be very satisfying, a little bit of sex often leaves an individual feeling less satisfied than he might otherwise have been. Accordingly, I prefer to speak of sexual activity in terms of sexual pleasure. The activities by which sexual feeling is removed are experienced as (an intensification of) pleasurable sexual feeling. When they cease to be pleasurable, that is to say, when the sexual feeling has been removed, the activities lose their specifically sexual character, and, unless there is some other reason for continuing, the behavior ceases.

Sexual perversions, then, will be all and only those activities which are dysfunctional (in the sense given above) in terms of sexual pleasure, or, as Thomas Nagel expresses it, "A sexual perversion must reveal itself in conduct that expresses an unnatural *sexual* preference" (77). However, as the quotation from Nagel shows, this is not quite adequate. Perversion, as a category, applies not only to activities, but to persons, in which case the perversion must reveal itself in an unnatural sexual *preference.* There are many sorts of activities from which we might derive sexual pleasure, some of which are undoubtedly perverted, but is it not the fact that a person might derive sexual pleasure from a given activity that makes him perverted; it is, rather, that he desires or prefers to engage in such sexual activities. We may say, accordingly, that a person will be sexually perverted if his sexual desires are for, or lead him to perform, activities which, given the adaptive function(s) of sexual activity (e.g., that it ends in reproduction), are counterproductive or maladaptive.

The definitions given here have some interesting implications, which may be best seen by contrasting them with the views taken by Ruddick. Ms. Ruddick is concerned, not so much with sexual perversion, as with what she calls "better sex," of which, on her account, pleasure, naturalness (nonpervertedness), and "completeness" are the three criteria (18). As I have developed the notion of sexual activity, however, it is clear that pleasure is a criterion not so much of better sex as of sex itself. Those activities

not serving to relieve sexual feeling, or from which no sexual pleasure is derived, would thus not be sexual activities at all. This at
first sight seems counterintuitive, since we often speak, for example, of a person's not enjoying (in the sense of deriving pleasure
from) sexual relations with his or her spouse. In this case, the difficulty lies, I think, with ordinary language. Sexual intercourse is
thought to be, and is spoken of as, sexual activity, because it is
that activity to which sexual desire paradigmatically leads. The
unacceptability of the ordinary-language criterion is best shown,
however, by the fact that, if we accept it, we are led to the unhap-
py conclusion that the rape victim has engaged in sexual activity,
although, from her point of view, the activity may not have been
sexual at all. It may make the analysis of sexual relations more
difficult, but there is nothing intrinsically objectionable in the suggestion that what is, from the point of view of one of the participants, a sexual activity, may not be so from the point of view of
the other. In fact, it would seem that ordinary language itself recognizes sexual pleasure as a criterion of sexual activity, at least
implicitly and on some occasions. For example, ordinary persons
are fond of bewailing the amount of sex and violence shown on
commercial television. Just what constitutes sex in this case, however, is not clear, since neither nudity nor the portrayal of it is, in
itself, a sexual activity. Were it so, the ordinary man, it seems to
me, would be forced to conclude that he engages in sexual activities far more frequently than he might otherwise think, e.g., in
taking a bath or changing his clothes. The only thing I can see in
this example in virtue of which televised nudity might be called
sexual is the fact that it is intended to, and in fact does, arouse
sexual feelings. The fact that it is so intended, however, may not
be crucial. To take another example, Dr. David Reuben relates
that, in the early days of the garment industry, women found that
the operation of treadle sewing machines could be employed as a
masturbatory technique,[2] and, to the extent that they so employed
it, I think it is clear that they would, in ordinary parlance, be said
to be engaging in sexual activity. We must assume, however, that
at some point the sexual possibilities of operating a treadle sewing
machine must have been discovered, presumably, at least in some
cases, by accident. Those women who made this discovery would
then have found themselves engaging in sexual activity quite unintentionally. They may or may not have found this a welcome discovery, but that is quite beside the point.

If these examples are compelling, and taken in sum I think they are, we are forced to the conclusion that what makes an activity a sexual activity, even in terms of ordinary language, is just the sexual nature of the pleasure deriving from it. Accordingly, it is quite possible that any activity might become a sexual activity and, as the last example shows, that it might become a sexual activity unintentionally. And, of course, it would follow too that no activity is a sexual activity unless sexual pleasure is derived from it. And, since no activity could be sexually perverted unless it were also a sexual activity, the same thing would hold for sexual perversion.

Although pleasure would thus seem to enter the analysis of sexual activity only as a matter of degree, as one means of determining the comparative worth, in sexual terms, of any given sexual experience, the notion of completeness would not appear to enter at all. Ruddick, who seems to take the notion principally from Nagel, defines it in this way:

A sex act is complete if each partner (1) allows himself to be "taken over" by desire, which (2) is desire not merely for the other's body but also for *his* desire, and (3) where each desire is occasioned by a response to the partner's desire (20).

Though she offers a defense of sorts for the claim that, in a complete sex act, the participant is "taken over" or "embodied" by his or her desire, Ruddick would seem to have no real argument in support of the other elements of her definition. In fact, she goes so far as to say at the end of her discussion of completeness that "incompleteness does not disqualify a sex act from being fully sexual" (23). Presumably, these other aspects of the completeness of a sex act are just accidental components, characteristics which may or may not be present but which serve to make the sex act "better" when they are. It should be noted, however, that when Ruddick comes to discuss the contribution that completeness makes to the sex act, it is not the sex act itself that is said to be improved. (This will not hold for the condition of "embodiment.") She argues, rather, that completeness contributes to the psychological and social well-being of the participants (29–30).

For Nagel, on the other hand, completeness would appear to be, at least partially, constitutive of sexual activity. Completeness, on his view, would appear to consist in a complex interaction between the desires of the two participants ("It is important that the partner be aroused, and not merely aroused, but aroused by the awareness of one's desire"–85), and he writes accordingly that

... this overlapping system of distinct sexual perceptions and interactions is the basic framework of any full-fledged sexual relation and that relations involving only part of the complex are significantly incomplete (83).

That Nagel should have attached such significance to the notion of completeness (a perversion is, for him, simply an incomplete sex act—85) is fairly easily explained. Nagel has incorrectly assumed that "sexual desire is a feeling about other persons." It "has its own content as a relation between persons." Accordingly, "it is only by analyzing that relation that we can understand the conditions of sexual perversion" (79–80). This mistake, as has already been pointed out, is understandable and is, furthermore, one we commonly make. Copulation is the paradigmatic object of sexual desire; it is just such a relation between persons that sexual desire has as its "characteristic object." But it is a mistake to go from this to the view that sexual desire has such an object as its content (or to the view that, in the analysis of sexual activity, the nature of sexual desire is in any way fundamental). A given desire is sexual, not because it has a particular object, but because it arises from a particular kind of feeling. Put differently, it is the desire (or feeling) itself that is sexual, and it is in terms of this that the activity it has as its object is perceived as a sexual activity. The relationship is not the other way around. If it were, it would be difficult, if not impossible, to see how many of the more exotic perversions could be considered sexual. One might characterize an activity such as masturbation (which Nagel apparently regards as a perversion—84–85) as sexual on the basis of some sort of family relation with coital activity, but this seems unlikely as a means of categorizing all sexual activities as sexual. Even in the case of masturbation this approach would raise problems (one could, for example, conceive a situation in which a person might masturbate, while feeling nothing at all—perhaps by using anesthetic ointments—for reasons having nothing to do with sexual desire or gratification—as part of a medical experiment, for instance. Would this activity in that case be sexual?), but one wonders what the family resemblance might be in the, admittedly strange, case of coprophilia described earlier.

This, however, is not the only difficulty with Nagel's notion of completeness, although I think it is the most serious. As Janice Moulton has argued, both Nagel and Robert Solomon (who sees the specific content of sexual desire in terms of interpersonal communication—sexual activity is a kind of "body language")[3] have "assumed that a model of flirtation and seduction constitute an adequate model of sexual behavior in general," whereas, as she argues, "most sexual behavior does not involve flirtation and seduction, and . . . what characterizes flirtation and seduction is not what characterizes the sexual behavior of regular partners."[4] This itself, however, leads Moulton into difficulties. She is forced to conclude that it is impossible to characterize sexual behavior, because there are two kinds of it: "sexual anticipation," which includes "flirtation, seduction, and traditional courtship," and "sexual satisfaction," which "involves sexual feelings which are increased by the other person's knowledge of one's preferences and sensitivities, the familiarity of their touch or smell or way of moving, and not by the novelty of their sexual interest" (111). "However, anticipation and satisfaction are often divorced" (111). But even this classification is too narrow, for, to the extent that satisfaction is here defined in interpersonal terms, "the *other* person's knowledge . . . the familiarity of *their* touch," etc., masturbation and related types of sexual activities would, again, be excluded from the possible range of sexual behaviors. However, there is, as we have seen, a means, if not of characterizing, at least of identifying behavior as sexual, and the ground here, sexual feeling, is independent of any particular model of sexual activity. Note that this is not equivalent to saying that, as Solomon puts it, "sex is pure physical enjoyment" (96). To put it in Solomon's words again, "this enjoyment accompanies sexual activity and its ends, but is not that activity or these ends" (94). Sexual activity may have many ends, interpersonal communication among them, but if we take the view that it is the end that identifies it as sexual, then we are left squarely facing the problem that any sexual activity that does not have that specific end is not, in fact, sexual activity or is somehow less than fully sexual. Thus, on Solomon's communication model, masturbation turns out to be like "talking to yourself" and therefore "clearly secondary to sexuality in its broader interpersonal context." And " 'Unadorned sexual intercourse' . . . becomes the ultimate perversion, since it is the sexual equivalent of hanging up the telephone without saying anything" (96). One is inclined to take the view, in fact, that, if Solomon has concentrated too narrowly on one model of sexuality, it is not that of anticipation, but of satisfaction. Like most men, Solomon seems to be fully persuaded of the fundamental role of genital-genital intercourse (which is entirely satisfactory from a male point of view) in human sexuality. There is evidence, however, to show that, at least from the female point of view, it is not (this sort of) intercourse, but masturbation that is crucial.[5] This may, of course, take place in an interpersonal context, and it may be preferable when it does. All it shows is that our models must not be so constructed as to exclude it.

II

What the foregoing discussion will show is that the classification of a given (type of) sexual behavior as perverted is purely descriptive. Which activities are and are not perverted will depend on what we ultimately discover the natural adaptive function of sexual activity to be, and this is a question whose answer must be given by the scientist whose business it is to study such things. Of course, if reproduction were, as some think, the sole function of sexual activity, the scientist would have no further questions to ask about the matter, and all nonreproductive sexual activity might correctly be described as perverted. However, it would seem that this is not the case. "Reproduction" is, as Nagel claims, a biological concept. As such, it includes such biological functions as conception, gestation, and birth, and, if men were fruit flies, sexual behavior might have been just that behavior minimally sufficient to ensure reproduction in this limited sense. Copulation, then, might have been enough to ensure conception; conception, enough to ensure gestation; and gestation, enough to ensure birth. The fact is, however, (and the world may or may not be better off for it) that men are not fruit flies, and reproduction in man includes far more than just the production of new individuals. Reproductive activity in man must be construed as the sum of all those activities minimally necessary to bring those new individuals themselves to reproductive maturity. Among other things, this would seem to include the formation and maintenance of well organized, stable societies and the establishment and maintenance of fairly stable male-female reproductive pairs. Since the latter would seem ultimately to depend on sexual attraction and since there is substantial evidence to show that many characteristics of human sexual behavior contribute as well to the former, it would seem probable at least that maintenance of that degree (and kind) of social organization and stability requisite to the maintenance of human society is a function that human sexual behavior has evolved to fulfill, and, if this is so, it is clear that the range of nonperverted sexual activity will be much broader than it has traditionally been taken to be. It may turn out, too, that the natural adaptive functions of human sexual activity are not culturally independent. In this case, a behavior that is maladaptive in one society may not be so in another. Thus, for example, male homosexual behavior may be maladaptive in a society with a high ratio of females to males and a birth rate too low to make the society viable. In another society, however, where the sex ratios are reversed, male homosexual behavior, by reducing sexual rivalry, might be adaptive. A similar argument would serve to demonstrate the possible adaptive character of such activities as masturbation, whatever the techniques used, including "intercourse with ... inanimate objects," which Nagel classes as a perversion. We could, perhaps, say then that variability of sexual objects is a natural characteristic, or natural adaptive function, of human sexual desire and that, where it contributes to (or, at least, does not detract from) the maintenance of the over-all social order, or to the long-term viability of society, such variability is adaptive (or, at least, not maladaptive) and nonperverted.

Of course, it may well be that, as many stalwarts claim, all and only those sexual activities traditionally approved in our society are natural (or adaptive) and nonperverted, and what the discussion so far will show is that those who agitate against the increasing sexual permissiveness of contemporary society on the ground that it is destructive of the family, presumably the bulwark of modern social institutions, are at least on the right track. However, if the view of the nature of sexual perversion taken here is correct, to uphold the claim that such practices are sexually perverted, it will be necessary to show that societies that encourage divergent sexual behaviors are, for that reason, substantially less viable than our own (since evolutionary theory regards the reproductive group rather than the individual, it should be noted, too, that a particular practice detrimental to a given group or institution may benefit the society as a whole), or that our own society, with its peculiar institutions, would be made substantially less viable, and not merely different, if it permitted or encouraged other sexual practices. In any case, the judgment whether or not a given activity is sexually perverted, to the extent that it is properly an answer to the factual question whether the behavior is or is not consonant with the natural adaptive function(s) of sexual activity, would be descriptive and nonevaluative and need not, therefore, carry any moral connotations.

This, of course, is not to say that sexual perversion is not immoral. In fact, depending on the moral view we take, there may well be ground for claiming that any and all sexual perversion is immoral. For example, one might adopt a moral view according to which the natural is the moral. This would not automatically brand sexual perversion as immoral, since it may be the case, as we have seen, that human sexual activity is naturally variable. If, however, this theory were cast in evolutionary terms, so that natural is taken to mean the naturally adaptive function of a given behavior, sexual perversion would, by definition, be immoral. I am not myself inclined to such a moral view. I am, rather, inclined to take a somewhat Hobbesian view, according to which morality is the sum of those rules minimally necessary to social cohesion. On this view, all sexual activities that are perverted by virtue of the fact that they disrupt the cohesiveness of society, assuming social cohesion is a natural function of human sexual activity, would be immoral. But it should be noted that this judgment is logically independent of the judgment that those activities are perverted. One might, therefore, make the suggestion, since 'perversion' has acquired such a strong pejorative connotation in our society, that the term be dropped from our sexual vocabulary all together. Other clearer and less emotive terms may just as easily be substituted for it.

But, whatever the moral implications, this much seems clear. If we have correctly defined what it is for behavior to be sexually perverted and, in that sense, "contrary to nature," as any practice or activity from which sexual pleasure is derived and which, given the natural adaptive function(s) of sexual activity, is counterproductive or maladaptive, we will at least have succeeded in putting the question, "What specific activities are and are not perverted?" in terms amenable to investigation by the behavioral sciences. In such questions as these, no more really can be asked of the philosopher.

NOTES

1. "On Sexual Morality," in James Rachels, ed., *Moral Problems*, 2nd ed. (New York: Harper & Row, 1975), pp. 23–24. See also Thomas Nagel, "Sexual Perversion," *The Journal of Philosophy* 66, No. 1 (1969), pp. 5–17. (This volume, pp. 76–88.)
2. *Everything You Always Wanted to Know About Sex* (New York: Bantam, 1971), pp. 201–202. (Originally: McKay, 1969.)
3. "Sexual Paradigms," *The Journal of Philosophy* 71, No. 1 (1974), pp. 336–345, p. 343. (This volume, pp. 89–98; p. 96.)
4. "Sexual Behavior: Another Position," *The Journal of Philosophy* 73, No. 16 (1976), pp. 537–546, p. 538 (This volume, pp. 110–118; p. 111.)
5. Shere Hite, *The Hite Report* (New York: Macmillan, 1976), pp. 229–252.

Donald Levy

Perversion and the Unnatural as Moral Categories

For whatever reasons, the recent revival of philosophical interest in problems relating to love and sexuality began with attempts to analyze the concept of sexual perversion. Is it essentially an incoherent idea, one we moderns ought to seek to do without in thinking about sex? Is a revival of one or another of the traditional theologically based accounts of sexual perversion to be undertaken, perhaps updated, by the addition of the latest psychiatric findings? Or does the concept conceal hitherto unsuspected patterns of meaning which philosophical analysis might uncover for the first time? If sexual perversion is to be taken seriously, problems of definition demand solution at the start; what makes a sexual practice perverted? What differentiates sexual perversions from

Reprinted by permission from *Ethics* 90, No. 2 (January 1980), pp. 191–202. This is an expanded version of a paper which originally appeared in *Ethics* in 1980. Essential advice and assistance in writing this paper was received from Marilyn M. Hamilton, David A.J. Richards and Alan Soble. It was presented, in part, before the Thirteenth Conference on Value Inquiry at SUNY College at Geneseo in April, 1979, before the Society for Philosophy and Public Affairs, New York Chapter, in November, 1975 and before the CUNY Ethics Colloquium in March, 1975.

non-sexual perversions, if there are any such things? What makes a human activity perverted at all?

The range of human sexual activities commonly called "sexual perversions" is very wide, and vague in outline. Its vagueness will be clear from the following list, which I have adapted from Michael Balint.[1]

1. First of all, there are the various kinds of homosexuality.
2. Next, the several forms of sadism and masochism.
3. Exhibitionism, voyeurism, use of other parts of the body (i.e., other than the genitals).
4. Fetishism, transvestism, possibly kleptomania.
5. Bestiality.
6. Necrophilia, pedophilia.

I should add that this list can be misleading by its abstractness; fetishism, for example, may cover a great variety of behaviors.

One can get some sense of the confusion in this field from the fact that Balint does not regard bestiality as a "proper" perversion—it never reaches the height of a proper perversion, he says, since it always comes about for want of something better. In addition, practices classified under necrophilia and pedophilia belong to the psychoses, he thinks. Even if we grant these unintuitive reasons for separating bestiality, necrophilia and pedophilia from the main group, it is not at all easy to see what the first four categories have in common that nothing else in the way of sexual behavior shares.

Given the vague outlines of the classification, it is not surprising that the definitions proposed for this concept have not been very satisfactory. Ideas about various of the perversions can be found in Freud's writings, though it is fairly clear that he does not regard the term as a specially psychoanalytic one, for whose definition he bears responsibility. In that sense, it is incorrect to speak of Freud as having a theory of the perversions at all. (Freud sometimes uses the word in quotes, and once even refers to narcissism, which is of course not even a sexual activity as sometimes having "the significance of a perversion".)[2] If this is understood, we can say that Freud does tend to think of perversion as the undisguised expression of an infantile sexual wish.[3] Normal sex differs from the perverted variety in integrating the infantile sexual wish with other sexual wishes, not isolating it, and in gratifying it in disguised form. The difference between normal and perverted is one of degree, however.[4]

The most acute criticism of the account I am attributing to

Freud comes from within psychoanalysis itself. Balint points out that many forms of homosexuality on the one hand, and of the sadomasochistic group on the other, are definitely not survivals of infantile forms of sexuality but rather are later developments. Balint's own attempt at definition focuses on perversions as

> . . . attempts to escape from the two main demands of mature genitality: (1.) accepting as real the intense need in ourselves for periodic regressions in the form of heterosexual coitus, and (2.) accepting the necessity of the work of conquest, i.e., changing an indifferent object into a cooperative genital partner."[5]

There are several reasons for doubting the adequacy of this approach. In the first place, Balint has made it clear that homosexuality is to be included among the perversions, yet he also maintains that in homosexual love "there is also the same bliss"[6] as in heterosexual love, from which it is reasonable to infer that the need for regression is felt and fulfilled in both alike. As for the second feature, Balint also asserts that "all the altruistically loving . . . features of heterosexual love can be found in homosexual love as well."[7] Besides, the first condition of Balint's definition would appear to make all celibates perverts; and the second condition would classify as perverted all selfish, crude, negligent—but heterosexual—lovers.

Recent philosophical attempts to define sexual perversion have not achieved any greater success than have the efforts of the psychoanalysts. Thomas Nagel conceives of sexual perversion in psychological terms, he says,[8] but it is nothing psychoanalytic he has in mind. Sexual perversions, according to Nagel, are incomplete versions of the "multi-level interpersonal awareness" which is "the basic psychological content of sexual interaction."[9] Perversions are incomplete versions of the complete configuration. Nagel's view seems close to the one usually ascribed to Freud— fixation on an infantile level being a kind of incompleteness. Nagel's view seems even closer to the idea contained in Catholic canon law, which defines as immoral any sex act which is "designed to be preparatory to the complete act" but which is "entirely divorced from the complete act."[10] Nagel does not indicate why it is important or noteworthy that some people seem to want only incomplete versions of sex instead of the complete ones, or why we need the classification "perversion" at all. (After all, we have no special designation for those who select their meals from the *a la carte* menu instead of ordering the complete dinner.) Another trouble with Nagel's view is that the prostitute, for example, who hardly participates at all in the interpersonal awareness Nagel refers to, would be perverted—yet neither ordinary usage nor any traditional classification of the perversions has such a result. (Nagel seems to be aware of this problem, but does not regard it as crucial.) Besides, the sadomasochistic pair do complete the psychological process Nagel refers to; that is, there is interpersonal awareness between them on many levels, yet they would commonly be classified as perverted. It is surprising and puzzling that Nagel claims that sexual perversions

... will have to be sexual desires or practices that can be plausibly described as in some sense unnatural, though the explanation of this natural/unnatural distinction is of course the main problem.[11]

Yet he does not attempt to explain the distinction, or relate the concept of perversion to it.

Sara Ruddick defines "perverse" sex acts as deviations from the natural—the natural being defined as "of the type that can lead to reproduction."[12] Thus far, her view resembles Aquinas' account of sex which is contrary to nature.[13] However, unlike Aquinas, she sees no moral significance to an act's being perverted.[14] Nevertheless, it seems odd to lump together masturbation, the use of birth-control, and (heterosexual) sex between sterile partners as perverted or unnatural, while remaining unclear whether the (heterosexual) child-molester is perverted or not. (A twelve-year-old girl may be capable of reproducing, yet sex with her by an adult male counts as pedophilia, regardless of that biological fact.)[15] Against Ruddick's view, an alternative account would be preferable if it explained why the perverted and the unnatural are not coextensive.

Robert C. Solomon faults Nagel's definition of perversion for emphasizing the form of the interpersonal awareness in sex rather than its content.[16] According to Solomon, sadism, for example, is not so much a breakdown in communication as

... an excessive expression of a particular content, namely the attitude of domination, perhaps mixed with hatred, fear, and other negative attitudes.[17]

Solomon offers no account explaining at what point the expression of attitudes of domination becomes excessive enough to warrant being labelled perversion; more important, it is hard to see why being excessive in the expression of domination should count as perversion at all, and not merely as rudeness, perhaps.

According to Charles Fried, a case of perversion exists when an actor uses another person to attain his end, and when it is a necessary constitutive element of that end that another person be used, but it is also a necessary element of the actor's "rational principle" that the other person thereby not attain an end of his own.[18] One objection to this is that it is too broad—the non-sexual joker, swindler or con man fit the definition, yet they are hardly perverted, certainly not sexually perverted. A sexual trickster also not excluded by Fried's definition would be the sterile man seeking sex with a woman who merely wishes to conceive by him. If he keeps his sterility a secret from her, his pursuit of her fits Fried's definition of perversion, though he would normally be called neither perverted nor sexually perverted—just malicious.[19] Secondly, the exclusive fetishist, transvestite, bestialist, is clearly beyond Fried's definition, yet Fried would probably accept them as being as genuine cases of perversion as any. Fried's view of perversion is unusual in providing an account of the concept apparently conceived in moral terms. (This seems to be his intent—though it is not clear that it would always be morally wrong for one person to use another in the way described in Fried's definition.) In this respect, Fried's account appears to be unique among recent philosophical discussions of perversion.

The opposite extreme is Alan H. Goldman's purely statistical interpretation, according to which those sexual desires are perverted which are statistically abnormal in form.[20] Identifying the form of a desire is problematic, however. Goldman gives the following examples of desires whose abnormality in form makes them perverted desires:

... desire, not for contact with another, but for merely looking, for harming or being harmed, for contact with items of clothing.[21]

Desiring to engage in sex continuously for three hours is not, it seems, abnormal in form in the requite sense.[22] Nevertheless, plausible counter-examples seem to be available; the male officeworker whose lustful desires are restricted exclusively to his female superiors would seem to be one, since his sexual desires are abnormal (statistically), yet hardly perverted. It might at first appear that this example involves only an abnormality in the content of the desire, not in its form. But if the officeworker case is dismissed as a case of perversion on account of the form/content distinction, there is the danger that the heterosexual transvestite, necrophiliac, child-molester, will also lie outside the definition of perversion. This problem with the form/content distinction arises again when Goldman writes

Raping a sheep may be more perverted than raping a woman, but certainly not more condemnable morally.[23]

It is hard to see how raping a woman could be perverted at all on Goldman's account, since the form of the act would appear to be normal.[24] (Incidentally, I doubt that it even makes sense to speak of raping a sheep, whose consent or lack of it cannot exist.)[25]

Evolutionary theory is the basis of Robert Gray's definition of perversion and the unnatural, which, following Ruddick, he equates.[26] Like Ruddick, he too regards these terms as descriptive and non-evaluative, carrying no moral connotations.[27]

If, then, we are able to show that there is some adaptive function or end that sexual activity evolved to fulfill, we may speak of sexual activity that departs from that function and, more clearly, of sexual activity that, by departing from that function, is maladaptive, as counterproductive and, in that sense, contrary to nature or unnatural. . . . Put more simply, those forms of sexual activity would be perverted which, in evolutionary terms, are dysfunctional.[28]

For Gray, the advantage of this definition is that it alone enables us to avoid cultural relativism in defining perversion.[29] This claim is puzzling, given his later remark that

It may turn out, too, that the natural adaptive functions of human sexual activity are not culturally independent. In this case, a behavior that is maladaptive in one society may not be so in another.[30]

However, a more serious problem with Gray's definition arises when he comes to consider what "the natural adaptive function" of sex in humans is. To the suggestion (perhaps Ruddick's) that reproduction is the sole function of sexual activity, Gray's reply is unclear. On the one hand, he seems to deny it:

. . . if reproduction were, as some think, the sole function of sexual activity, the scientist would have no further questions to ask about the matter, and all nonreproductive sexual activity might correctly be described as perverted. However, it would seem that this is not the case.[31]

But on the other hand, the reasons he gives for denying it point in the opposite direction—instead of considering other functions sex might fulfill, or the possibility that sex need not serve any function at all, his denial seems to rest on interpreting reproductive activity to include

. . . all those activities minimally necessary to bring those new individuals themselves to reproductive maturity. Among other things, this would seem to include the formation and maintenance of well organized, stable societies and the establishment and maintenance of fairly stable male-female reproductive pairs.[32]

From this it follows that

... maintenance of that degree (and kind) of social organization and stability requisite to the maintenance of human society is a function that normal sexual behavior has evolved to fulfill, and, if this is so, it is clear that the range of non-perverted sexual activity will be much broader than it has traditionally been taken to be.[33]

Therefore, it would not be strained to ascribe to Gray the view that reproduction is "the natural adaptive function" of sex, but that reproduction includes very much more than usually supposed.

The trouble with this account is not, however, in its determination of what the natural adaptive function of sex is—anyway, Gray claims no special authority or expertise in the question, which he regards as answerable only by the scientist.[34] More problematic is the essentially utilitarian nature of Gray's use of evolutionary theory in defining perversion. This comes out in his appeals to "the maintenance of human society,"[35] "the maintenance of the over-all social order,"[36] and "the long-term viability of society"[37] as the crucial considerations in deciding which sexual activities are perverted. As with any utilitarian theory, paradoxical implications can be expected, and one does seem to be implicit in Gray's view. Consider, for example, a society in which artificial insemination has become the form of reproduction most conducive to "the long-term viability of society." (Given certain global conditions, we might imagine this to be true of the whole species, i.e., of all human societies.) Then, heterosexual sex (between loving spouses, in the missionary position) would turn out to be perverted by the functional criteria Gray suggests. This paradoxical result will be derivable even if some function (or functions) other than reproduction is decided upon by the experts to be "the natural adaptive function" of sex. Whatever the function or functions might be, nothing guarantees that normal, heterosexual sex performs this function more effectively than any other sexual practice (or combination of sexual and non-sexual practices). In some conditions, heterosexual sex may perform the function or functions of sex far less effectively than other practices, and will then have to be categorized as a sexual perversion, according to Gray's definition.

Perhaps in despair at the problems such efforts at definition as these confront, the temptation arises to declare the concepts of perversion and the unnatural to be empty, idle, or meaningless. Such a trend (with regard to the unnatural) can be traced as far back as Mill's essay *On Nature*, Diderot's *D'Alembert's Dream*, Descartes' *Sixth Meditation*, and perhaps the ancient sophists. The most recent expression of this position is Michael Slote's "Inapplicable Concepts and Sexual Perversion."[38] The best response to this temptation would be a theory of perversion and the unnatural—one that succeeds in overcoming the difficulties to be found in Nagel, Ruddick, Solomon, Fried, Goldman, Gray and Slote.

In offering the following theory, I have started by trying to do something different from what has been previously attempted. In the first place, I have tried to separate analysis of the concepts of perversion and the unnatural from the discussion of the criteria to be employed in applying these terms to particular cases. (The separation of concept analysis from consideration of criteria is at least as old as the philosophy of love and sexuality itself; in the *Symposium* Socrates proposes "first to treat of the nature of Eros and then to treat of his acts." (199C5-6; 201E1-2).) Also, I believe the account to be sketched here makes better sense of the differences between calling something unnatural and calling it perverted than have the accounts of the seven philosophers I have reviewed. (For the most part, they do not concern themselves with this at all.) Secondly, I have set out to provide a moral theory of perversion and the unnatural. Regardless of whether or not commonly held, unreflective applications of the terms "perversion" and "unnatural" are agreed to, there seems to be little point in providing a definition emptying them of their most obvious feature—that is, that their normal use is as terms of serious moral condemnation. I have accordingly tried to provide an account that preserves and explains this aspect of their use. To seek a theory of sexual perversion which accounts for our having such a concept at all in purely psychological, aesthetic, biological or statistical, terms seems a futile endeavor. Thirdly, a theory of sexual perversion ought to make it possible to revise some of our moral judgments in applying the concept. It ought to enable us to make more reasoned judgments, recognizing that some of what has been labelled "perversion" in the past may have been mistakenly so labelled, as well as enabling us to add to the class of perversions acts that may not have been traditionally included there.

A good way to begin is to return to the historical origin of the idea of the unnatural, which is philosophical. It apparently first occurs in Plato's *Phaedrus*, where Socrates refers to "unnatural pleasure" (251A), but Plato's *Laws* (Book VIII, 836ff) contains the earliest occurrence of an argument for the unnaturalness of a human action (here, a sexual practice, homosexuality). Plato is thinking of male homosexuality, but male masturbation is perhaps also forbidden as unnatural, too. Two sorts of reasons are given; one (at 838E) is that since the natural purpose of the sex act is procreation, an unnatural sex act is one in which the purpose is other than procreation. A quite different sort of consideration is offered earlier, however (at 836D):

Will the spirit of courage spring to life in the soul of the seduced person? Will the soul of the seducer learn habits of self-control?

the Athenian asks. Speaking of homosexuality he says

. . . such practices are incompatible with what in our view should be the constant aim of the legislator—that is, we're always asking 'which of our regulations encourages virtue, and which does not?' . . . Everyone will censure the weakling who yields to temptation, and condemn his all-too-effeminate partner who plays the role of the woman.[39]

I believe this passage (at 836D) provides the basis for a defensible view of the unnatural even if its application by Plato is questioned. Certainly the other definition of Plato's, the one that depends upon identifying the natural purpose of sex, is more familiar, having marked one dominant trend in traditional sexual morality. But in this passage, Plato speaks of an unnatural sex act as involving the denial to someone (whether oneself or another) of a vital capacity—courage or self-control—by seduction.

First of all, the traditional treatments (in Plato, Aquinas and Kant, for example) discuss perversion under the heading of the unnatural, and this is where I shall begin, too. Modern philosophers tend to ignore the concept of the natural—and so, too, of the unnatural—perhaps out of verificationist concern about the apparent impossibility of giving non-emotive sense to talk about the unnatural in moral matters, and perhaps also out of considerations of the sort Sartre offers in *Existentialism Is a Humanism*. To talk of human nature, he argues, is possible only on the assumption that man is an artifact, a product of divine handicraft, made for a purpose. Apart from that framework, that view of the universe, no sense can be given to talk of human nature. I intend to take issue with that view; indeed, my argument will have the implication that, whatever may be the case with other things in the universe, man is one thing we can know has a nature—we can know man's nature regardless of whether man is seen as created for a purpose, or created at all.

To define the unnatural, of which the perverted is a subcategory, I shall need first to make a distinction between a limited set of basic human goods on the one hand, and the indefinitely large set of non-basic, non-essential goods on the other. Among the latter I include such things as enjoying one's dinner, getting to be famous in one's profession, winning at the next drawing of the state lottery, winning at some drawing or other of the state lottery, having children of whom one can be proud. It should be clear from these examples that classifying something as a non-basic human good is not at all to claim that it is unimportant. By contrast, what I count as the basic human goods can be rather completely listed—life, health, control of one's bodily and psychic functions, the capacity for knowledge and love. These goods seem to be basic in the (Rawlsian) sense that these will be desired whatever else will, insofar as they are necessary for the getting of any other human goods; but two other ways occur to me to identify the basic human goods and to distinguish them from the others.

One mark of a basic human good is that it is hard to make literal sense of the claim that a person has too much of it—what is commonly called being loved too much, i.e., being spoiled, is really a case of having been loved badly.[40] Hence, too, I exclude wealth from the list. I doubt that much disagreement about what belongs on the list is possible, though different cultures may order them differently in importance. My reasons for claiming much disagreement is not possible may be connected with the other, major, way of picking out the basic human goods, which is this—a basic human good is a feature of human life one can actively seek to reduce to a minimum among humans only at the expense of one's own status as a human being. For example, a creature (perhaps human in appearance) who acts out of a "moral" obligation to reduce health among humans as much as possible (in much the same way we normally feel obliged, on principle, to avoid causing disease as much as possible) would be a creature whom we would not perceive as human. (Imagine a creature who sincerely offered excuses for having failed to spread disease in a particular situation in which he had the opportunity.) It is at that point that simple people begin to speak of creatures as being possessed by evil demons, that is, the point at which a creature manifests negative concern for the basic human goods. (The zombie and Frankenstein's monster are variants of demon-possession: in them, absence of awareness or care about the basic human goods is manifested.)

People around the world intuitively avoid dealing with human wickedness as if it consisted of an infinite continuum with no lower end; instead, they cut off at a certain point and call whatever lies on the other side alien, non-human, demonic, possessed. I offer this general (though not universal) fact as evidence of a deep distinction between basic and non-basic human goods; it also seems to me to pick out as basic those goods I listed as such. Any creature, however rational or articulate, who does not value the basic human goods is not human. The basic human goods may be defined as those aspects of human existence such that principled lack of concern for them by a creature is a sufficient condition of the creature's non-humanity.[41]

As a first approximation, I suggest that an unnatural act is one that denies a person (oneself or another) one or more of these basic human goods without necessity, that is, without having to do so in order to prevent losing some other basic human good. A person might intelligibly deny himself or another one or more of these basic human goods for the sake of another basic human good; a priest might adopt celibacy, admitting that it is against nature to seek to live without human love. An artist might sacrifice his health for his art. (A sacrifice is the giving up of something valued; we cannot sacrifice our garbage to the city dump.) But denying oneself or another a basic human good without some other basic human good being expected or intended to be made possible thereby is always wrong; it is also, as I shall show, a necessary condition of perversion. Sports-car racers enjoy risking their lives, partly at least for the gain in skill achieved thereby. Although the likelihood may be great that they may die in a racing accident, it is not probable that they will die in any particular race. If this were likely, their participation in that race might well seem unnatural. Similar arguments apply in the case of the smoker, the drinker and the drug user.[42]

The perverted is a sub-class of the unnatural. When a person denies himself or another one of the basic human goods (or the capacity for it) and no other basic human good is seen as resulting thereby, and when pleasure is the motive of the denial, the act is perverted. When the pleasure is sexual, the perversion is sexual. It should be clear from this definition of perversion that pleasure is assumed not to be a basic human good. First, because one can have too much of it—to see this, consider the case of a person hooked up to a machine stimulating the pleasure center of the brain. Suppose he were unwilling to disconnect himself even long enough to obtain food to sustain life. He would have died for a bit of extra pleasure. Besides, a person can seek to minimize human pleasure quite generally (perhaps as an obstacle to the maximization of knowledge or other basic human goods) without casting his humanity into doubt—a rather extreme puritan might illustrate this.

This account distinguished sexual from non-sexual perversions. An example of the latter would be the man who takes pleasure in frightening small children by holding them close up to speeding trains. His pleasure would be perverted, since the effects on his victims can be expected to be traumatic. Killing for pleasure, or maiming for the fun of it, would of course also be perverted, but not a sexual perversion. A surgeon who performs operations for the excitement, when not required for the health of the patient, is perverted. In individual cases it may be difficult to determine just what motivated someone to do what he did—rationalizations may be common. But this uncertainty of verification is distinguishable from the blurring of the line *defining* perverted and non-perverted acts. I shall assume that the child-molester is a case of sexual perversion, even though it is not the sort of case central to (or even mentioned in) several familiar accounts of the concept. It has the requisite completeness for natural sex in the canon law sense, its form is normal, and it can lead to reproduction; thus Aquinas does not consider it in his treatment of the unnatural in sex. Nevertheless, the young girl, for example, who is sexually initiated by an older person can easily be traumatized; that there is no way of undoing the harmful effects with the ease and certainty with which they were induced establishes the correctness of classifying the case as one of sexual perversion. (The mere intensity of an adult's sexual feeling can be traumatic to a child, even if the adult is not strange or threatening.)[43]

The sort of damage I refer to is properly called degradation, corruption. *Perversion degrades* is a necessary truth (perhaps a trivial one) as I have defined perversion.[44] To categorize some activity as perverted is to say something important about what is wrong with it.[45] One advantage of this account of sexual perversion is that accepting it does not commit us to accepting any of the common views of particular sex acts, although it does in fact capture many of our intuitions about what is perverted. How the concept of perversion as defined here would apply, for instance to homosexuality, is not obvious, if only because homosexuality is a complex phenomenon—it can be viewed merely as an activity, one among many engaged in by those whose lives at the same time include other sexual activities such as heterosexual ones. But homosexuality can also occur as an institution, which it is in many societies other than our own; there, it is often typical of one stage of normal development, leading to, and compatible with, heterosexual functioning in marriage. Lastly, homosexuality can also be considered as a form of life, when it practically excludes heterosexuality. It is this meaning that modern gay liberation intends, and about which little can be learned from other societies. However, consideration of homosexuality as a form of life would take us far from the question of perversion and the unnatural.

Although the definition of the concept does not, by itself, produce criteria strong enough to allow us to be decisive in the important case of homosexuality,[46] the definition might seem to require rape to be included among the sexual perversions, contrary to the traditional accounts.[47] Rape does degrade—this would seem to be a necessary truth—but whether in the way the definition of perversion requires, is unclear. (All perversions degrade, but not all degrading acts or experiences are cases of perversion.) What more must be added to the definition of perversion in order to generate criteria applicable to homosexuality deserves a paper of its own, as does the question of why rape has not traditionally been perceived as perversion at all.

NOTES

1. Michael Balint, "Perversions and Genitality" in *Primary Love and Psycho-analytic Technique* (New York: Liveright, 1965), pp. 136–144.

2. Sigmund Freud, "On Narcissism: An Introduction" *Standard Edition* XIV (London: Hogarth Press 1957), p.73.

3. Sigmund Freud, *Three Essays on the Theory of Sexuality, Standard Edition* VII (London: Hogarth Press 1953), p. 231.

4. Valuable accounts of the perversion concept in psychoanalysis can be found in J. Laplanche and J. B. Pontalis, *The Language of Psycho-Analysis* (New York: W. W. Norton, 1973), pp. 306–309; H. Nagera, ed., *Basic Psychoanalytic Concepts on the Libido Theory*, vol. I of The Hempstead Clinic Psychoanalytic Library (New York: Basic Books, 1969), chapter 23, pp. 158–170; post-Freudian as well as Freudian developments are discussed in J.R. Bemporad, "Sexual Deviation: A Critical Review of Psychoanalytic Theory" in E. T. Adelson, ed., *Sexuality and Psychoanalysis* (New York: Brunner/Mazel, 1975), pp. 267–290.

5. Balint, *op. cit.*, p. 144.

6. *Ibid.*, p. 137.

7. *Ibid.*, p. 137.

8. Thomas Nagel, "Sexual Perversion," *Journal of Philosophy* 66 (1969), pp. 5–17, at p. 6. (This volume, pp. 76–88; p. 77.)

9. Nagel, *op. cit.,* this volume, p. 86

10. H. C. Gardiner, S. J., "Moral Principles Toward A Definition of the Obscene," *Law and Contemporary Problems* 20 (Autumn, 1955), pp. 560–620, at p. 564.

11. Nagel, *op. cit.,* this volume, p. 76.

12. Sara Ruddick, "Better Sex," in Robert Baker and Frederick Elliston, eds., *Philosophy and Sex* (Buffalo: Prometheus, 1975), p. 91.

13. St. Thomas Aquinas, "The Reasons Why Simple Fornication Is a Sin According to Divine Law, and That Matrimony Is Natural," in V. J. Bourke, trans., *On The Truth of the Catholic Faith (Summa Contra Gentiles)*, Book III, Part 2, *Providence* (Garden City, N.Y.: Doubleday, 1956), Ch. 22, pp. 142–147 at p. 144.

14. Ruddick, *op. cit.,* p. 95.

15. Ruddick's later complete formulation is apparently designed to avoid these odd consequences, at least in the sterile couple case (perhaps the use of birth-control, too, is meant to be exempt). She writes—

> The perversity of sex acts does not depend upon whether they are intended to achieve reproduction. "Natural" sexual desire is for heterosexual genital activity, not for reproduction. The ground for classifying that desire as natural is that it is so organized that it *could* lead to reproduction in normal physiological circumstances. (*Ibid.*, p. 92.)

I shall assume that Ruddick means to refer to sex *acts*, not desires, whose organization makes them capable of leading to reproduction, in the last quoted sentence; then Ruddick's argument can be represented as follows—

(1.) All sex acts which could lead to reproduction in normal physiological circumstances are natural.

(2.) All heterosexual genital activities are sex acts so organized that they could lead to reproduction in normal physiological circumstances.

(3.) Therefore, all heterosexual genital activities are natural.

There is a problem, however, in interpreting (2.). For how might "in normal physiological circumstances" be specified in it? After all, on a sufficiently wide interpretation of that expression, it might be said of masturbation and even of homosexual acts that they could lead to reproduction if they took place in normal physiological circumstances. More to the point—heterosexual sex between elderly partners cannot lead to reproduction in normal physiological circumstances. Unless we are merely to mean by that expression "circumstances in which reproduction could result," in which case (2.) is redundant and false, since the sterile couple is excluded as before—it must be possible to specify the meaning of "in normal physiological circumstances" without simply defining it to be true that reproduction is possible whenever physiological circumstances are normal. However, if we succeed in providing a specification of the meaning "in normal physiological circumstances" that leaves it open whether or not reproduction could result from heterosexual genital activities engaged in in normal physiological circumstances, then (2.) seems to be self-contradictory, since it will then state that

(2*.) All heterosexual genital activities are so organized that they could lead to reproduction whether or not physiological circumstances are such that reproduction could result (i.e., even if physiological circumstances are such that reproduction could not result).

If we reject (2.), and so the revised formulation of Ruddick's definition, we are left with her first account, which classifies masturbation, birth-control, and heterosexual sex between sterile partners as perverted.

Is the heterosexual child-molester perverted? Ruddick writes—

"Natural" sexual desire has as its "object" living persons of the opposite sex, and in particular their post-pubertal genitals. (*Ibid.*, p. 91.)

"Post-pubertal genitals" probably means here "genitals able to reproduce"—but then many cases of sex between adult males and twelve year old girls, e.g., will count as natural, hence not perverted, sex. "Post-pubertal genitals" might mean merely "genitals of one past a certain age (say, twelve or over)"; but then Ruddick's remark would entail that some cases of natural sex exist in which reproduction is not (yet) possible, contrary to her earlier formulation. Aquinas' difficulties with the sterile couple case are discussed in J. T. Noonan, Jr., *Contraception* (Cambridge, Mass.: Harvard University Press, 1965), pp. 238–246 and pp. 289–292. See especially page 242—"In the acts of nonprocreative intercourse accepted as natural, semen can be deposited in the vagina. In the acts stamped as unnatural, insemination has been made impossible. What is taken as sacral is the act of coitus resulting in insemination." Noonan does not comment here on the implications of this distinction for determining the naturalness of artificial insemination, nor is it clear how to apply the distinction to forms of birth control that do not interfere with the deposition of semen in the vagina.

16. Robert C. Solomon, "Sexual Paradigms," *Journal of Philosophy* 71 (1974), pp. 336–345, at p. 344. (This volume, pp. 89–98; p. 97.)

17. Solomon, *op. cit.*, this volume, p. 97.

18. Charles Fried, *An Anatomy of Values* (Cambridge, Mass.: Harvard University Press, 1970), p. 50.

19. I owe this example to Paul Shupack.

20. Alan H. Goldman, "Plain Sex," *Philosophy and Public Affairs* 6, No. 3 (Spring, 1977), pp. 267–287, at p. 284. (This volume, pp. 119–138; pp. 134–135.)

21. *Ibid.,* this volume, pp. 134–135.
22. *Ibid.,* this volume, p. 134.
23. *Ibid.,* this volume, p. 136.
24. Alan Soble pointed this out to me.
25. Goldman ascribes to Nagel and Solomon evaluative accounts of perversion (this volume, p. 135)—but the value, if it is there at all, seems not to be moral, only perhaps aesthetic. Compare Nagel (this volume, pp. 76–78, 87–88) and Solomon (this volume, p. 98): ". . . perverse sex is not necessarily bad or immoral sex."
26. Robert Gray, "Sex and Sexual Perversion," *Journal of Philosophy* 75 (1978), pp. 189–199, at p. 189. This volume, pp. 158–168; p. 159.)
27. *Ibid.,* this volume, p. 167.
28. *Ibid.,* this volume, p. 159.
29. *Ibid.,* this volume, p. 159.
30. *Ibid.,* this volume, pp. 166–167.
31. *Ibid.,* this volume, p. 166.
32. *Ibid.,* this volume, p. 166.
33. *Ibid.,* this volume, p. 166.
34. *Ibid.,* this volume, p. 168.
35. *Ibid.,* this volume, p. 166.
36. *Ibid.,* this volume, p. 167.
37. *Ibid.,* this volume, p. 167.
38. Michael Slote, "Inapplicable Concepts and Sexual Perversion" in Robert Baker and Frederick Elliston, eds., in *Philosophy and Sex* (Buffalo: Prometheus, 1975), pp. 261–267.
39. Plato, *Laws,* trans. by T. J. Saunders (Harmondsworth: Penguin, 1970), 836 D.
40. Descartes seems to mean something like this when he says that in certain conditions love "can never be too great," *The Passions of the Soul,* Part II, article CXXXIX, in E. S. Haldane and G. R. T. Ross, trans. *Philosophical Works of Descartes* I (N.Y.: Dover, 1955), p. 383.
41. There is something essentially incomprehensible about principled lack of concern for the basic human goods; in this respect, there appears to be a categorical contrast with the way we think about the insane. However serious their disturbance, the mentally ill seem to us to be distorted versions of creatures like ourselves, with original instincts (if there are such things) like ours. This way of regarding the insane, as comprehensible, remains intact even when we do not know what motivates them, or might be motivating them. Making the distinction between the demonic and the insane in this way conflicts with Joel Feinberg's discussion in "What Is So Special About Mental Illness?" [in *Doing and Deserving* (Princeton, N.J.: Princeton University Press, 1970), pp. 272–292], since he appears to regard the motivations of the mentally ill, and certainly of the criminally insane, as unintelligible, senseless, and incoherent. I believe he would not think this if he did not also implicitly accept a somewhat Olympian conception of the non-insane, non-criminal individual, whose motives

Feinberg seems to think fit together and make a coherent whole (*Ibid.*, p. 287). Such a person, he suggests, has an overriding interest in personal integration and internal harmony and is thus comparable to a machine in proper working order (*Ibid.*, p. 288). I doubt that there are many non-criminals of the sane category who fit this description; no one, however sane, whose view of life is tragic, does. Besides, the demonic creatures I hypothesize may have motives that fit together in coherent wholes, etc. What makes us perceive them as demonic is our inability to understand why anyone would have the motives they have, not the lack of fit of these motives with each other. (Fairness to Feinberg requires that I note that his position is more complex than indicated here; but it is not different.)

42. Defining the unnatural in this way, as a certain definite kind of exchange of basic for non-basic human goods presupposes that the basic human goods I have specified are not "culturally relative." This has been questioned, however; writing in response to Rawls's list of *primary goods* which my list of basic human goods closely resembles, Michael Teitelman writes:

> . . . some things may be primary goods only relative to the social institutions in which persons who have these preferences find themselves, but we might be inclined to regard these as primary goods *simpliciter* because of a failure to appreciate the role of social circumstances. I think this holds of some of the things that Rawls regards as primary. Wealth and power, for instance, may be essential for the attainment of a person's ends in some kinds of societies but not in others. Indeed, there are possible life plans in which possession of wealth and power are genuine nuisances. ["The Limits of Individualism," *Journal of Philosophy* 69 (5 October, 1972), pp. 545–556, at pp. 550–551.]

Since the list of basic human goods does not, on principle, include wealth or power, the only one of the basic human goods about which the problem of social relativity might be raised is the capacity for love, I believe. Those thinkers to whom love has appeared not to be a basic human good can be divided into two groups; (1.) those, like Plato, for whom love is neither good nor bad in itself (Socrates and Diotima agree about this in the *Symposium*, 201B–202B); and (2.) those who appear to hold that we ought to minimize love on principle. They appear to regard love as evil. Concerning the first group, I would point out merely that the refusal to treat love as a basic human good does not seem to be the result of social relativity, but of genuine difference in philosophical viewpoint, i.e., of different conceptions about what love really consists in, about the definition of love. They do not pose the sort of problem the second group appears to present. (If the difference in viewpoint between Plato and us were attributable to social relativity, one would expect all other Athenians of his time to agree with him. That this was not so is evident from the earlier speeches in the *Symposium*.)

It is only the second group that seems to maintain that we ought to minimize love on principle, a claim which I have characterized as an unintelligible proposal for a human being to make. Two apparent examples of the second group would be the Buddha, who is sometimes thought to have explained all suffering as derived from desire, and the Gnostics, e.g., Marcion and Mani, who abstained from sex and marriage as inherently evil. In the case of Buddha, however, it is not desire, but craving, grasping desire, in which suffering originates, according to him; and the Gnostics rejected sex and marriage not because they placed negative value on love itself, but because of hopes to obstruct what they took to be the evil of the creation and its maker, which reproduction would prolong. Man's 'native realm of light' and the transmundane god were worthy of love, however. [See articles on "Buddhism," "Gnosticism," "Mani and Manichaeism," and "Marcion" in *The Encyclopedia of Philosophy*, P. Edwards, ed. (New York: Macmillan and the Free Press, 1967).] This pattern will be repeated in other likely cases, I believe. It is not love itself which is held to be evil; on the contrary, the value placed on one sort of love or object of love leads to rejection of all others.

43. The dominant view of the effects of pedophilia, opposed to this one, is well represented in L. Bender and A.E. Grugett, Jr., "A Follow-up Report on Children Who Had Atypical Sexual Experience," *American Journal of Orthopsychiatry* 22 (1952), pp. 825–837.

Whether coprophilia or necrophilia are covered by the definition of perversion proprosed here has been questioned. What basic human good is a person deprived of in engaging in either of these practices? Briefly, each involves the use of a fetish, which Charles Rycroft defines as "an object which a *fetishist* endows with sexual significance and in the absence of which he is incapable of sexual excitement. A sexual fetish is either an inanimate object or nonsexual part of a person . . . ," *A Critical Dictionary of Psycho-analysis* (Totowa, New Jersey: Littlefield, Adams, 1973), p. 51. So, the coprophiliac or necrophiliac has lost the ability to love another human being sexually in pursuing pleasure with some inanimate object.

44. It would not make sense, I think, to substitute "perversity" for "perversion" in the italicized sentence; this suggests that those dictionaries are wrong which define the terms as synonyms in any of their senses. Perverse acts might be thought of as defective cases of the perverted, since the harm enjoyed in a perverse act is the denial of a good, but not the denial of a basic human good. Such acts are not necessarily degrading; a person who enjoys (temporarily) depriving someone of comfort, information, pleasure, does not degrade himself or anyone else necessarily, though he may ruin their evening.

45. Sexual perversion, as interpreted here, is not the perversion *of* sex, of the sexual function or of the sex organs—anymore than sex*ual* relations are relations *of* the sex organs. The genitals of two people may have all sorts of relations (e.g., spatial relations, relations of resem-

blance) without there being any sexual relations between them. The expression "sexual perversion" signifies perversion (as defined) *by way of* sex. The harm in sexual perversion is not to the organs, but to the person or persons whose organs they are. Sexual perversion is perversion, sexual in form. There is no such thing as perversion of sex or of the sex organs, since such entities are not human beings, and therefore cannot be deprived of basic human goods. For the same reason, there is no such thing as perversion of the teeth or of mastication, of the eyes or of sight. A person who enjoys biting off the caps from soda-pop bottles is not perverting his teeth, even if they fall out as a result. In denying there can be a perversion of a human bodily organ or function apart from the harm to the person (or persons) whose organ's function it is, I am in conflict with Aquinas, it seems, and certainly with Nagel. Aquinas writes—

> Now, it is good for each person to attain his end, whereas it is bad for him to swerve away from his proper end. Now, this should be considered applicable to the parts, just as it is to the whole being; for instance, each and every part of man, and every one of his acts, should attain the proper end . . . every emission of semen, in such a way that generation cannot follow, is contrary to the good for man. And if this be done deliberately, it must be a sin. Now, I am speaking of a way from which, *in itself,* generation could not result: such would be any emission of semen apart from the natural union of male and female. For which reason, sins of this type are called *contrary to nature. (Op. cit.,* pp. 143–144.)

If "the parts" in the second sentence quoted refers to the parts of an individual human being's body, then Aquinas appears to be saying that an act contrary to nature could consist merely in some organ not attaining its proper end, even if no harm occurs to the individual whose organ it is. However, Aquinas seems to be thinking of the harm done in such an act as harm to the human race as a whole. But it is hard to see that it is true in all cases that "every emission of semen, in such a way that generation cannot follow, is contrary to the good for man," if "man" here means the human race; for the statement now means what Gray meant when he appealed to "the maintenance of human society" to define natural sex, and which I have criticized above as an essentially utilitarian claim. Nagel writes of a perversion of hunger, but his examples are rather fantastic *(Op. cit.,* p. 78); a preference for eating cookbooks over ordinary food, seeking satisfaction of hunger by fondling a napkin or ashtray from a favorite restaurant. This last, he says, it would be natural to describe as a case of gastronomical fetishism. (One wonders if a person on a diet might not reasonably adopt such a habit, if it worked, to lose weight.) He writes—

> . . . there is little temptation to describe as perverted an appetite for substances that are not nourishing. We should probably not

consider someone's appetite as *perverted* if he liked to eat paper, sand, wood, or cotton. Those are merely rather odd and very unhealthy tastes: they lack the psychological complexity that we expect of perversions. (*Op. cit.,* p. 78.)

This psychological complexity he explains as follows—

Displacements or serious restrictions of the desire to eat could then be described as perversions, if they undermined that direct relation between man and food which is the natural expression of hunger. This explains why it is easy to imagine gastronomical fetishism, voyeurism, exhibitionism, or even gastronomical sadism and masochism. Indeed some of these perversions are fairly common. (*Ibid.,* p. 79.)

This claim appears to treat Freud's interpretive ideas about perversions (mechanisms of displacement, isolation) as constitutive of them, even though these same mechanisms are employed by Freud in interpreting many other phenomena besides perversions, e.g., dreams. Presumably, liking to eat paper, sand, wood, or cotton would be explainable by reference to these same mechanisms. By contrast, there is a real disturbance of appetite, called *pica*, which the *Oxford English Dictionary* defines as "a perverted craving for substances unfit for food . . . ." I take it to be confirmatory of my claim that there can be no perversion of a natural function as such, that is, apart from harm to the person (or persons) whose organ's function it is, that the earliest explanatory occurrence recorded for the term *pica* in the *OED* is "1584 Fenner *Def. Ministers* (1587) 49 When one is oppressed with the disease Pica, so that hee can not eate anie thing but pitche." If there are any perversions of hunger, they must consist in more than the mere craving for non-food substances. At least they must also be cravings whose satisfaction is dangerously unhealthy to the person, as eating nothing but pitch would be. (A perversion of appetite would also have to have pleasure as the goal of the craving, which is not clearly so in cases of pica.) Nagel does not regard danger to the health (or other basic human good) of the person as necessary to perversion of appetite, whereas my account does; Nagel regards explainability by Freudian mechanisms ('psychological complexity') as sufficient for perversion, whereas my account does not—only a certain kind of moral complexity would be sufficient on my view.

The confusion concerning the analysis of the concept of perversion sketched here is not confined to philosophers reflecting on sex and hunger. The neurologist Walter Freeman and his associate in neurosurgery J. W. Watts claim, in their work on prefrontal lobotomy, *Psychosurgery* (Springfield, Ill., Baltimore, Md.: Charles C. Thomas, 1942), p. vii, Preface, that

. . . certain individuals may suffer from perverted activity of these areas [the frontal lobes] and may become capable of better adaptation when these lobes are partially inactivated. Theories

> are developed [by Freeman and Watts] concerning the mecha-
> nism by which the perverted activity of the frontal lobes pro-
> duces deviation in behavior; . . .

Referring to the pioneering surgery of G. Burckhardt on a schizophrenic patient, they write

> Thinking that the hallucinations were at the base of the dis-
> turbed behavior, Burckhardt argued further that perverted
> speech mechanisms prevented potentially normal associations.
> This patient was particularly active in response to outside
> noises, so that attention was paid to the hearing center. "If one
> could remove these exciting impulses from the brain mecha-
> nism, the patient might be transformed from a disturbed to a
> quiet dement." (p. 7.)

I believe it would be fair to say that a whole medical ideology is contained in this confusion of meanings.

46. This point has been pursued in David A. J. Richards' *The Moral
Criticism of Law* (Encino, California: Dickenson, 1977), Ch. 3. A
fuller expansion of these ideas can be found in the same author's
"Unnatural Acts and the Constitutional Right to Privacy: A Moral
Theory," *Fordham Law Review* XLV, No. 6 (May, 1977), pp. 1281–
1348.

47. Sara Ruddick says rape "can constitute perversion if rape, rather
than genital intercourse, is the aim of desire" (*op. cit.*, p. 99).

L. Nathan Oaklander

Sartre on Sex

Sartre's analysis of sexual desire is the culmination of some of the most central themes of *Being and Nothingness*. It has, however, scantly received the attention it deserves, and when it is considered, some of his interpreters seem to misunderstand him.[1] Perhaps the reason why Sartre's analysis of sexual desire is misunderstood is that once it is clearly spelled out, it seems to lead to the rather paradoxical conclusion that all sexual activity is a kind of perversion. Some are unwilling to accept that Sartre could have maintained such a view, and misintepretations arise. It seems to me, however, that in some sense Sartre's analysis of sexual desire *does* entail that all sexual activity is a "perversion." One aim of this paper is to defend that claim. Since Sartre's analysis of sexuality cannot be understood apart from some of his most fundamental ontological views, it will be necessary to proceed by first briefly discussing Sartre's analysis of consciousness and its relation to the world. Then I will briefly consider Sartre's account of the meaning of the Other's look. Thirdly, I will criticize Robert Solomon's account of Sartre's views on sex, offer what I consider to be the correct interpretation of Sartre, and then compare it with Jerome Shaffer's views on sexual desire. Finally, I will indi-

An earlier version of this paper was delivered at the Annual Meeting of the Michigan Academy of the Arts and Sciences in Mt. Pleasant on March 18, 1977, and at the Western Division Meetings of the American Philosophical Association in Chicago, Illinois on April 30, 1977.

cate the connection between sexual desire and sexual perversion (activity) in Sartre's view, and then respond to objections.

I. CONSCIOUSNESS AND THE WORLD

In examining the system of a great philosopher, we inevitably are led to one or more basic gambits that serve as the foundation of what is to follow. In Sartre's philosophy of man, one basic gambit is his analysis of consciousness as an "indivisible, indissoluble unity" of *both* positional and non-positional consciousness. His idea is that all consciousness is a unity that involves both a positional or thetic consciousness of an object and a non-positional or non-thetic consciousness of itself. For example, at the moment when I am perceiving a tree, I am conscious of the tree and (non-positionally) conscious of *perceiving* as opposed to say, remembering or thinking of the tree. These are the phenomenological facts; the original Sartrean thesis concerning them is that the non-positional consciousness of the positional perceiving consciousness is *one* with the perceiving consciousness.[2]

One consequence of Sartre's gambit is that consciousness is nothing. That is, consciousness is not an entity, a thing, or an object in the world. He reasons that all objects or things in the world have a certain hidden nature. When I look at a table I can only see its front surface; consequently much of the table is hidden from me. By contrast, since all consciousness is self-consciousness, when I see a table there is nothing about my *seeing* that is hidden from me. Consciousness is entirely translucent; it is what it appears to be and appears to be what it is.[3] Thus, in virtue of his first gambit which asserts the unity of positional and non-positional consciousness, consciousness is nothing.[4]

In virtue of Sartre's second basic gambit, consciousness may be said to be everything. His second gambit is that consciousness, although not responsible for the existence of its objects, is responsible for producing out of being-in-itself a world in which classifications can be made and distinctions can be drawn. In other words, it is in virtue of consciousness that objects can be divided into kinds, and actions can be given meaning and valuations. Thus, conscious is everything because it determines what objects and actions are understood to be.

Given Sartre's two basic gambits and some consequences of them, the relation between consciousness and the world may be stated briefly: Consciousness is not an object or thing in the world, but rather consciousness is the creator of the worldliness of the world in virtue of introducing meaning, values, and differences into the undifferentiated totality of being-in-itself.

II. THE MEANING OF THE OTHER'S LOOK

A good passage that connects these two Sartrean gambits with his view on the Other is the following:

> ... my objectivity cannot itself derive *for me* from the objectivity of the world since I am precisely the one by whom *there is* a world; that is, the one who on principle cannot be an object for himself.[5]

In other words, for me, apart from my relations with the Other, I cannot have a conception of myself as an object. Sartre's point is that if I reflect upon "my" past consciousness, then I am not the consciousness reflected upon (i.e., the object), but rather, I am the reflecting consciousness.[6] For myself, I am, as it were, at the center of the world. I am the creator and master of the world in the sense that *qua* consciousness I am the source of the world's structure and I am responsible for creating myself in the light of all the possibilities that are open to me. For myself I am *nothing* except consciousness (transcendence).

Yet, there is another aspect to my being—my facticity—my body and my nature or essence as revealed through my actions. The look of the Other makes me non-positionally conscious of this other aspect of me. For, from the point of view of the Other's consciousness, I have become a part of the world. Consequently, I have lost myself as a for-itself (or consciousness) and for the first time I discover myself as a being-in-the-world. As Sartre says:

> To apprehend myself as seen is, in fact, to apprehend myself *as seen in the world* and from the standpoint of the world.[7]
> For the Other *I am seated* as this inkwell is on the table; for the Other, *I am bending over* the keyhold as this tree *is bent* by the wind. Thus for the Other I have stripped myself of my transcendence.[8]

It is consciousness which creates the world and thus the appearance of the Other's consciousness signals the loss of my world. That is, the loss of my freedom to structure the world and create myself. Sartre makes this point in the following passages:

> ... suddenly the alienation of myself, which is the act of being-looked-at, involves the alienation of the world which I organize. The appearance of the Other in the world corresponds therefore to a congealed sliding of the

whole universe, to a decentralization of the world which undermines the centralization which I am simultaneously effecting.[9]

The Other steals my world and reduces me to a mere object. Here we have the most fundamental sense of alienation: I am alienated from what I am as a for-itself.

The loss of my transcendence or, myself as a for-itself, does have some compensation. Insofar as I am an object for the Other I avoid my being "nothing" and thus I avoid the infinite responsibilities that accrue to the consciousness that lies at the center of the world. And yet, "conflict is the original meaning of being-for-others."[10] I want to recover my world and freedom, for although my emergence in the world as an entity with a certain kind of character depends on the Other, I am responsible for what the Other finds. Herein lies the rub: the Other is the foundation of what I am for-myself—he determines my essence or nature (i.e., the meaning of my acts)—and yet in virtue of my transcendence, I am responsible for what the Other creates or determines.[11] Thus, I want to reaffirm myself as a for-itself. The question we must now consider is how, according to Sartre, are we to recapture our identity as a for-itself (consciousness)?

Clearly, Sartre's views on sex are inextricably bound up with his answer to this question, but the connection between sex and the reaffirmation of our freedom is not as simple as some of Sartre's critics would have us believe. One interpretation of Sartre's view on sex is that the sole aim or goal of sex is domination or power over the Other. It is maintained that in the sexual situation we recover our freedom by making the Other into an object. Robert Solomon expresses this understanding of Sartre in the following passage:

> For Sartre, sexual desire is the desire to possess, to gain recognition of one's own freedom at the expense of the Other. By 'incarnating' and degrading him/her in flesh, one reduces him/her to an object. Sadism is but an extension of this domination over the Other. Or one allows himself to be 'incarnated' as a devious route to the same end, making the Other his/her sexual slave. . . . On this model, degradation is the central activity of sex, to convince the Other that he/she is a slave, to persuade the Other of one's own power, whether it be through the skills of sexual technique or through the passive demands of being sexually served.[12]

Solomon seems to be claiming that, for Sartre, the central aim of *both* sexual desire and sexual activity is to reduce the Other to an object and elevate oneself in power. I shall argue that, for Sartre, the goal of sexual desire is *never* to reduce the Other to a mere object, and that in sexual activity that goal is sometimes but by no means always sought after. My argument will begin by first considering Sartre's analysis of sexual desire.

III. SEXUAL DESIRE

Sexual desire is a unique state of consciousness in which, as Sartre says, ". . . it seems that one is invaded by facticity."[13] In sexual desire I am not only a clear and translucent for-itself, since my consciousness becomes immersed in and identical with my body. To see what is involved, let us follow Sartre and explain sexual desire by means of a contrast and an analogy. Sartre contrasts sexual desire with the desire for food. Both hunger and sexual desire presuppose a certain state of the body, but in hunger the desiring consciousness flees the body and is completely absorbed in its future possibles, i.e., the future ways of satisfying hunger. On the other hand, in sexual desire one does not flee from one's body but rather one coalesces with it. According to Sartre,

The desiring consciousness exists this facticity; it is *in terms of this* facticity—we could even say *through* it—that the desired body appears as desirable.[14]

In other words, when I desire another I am conscious of the Other's body and at the same time non-positionally conscious of my own body. To quote Sartre once more,

Desire is not only the desire of the Other's body; it is—within the unity of a single act—the nonthetically lived project of being swallowed up in the body.[15]

Sartre calls a sexual desiring consciousness a "troubled" consciousness and compares it with "troubled" or muddy water. "Troubled" water remains water, but it is disturbed and changed by the presence of something that is not clearly distinguishable from the water itself. Similarly, a desiring consciousness is consciousness, that is, it is a direction toward an object, and a non-positional consciousness of itself, but it is not only that. For in sexual desire my consciousness is disturbed by my body which at that time is indistinguishable from it. Thus, using Sartre's terminology we may say that in sexual desire and only in sexual desire there is an "incarnation of consciousness." Or, as Sartre also puts it, "The being which desires is consciousness *making itself body*.''[16] We are now ready to understand how, according to Sartre, we are to reaffirm our identity as a consciousness or a for-it-self.

Sexual desire is the mechanism by which I recover my world from the Other, but that does *not* mean that through sexual desire I degrade the other or turn him/her into an object. Rather, it means that I recover my world by producing in the Other sexual desire towards me. In sexual desire I incarnate my own consciousness (i.e., I make myself flesh) so as to produce a similar incarnation in the Other. That is, sexual desire is intentionally seductive: the goal of sexual desire is to produce an identity of consciousness and body in the Other as exists in myself. Sartre sums up the matter in a quote that I hope the foregoing makes clear:

> Thus, the revelation of the Other's flesh is made through my own flesh; in desire and in the caress which expresses desire. *I incarnate myself in order to realize the incarnation of the Other....* I make her enjoy my flesh through her flesh in order to compel her to feel herself flesh. And so possession truly appears as a double reciprocal incarnation.[17]

In sexual desire there is a positional consciousness of the Other's consciousness and body and a non-positional consciousness of one's own consciousness and body. The motive for this reciprocal incarnation is two-fold: (1) Insofar as the Other is conscious of his/her body, I reaffirm my identity as a consciousness, and (2) insofar as the Other is conscious of me, I can retain my identity as a being-in-the-world. Thus, in sexual desire lies the resolution of the conflict in human relationships, for in sexual desire I achieve and the Other achieves an ideal situation in which we preserve our freedom (consciousness, transcendence) while retaining our security as being an object-in-the-world. Therefore, Solomon is mistaken when he says that sexual desire aims "at the recognition of one's own freedom at the expense of the Other."[18]

The question remains regarding whether Sartre maintains that the goal of all sexual *activity* is power or domination over the Other. In the final section I shall consider this question and explain my belief that, according to Sartre, all sexual activity is a kind of perversion. Before turning to those issues, however, it will be helpful to our understanding of Sartre's views on sexuality to compare them with the views of Jerome Shaffer.

In his article on "Sexual Desire," Shaffer first attempts to refute what he calls the Propositional Theory of sexual desire, and then he offers his own account of sexual desire. According to Shaffer, the Propositional Theory holds the following:

"At t, S sexually desires 0" = Df. "At t, S desires that he or she have sex with 0."[19]

Shaffer leaves open what is to count as "having sex" but it is clear that for him, to "have sex" means to engage in some form of sexual activity. He argues quite convincingly that sexual desire does not entail desiring sexual activity. Sartre would agree in rejecting the Propositional Theory as Shaffer understands it for he says,

. . . desire by itself by no means implies the sexual act; desire does not thematically posit it, does not even suggest it in outline, as one sees when it is a question of the desire of very young children or of adults who are ignorant of the 'technique' of love. Similarly, desire is not a desire of any special amorous practice; this is sufficiently proved by the diversity of sexual practices, which vary with social groups.[20]

Sartre would, however, entirely disagree with the conclusion that Shaffer draws from his rejection of the Propositional Theory, namely, that "sexual desire as such has no necessary connection with some goal, aim, or end in view" and that "sexual desire does not entail any *desirings that* nor do any *desirings that* entail sexual desire." It is true that sexual desire does not aim at, or have as its goal, engaging in sexual activity, but it does, nevertheless, have a goal according to Sartre. The goal of sexual desire is to produce in another sexual desire towards me. Moreover, if I *desire that* the Other desire me, then I must sexually desire the Other, and if I sexually desire the Other, then I desire that the Other sexually desire me. As Sartre says,

But my *incarnation* is not only the preliminary condition of the appearance of the Other as flesh *to my eyes*. My *goal* is to cause him to be incarnated as flesh *in his own eyes*. . . . Thus the other meaning of my incarnation—that is, of my troubled disturbance—is that it is a magical language. I make myself flesh so as to fascinate the Other by my nakedness and to produce in her the desire for my flesh—exactly because this desire will be nothing else in the Other but an incarnation similar to mine. Thus, desire is an invitation to desire.[21]

The difference between Shaffer and Sartre can be understood as a disagreement over what is meant by "having sex." According to Shaffer, to "have sex" means to "engage in sexual activity.[22] Thus, having sex is something that is contingently based on the fact that we have sexual organs. For Sartre, on the other hand, to "have sex" means "to exist sexually for an Other who exists sexually for

me."[22] According to Sartre, to "have sex" is, in its most fundamental sense, not to engage in some sort of physical activity involving our sexual organs but to be in a state of double reciprocal
incarnation, or mutual awareness. Consequently, if we take "having sex" in accordance with Shaffer's definition, then Sartre
would disagree with the Propositional Theory, but if we take
"having sex" in Sartre's sense, then Sartre would agree with the
Propositional Theory. The disagreement between Shaffer and Sartre is not, however, merely verbal. It indicates a basic difference in
their attitudes toward the nature of sexuality, and more specifically in their accounts of sexual desire. To see what is involved in
this last point, let us turn to Shaffer's positive account of sexual
desire.

According to Shaffer, sexual desire is a case of *desire* because it
is directed toward an object and it "is necessarily connected with
the idea of *satisfaction* (or frustration)."[23] What makes a desire a
sexual desire is that it is necessarily connected with *sexual* satisfaction. To avoid the obvious circularity Shaffer goes on to say,

What makes desire and satisfaction *sexual in the intervening state of sexual arousal*, which is directly sexual in that it involves the sexual parts,
viz., the genital areas.[24]

And again,

It is the special features of the arousal stage which serve to define sexual
desire as *sexual.* . . . [25]

The essential place of sexual arousal in Schaffer's analysis of sexual desire is reaffirmed in the following example:

What makes the touching of Claire's knee the *sexual* satisfaction of a sexual desire is the occurrence of the intervening sexual excitement and the
sense of resolution of that excitement in which satisfaction consists. Otherwise, it would be merely the desire to touch her knee and the eventual
fulfillment of that desire.[26]

These passages imply that for Shaffer, it is sexual arousal, i.e., "lo-
catable physiological processes and the sensations concomitant
with them"[27] that is the fundamental aspect of our *sexual* life. In
other words, according to Shaffer, the fact of our sexuality in general and sexual desire in particular is a contingent accident bound
to our physiological nature. For Shaffer, man is a sexual being because he possesses sexual organs and has sensations associated
with the areas in which they are located.

Shaffer's view of sexual desire is diametrically opposed to Sartre's. For Sartre, sexual desire does *not* derive its origin from *sex*

as a physiological and contingent determination of man. Rather, sexuality is an ontological or necessary structure of our concrete relations with others. The distinction between these two ways of viewing sexuality is nicely stated by Sartre in the following passage:

It is evident that if sexuality derives its origin from *sex* as a physiological and contingent determination of man, it cannot be indispensible to the being of For-Others. But do we not have the right to ask whether the problem is not per chance of the same order as that which we encountered apropos of sensations and sex organs? Man, it is said, is a sexual being because he possesses a sex. And if the reverse were true? If sex were only the instrument and, so to speak, the *image* of a fundamental sexuality? If man possessed a sex only because he is originally and fundamentally a sexual being as a being who exists in the world in relation with other men?[28]

The issue between Sartre and Shaffer is clear, but how are we to decide between these two conceptions of sexuality?

Sartre mentions some facts about sexual desire that are worth considering and seem to go against Shaffer's view. He says,

Infantile sexuality precedes the physiological maturation of the sex organ. Men who have become eunuchs do not thereby cease to feel desire. Nor do many old men. The fact of being able to *make use of* a sex organ fit to fertilize and to procure enjoyment represents only one phase and one aspect of our sexual life. But there are other modes of sexuality . . . , and if we take these modes into account we are forced to recognize that sexuality appears with birth and disappears only with death.[29]

Indeed, Shaffer himself criticizes the James-Lange account in which desire is sexual because it is accompanied by certain bodily events and/or bodily sensations in various areas of the body which are called "sexual." Shaffer notes that, "In the case of sexual desire, male paraplegics, who have become paralyzed and unfeeling from the trunk down, seem still to have sexual desire."[30] How then can Shaffer identify sexual desire as *sexual* by appealing to the intervening state of sexual arousal, for in cases that he himself recognizes there is sexual desire *without* sexual arousal? Shaffer avoids the problem by lapsing into inconsistency. He says that on his account, "it is *not necessary* that the original state (*viz.*, sexual desire) actually lead to sexual arousal. . . . "[31] And that,

I have claimed that it is the special features of the arousal state which serve to define sexual desire as *sexual, even though they may not be present in every case of sexual desire.*[32]

If we compare these passages with his other comments, it would appear to be the case that Shaffer is committed to maintaining both that sexual arousal is and is not necessary in order for there to be a case of sexual desire. Moreover, if we accept his remarks that arousal need not be present in all cases of sexual desire, then we are still left with the question, "What makes sexual desire sexual?" Later we will examine Roger L. Taylor's non-Sartrean answer to this question, but first we must return to the central issue of this paper which is to explain my belief that, according to Sartre, all sexual activity is a kind of perversion.

IV. SEXUAL ACTIVITY AND SEXUAL PERVERSION

There is, as we all know, a connection between sexual desire and sexual activity: the former, given the appropriate conditions, leads to the latter. Now, it is precisely because sexual desire leads to sexual activity that Sartre says that "desire is itself doomed to failure."[33] Sartre's point is that sexual activity entails a breakdown of the double reciprocal incarnation brought about by sexual desire, because sexual activity involves either a concentration on one's own bodily pleasure or "a desire of taking and of appropriating"[34] the Other's body. If I concentrate on my own pleasure, then I am forgetful of the Other's incarnation and reduce myself to an object, thus remaining a slave to the Other. If, on the other hand, I ignore my own pleasure and concentrate on appropriating the Other's body, that is, I attempt to seize the Other's body, to unite with it, and so on, then the Other ceases to be an incarnated consciousness and becomes a mere object in the midst of the world. Thus, Sartre says that desire "brings about the rupture of that reciprocity of incarnation which was precisely the unique goal of desire."[35] Or, still differently, sexual desire issues in the death of desire, and hence it is "doomed to failure."

Given the foregoing understanding of sexual activity, it follows that domination or power is not the sole aim of sexual activity. For, when I pay attention to my own pleasure the Other-as-object (or incarnated consciousness) disappears, and the Other-as-consciousness (or look) appears. If one is to speak of an aim of this sort of sexual activity, then we can best quote Sartre where he says:

. . . consciousness apprehending itself in its facticity demands to be apprehended and transcended as body-for-the-Other by means of the Other's consciousness.[36]

Clearly then, the aim of *all* sexual activity is not to dominate, or to degrade the Other by reducing him/her into an object.

It remains to be shown that it follows from Sartre's analysis of sex that all sexual activity is a kind of perversion. Fortunately, the argument is really quite simple. We have seen that for Sartre, sexual desire is the ideal state for individuals to be in because it involves a double reciprocal incarnation and thus a solution to the fundamental conflict between ourselves and Others. In sexual desire I desire the Other as the Other desires me; not as a body, and not as a consciousness, but as a human being, that is, as a *unity* of consciousness and body. To quote Sartre once more,

> I desire a human being, not an insect or a mollusk, and I desire him (or her) as he is and I am in situation in the world and as he is an Other for me and as I am an Other for him.[37]

We have also seen that sexual desire leads to sexual activity which destroys the reciprocal incarnation. If the destruction is accomplished by attention to pleasure, then the situation is masochistic; if the destruction is accomplished by appropriating the Other, then the situation is sadistic. In either case, sexual activity is a kind of perversion, i.e., a movement away from the state of sexual desire. This way of reading Sartre is not only structurally sound, it also has textual support. Consider for example, a passage that occurs during Sartre's discussion of sadism:

> . . . as soon as I seek to take the Other's body which through my own incarnation I have induced to incarnate itself, I break the reciprocity of incarnation, I transcend my body toward its own possibles, and I orient myself in the direction of sadism. Thus, sadism and masochism are the two reefs on which desire may founder—whether I transcend my troubled disturbance toward an appropriation of the Other's flesh or, intoxicated with my own disturbance, pay attention only to my flesh and ask nothing of the Other except that he should be the look which aids me in realizing my flesh. It is because of this inconstancy on the part of desire and its perpetual oscillation between these two perils that 'normal' sexuality is commonly designated as 'sadomasochistic.'[38]

This passage, I submit, supports my thesis that, for Sartre, *all* sexual activity is a kind of perversion. In other words, even normal sexuality, what Nagel calls "unadorned sexual intercourse," will be a perversion since it involves a rupture of the double reciprocal incarnation brought about by sexual desire.

The case for interpreting Sartre as I do depends on supposing that according to him, the goal of sexual desire is realizable, for it is only by allowing sexuality to achieve its goal on occasion that we can provide the concept of perversion with a foothold. Fortunately, there are passages that do strongly suggest that the goal of sexual desire is realizable. For example, after a brief discussion of the caress Sartre says,

At this moment the communion of desire is realized; each consciousness by incarnating itself has realized the incarnation of the Other; each one's disturbance has caused disturbance to be born in the Other and is thereby so much enriched. By each caress I experience my own flesh, and I am conscious that this flesh which I feel and appropriate through my flesh is flesh-realized-by-the-Other.[39]

In spite of that passage, Nagel has claimed that on Sartre's view the aim of sexual desire cannot be accomplished and thus he cannot admit the concept of perversion. Nagel writes,

According to Sartre, all attempts to incorporate the other into my world as subject, that is, to apprehend him at once an object for me and a subject for whom I am an object, are unstable and doomed to collapse into one or the other of the two aspects. This has the consequence that there can be no such thing as a *successful* sexual relation, since the deep aim of sexual desire cannot in principle be accomplished. It seems likely, therefore, that this view will not permit a basic distinction between successful or complete, and unsuccessful, or incomplete, sex and therefore cannot admit the concept of perversion.[40]

Although Nagel does not give any textual support for his interpretation, there are passages that do indeed suggest that the goal of sexual desire is unattainable. Sartre says that desire is "doomed to failure," "that it bears within itself the cause of its own failure," and that it is an "impossible ideal."[41] In the light of these and other passages can it still be maintained that sexual desire is realizable and consequently that sexual activity is a perversion of desire? I think, perhaps, that it can.

When Sartre says that "desire bears within itself the cause of its own failure" I suggest that he means that the *necessary result* of attaining desire is the collapse or destruction of desire. Let me explain. A sexually desiring consciousness is, in a sense, a contradiction. For is it not a contradiction to suppose that two radically different kinds of being-my facticity and my transcendence-can be indivisibly united in desire? Indeed, it is a contradiction, but why should that prove it has no being? If my account of Sartre's analysis of consciousness as being an indivisible unity of positional and non-positional consciousness is correct, then he has already admitted a contradictory being into his ontology. (The contradiction is that positional consciousness is intentional, non-positional consciousness is not intentional, and yet together they form a single consciousness.) Thus, the fact that sexual desire is a contradictory being does entail that desire contains within itself the cause of its own failure. For, due to its being contradictory, a desiring consciousness is radically unstable in that the immediate *result* of its disintegration into one or another of aspects that comprise it. More specifically, at the moment at which desire is realized there is a shift of consciousness to my own incarnation or the incarnation of the Other. In other words, the *result* of attaining the goal of sexual desire is the breakdown of the double reciprocal incarnation into a subject-object or sadomasochistic dichotomy. In either case, as Sartre says, "there is a rupture of contact and desire misses its goal."[42] It is this "rupture of contact" that constitutes a perversion, and since all sexual activity involves such a breakdown, it follows that all sexual activity is a perversion.

A critic may reply that even if we accept this interpretation of Sartre, and allow that sexual desire has a realizable goal, we need not accept Sartre's conclusion that all sexual activity is a perversion. More specifically, one might raise the following objection:

Why should we call something perverted just because it is not ideal? This leaves our supply of negative evaluative terms in a state of unjustified poverty. We have no range at all if something must be either ideal or perverted.[43]

This argument is invalid because by saying that all sexual activity is a perversion we are not committed to limiting our range of negative evaluative terms. What has to be understood is that for Sartre, the notion of a "perversion" is at its most fundamental level an ontological and not an evaluative notion. For Sartre, sexual perversions are the inevitable consequence of all our concrete relations with Others. But they are inevitable, not because humans are essentially morally wrong or bad creatures, but because of the very nature of consciousness. Thus, to talk about all sexual activity being a perversion does not imply that all sexual activity is morally wrong or of no value. If my interpretation of Sartre is correct, then he would maintain that the concept of perversion must be removed from the moral sphere and placed into the ontological sphere. Indeed, this is perfectly compatible with Sartre's insistence on the fact that sexuality is a fundamental and necessary structure of our being for Others. Furthermore, Sartre's view is also perfectly compatible with there being a range of negative and positive evaluative terms. The notion of perversion does not overlap with that of wrong or bad and consequently, we can make positive evaluative judgments about perverted sex or negative value judgments about unperverted sex (sexual desire). For example, ideal sex might be bad from the point of view of quantity of pleasurable sensations, and perverted sex, e.g., sexual intercourse, might be good from that point of view. Thus, even though only sexual desire is unperverted, we can make a range of negative and positive value judgments concerning perverted sex.[44]

Another argument against Sartre's analysis of sexuality is found in Roger L. Taylor's article, "Sexual Experiences." He says,

There may be a number of distinct ways in which we might try to explain sexual concern by reference to what persons seek of other persons, but what is clear, is that Sartre's conclusions here fail to convince that these are our reasons for sexual concern. . . . Would anyone really avow that he . . . sexually desired in order to reduce another's consciousness to a consciousness of himself as flesh only, or this was what he attempted in sexually desiring?[45]

The tone in which Taylor asks this rhetorical question clearly implies that he believes that the answer is no. Yet, it is by no means evident that the phenomenological facts bear him out. The various descriptions of sexual desire that Sartre offers do fit my experience. Furthermore, although we do not often think of desire in terms of "reducing another's consciousness to a consciousness of oneself as flesh only," we do think of and experience desire as a mutual awareness, or as a desire that the Other desire me as I desire the Other, and that is essentially what Sartre means by the enigmatic phrase. Sartre cannot be refuted by a simple appeal to our experience.

Taylor's own view is that we can sufficiently explain sexual desire in terms of relationships between persons and objects, i.e., things lacking consciousness. If Taylor's view is correct, then Sartre's is mistaken, since Sartre insists that in sexual desire we aim at persons as persons. As part of Taylor's defense of his position against Sartre's he offers the following definition of sexual desire:

The translation of sexually desiring *a* is, to sexually desire to enter into physical contact with a particular fleshy object.[46]

Prima facie there is an element of circularity in Taylor's definition since "sexually" occurs in the *definiens* and the *definiendum*. Even if we ignore that problem, his translation still does not show that sexual desire can be understood in terms of a relationship between persons and objects. The notion of a "fleshy object" is ambiguous. It can be understood as (1) a purely material object or, along Sartrean lines, as (2) a material object (body) in which con-

204   THE PHILOSOPHY OF SEX

sciousness is incarnated or ensnarled. If we understand "fleshy object" in the first sense, then Taylor's definition of sexual desire is inadequate. A person at the death of his beloved might desire to enter into physical contact, (to touch) his beloved's flesh, although the desire is *not a sexual* desire. On the other hand, if "fleshy object" is understood in the second sense, then it would turn out that sexual desire is a relationship between persons, since to desire to enter into physical contact with a particular fleshy object would amount to a desire to enter into physical contact with a conscious body, i.e., a person. Thus, on either interpretation of "fleshy object," Taylor's analysis of sexual desire does not succeed in undermining Sartre's.

I have two closing remarks. First, a common theme in existentialist literature is that life is meaningless and that the human condition is hopeless. My interpretation of Sartre on sex makes clear at least one meaning of these vague slogans. What makes the human condition so hopeless is that unperverted relationships between human beings require an ideal state of sexual desire that is fleeting and rarely achieved. And further, shortly after it is achieved, it inevitably leads to its own destruction. Second, Sartre's views on sex would also make clear why the basic problems of human relationships cannot be solved in bed. As Solomon facetiously, but perhaps not inaccurately puts it, "Sartre's notion of sexuality, taken seriously, would be enough to keep us out of bed for a month."[47]

NOTES

1. Thomas Nagel, "Sexual Perversion," this volume, pp. 76–88. Maurice Natanson, *A Critique of Jean-Paul Sartre's Ontology* (Lincoln: University of Nebraska Press, 1951), pp. 42–46. Jacques Salvan, *To Be and Not To Be: An Analysis of Jean-Paul Sartre's Ontology* (Detroit: Wayne State University Press, 1962), pp. 93–95. Robert Solomon, "Sexual Paradigms," this volume, pp. 89–98.
2. Jean-Paul Sartre, *Being and Nothingness: An Essay on Phenomenological Ontology,* translated with an introduction by Hazel E. Barnes (New York: Philosophical Library, 1956), pp. 13–14. (Hereafter referred to as *B&N.*)
3. Jean-Paul Sartre, *The Transcendence of the Ego: An Existentialist Theory of Consciousness*, translated with an introduction by Forrest Williams and Robert Kirkpatrick (New York: The Noonday Press, 1957), pp. 40–42.

4. There are other senses in which consciousness is nothing, according to Sartre. Pointing out this one sense is, however, sufficient for our purposes.
5. Sartre, *B&N*, *op. cit.*, p. 345.
6. Sartre, *The Transcendence of the Ego, op. cit.,* pp. 44–49.
7. Sartre, *B&N*, *op. cit.*, p. 353.
8. *Ibid.*, p. 352.
9. *Ibid.*, p. 353, 343.
10. *Ibid.*, p. 475.
11. *Ibid.*, p. 475.
12. Solomon, *op. cit.,* p. 95 in this volume. My emphasis.
13. Sartre, *B&N*, *op. cit.*, p. 504.
14. *Ibid.*, p. 504.
15. *Ibid.*, p. 505.
16. *Ibid.*, p. 506.
17. *Ibid.*, p. 508. My emphasis.
18. Solomon, *op. cit.,* p. 95 in this volume.
19. Jerome Shaffer, "Sexual Desire," *Journal of Philosophy* 75 (1978), p. 176.
20. Sartre, *B&N*, *op. cit.*, p. 501.
21. *Ibid.*, p. 514.
22. *Ibid.*, pp. 499–500.
23. Shaffer, *op. cit.*, p. 183.
24. *Ibid.*, p. 187. My emphasis except for the first "sexual."
25. *Ibid.*, p. 188.
26. *Ibid.*, pp. 186–187.
27. *Ibid.*, p. 188.
28. Sartre, *B&N*, *op. cit.*, p. 499.
29. *Ibid.*
30. Shaffer, *op. cit.*, p. 185.
31. *Ibid.*, p. 187.
32. *Ibid.*, p. 188. My emphasis except for the second "sexual."
33. Sartre, *B&N*, *op. cit.*, p. 515.
34. *Ibid.*, p. 516.
35. *Ibid.*, p. 517.
36. *Ibid.*, p. 516.
37. *Ibid.*, p. 499.
38. *Ibid.*, p. 524.
39. *Ibid.*, p. 514.
40. Nagel, *op. cit.,* p. 81 in this volume.
41. Sartre, *B&N*, *op. cit.*, p. 512.
42. *Ibid.*, p. 516.
43. Attributed to Sara Ann Ketchum by Christine Pierce in her comments, read at the Western Division Meetings of the APA (Chicago, 1977), on an earlier version of this paper. See also Sara Ann Ketchum, "The Good, the Bad and the Perverted," in this volume, pp. 139–157.

44. In Christine Pierce's reply to an earlier version of this paper she offers her own interpretation of why, for Sartre, all human relationships are sadomasochistic. Her interpretation rests on two claims: (1)
"In *Being and Nothingness* Sartre identifies Being-for-itself and male
and Being-in-itself as female." (2) "Traditional relationships between
the sexes become for Sartre the model of human relationships in general." See Christine Pierce and Marjorie L. Collins, "Holes and
Slime: Sexism in Sartre's Psychoanalysis," *The Philosophical Forum,*
5 (1973–1974), pp. 112–127. Even if we grant Pierce's first questionable claim, and identify Being-for-itself with male and Being-in-itself
with female, it is still unclear how that helps to explain Sartre's claim
that all human relationships are sado-masochistic. For, Pierce's second claim, "that traditional relationships between the sexes become
for Sartre the model of human relationships in general" is mistaken.
A passage from the chapter on "Concrete Relations With Others"
should make this evident.

> To have sex means . . . to exist sexually for another who exists
> sexually for me. And it must be well understood that at first this
> Other is not necessary *for me—nor* I for him—a *heterosexual*
> existent but only a being who has sex. My *first* apprehension of
> the Other as having sex does not come when I conclude from the
> distribution of his hair, from the coarseness of his hands, the
> sound of his voice, his strength that he is of the masculine sex.
> We are here dealing with derived conclusions which refer to an
> original state. The first apprehension of the Other's sexuality . . .
> can be only desire; it is by desiring the Other . . . or by appre-
> hending his desire for me that I discover my being-sexed and his
> being-sexed. Here therefore in order to decide the nature and
> ontological position of sex we are referred to the study of desire.
> (p. 384).

Since Sartre is claiming that desire is an original state from which
masculine and feminine are derived, Pierce is mistaken in maintaining that, for Sartre, all human relationships are based on traditional
relationships between the sexes. Consequently, Pierce's interpretation
leaves unexplained Sartre's pessimism concerning human relationships.

Sartre's general conclusions about the nature of human relationships and his specific conclusion that all sexual activity is a perversion are not, perhaps, ones that we can comfortably accept. But if we
want to attack them we must turn to the *ontological* suppositions
upon which they rest and not to sex.

45. R. Taylor, "Sexual Experiences," this volume, pp. 59–75; pp. 71–72.
46. *Ibid.,* p. 65 in this volume.
47. R. Solomon, *op. cit.,* p. 95 in this volume.

II
Sexuality And Society

Irving Singer

The Sensuous and
the Passionate

There are many ways in which human sexuality can be analyzed. In distinguishing between the sensuous and the passionate, I refer to elements that occur in everyone's experience but often at different times and in different ways. We encounter one another through our senses, and we enjoy the encounter only as they are gratified. We perceive each other through our ability to see, to touch, to hear, to smell, and even to taste. Our sensations are generally localized in specific areas of the body, even though they contribute to responses that unify them into a single system of pleasurability. In sexual behavior, a man or woman may concentrate upon sensory pleasure and even seek to prolong it indefinitely; they may give it special importance in their life together, bestow value upon it, create ideals that dignify and further its occurrence. For some people, sexual experience amounts to little more than the sensuous, and even the end-pleasure of orgasmic relief becomes subordinate to the delights of sensory enjoyment. For others, however, sexuality is charged (on some occasions at least)

This selection is reprinted from *The Goals of Human Sexuality* by Irving Singer, Ph.D., with the permission of W.W. Norton & Company, Inc. © 1973 by Irving Singer. Reproduced by permission of Wildwood House, London. Reprinted by Schocken, 1974.

with emotions of yearning, craving, hope, anticipation, joy, oneness: overwhelming tension followed by a dying or dissipation of feeling, a final release of sexual energies.

This variable complex of warm and turbulent emotions—in contrast to the cooler and less demanding ones that characterize the sensuous—has always been recognized as the passionate aspect of sexuality. But its relationship to instinct or innate patterns of response has never been understood, nor its dependence upon cultural and environmental influence, nor even its relationship to the sensuous element. For the passionate requires at least a modicum of the sensuous in order for it to occur. Erotic emotions are always mediated by some form of sensory experience, which then becomes submerged in the needs and consummations of the passionate mode. For its part, the sensuous would not be felt as something sexual that relates us to another human being unless it also involved the passionate to some degree. The two elements may be contrasted, but one need not assume that they exist in perfect isolation even though they define different attitudes. And while these sexual attitudes may approximate a virtual independence, they may also cooperate harmoniously within a person's experience.

When the sensuous and the passionate become alienated from one another, those who believe in passion tend to think of the sensuous as evil or undesirable. In English the word "sensual" bears that connotation. For their part, those who believe in the sensuous often feel that the passionate is emotionally aberrant, romantic in a bad sense. But these negative judgments are unreliable. There is nothing necessarily good or bad about either aspect of sexuality. And nothing, even in their unfortunate isolation, prevents either one from being administered with love. For that term refers to the *manner* in which we relate to other people, *how* we are sensuous or passionate towards them. Perhaps the confusion about love results from the fact that "falling in love" implies a violence of emotional involvement that bespeaks the passionate and sometimes excludes the sensuous. But falling in love is not the only kind of love, and frequently it is not really love at all. When it entails no clear perception of the other person, it is not love; when it is determined by the lover's need but not the beloved's welfare, it is not love; when it is possessive rather than being a bestowal of value, it is not love. To love another person passionately, one must have both love and passion for that person. But the two are different, and passion alone is no guarantee of love.

On the other hand, we often use the word "love" to mean a sensuous interest that one person may have in another. This may or may not be a misuse of the other person; and it may or may not be love in the honorific sense that word usually implies. The sensuous is closely related to the playful. But one can play with someone either as a cat plays with a mouse or as a doting mother plays with her baby. Play can be destructive or creative, a murderous confrontation or a joyous interaction. When it effects a mutuality of enjoyment, the sensuous belongs to a loving attitude no less than the passionate—and whether or not it is accompanied by the passionate.

In the western world the sensuous and the passionate have often been pitted against one another. Each has been idealized by some people and denigrated by others. For the last two thousand years their partisans have fought in constant warfare against each other. All men and women have participated in the battle; and all have suffered for it. One cannot hope to find a single reason for the struggle. At different times, different attitudes have prevailed; and later developments served as reactions to earlier ones. Before describing the psychodynamics of the conflict, I shall trace the history of its development—but without trying to find one or only one means of explaining it.

Ξ

If it seems strange to say that love can be sexual and yet not passionate, the reason can be found in ideas we have inherited from the past. We have been taught to believe that love as something desirable takes us beyond the pleasures of the senses. The very concept of love as a condition worthy of aspiration arose among people who were ashamed of their bodies. They therefore sought to dignify sex by interpreting it as an ardent desire for something else. In the *Phaedrus*, for example, Plato begins with a paradigmatic situation of sexual interest between two persons. The sensuous components he discounts as merely physical, but the passionate obviously intrigues him. That the lover *yearns* for the beloved signifies to him a search for goodness which underlies all empirical nature. Once the lovers purify their passion by directing it towards the good itself, their relationship becomes what Plato calls "true love." Without this transcendental function, passion could only be self-indulgent lust, a burning appetite that can never be satisfied. As such, it was something to be feared, avoided, cured, and exorcised like all the other evils of the body. In the ancient world, passion was often related to insanity. But also it symbolized a "divine madness" that took men out of themselves and enabled them to communicate with the gods. Plato eliminates the materiality of passion by directing it towards an ideal entity—the Good or Beautiful. This preserved the value of the passionate, but at the expense of making it inhuman and *non*-sexual. The Good is not a person, and we cannot desire it as we would desire another human being.

In its attempt to rectify the deficiencies of Greek philosophy, Christianity merged Platonism with the mystery religions of antiquity. These had celebrated the passional element of sex both in itself and as the means to oneness with a personal deity. Like Platonism, Christianity condemned sexual passion; but like the pagan mysteries, it cultivated the passionate striving for God. In effect, it tried to satisfy human passions by means of the mystical encounter. Though later theologians modified the original design, Christianity conceived of man's love for God as a passionate experience that would make all other passionate experiences unnecessary. Not only unnecessary but even harmful to the soul and actually sinful. With this restriction the ideal of passion survived though greatly transmuted, for now it belonged to love directed towards a spiritual entity. But since that entity was a person, a Supreme Being and yet a person all the same, the ideal could still involve passion not *wholly* different from the passion in sexuality. As Christ had given himself in the nonsexual agony of his Passion, so too would the devout believer achieve salvation through a love that duplicates the union of two passionate lovers but does so at the higher level of pure spirituality.

There were two unfortunate consequences that followed upon the Christian idealization of passion. First, it meant that passionate experience as something good was reserved for the love of God to the exclusion of everything and everyone else. Second, it meant that passion directed towards any other object would have to be utterly prohibited. For the ancient world, passion was frightening because it withdrew a man from society and the influence of other men. But for Christianity its occurrence in sexuality was even worse: a sacrilege towards God himself. It is in this context that one must understand Saint Jerome's dictum that "he who loves his own wife too ardently is an adulterer." Since the legitimate spouse is really God, passion directed towards another—even the woman one has married in church—is adultery *more* terrible than when a married man sleeps with someone who is not his wife. "A wise man ought to love his wife with judgment, not with passion. Let a man govern his voluptuous impulses, and not rush headlong into intercourse."[1]

This opinion of Saint Jerome was repeated by all the doctors of the Church in the Middle Ages. Sexuality as such was not the enemy they fought. They feared, and therefore considered diabolical, the very possibility of passionate love between human beings. When Saint Paul said it is better to marry than to burn, he spoke as one who wished to avoid the pleasures as well as the pains of burning. Marriage being a sacrament, the conjugal act could not be evil in itself. Indeed, it was a meritorious means of propagating the species. Nor did most thinkers believe that sexual impulse was sinful. Although there was much debate about whether desire for sexual intercourse preceded the Fall of Adam and whether it was original sin or merely the punishment for original sin, medieval philosophers and theologians generally agreed that sexuality— properly administered—could be innocent. Saint Thomas insisted that neither the desire for sexual pleasure nor even the pleasure itself was evil, but only the subordination of reason to emotionality which often accompanied them. It was the passionate element that deflected man from his rational search for the Highest Good, thereby leading him into sin or mortal error.

It followed from this position that the sensuous could still find a place in Christianity. Sex being a natural function of man, his sensuous pleasures merely indicated that he was doing what he was made to do with the enjoyment that comes from efficiency. The sensuous was not to be pursued for its own sake, but nothing prevented it from belonging to a life in which everything happened for the sake of God. As long as personal emotions did not intrude, bodily pleasure was morally of little interest to the Church; and in fact, the sensuous was never condemned in the way that passional sex was. As a result, the split between the modes of sexuality hardened even further; and when the humanization of Christian doctrine occurred in the late Middle Ages, it too divided into two separate camps. On the one hand, there were those who tried to elevate the love of man and woman by duplicating within its structure the same passionate devotion that the Church reserved for the love of God. The heresy of courtly love, in the troubadours for example, consisted in the desire to treat a woman with the same spiritual yearning that only God deserved.

Though the troubadours generally considered themselves good Christians, the Church attacked their humanism as an insidious mockery of orthodox doctrine.

On the other hand, there were those who capitalized upon Christianity's acceptance of the sensuous to make it the principal focus of sexual experience. Alongside of courtly love there developed a lusty and carefree attitude towards the nonpassional pleasures of sex. Goliardic poetry is filled with it. In the *Carmina Burana* we see its infiltration into the monastery; in Boccaccio and Chaucer it dominates the *Decameron* and *The Canterbury Tales*, though not the *Filostrato* or *Troilus and Criseyde*, which belong to the passionate element. In the *Roman de la Rose*, the first part celebrates the passions of courtly love while the second part (written by another hand) reviles them for the greater glory of the sensuous. Within the writings of even the earliest troubadours—Guillaume IX, Marcabru, Cavalcanti, and many others—the two approaches to sexual love occur together, always separate and distinct but coexisting as viable alternatives in human relations. Though the troubadours generally favored the passionate over the sensuous, some of their poems make us wonder about their ultimate preference. And by the time we reach the Renaissance, it is often impossible—as in the love songs of Lorenzo de' Medici—to determine which of the two attitudes is authentic and which is merely a poetic façade. Sometimes the two are blended and thoroughly harmonized with one another, in Lorenzo's poetry as well as in the writings of other Renaissance authors.

For the most part, the modern world has retained the division that began in the Middle Ages. Luther and the Reformation as a whole reversed the earlier tradition in Christianity by considering the sensuous to be ultimately as sinful as the passionate. But also, Luther treated sexuality as a natural appetite that became dangerous only when its frustration gave it undue importance. It was to be satisfied (twice a week) with a regularity that made emotional extravagance impossible. At the same time, however, Luther unwittingly enabled the passionate to flourish in a way that it never had before. For in arguing that man could not hope to love God, Luther concluded that God's love descended to the level of humanity and showed itself in the ardent bonds that drew one person to another. This love could manifest itself in society at large but also between men and women, particularly in their sexual relations when sanctified by marriage. While man was still sinful merely in having sensuous inclinations, the passionate union of a married couple could be taken as evidence of their participation in God's love. Having this potentiality for holiness, passion had only to emancipate itself of the Christian dogmas in order to be idealized on its own.

The liberation of the passionate occurs in the romanticism of the eighteenth and nineteenth centuries. Love then *becomes* God, working miracles through its sheer emotionality. Romantic love defines itself either exclusively as passion or else as the passionate completion of sensuous interests that would be base and even despicable without it. For its part, the sensuous was also liberating itself. In the seventeenth and eighteenth centuries it successfully rebelled against all religious or edifying categories. Though sometimes violent in its rejection of restraints imposed by both the Reformation and the Counter-Reformation, the sensuous cause—as in Montaigne and Rabelais—had only to return to the medieval belief in the fundamental goodness of sexual pleasure. Being merely the contact between two epidermises, as Sébastien Chamfort called it, sexuality pertained to the class of innocent appetites— like a taste for mutton or a penchant for lovely colors. If sex inspired strong emotions, so much the worse. For what breaks through the skin can always be painful. Better to limit oneself to pleasures that could be controlled and easily modified, and in sexuality these are always sensuous.

In subordinating the sensuous to the passionate, or even eliminating the sensuous entirely as in the romantic puritanism of Rousseau, the nineteenth century wrapped sexuality in an aura of mystery. At one and the same time, it was the holiest and the most forbidding of human activities. Sexual love purified and ennobled mankind, and yet sex was the one area in which curiosity—and even scientific investigation—could not be tolerated. Novels, dramas, operas, and even the ballet seemed to concern themselves with nothing but the terrors and the joys of passion, but without the physical union or sensuous interest that accompanies sexuality in the real world. One can see and hear the passion of Tristan and Isolde, but one can hardly imagine these Wagnerian characters *making love*. In them, as in many products of latter-day romanticism, passion exists at such a distance from the physical possibilities of sex that it can only appear as a ritual that transcends ordinary experience. It once again becomes a part of religion, though now a fanciful and fictionalized religion, instead of being a part of life.

In a young and healthy organism, passion would not depend

upon frustration: between each consummation it would swell as sexual needs increased. But in all organisms, passion can be made to flourish as a result of frustration. With its puristic morality, its Victorian restraints, and its extraordinary sense of decorum, the nineteenth century constantly frustrated sensuous impulses and thus augmented the passionate. It is almost as if frustration was increased *for the sake of* creating more and greater passion. In any event, that was the consequence, and quite clearly it was the passionate life—often but not always spiritualized—that the age valued more than anything else.

Thus far, the twentieth century has largely been a flight away from passion. To us in the 1970s it is difficult (though not impossible) to take the tragedy of Tristan and Isolde at its face value. We have found easier, and more delightful, ways of satisfying our sexual needs: sensuous ways based upon a free acquaintance with the body rather than a numinous secrecy that magnifies its emotional importance. With its open tolerance of all and every kind of sex, it is easy to see the contemporary world as a return to the swinging eighteenth century. But the experience of romanticism is not that easily forgotten, and in the present-day acceptance of the sensuous we may be closer to a wholesome reconciliation than at any time in the past.

Ξ

Without the sensuous, sexual experience would not be the kind of enjoyment that it is for human beings. It would be the expression of burning desire, a gnawing tension, a savage hunger that came upon people for reasons too deep to fathom—an emotional occasion driven by psychological and physiological causes that may hardly enter into consciousness. Without the passionate, sexual experience might be enjoyable enough but not especially meaningful or imperious. It would be calm, relaxing, delectable, and quieting to the nerves though also affording moments of exquisite, even excruciating, pleasure. The sensuous aspect of human sexuality must surely approximate what monkeys and apes enjoy while being groomed by one another. To western man the sensuous has often seemed passive, unworthy of his questing spirit. Like Odysseus in the land of the lotus-eaters, he feels threatened by the tranquillizing effect of mere sensuousness, and by the fact that getting something directly through the senses is rarely as exciting as yearning for it in erotic imagination. This applies to the ancients as well as the moderns. We are not surprised to hear

Byron say that "passion is the element in which we live: without it we but vegetate";[2] but even Plutarch approvingly reports that Lycurgus recommended continence in newly wedded Spartans because "it continued in both parties a still burning love and a new desire of the one to the other."[3]

Neither Lycurgus nor Plutarch believed that passion is "the element in which we live," that it defines the normal or proper function of sexuality. Yet they realized that intimacy seems more valuable to husband and wife when they desire each other ardently. The passionate always runs the risk of being painful or mad; but it contributes a sense of importance that cannot come from the sensuous alone. For its part, the sensuous provides a taste for beauty and pervasive pleasure. Though it often seems mindless and superficial, it satisfies a network of appetites as surely as food or drink.

In sexual experience, the sensuous functions in two ways. First, it is an extremely effective means of awakening libidinal interest. It arouses the male or female, stimulates their desire for one another, and brings the genitals into that condition of excitement which is necessary for their satisfactory operation. In men the visual and auditory senses are highly developed as an agency of sensuousness. That erotic scopophilia, love of looking, which characterizes the human male serves as an anticipatory response to sexual possibilities. Whether he is sitting at a café, waiting for a train, walking through a shop, looking at a painting, or watching a movie, the male uses his eyes for visual consummations which are clearly sexual even if they do not lead to orgasm. Compared to men, women are less often stimulated by sensations of sight or hearing; they tend to rely more on direct physical contact. In both men and women, though especially in women, the tactile sense facilitates like nothing else that experience which is itself what D. H. Lawrence called "the closest touch of all." Directly or indirectly, proximately or at a distance, these sensuous acuities create the appetite for sexual experience. And within the experience itself, foreplay intensifies desire merely by means of the sensuous. Looking, touching, tasting, hearing, smelling—each in accordance with individual preference and momentary inclination—brings about a heightening of interest in the other person and in his sexual availability. Without sensuous foreplay, coitus might occur in ways that could certainly propagate the species. But unless there were some prelude of this sort, however brief or limited, sexual intercourse would hardly be pleasurable for either male or female.

It is this pleasurability that indicates the second function of the sensuous. Quite apart from its capacity to awaken appetite, the sensuous is simply enjoyable in itself. The man who watches a woman undress may do so as a means of stimulating himself; but more often, he takes pleasure in the somewhat passive experience of looking. The naked body, when it is handsome or suggestive, is a delightful thing to see. Seeing it need not necessarily lead on to anything else. It would be a pity to live with nothing but the sexual pleasures of looking, seeing, watching. But one does not have to justify such interests by citing another activity or experience to which they lead. Their justification consists in their inherent enjoyability as purely sensuous moments, and not as mere instrumentalities. In coitus itself, the sensuous does more than just arouse appetites. It also has its own way of satisfying them. The tensions that sensuous foreplay creates issue into orgasmic release which may itself be a function of the sensory excitation rather than a passionate drive or any vehement need for explosive end-pleasure. Though the orgasm is often felt as a response that convulses the entire organism, its pleasures are also localized in genital sensations and sometimes these are not accompanied by strong emotions. In the passionate mode, orgasms tend to be emotionally very powerful. But even so, they may not be more satisfying, and often they are less enjoyable, than the pleasures of the sensuous. And that is why some people are willing to forego the passionate for the sake of sensuous consummations that are easier to attain or more desirable under the circumstances.

For many people, however, sexual behavior would not be satisfying unless it also involved the kind of emotional discharge that the passionate provides. The sensuous then operates not only to stimulate desire and to create pleasures that come from its arousal, but also to direct libidinal interests towards a final release that takes them beyond sensation. Without the mediation of the senses, people would not exist for one another. But their *affinity* to each other is more than merely sensory. Human beings gravitate within each other's sexual orbit through an urgency and compulsion that cannot be explained in terms of sight or touch or any other sense modality. This mutual craving is a need for release resulting from tensions that are partly organic and partly interpersonal. Yearning becomes stronger as the tensions build up; if they are not released enjoyably, yearning can change into anger and hatred. And since frustration and orgasmic failure are always possible, the tensions may be accompanied by fear long before their release is even feasible. In the male, this often results in impotence; in the female, in a thwarting of desire that makes it difficult for her to be sexually aroused. In either event, passion disappears and tends to undermine the sensuous as well. But often they strengthen one another. The sensuous induces sensory awareness, which may then be experienced as a passionate yearning; the passionate impels the sexes into each other, and this may lead to sensory gratification as well as emotional ecstasy. Insofar as they define different attitudes, the sensuous and the passionate are separable from one another; and to some extent, each attitude can often survive without the other. How they may be harmonized, and whether they need to be, is one of the major problems to which this book will continually return.

Since the two modes of sexuality interweave so massively, one may well wonder how it is *possible* for them to separate and even conflict. One feels that left to itself sexual experience would naturally bring about their harmony and joint cooperation. But sexuality cannot be left to itself; it does not exist apart from the rest of human reality. Man differs from all other animals, even the nonhuman primates, in the extent to which his sexual responsiveness pervades each moment and every aspect of his being. As a result, sex frequently conflicts with other interests. It is a threat to many economic, political, and spiritual aspirations whose goals are not always consistent with either erotic element. Civilization in general has evolved as a complex of institutions that often control the sexual for the sake of other ends. This is not to say that civilization must be repressive. It can further each of the modes of sexuality, and in some respects it always has. Moreover, the conflict between sensuous and passionate may not be entirely related to social repressiveness. Even if society were to devote itself to the harmonization of the two aspects, and to the fullest expression of each, there may be something in sexuality itself that could always renew their internal warfare. Let us consider what that might be, and whether it is related to what Freud called "organic repression."

Ξ

If it were easy to harmonize the sensuous and the passionate, many of the problems of sexuality would quickly disappear. But the fact that whole ideologies have been constructed out of the need to separate the two, and out of the desire to favor one rather than the other, indicates that something very profound impedes a satisfactory harmonization. In his pervasive pessimism about sexual happiness, Freud often stressed the difficulties in satisfying the two modes of sexuality. Discussing the relationship between freedom and total satisfaction, he remarks that not only repression is injurious to human beings but also unrestrained sexual liberty. He then says:

It is easy to show that the value the mind sets on erotic needs instantly sinks as soon as satisfaction becomes readily obtainable. Some obstacle is necessary to swell the tide of the libido to its height; and at all periods of history, wherever natural barriers in the way of satisfaction have not sufficed, mankind has erected conventional ones in order to be able to enjoy love. This is true both of individuals and of nations. In times during which no obstacles to sexual satisfaction existed, such as, may be, during the decline of the civilizations of antiquity, love became worthless, life became empty, and strong reaction-formations were necessary before the indispensable emotional value of love could be recovered. In this context it may be stated that the ascetic tendency of Christianity had the effect of raising the psychical value of love in a way that the heathen antiquity could never achieve; it developed greatest significance in the lives of the ascetic monks, which were almost entirely occupied with struggles against libidinous temptation.[4]

The obstacles to which Freud refers are the usual repressive devices that tend to increase passion. In saying that they are needed for the "indispensable emotional value of love" and "to swell the tide of the libido to its height," he would *seem* to be arguing for the desirability of the passionate as well as the sensuous. But Freud's argument implies that they cannot both be satisfied. If erotic experience is readily attainable, the sensuous can be gratified; but then—Freud assures us—passion disappears and sexuality ceases to be valuable. Without the barriers of frustration and restraint, love becomes "worthless." For it to recover its emotional importance, sexuality has to defeat its own ends as in the extreme case of Christian asceticism. When that happens, however, the pleasures of the sensuous are also denied. By choosing lesser obstacles to satisfaction, Freud might have envisaged a condition in which some passion, at least, would be compatible with sensuous pleasure. But in this place, he sounds as if the mere fact of being "readily available" deprives sexual experience of its value in either mode.

Freud's argument is plausible from the point of view of those who identify love with passion and think that passion can only originate through obstacles. For if this were true, love would lose its value once the obstacles that create passion have been re-moved. Like many another raised in the nineteenth century, Freud states more than once that a woman can expect to lose her lover on the very day that she takes him as her husband. He obvi-ously means a lover not in the sense of one who *loves* the woman, but rather in the sense of passionate sexual desire. To those who believe in the sensuous, it will seem strange that sexual love should thus be defined in terms of passion alone. Through the in-timacy that marriage affords, lovers can have access to more ex-tensive sensuous pleasure than could ever have been available at a distance. Having overcome the obstacles that separated them, they may enjoy the pleasures of the senses with greater security, greater leisure, and greater likelihood of success. Provided, of course, that sensuousness is valued in itself. If so, the love that *it* defines can never be worthless to those who enjoy the sensuous with utter freedom.

But while Freud neglects the goodness of purely sensuous love, he is not an advocate of passion either. From the paragraph I just quoted, one might have thought he would be. Reared in the ro-mantic tradition, he nevertheless turns against it as one of its most profound critics. In many places he seems horrified at the turmoil and emotional stress that passion involves. Though erotic needs sink in value once obstacles are removed, Freud is sensitive to the way in which the obstacles lead to neurosis and sexual misery. In this respect, he closely resembles Lucretius, who also thought that the power and importance of passion resulted from the frustration of erotic impulses, and who also recommended the regularity of marriage as a means of *eliminating* passion. To both Freud and Lucretius, romantic love is not really valuable: it is only valued, or overvalued, by the passionate interest itself. This has the effect of swelling the tide of the libido, but that has so many unfortunate consequences that neither Lucretius nor Freud thinks that it can lead to sexual happiness.

At other times, however, Freud seemed to hold views of a total-ly different sort. Together with his pessimism, and even negativ-ism, one also finds indications that possibly he did believe in some kind of harmony between the sensuous and the passionate. When he lists the ingredients in a happy marriage, or what he calls the "completely normal attitude" towards sex, he names the elements of *Sinnlichkeit* and *Zärtlichkeit*.[5] The latter is tenderness or affec-tion. The former his translators render as "sensuality"; but since Freud uses the word with no pejorative intention, I think my term "sensuousness" is more appropriate. The question now arises: Does the fusion of *Sinnlichkeit* and *Zärtlichkeit* also include the passionate?

Freud was not writing with my distinction in mind, and one cannot hope to answer such a question too precisely. But in describing what he considers to be normal sexuality, Freud cites obstacles to final satisfaction which would necessarily seem to foster the passionate throughout maturity. Tracing the libido to infantile demands upon the parents which are unrealistic as well as unsatisfiable, he remarks that adult sexuality is inherently imperfect, inherently incapable of being fully satisfied. Whether this results from organic repression he does not say, but he does refer to universal incest-taboos as the cause of childhood yearnings which inevitably linger on in the adult libido. If this is so, the structure of all sexual love would seem to create passion within itself. To the extent that the beloved is always and necessarily an imago of a parental figure—as Freud insists—a sensuous interest *must* be accompanied by some degree of passionate longing for an unobtainable object. This in turn could prevent even sexual experience that was readily attainable from losing value or becoming wholly worthless.

Given his belief in parental imagoes and their effect upon the emotions, it seems likely that Freud did mean to include the passionate as well as the sensuous in the sexuality of a happy marriage. Discussing the merging of *Sinnlichkeit* and *Zärtlichkeit*, he says that the libidinal objects of maturity "will still be chosen on the model (imago) of the infantile ones, but in the course of time they will attract to themselves the affection that was tied to the earlier ones. A man shall leave his father and his mother—according to the biblical command—and shall cleave unto his wife; affection and sensuality are then united. The greatest intensity of sensual passion [*"sinnlicher Verliebtheit"*] will bring with it the highest psychical valuation of the object—this being the normal overvaluation of the sexual object on the part of a man."[6]

In speaking of "overvaluation," Freud confuses us again. For he uses that term throughout his writings to signify an unwarranted expenditure of libido. It is the dangerous and unrealistic element in all romantic excitement; it is the madness in the condition known as "falling in love." When Freud condemns passion, he does so because he thinks it always leads to overvaluation.[7] Nevertheless, what Freud says in this place would definitely imply that normal sexuality satisfies both the sensuous *and* the passionate by choosing an object which reawakens childhood needs while also being readily accessible. And perhaps it is this theme that we ought to emphasize in his writings. Far from leading us to assume that the sensuous and the passionate are necessarily antagonistic, his argument would then encourage us to try to find the circumstances in which they cooperate. Despite his ambiguities, I think that was Freud's intention. But he did not carry it out, and our age will have to discover new ways of doing so.

Ξ

It is too early in the development of the life sciences for us to resolve the difficulties we have been examining. But I would like to walk about them a little longer, to understand them better before the following chapters reformulate them in terms of various sexological problems.

I begin, or begin again, by asserting that the sensuous attitude is basically innocent. It is just a playful enjoyment of the body, and of the human personality as it expresses itself through the senses. The sensuous is an aesthetic interest whose materials are sensations related to the genitals and other erotogenic zones. Whether its pleasures lead to orgasm or not, whether it limits itself to foreplay or goes beyond, whether it is experienced with a single partner or many at once, whether it is heterosexual or homosexual, whether it employs the mouth, the anus, the vagina, or any other orifice of the body, it can be approached as an artistic activity designed to maximize and prolong human pleasure. When Ovid speaks of the "art of love," he principally has in mind this aspect of sexuality. And as savages have often been idealized as living at the level of mere sensation, the sensuous is frequently represented by an idyllic image of man in nature. Thus, Stendhal—who distinguishes between sensuous love, passionate love, vanity love, and sympathy love—describes *l'amour sensuel* as an erotic extension of the hunt: "Whilst out shooting, to meet a fresh, pretty country girl who darts away into a wood. Everyone knows the love founded on pleasures of this kind: however unromantic and wretched one's character, it is there that one starts at the age of sixteen."[8] In the visual arts, we often encounter a similar scene—Boucher and Fragonard have captured it to perfection.

Stendhal himself wishes to transcend the sensuous in the direction of the passionate. But nowhere does he insist upon a necessary conflict between the two. And though his entire book on love is devoted to the possibilities of passion love, he also recognizes that it can sometimes be harmful in thwarting man's sensuous nature. In the chapter entitled "Failures" in *De l'Amour*, he shows how the passionate attitude can lead to male impotence resulting from a fear of performance, thereby robbing the lovers of sensory pleasure. And despite his faith in passion as such, Stendhal continually makes remarks such as this one: "Some virtuous and affectionate women have almost no idea at all of sensuous pleasure; they have only very rarely laid themselves open to it, if I may put it so, and even then the raptures of passion love have almost made them forget the pleasures of the body."[9] When he discusses the birth of love, Stendhal gives the sensuous at least as much importance as the passionate: "To love is to derive pleasure from seeing, touching, and feeling through all one's senses and as closely as possible, a lovable person who loves us."[10]

Stendhal does not take the defense of the sensuous any further; and in his novels, its role and its significance are always tantalizingly unclear. But in seeking to harmonize it with passion love, he accords the sensuous a dignity that many of his contemporaries found shocking. In eastern philosophy this dignity has often turned into spiritual idealization, the sensuous being refined into a method for *extirpating* man's passionate cravings. In the sexual yoga of Hinduism, Buddhism, and Taoism, male and female bodies achieve spiritual oneness through a spontaneous and unforced sharing of sensory pleasures. Intercourse occurs not through any action or doing, not because of any "grasping desire," but rather as a passionless enjoyment of contemplative love: "One finds out what it can mean simply to look at the other person, to touch hands, or to listen to the voice. If these contacts are not regarded as leading to something else, but rather allowed to come to one's consciousness as if the source of activity lay in them and not in the will, they become sensations of immense subtlety and richness."[11]

In recommending the sensuous as they do, the eastern philosophers have one thing in common with western hedonists like Ovid. As in much erotic literature both eastern and western, they strengthen the sensuous approach by making sexual experience routine and even casual—though also very sophisticated in the ways of maximizing pleasure. But easygoing sex is rarely cathartic; and cleverness in the use of the body need not lead to powerful emotions. Can anyone following minute instructions about positions and techniques, of the sort to be found in the *Kama Sutra* for instance, really get carried away by an ardent longing for the beloved? Lovemaking can be taught, but not passion itself. The same applies to much of contemporary sexology. Readers of the works of Masters and Johnson may learn a great deal that can liberate their propensity to sensuous pleasure. But in their attempt to make sexuality less mysterious, less inhibited, and also less frightening, such studies do nothing to facilitate the passionate response. Perhaps that is why the therapeutic advice that has issued from this research seems to minimize the desirability of passion. In their book on sexual inadequacy, Masters and Johnson caution against that "pattern of demanding pelvic thrusting" in which passion generally manifests itself: "The wife repeatedly must be assured that this forceful approach will not contribute to facility of response. If the husband initiates the driving, thrusting coital pattern, the wife must devote conscious effort to accommodate to the rhythm of his thrusting, and her opportunity for quiet sensate pleasure in coital connection is lost."[12] This emphasis upon "sensate focus," and in general the sensuous attitude, may be interpreted as merely therapeutic; but as we shall see throughout this book, there may be no way of differentiating between therapeutic means and permanent conditioning in Masters' and Johnson's approach to sexual possibilities.

Since passion so often originates in pathology, one may not want to increase it on many occasions. To do so, however, involves something more than a concern for sensuous techniques. It requires a *yearning* for the person one is with, a *craving* to penetrate her and to be penetrated by him, a *striving* for the deepest contact, a *need* for emotional union that enables each to participate in the other, to appropriate the other, and possibly to give oneself as well.

Whence arises this passionate need that people often have for one another, and that they express in sexuality? From person to person it varies greatly. Some theorists even postulate a fixed quantity with which an individual is endowed. If this were the case, passion would be an emotional constant for each person, analogous to temperament or musical talent or mathematical genius. As there are volatile spirits and others that are more sedate, so too would there be human beings fundamentally more or less passionate than others. At the same time, however, we know that sexual passion is correlated with physiological maturation. In people who are repressed at least to the extent characteristic of the western world, passion extends from adolescence into middle age. The time span varies greatly, but most young people go through a period of passionate potential that eventually becomes kinetic in relation to at least one erotic object. Through the middle years passion tends to diminish, though the onset of menopause makes the decline more noticeable in women then in men. In both sexes the trend often reverses itself in the late thirties, the forties, or even the fifties, with an outburst of passional interest that some people call the middle-age adolescence. As if to compensate for the gradual loss of emotional capability, nature gives men and women another chance to feel towards some beloved that youthful turmoil which everyone cherishes but no one manages properly when it first appears.

Fictional literature often centers about the vicissitudes of human experience at these two periods in a person's life. They set the biological time for tragedy as well as comedy. One would have difficulty understanding *Phaedra* in any of its versions unless one realized that the heroine has reached the time of sudden recrudescence in passion that many women experience as they approach the menopause. On the other hand, the dilemma that Shaw's doctor undergoes in *The Doctor's Dilemma* would not exist if Ridgeon were ten years younger or ten years older. Having reached the age of forty in a somewhat celibate condition, Ridgeon complains of a curious and unlocalized "aching." Sir Patrick, his older colleague, diagnoses the ailment quite correctly: "It's very common between the ages of seventeen and twenty-two. It sometimes comes on again at forty or thereabouts. You're a bachelor, you see. It's not serious—if you're careful."[13]

Though geared to physiological developments common to the species, these temporal factors are also a function of social and psychological determinants. Some people never fall in love, others seem to do so all the time. Furthermore, the state of passionate desire is so highly prized by men and women in the western world that a great deal of effort goes into trying to awaken or reawaken it throughout the years of maturity. What came so easily in early youth has to be carefully cultivated later on. Even in first love, however, passion is obviously psychogenic to a considerable degree. Theodor Reik has argued that passionate love arises as part of the adolescent's attempt to fulfill some ego ideal. Having been frustrated in our striving for self-perfection, he says, we transfer the image of this ideal to another person. Since no one can *really* provide the perfection we crave, love must always be illusory: "All love is founded on a dissatisfaction with oneself. It is an attempt to escape from oneself in search of a better, an ideal self. The lover imagines that he has found it in his object. Is love thus an illusion? Of course it is. . . . "[14] Romantic love or the state of falling in love would thus differ from other love only in its emotional intensity. Its passional ferocity Reik explains as an effort, a desperate effort, to rescue a menaced ego through the attempt to appropriate that perfect goodness promised by one's illusory image of the beloved.

I have elsewhere[15] suggested that, even at its most ardent, love is not necessarily an illusion. But Reik is also wrong in thinking that dissatisfaction accounts for passion. Strong sexual impulse is part of the sheer human vitality that *everyone* prizes, not merely those who are dissatisfied with themselves. Passionate desire is not greater in those who are more dissatisfied with themselves, or diminished in those who are less dissatisfied. It is true that passion implies a compelling need. Unless one wants the woman or man, this particular woman or man on this particular occasion, one will not feel a passionate drive. But to say this is not to say that there is a perfection which we lack and which causes us to be dissatisfied with ourselves and which we hope to attain by possessing the woman or the man. What we lack is precisely the state of oneness with this other person which we achieve by means of our passion. Making love is more than just the removing of a dissatisfaction. It can also be an emergent condition, an emotional unity, desirable in itself and not as the mere remedy for a menaced ego. The ego may feel menaced if it has no passionate desires; but passion does not arise—except in pathological cases—as a device for escaping prior failures in oneself.

It is passion which enables us to *care* about other people, to want them and to want to be wanted by them. It provides that vital urgency without which we could not identify with fellow creatures struggling like ourselves in a world we never made. It overcomes loneliness and isolation by making us yearn to be with other men and women. If we had no such feeling, could they be persons who matter to us? Could we be persons for them as well? The answers to these questions may be affirmative since the sensuous mode creates its own social joys—friendly consummations which are often gentler and more pacific than those that result from the passionate. But without the impetus of passion, a purely sensuous society could not mold those affective bonds which ordinarily belong to the very concept of a person.

Since the beginning of time, human beings have always sought means of increasing passional desire in one another and in themselves. One could write a history of mankind by reference to love potions alone. Even those who idealize the sensuous recognize the importance that passion has for most people. In Balzac's book on the physiology of marriage he defines love as "the poetry of the senses"; yet he constantly reminds us that even sensory pleasure deteriorates unless passion is also aroused. In the western world men have generally sought to awaken desire in the female by their status in society, whereas women were expected to increase the male's libidinal interest through the beauty of their face and figure. Liberated women who nowadays complain that men have used them as physical contrivances are right to protest against such treatment. But they will never understand the condition unless they realize that these roles have existed partly because women saw no other way of increasing masculine desire. In the rudimentary sex act the female does not need to get anything ready, while the man must have an erection. And this is more likely to occur if the man feels secure and even admirable. For reasons of their own, sometimes good and sometimes bad, women (not all women, but many) have been willing to submit to almost anything that will create this feeling in the male—and thereby augment his ardor for the female.

As a symbol of this sociobiological relationship, one need only consider the institution of the dancing-girl or striptease artist. With his greater sexual interest in visual sensations, the male enjoys the exhibition of female flesh more than the female enjoys the exhibition of male flesh. In all societies women have regularly provided such enjoyment. In doing so, however, the self-exhibiting female systematically hides as much as she reveals. She causes frustration through her teasing and evasive movements, through the repressive suggestion that there is something naughty or forbidden in the presentation of her nudity, and through the distance that her performance imposes upon the male who can watch but cannot touch her. Frustration of this sort may challenge a man but it does not threaten him. The performance is itself a means of flattering his sexual interests. It arouses desire, and sometimes passion, in the male.

Dancing-girls and stripteasers make up a tiny percentage of the female population. Moreover, they are relegated to the lower classes as a way of assuring men that the male is ultimately superior to the female despite her sexual powers. Nevertheless, the dancing-girl represents all women inasmuch as she specializes in arousing masculine desire through the use of her body, and that is one of the principal roles which western society has demanded of women in general. The equivalent among men—crooners, movie idols, and others who devote themselves to arousing women—have no comparable importance. They do not represent attitudes expected of men as a whole. On the contrary, those who excite women merely by entertaining them have generally been scorned by other men, or even hounded by society as in the Don Juan myth. Men want women to be passionate, but only when they admire masculine achievements that belong to the world of men and that men themselves respect. The male entertainer does not live in that world, at least not in the way that the politician, the soldier, and the football player do. To some extent, this phenomenon is culturally determined. To some extent, however, it is related to the fact that women often fear the consequences of their passion and will yield to its ecstatic abandon only when they feel protected by a vigorous and masterful male. Don Juan seduces them by pretending to be that kind of man. When they realize he is not, they turn on him with all the fury that passion has created in them.

Ξ

As Freud suggests in that passage I quoted earlier, natural barriers and artificial obstacles tend to increase passion and magnify its value. In the western world the tradition that stems from Plato sets up obstacles by means of the very idealizations that structure its attitudes towards love. Plato defines eros as the desire for the Good; but then he tells us that the Good is unattainable in experience. All human desire must therefore be a striving after perfection which is both hopeless and inescapable. If one could really *live* this philosophy, one's life would be a throbbing passion from beginning to end. That being impossible, courtly and romantic love make lesser arrangements among mere human beings. Like Platonism, they augment the passionate by means of alternate inducements and repressions not wholly different from the striptease. The medieval lady was revered as the visible exemplar of beauty but always worshiped from afar, accessible to the poetic imagination but never to be touched or enjoyed through carnal intercourse. In the nineteenth century, the courtly concepts were universalized so that *every* woman could become an angel in the household. She was to shine forth as the image of a perfect goodness men desired without herself being subject to passions that might have quieted the endless yearnings of her husband. Her theoretical lack of sexual interest served as a final and limiting obstacle that men could use to maximize their own passion. Whenever the authentic feelings—sensuous *or* passionate—of a normally sexual woman burst through the conventional barriers, she was made to feel guilty or sick. Only in our century has society come to recognize that the lustful woman is not abnormal, certainly no more so than the lustful male.

In our day the women's liberation movement, and in general the toughness of the female, may provide (may even be *designed* to provide) a new enticement to the male. In their professed belligerence women may be changing tactics but not the strategy; as in Aristophanes' *Lysistrata*, they get what they want by frustrating men as women always have. But times *do* change. If some liberationists rebel against all heterosexual possibilities, perhaps it is because they do not realize that the major battle has been won. Women are now free to enjoy sexual experience in any way they can. And so are men. The old barriers no longer exist. We shall have to find more positive ways of making sex intense and meaningful as well as delectable.

In making this attempt, we may begin by recognizing that Plato was right to associate passion with a search for ideals. Though the Good is too abstract a notion to be of much use, it may very well be the case that without standards of value the phenomenon of passion could not exist. The passionate is not wholly reducible to the drive for coitus, or even the need for orgasmic consummation. These may serve as characteristic ingredients of sexual passion, but they themselves presuppose a craving to unite and a feeling that it is *important* to do so. Passion would not arise unless the desired person, or the activity of uniting, or both, were cherished by the lover as something *worthy* of his desire. As a basis for this valuation, there may be any number of biological, psychological, and sociological causes. But they are not always the same, and no one of them is either necessary or sufficient. There must be something in valuation itself which engenders the passionate. I have suggested that in a healthy organism passion arises spontaneously during the years of sexual maturity, and therefore that it is not entirely a function of artificial barriers. If this is true, perhaps it results from the fact that healthy organisms create standards of value as part of their response to reality. Far from being artificial, the social restraints that increase passion may often derive from a pervasive need to create values.

These are merely speculations, however, and will remain so until they can be verified by the empirical sciences. In the following chapters we shall be studying various problems in the theory of sex which are both empirical and philosophical. They are all related to the conflict between the sensuous and the passionate; and they all involve ambiguities in the use of terms like "libido,"

"drive," "desire," "consummation," "orgasm," and even "sex."
In the male and in the female, the sensuous and the passionate express themselves through different behavioral dispositions and different orgasmic consummations that need to be delineated with as
much precision as science can presently afford. If the passionate is
"natural" in the sense of being more than just a product of artificial barriers, one must determine what its natural condition may
be. And since the sensuous and the passionate conflict in so much
of human experience, one must consider ways in which they may
be harmonized. It is also possible that harmonization is not desirable, or even feasible, for all people on all occasions. In formulating a pluralistic approach to sexological problems, we cannot
assume that any one solution is necessarily the right one for all the
situations that constitute human experience.

NOTES

1. Saint Jerome, *Against Jovinian.*
2. Quoted in Countess of Blessington, *Journal of the Conversations of Lord Byron*, 1834, p. 317.
3. Lycurgus, quoted in De Rougemont, D., *Love in the Western World* (New York: Anchor Books, 1957), p. 50.
4. Freud, S., "The Most Prevalent Form of Degradation in Erotic Life," in *Sexuality and the Psychology of Love* (New York: Collier Books, 1963), p. 67. I prefer this translation to the one in *SE*, Vol. XI, pp. 187–88.
5. *Ibid.*, in *SE*, Vol. XI, p. 180; Freud, S., "Über die allgemeinste Ernie-drigung des Liebeslebens," *Beiträge zur Psychologie des Liebeslebens II, Gesammelte Schriften von Sigmund Freud, Fünfter Band* (Leipzig, Internationaler Psychoanalytischer Verlag, 1924), p. 201.
6. *Ibid.*, in *SE*, Vol. XI, p. 181.
7. I have discussed this at greater length in my chapter on Freud in *The Nature of Love* (New York: Random House, 1966).
8. Stendhal, *On Love* (New York: Grosset & Dunlap, 1967), p. 2.
9. *Ibid.*, p. 3.
10. *Ibid.*, p. 5.
11. Watts, A. W., *Nature, Man, and Woman* (New York: Mentor Books, 1958), p. 167.
12. Masters, W. H. & Johnson, V. E., *Human Sexual Inadequacy* (Boston: Little, Brown, 1970), p. 309.
13. Shaw, G. B., *The Doctor's Dilemma*, Act I.
14. Reik, T., *Of Love and Lust* (New York, Farrar: Straus & Giroux, 1957), p. 190.
15. In Part I of *The Nature of Love.*

Ann Ferguson

Androgyny as an Ideal for Human Development

In this paper I shall defend androgyny as an ideal for human development. To do this I shall argue that male/female sex roles are neither inevitable results of "natural" biological differences between the sexes, nor socially desirable ways of socializing children in contemporary societies. In fact, the elimination of sex roles and the development of androgynous human beings is the most rational way to allow for the possibility of, on the one hand, love relations among equals, and on the other, development of the widest possible range of intense and satisfying social relationships between men and women.

Ferguson, Ann. "Androgyny as an Ideal for Human Development," in Mary Vetterling-Braggin, Frederick Elliston and Jane English, eds. *Feminism and Philosophy* (Totowa, N.J.: Littlefield, Adams and Co., 1977), pp. 45–69. Reprinted by permission.

I'd like to acknowledge the help and encouragement of the socialist and feminist intellectual communities at the University of Massachusetts in Amherst, particularly the help of Sam Bowles, Jean Elshtain, and Dennis Delap, who read and commented extensively on earlier drafts of this paper. John Brentlinger and Susan Cayleff also provided feedback and comments. Many students who read the paper were helpful and supportive. A first version of this paper was read in the fall of 1974 at Bentley College, Boston, Massachusetts.

I. ANDROGYNY: THE IDEAL DEFINED

The term "androgyny" has Greek roots: *andros* means man and *gynē*, woman. An androgynous person would combine some of each of the characteristic traits, skills, and interests that we now associate with the stereotypes of masculinity and femininity. It is not accurate to say that the ideal androgynous person would be both masculine and feminine, for there are negative and distorted personality characteristics associated in our minds with these ideas.[1] Furthermore, as we presently understand these stereotypes, they exclude each other. A masculine person is active, independent, aggressive (demanding), more self-interested than altruistic, competent and interested in physical activities, rational, emotionally controlled, and self-disciplined. A feminine person, on the other hand, is passive, dependent, nonassertive, more altruistic than self-interested (supportive of others), neither physically competent nor interested in becoming so, intuitive but not rational, emotionally open, and impulsive rather than self-disciplined. Since our present conceptions of masculinity and femininity thus defined exclude each other, we must think of an ideal androgynous person as one to whom these categories do not apply—one who is neither masculine nor feminine, but human: who transcends those old categories in such a way as to be able to develop positive human potentialities denied or only realized in an alienated fashion in the current stereotypes.

The ideal androgynous being, because of his or her combination of general traits, skills, and interests, would have no internal blocks to attaining self-esteem. He or she would have the desire and ability to do socially meaningful productive activity (work), as well as the desire and ability to be autonomous and to relate lovingly to other human beings. Of course, whether or not such an individual would be able to *achieve* a sense of autonomy, self-worth, and group contribution will depend importantly on the way the society in which he/she lives is structured. For example, in a classist society characterized by commodity production, none of these goals is attainable by anyone, no matter how androgynous, who comes from a class lacking the material resources to acquire (relatively) nonalienating work. In a racist and sexist society there are social roles and expectations placed upon the individual which present him/her with a conflict situation: either express this trait (skill, interest) and be considered a social deviant or outcast, or repress the trait and be socially accepted. The point, however, is that the androgynous person has the requisite skills and interests to be able to achieve these goals if only the society is organized appropriately.

II. LIMITS TO HUMAN DEVELOPMENT: THE NATURAL COMPLEMENT THEORY

There are two lines of objection that can be raised against the view that androgyny is an ideal for human development: first, that it is not possible, given the facts we know about human nature; and second, that even if it is possible, there is no reason to think it particularly desirable that people be socialized to develop the potential for androgyny. In this section I shall present and discuss Natural Complement theories of male/female human nature and the normative conclusions about sex roles.

There are two general facts about men and women and their roles in human societies that must be taken into account by any theory of what is possible in social organization of sex roles: first, the biological differences between men and women—in the biological reproduction of children, in relative physical strength, and in biological potential for aggressive (dominant, demanding) behavior; and second, the fact that all known human societies have had a sexual division of labor.

According to the Natural Complement theory, there are traits, capacities, and interests which inhere in men and women simply because of their biological differences, and which thus define what is normal "masculine" and normal "feminine" behavior. Since men are stronger than women, have bodies better adapted for running and throwing, and have higher amounts of the male hormone androgen, which is linked to aggressive behavior,[2] men have a greater capacity for heavy physical labor and for aggressive behavior (such as war). Thus it is natural that men are the breadwinners and play the active role in the production of commodities in society and in defending what the society sees as its interests in war. Since women bear children, it is natural that they have a maternal, nurturing instinct which enables them to be supportive of the needs of children, perceptive and sensitive to their needs, and intuitive in general in their understanding of the needs of people.

The Natural Complement theory about what men and women should do (their moral and spiritual duties, ideal love relations, etc.) is based on this conception of what are the fundamental biologically based differences between men and women. The universal human sexual division of labor is not only natural, but also desirable: men should work, provide for their families, and when necessary, make war; women should stay home, raise their children, and, with their greater emotionality and sensitivity, administer to the emotional needs of their men and children.

The ideal love relationship in the Natural Complement view is a heterosexual relationship in which man and woman complement each other. On this theory, woman needs man, and man, woman; they need each other essentially because together they form a whole being. Each of them is incomplete without the other; neither could meet all their survival and emotional needs alone. The woman needs the man as the active agent, rationally and bravely confronting nature and competitive social life; while the man needs the woman as his emotional guide, ministering to the needs he doesn't know he has himself, performing the same function for the children, and being the emotional nucleus of the family to harmonize all relationships. Love between man and woman is the attraction of complements, each being equally powerful and competent in his or her own sphere—man in the world, woman in the home—but each incompetent in the sphere of the other and therefore incomplete without the other.

The validity of the Natural Complement theory rests on the claim that there are some natural instincts (drives and abilities) inherent in men and women that are so powerful that they will determine the norm of masculine and feminine behavior for men and women under any conceivable cultural and economic conditions. That is, these natural instincts will determine not only what men and women can do well, but also what will be the most desirable (individually satisfying and socially productive) for them.

Even strong proponents of the Natural Complement theory have been uneasy with the evidence that in spite of "natural" differences between men and women, male and female sex roles are not inevitable. Not only are there always individual men and women whose abilities and inclinations make them exceptions to the sexual stereotypes in any particular society, but there is also a wide cross-cultural variation in just what work is considered masculine or feminine. Thus, although all known societies indeed do have a sexual division of labor, the evidence is that what behavior is considered masculine and what feminine is *learned* through socialization rather than mandated through biological instincts. So, for example, child care is said by the proponents of the Natural Complement theory to be women's work, supposedly on the grounds that women have a natural maternal instinct that men lack, due to women's biological role in reproduction. And it is true that in the vast majority of societies in the sexual division of labor women do bear a prime responsibility for child care. However, there are some societies where that is not so. The Arapesh have both mother and father play an equally strong nurturant role.[3] A case of sex-role reversal in child care would be the fabled Amazons, in whose society those few men allowed to survive past infancy reared the children. In the case of the Amazons, whose historical existence may never be conclusively proved, what is important for the purposes of our argument is not the question of whether such a culture actually existed. Rather, insofar as it indicated that an alternative sexual division of labor was possible, the existence of the myth of the Amazon culture in early Western civilizations was an ongoing challenge to the Natural Complement theory.

It is not only the sexual division of labor in child care that varies from society to society, but also other social tasks. Natural Complement theorists are fond of arguing that because men are physically stronger than women and more aggressive, it is a natural division of labor for men to do the heavy physical work of society as well as that of defense and war. However, in practice, societies have varied immensely in the ways in which heavy physical work is parceled out. In some African societies, women do all the heavy work of carrying wood and water, and in most South American countries Indian men and women share these physical chores. In Russia, women do the heavy manual labor involved in construction jobs, while men do the comparatively light (but higher-status) jobs of running the machinery.[4] In predominantly agricultural societies, women's work overlaps men's. From early American colonial times, farm women had to be prepared to fight native American Indians and work the land in cooperation with men. Israeli women make as aggressive and dedicated soldiers as Israeli men. Furthermore, if we pick any *one* of the traits supposed to be primarily masculine (e.g., competitiveness, aggressiveness, egotism), we will find not only whole societies of both men *and* women who seem to lack these traits, but also whole societies that exhibit them.[5]

Further evidence that general sex-linked personality traits are learned social roles rather than inevitable biological developments is found in studies done on hermaphrodites.[6] When children who are biological girls, but because of vestigial penises are mistaken for boys, are trained into male sex roles, they develop the cultural traits associated with males in their society and seem to be well adjusted to their roles.

Faced with the variability of the sexual division of labor and the evidence that human beings as social animals develop their self-concept and their sense of values from imitating models in their community rather than from innate biological urges, the Natural Complement theorists fall back on the thesis that complementary roles for men and women, while not inevitable, are desirable. Two examples of this approach are found in the writings of Jean-Jacques Rousseau (in *Émile)* and in the contemporary writer George Gilder (in *Sexual Suicide*).[7] Both of these men are clearly male supremacists in that they feel women ought to be taught to serve, nurture, and support men.[8] What is ironic about their arguments is their belief in the biological inferiority of men, stated explicitly in Gilder and implicitly in Rousseau. Rousseau's train of reasoning suggests that men can't be nurturant and emotionally sensitive the way women can, so if we train women to be capable of abstract reasoning, to be self-interested and assertive, women will be able to do both male and female roles, and what will be left, then, for men to excel at? Gilder feels that men need to be socialized to be the breadwinners for children and a nurturant wife, because otherwise men's aggressive and competitive tendencies would make it impossible for them to cooperate in productive social work.

The desirability of complementary sex roles is maintained from a somewhat different set of premises in Lionel Tiger's book *Men in Groups.*[9] Tiger argues that the earliest sexual division of labor in hunting and gathering societies required men to develop a cooperative division of tasks in order to achieve success in hunting. Therefore, men evolved a biological predisposition toward "male bonding" (banding together into all-male cohort groups) that women lack (presumably because activities like gathering and child care didn't require a cooperative division of tasks that would develop female bonding). Because of this lack of bonding, women are doomed to subjection by men, for this biological asset of men is a trait necessary for achieving political and social power.

It is hard to take these arguments seriously. Obviously, they are biased toward what would promote male interests, and give little consideration to female interests. Also, they reject an androgynous ideal for human development, male and female, merely on the presumption that biological lacks in either men or women make it an unattainable ideal. It simply flies in the face of counter-evidence (for example, single fathers in our society) to argue as Gilder does that men will not be providers and relate to family duties of socializing children unless women center their life around the nurturing of men. And to argue as Tiger does that women cannot bond ignores not only the present example of the autonomous women's movement, but also ethnographic examples of women acting as a solidarity group in opposing men. The women of the Ba-Ila in southern Africa may collectively refuse to work if one has a grievance against a man.[10] A more likely theory of bonding seems to be that it is not biologically based, but learned through the organization of productive and reproductive work.

III. HISTORICAL MATERIALIST EXPLANATIONS OF SEX ROLES

Even if we reject the Natural Complement theory's claims that sex roles are either inevitable or desirable, we still have to explain the persistence, through most known societies, of a sexual division of labor and related sexual stereotypes of masculine and feminine behavior. This is due, I shall maintain, to patriarchal power relations between men and women based initially on men's biological advantages in two areas: that women are the biological reproducers of children, and that men as a biological caste are, by and large, physically stronger than women.[11] As Shulamith Firestone argues in *The Dialectic of Sex* and Simone de Beauvoir suggests in *The Second Sex*, the fact that women bear children from their bodies subjects them to the physical weaknesses and constraints that pregnancy and childbirth involve. Being incapacitated for periods of time makes them dependent on men (or at least the community) for physical survival in a way not reciprocated by men. Breast-feeding children, which in early societies continued until the children were five or six years old, meant that women could not hunt or engage in war. Men have both physical and social advantages over women because of their biological reproductive role and the fact that allocating child-rearing to women is the most socially efficient division of reproductive labor in societies with scarce material resources. Thus, in social situations in which men come to perceive their interests to lie in making women subservient to them, men have the edge in a power struggle based on sexual caste.

It is important to note at this point, however, that these biological differences between men and women are only *conditions* which may be *used* against women by men in certain economic and political organizations of society and in social roles. They are like *tools* rather than mandates. A tool is only justified if you agree with both the tool's efficiency and the worth of the task that it is being used for, given other available options in achieving the task. In a society with few material resources and no available means of birth control, the most efficient way of ensuring the reproduction of the next generation may be the sexual division of labor in which women, constantly subject to pregnancies, do the reproductive work of breast-feeding and raising the children, while the men engage in hunting, trading, and defense. In a society like ours, on the other hand, where we have the technology and means to control births, feed babies on formula food, and combat physical strength with weapons, the continuation of the sexual division of labor can no longer be justified as the most efficient mode for organizing reproductive work.

It seems that we should look for a social explanation for the continued underdevelopment and unavailability of the material resources for easing women's reproductive burden. This lack is due, I maintain, to a social organization of the forces of reproduction that perpetuates the sexual division of labor at home and in the job market, and thus benefits the perceived interests of men, not women.

The two biological disadvantages of women, relative male strength and the female role in biological reproduction, explain the persistence of the sexual division of labor and the sexual stereotypes based on this. Variations in the stereotypes seem to relate fairly directly to the power women have relative to men in the particular society. This, in turn, depends on the mode of production of the society and whether or not women's reproductive work of raising children is in conflict with their gaining any power in the social relations of production.

There are disagreements between anthropological theorists as to whether early human history contained matriarchal societies, in which bloodlines and property were traced through the maternal side and in which women had the edge over men in political and economic power. Early theorists like Engels and Morgan[12] argue that the social organization of the family and women's power in society is directly related to women's role in production. In primitive hunting-and-gathering and agricultural societies, organization of production is communal and tribal. Women have a central role in production and reproduction, there is no separation of productive work from home and reproductive work, and bloodlines are matrilineal. Moreover, Engels uses examples like the Iroquois Indians, and Bachofen, myths of powerful goddesses, to argue that these societies were not just matrilineal but also matriarchal. According to Engels' theory, the "world-historical defeat of the female sex" came when the mode of production changed to an animal-herding economy, and the sexual division of labor thus gave men control over production and over any surplus. Men thus gained political and economic power over women, whose productive and reproductive work was concentrated on production for use in the home rather than for exchange.

Engels' theory is somewhat too simple. It doesn't sufficiently account for the fact that in *any* non-communal mode of production, the ability to control biological reproduction (progeny, future labor power) is a material power to be struggled for, and that there will be a dialectical struggle to control both production and reproduction in all but the most simple tribal societies.[13] It also doesn't take into account the possibility that even in communal modes of production there may be patriarchal power relations between men and women caused by male fear of women's biological ability to reproduce. This may result in "womb-envy," and in male attempts to compensate for women's reproductive power by setting up male-dominated areas in economic, political, and religious relations.[14]

Whatever the origin of the power struggle between men and women to control reproduction, the fact seems to be that the degree of a woman's oppression in a society is related to the amount of power she has at any particular historical period in the relations of reproduction in the family as well as the relations of production in society. Her oppression is this relative to her class position as well as to her power in relation to men in her family.

There is no easy formula by which to determine the amount of power women have by simply looking at how much productive work and child care they do relative to men in a certain historical period. What is important is not the *amount* of work done, but the control a woman has over her work and the kind of independence this control offers her in the case of actual or potential conflicts with men over how the work should be done. Thus, although American slave women did as much productive work as slave men, and were almost totally responsible for the child care not only for their own children but for those of the plantation owner as well, slave women had no control over this work. Their children could be sold away from them, and they could be brutally punished if they refused to do the work assigned them by their masters. The lady of the plantation, on the other hand, did little productive work. She was more in a managerial position, usually responsible for managing the health care, clothing, and food of the slaves. She usually had little say in economic decisions about the plantation, since she was not considered a joint owner. On the other hand, the Victorian sexual division of labor and the Cult of True Womanhood gave the wealthy white woman almost total control over her children in decisions about child-rearing. Relative to her husband, all in all, she had less power; relative to her female slave she had more; and her female slave in turn had more power than the male slave because of her central role in child-rearing and the greater likelihood that fathers rather than mothers would be sold away from children.

IV. THE SOCIAL ARTICULATION OF THE NATURAL COMPLEMENT THEORY

If we look at the beliefs of different societies about the proper roles for men and women, we note that these beliefs vary widely. We also see that societies always tend to appeal to the Natural Complement theory to back up their socially relative allocations of sex roles. The question arises, then: why, in the light of this obvious social variation, do people *persist* in clinging to the belief that there are inherent natural roles for men and women?

It would be simplistic to maintain that the ideology of sex roles directly reflects the degree of women's power in relation to men at a given historical period in a society. The Medieval religious view of women was extremely low,[15] yet there is evidence that women had more power than the simple reflective view of ideology would lead us to believe. In fact, there were women who were sheriffs, innkeepers, and managers of large households. The elevation of the Virgin Mary as the ideal woman on a pedestal seems to contradict the other elements in the Medieval religious view of women, and, indeed, it should make us wary of assuming a one-to-one correlation between ideology and reality. So, for example, 19th-century Americans placed women on a pedestal where they were considered morally superior to men; but this, ironically, was in an economic, legal, and political context where they had less power than their Puritan ancestors.[16] Middle-class women had no role in commodity production, which had become the dominant mode of production in the 19th century. Women could not own property if they were married, nor receive an education, nor hold political office, nor vote. Their husbands had complete legal control over children in case of divorce.

There is a more plausible way to understand how the ideology of sex roles is connected to the actual social and historical roles of men and women. Sex-role ideologies mystify the existing power relations between men and women and economic classes. This mystification justifies the social and economic roles of two dominant groups: men as a caste, on the one hand, and the dominant economic class on the other.

If we look at 19th-century America, we see the prevailing ideology, which held that women are too frail, "moral," and emotional to take part in commodity production (the amoral, competitive world of business). This ideology ignored the reality of black slave women, treated the same as male slaves and forced to do field work under brutal conditions. It ignored immigrant women, who worked long hours in crowded factories under conditions that caused many sicknesses and deaths. And it ignored farm women, who continued production for use on the farm. These working women made up the majority of the female population, yet the reality of their productive role was overlooked.

Why? A number of factors seem to be at work here. All end by supporting the interests and maintaining the status-quo power relations of the white male bourgeoisie. The first factor was the need to pacify bourgeois wives, whose role in production had evaporated but who were crucial to maintaining the system by lending emotional support and being subservient to their husbands, and by training their children, the future owners and controllers of capital. There was also a need for the bourgeois male to justify his position of dominance over his wife in legal, political, and financial matters. Second, the hierarchical control that the bourgeois male enjoyed over men of the lower classes was seen as inevitable (after all, it is masculine nature to be competitive and avaricious, and may the best man win!). Third, lower-class working women were thought to be fallen women, degraded and unnatural because of their role in production, and this conveniently made them free targets for bourgeois men (with their "natural" sexual appetites) to lure into prostitution. Finally, as production became more alienating, hierarchical, and competitive, working-class men as well needed the haven of women's emotional support and also the male dominance that being the breadwinner allowed them. As a result, both the men and the women of the working class struggled to achieve the ideal complementary sex-role relationships of woman-at-home/man-as-breadwinner that the Cult of True Womanhood assumed.

V. CONCLUSIONS ABOUT THE NATURAL COMPLEMENT THEORY

We have discussed several different views of the "natural" sex differences between men and women prevalent in different historical periods. When we observe the shift in ideology as to what constitutes "true" female and male nature, we note that the shift has nothing to do with the further scientific discovery of biological differences between men and women. It seems rather to correlate to changes in the relation between men's and women's roles in production and reproduction, and to what serves the interests of the dominant male economic class. Given this fact of its ideological role, the Natural Complement theory, and any other static universal theory of what the "natural relationship" of man to woman should be, loses credibility.

Instead, it seems more plausible to assume that human nature is plastic and moldable, and that women and men develop their sexual identities, their sense of self, and their motivations through responding to the social expectations placed upon them. They develop the skills and personality traits necessary to carry out the productive and reproductive roles available to them in their sociohistorical context, given their sex, race, ethnic identity, and class background.

If we wish to develop a realistic ideal for human development, then, we cannot take the existing traits that differentiate men from women in this society as norms for behavior. Neither can we expect to find an ideal in some biological male and female substratum after we strip away all the socialization processes we go through to develop our egos. Rather, with the present-day women's movement, we should ask: what traits are desirable and possible to teach people in order for them to reach their full individual human potential? And how would our society have to restructure its productive and reproductive relations in order to allow people to develop in this way?

VI. AN IDEAL LOVE RELATIONSHIP

One argument for the development of androgynous personalities (and the accompanying destruction of the sexual division of labor in production and reproduction) is that without such a radical change in male and female roles an ideal love relationship between the sexes is not possible. The argument goes like this. An ideal love between two mature people would be love between equals. I assume that such an ideal is the only concept of love that is historically compatible with our other developed ideals of political and social equality. But, as Shulamith Firestone argues,[17] an equal love relationship requires the vulnerability of each partner to the other. There is today, however, an unequal balance of power in male-female relationships. Contrary to the claims of the Natural Complement theory, it is not possible for men and women to be equal while playing the complementary sex roles taught in our society. The feminine role makes a woman less equal, less powerful, and less free than the masculine role makes men. In fact, it is the emotional understanding of this lack of equality in love relations between men and women which increasingly influences feminists to choose lesbian love relationships.

Let us consider the vulnerabilities of women in a heterosexual love relationship under the four classifications Juliet Mitchell gives for women's roles:[18] production, reproduction, socialization of children, and sexuality.

1. *Women's role in production.* In the United States today, 42 percent of women work, and about 33 percent of married women work in the wage-labor force. This is much higher than the 6 percent of women in the wage-labor force around the turn of the century, and higher than in other industrialized countries. Nonetheless, sex-role socialization affects women's power in two important ways. First, because of job segregation by sex into part-time and low-paying jobs, women, whether single or married, are at an economic disadvantage in comparison with men when it comes to supporting themselves. If they leave their husbands or lovers, they drop to a lower economic class, and many have to go on welfare. Second, women who have children and who also work in the wage-labor force have two jobs, not one: the responsibility for the major part of child-raising and housework, as well as the outside job. This keeps many housewives from seeking outside jobs, and makes them economically dependent on their husbands. Those who do work outside the home expend twice as much energy as the man and are less secure. Many women who try to combine career and motherhood find that the demands of both undermine their egos because they don't feel that they can do both jobs adequately.[19]

2. *Women's role in reproduction.* Although women currently monopolize the means of biological reproduction, they are at a disadvantage because of the absence of free contraceptives, adequate health care, and free legal abortions. A man can enjoy sex without having to worry about the consequences the way a woman does if a mistake occurs and she becomes pregnant. Women have some compensation in the fact that in the United States today they are favored legally over the father in their right to control of the children in case of separation or divorce. But this legal advantage (a victory won by women in the early 20th century in the ongoing power struggle between the sexes for control of children, i.e. control over social reproduction) does not adequately compensate for the disadvantages to which motherhood subjects one in this society.

3. *Women's role in socialization: as wife and mother.* The social status of women, and hence their self-esteem, is measured primarily in terms of how successful they are in their relationships as lovers, wives, and mothers. Unlike men, who learn that their major social definition is success in work, women are taught from childhood that their ultimate goal is love and marriage. Women thus have more invested in a love relationship than men, and more to lose if it fails. The "old maid" or the "divorcee" is still an inferior status to be pitied, while the "swinging bachelor" is rather envied.

The fact that men achieve self- and social definition from their work means that they can feel a lesser commitment to working out problems in a relationship. Furthermore, men have more options for new relationships than do women. The double standard in sexuality allows a man to have affairs more readily than his wife. Ageism is a further limitation on women: an older man is considered a possible lover by both younger and older women, but an older woman, because she is no longer the "ideal" sex object, is not usually considered a desirable lover by either male peers or by younger men.

A woman's role as mother places her in a more vulnerable position than the man. Taking care of children and being attentive to their emotional needs is very demanding work. Many times it involves conflicts between the woman's own needs and the needs of the child. Often it involves conflict and jealousy between husband and children for her attention and emotional energy. It is the woman's role to harmonize this conflict, which she often does at the expense of herself, sacrificing her private time and interests in order to provide support for the projects of her husband and children.

No matter how devoted a parent a father is, he tends to see his time with the children as play time, not as work time. His job interests and hobbies take precedence over directing his energy to children. Thus he is more independent than the woman, who sees her job as making husband and children happy. This is the sort of job that is never completed, for there are always more ways to make people happy. Because a woman sees her job to be supporting her husband and mothering her children, the woman sees the family as her main "product." This makes her dependent on their activities, lives, and successes for her own success, and she lives vicariously through their activities. But as her "product" is human beings, when the children leave, as they must, to live independent lives, middle age brings an end to her main social function. The woman who has a career has other problems, for she has had to support her husband's career over hers wherever there was a conflict, because she knows male egos are tied up with success and "making it" in this competitive society. Women's egos, on the other hand, are primed for failure. Successful women, especially successful women with unsuccessful husbands, are considered not "true" women, but rather as deviants, "castrating bitches," "ballbusters," and "masculine women." For all these reasons, a woman in a love relationship with a man is geared by the Natural Complement view of herself as a woman to put her interests last, to define herself in terms of husband and children, and therefore to be more dependent on them than they are on her.

A woman is also vulnerable in her role as mother because there are limited alternatives if, for example, she wishes to break off her relationship with the father of her children. As a mother, her social role in bringing up children is defined as more important, more essential for the well-being of the children than the man's. Therefore, she is expected to take the children to live with her, or else she is considered a failure as a mother. But the life of a divorced or single mother with children in a nuclear-family-oriented society is lonely and hard: she must now either do two jobs without the companionship of another adult, in a society where jobs for women are inadequate, or she must survive on welfare or alimony with a reduced standard of living. When this is the alternative, is it any wonder that mothers are more dependent on maintaining a relationship—even when it is not satisfying—than the man is?

4. *Women's role in sexuality.* A woman's sexual role is one in which she is both elevated by erotic romanticism and deflated to being a mere "cunt"—good for release of male sexual passions but interchangeable with other women. Because women play a subordinate role in society and are not seen as equal agents or as equally productive, men must justify a relationship with a particular woman by making her something special, mystifying her, making her better than other women. In fact, this idealization doesn't deal with her as a real *individual*; it treats her as either a beautiful object or as a mothering, supportive figure.

This idealization of women which occurs in the first stages of infatuation wears off as the couple settles into a relationship of some duration. What is left is the idea of woman as passive sex object whom one possesses and whose job as wife is to give the husband pleasure in bed. Since the woman is not seen as (and doesn't usually see herself as) active in sex, she tends to see sex as a duty rather than as a pleasure. She is not socially expected to take the active kind of initiative (even to the extent of asking for a certain kind of sex play) that would give her a sense of control over her sex life. The idea of herself as a body to be dressed and clothed in the latest media-advertised fashions "to please men" keeps her a slave to fashion and forces her to change her ego-ideal with every change in fashion. She can't see herself as an individual.

VII. ANDROGYNY AS A PROGRESSIVE IDEAL

It is the sexual division of labor in the home and at work that perpetuates complementary sex roles for men and women. In underdeveloped societies with scarce material resources such an arrangement may indeed be the most rational way to allow for the most efficient raising of children and production of goods. But this is no longer true for developed societies. In this age of advanced technology, men's relative strength compared to women's is no longer important, either in war or in the production of goods. The gun and the spinning jenny have equalized the potential role of men and women in both repression and production. And the diaphragm, the pill, and other advances in the technology of reproduction have equalized the potential power of women and men to control their bodies and to reproduce themselves.[20] (The development of cloning would mean that men and women could reproduce without the participation of the opposite sex.)

We have seen how complementary sex roles and their extension to job segregation in wage labor make an ideal love relationship between equals impossible for men and women in our society. The questions that remain are: would the development of androgynous human beings through androgynous sex-role training be possible? If possible, would it allow for the development of equal love relationships? What other human potentials would androgyny allow to develop? And how would society have to be restructured in order to allow for androgynous human beings and equal love relationships?

There is good evidence that human babies are bisexual, and only *learn* a specific male or female identity by imitating and identifying with adult models. This evidence comes from the discovery that all human beings possess both male and female hormones (androgen and estrogen respectively), and also from concepts first developed at length by Freud. Freud argued that heterosexual identity is not achieved until the third stage of the child's sexual development. Sex identity is developed through the resolution of the Oedipus complex, in which the child has to give up a primary attachment to the mother and learn either to identify with, or love, the father. But Shulamith Firestone suggests that this process is not an inevitable one, as Freud presents it to be. Rather, it is due to the power dynamics of the patriarchal nuclear family.[21] Note that, on this analysis, if the sexual division of labor were destroyed, the mechanism that trains boys and girls to develop heterosexual sexual identities would also be destroyed. If fathers and mothers played equal nurturant roles in child-rearing and had equal social, economic, and political power outside the home, there would be no reason for the boy to have to reject his emotional side in order to gain the power associated with the male role. Neither would the girl have to assume a female role in rejecting her assertive, independent side in order to attain power indirectly through manipulation of males. As a sexual identity, bisexuality would then be the norm rather than the exception.

If bisexuality were the norm rather than the exception for the sexual identities that children develop,[22] androgynous sex roles would certainly be a consequence. For, as discussed above, the primary mechanism whereby complementary rather than androgynous sex roles are maintained is through heterosexual training, and through the socialization of needs for love and sexual gratification to the search for a love partner of the opposite sex. Such a partner is sought to complement one in the traits that one has repressed or not developed because in one's own sex such traits were not socially accepted.

VIII. THE ANDROGYNOUS MODEL

I believe that only androgynous people can attain the full human potential possible given our present level of material and social resources (and this only if society is radically restructured). Only such people can have ideal love relationships; and without such relationships, I maintain that none can develop to the fullest potential. Since human beings are social animals and develop through interaction and productive activity with others, such relationships are necessary.

Furthermore, recent studies have shown that the human brain has two distinct functions: one associated with analytic, logical, sequential thinking (the left brain), and the other associated with holistic, metaphorical, intuitive thought (the right brain). Only a person capable of tapping both these sides of him/herself will have developed to full potential. We might call this characteristic of the human brain "psychic bisexuality,"[23] since it has been shown that women in fact have developed skills which allow them to tap the abilities of the right side of the brain more than men, who on the contrary excel in the analytic, logical thought characteristic of the left side. The point is that men and women have the potential for using both these functions, and yet our socialization at present tends to cut us off from one or the other of these parts of ourselves.[24]

What would an androgynous personality be like? My model for the ideal androgynous person comes from the concept of human potential developed by Marx in *Economic and Philosophical Manuscripts*. Marx's idea is that human beings have a need (or a potential) for free, creative, productive activity which allows them to control their lives in a situation of cooperation with others. Both men and women need to be equally active and independent; with an equal sense of control over their lives; equal opportunity for creative, productive activity; and a sense of meaningful involvement in the community.

Androgynous women would be just as assertive as men about their own needs in a love relationship: productive activity outside the home, the right to private time, and the freedom to form other intimate personal and sexual relationships. I maintain that being active and assertive—traits now associated with being "masculine"—are positive traits that all people need to develop. Many feminists are suspicious of the idea of self-assertion because it is associated with the traits of aggression and competitiveness. However, there is no inevitability to this connection: it results from the structural features of competitive, hierarchical economic systems, of which our own (monopoly capitalism) is one example. In principle, given the appropriate social structure, there is no reason why a self-assertive person cannot also be nurturant and cooperative.

Androgynous men would be more sensitive and aware of emotions than sex-role stereotyped "masculine" men are today. They would be more concerned with the feelings of all people, including women and children, and aware of conflicts of interests. Being sensitive to human emotions is necessary to an effective care and concern for others. Such sensitivity is now thought of as a "motherly," "feminine," or "maternal" instinct, but in fact it is a role and skill learned by women, and it can equally well be learned by men. Men need to get in touch with their own feelings in order to empathize with others, and, indeed, to understand themselves better so as to be more in control of their actions.

We have already discussed the fact that women are more vulnerable in a love relationship than men because many men consider a concern with feelings and emotions to be part of the woman's role. Women, then, are required to be more aware of everyone's feelings (if children and third parties are involved) than men, and they are under more pressure to harmonize the conflicts by sacrificing their own interests.

Another important problem with a non-androgynous love relationship is that it limits the development of mutual understanding. In general, it seems true that the more levels people can relate on, the deeper and more intimate their relationship is. The more experiences and activities they share, the greater their companionship and meaning to each other. And this is true for emotional experiences. Without mutual understanding of the complex of emotions involved in an ongoing love relationship, communication and growth on that level are blocked for both people. This means that, for both people, self-development of the sort that could come from the shared activity of understanding and struggling to deal with conflicts will not be possible.

In our society as presently structured, there are few possibilities for men and women to develop themselves through shared activities. Men and women share more activities with members of their own sex than with each other. Most women can't get jobs in our sexist, job-segregated society which allow them to share productive work with men. Most men just don't have the skills (or the time, given the demands of their wage-labor jobs) to understand the emotional needs of children and to share the activity of child-rearing equally with their wives.

How must our society be restructured to allow for the development of androgynous personalities? How can it be made to provide for self-development through the shared activities of productive and reproductive work? I maintain that this will not be possible (except for a small privileged elite) without the development of a democratic socialist society. In such a society no one would benefit from cheap labor (presently provided to the capitalist class by a part-time reserve army of women). Nor would anyone benefit from hierarchical power relationships (which encourage competition among the working class and reinforce male sex-role stereotypes as necessary to "making it" in society).

As society is presently constituted, the patriarchal nuclear family and women's reproductive work therein serve several crucial roles in maintaining the capitalist system. In the family, women do the unpaid work of social reproduction of the labor force (child-rearing). They also pacify and support the male breadwinner in an alienating society where men who are not in the capitalist class have little control of their product or work conditions. Men even come to envy their wives' relatively nonalienated labor in child-rearing rather than dealing with those with the real privilege, the capitalist class. Since those in power relations never give them up without a struggle, it is utopian to think that the capitalist class will allow for the elimination of the sexual division of labor without a socialist revolution with feminist priorities. Furthermore, men in the professional and working classes must be challenged by women with both a class and feminist consciousness to begin the process of change.

In order to eliminate the subordination of women in the patriarchal nuclear family and the perpetuation of sex-role stereotypes therein, there will need to be a radical reorganization of child-rearing. Father and mother must have an equal commitment to raising children. More of the reproductive work must be socialized—for example, by community child care, perhaps with parent cooperatives. Communal living is one obvious alternative which would de-emphasize biological parenthood and allow homosexuals and bisexuals the opportunity to have an equal part in relating to children. The increased socialization of child care would allow parents who are incompatible the freedom to dissolve their relationships without denying their children the secure, permanent loving relationships they need with both men and women. A

community responsibility for child-rearing would provide children with male and female models other than their biological parent—models that they would be able to see and relate to
emotionally.

Not only would men and women feel an equal responsibility to
do reproductive work, they would also expect to do rewarding,
productive work in a situation where they had equal opportunity.
Such a situation would of course require reduced work-weeks for
parents, maternity and paternity leaves, and the development of a
technology of reproduction which would allow women complete
control over their bodies.

As for love relationships, with the elimination of sex roles and
the disappearance, in an overpopulated world, of any biological
need for sex to be associated with procreation, there would be no
reason why such a society could not transcend sexual gender. It
would no longer matter what biological sex individuals had. Love
relationships, and the sexual relationships developing out of them,
would be based on the individual meshing-together of androgynous human beings.

NOTES

1. I owe these thoughts to Jean Elshtain and members of the Valley
   Women's Union in Northampton, Massachusetts, from discussions
   on androgyny.
2. See Roger Brown, *Social Psychology* (New York: Free Press, 1965).
3. For information on the Arapesh and variations in male/female roles
   in primitive societies, see Margaret Mead, *Sex and Temperament*
   (New York: William Morrow, 1963).
4. See "The Political Economy of Women," *Review of Radical Political
   Economics*, Summer 1973.
5. Contrast the Stone Age tribe recently discovered in the Philippines,
   where competition is unknown, with the competitive male and female Dobus from Melanesia. See Ruth Benedict, *Patterns of Culture*
   (Boston: Houghton Mifflin, 1934).
6. See Eleanor E. Maccoby, ed., *The Development of Sex Differences*
   (Stanford, Calif.: Stanford University Press, 1966).
7. George Gilder, *Sexual Suicide* (New York: Bantam Books, 1973).
8. Rousseau says, in a typical passage from *Émile*, "When once it is
   proved that men and women are and ought to be unlike in constitution and in temperament, it follows that their education should be
   different." And on a succeeding page he concludes, "A woman's education must therefore be planned in relation to man. To be pleasing

in his sight, to win his respect and love, to train him in childhood, to tend him in manhood, to counsel and console, to make his life pleasant and happy, these are the duties of woman for all time, and this is what she should be taught while she is young. The further we depart from this principle, the further we shall be from our own good, and all our precepts will fail to secure her happiness or our own" (trans. Barbara Foxley [New York: E. P. Dutton, 1911] pp.326–328).

Gilder's conclusion is as follows: "But at a profounder level the women are tragically wrong. For they fail to understand their own sexual power; and they fail to perceive the sexual constitution of our society, or if they see it, they underestimate its importance to our civilization and to their own interest in order and stability. In general across the whole range of the society, marriage and careers—and thus social order—will be best served if most men have a position of economic superiority over the relevant women in his [sic] community and if in most jobs in which colleagues must work together, the sexes tend to be segregated either by level or function." *Sexual Suicide*, p. 108.

9. Lionel Tiger, *Men in Groups* (New York: Random House, 1969).
10. Edwin W. Smith and Andrew M. Dale, *The Ila-Speaking Peoples of Northern Rhodesia* (London: Macmillan, 1920).
11. It is not simply the fact that men are physically stronger than women which gives them the edge in sexual power relations. It is also women's lesser psychological capacity for violence and aggressiveness. However, this has as much to do with socialization into passive roles from early childhood as it does with any inequality in the amount of the male hormone androgen, which is correlated to aggressive behavior in higher primates. As Simone de Beauvoir points out in *The Second Sex* (New York: Knopf, 1953), male children develop training in aggressive behavior from an early age, while female children are kept from the psychological hardening process involved in physical fights. Feeling that one is by nature submissive will cause one to be submissive; so even women who are equal in strength to men will appear to themselves and to men not to be so.
12. See Friedrich Engels, *The Origin of the Family, Private Property and the State* (New York: International Publishers, 1942); also Lewis Morgan, *Ancient Society*, ed. Eleanor Leacock (New York: World Publishing Co., 1963).
13. Perhaps part of the reason for the solidarity in these societies is due to the meager resources to be struggled for.
14. Karen Horney develops this theory in her book *Feminine Psychology* (New York: W.W. Norton, 1967); as does Eva Figes in *Patriarchal Attitudes* (New York: Stein & Day, 1970). Note the striking difference between Horney's and Tiger's (*op. cit.*) explanations of the phenomenon of male bonding.

15. Catholic Church doctrine maintains a dualism between soul and body. The soul is thought to be rational and spiritual, the valuable part of the self that loves God; while the body is sinful, animal, given to sexual lusts and passions. Women are identified with the body because of their childbearing function, hence with sexuality, evil, and the devil. (The story of Eve in Genesis was used to support this view.) It is women who lead men away from the pure spiritual life and into the evils of sexuality: they are thus inferior beings whose only positive function is the reproduction of children. Even in this role they are merely receptacles, for the theory of reproduction is that woman is the lowly, unclean vessel into which man puts the seed of life.

16. In the Cult of True Womanhood prevalent in America and England in the 19th century, women are thought to be passive and emotional but *not* sexual or tied to the body. Rather, the woman is the moral and spiritual guardian of the male, who is thought to be more naturally sinful than she—avaricious, competitive, self-interested, and imbued with sexual passions. The one sphere, then, in which woman is thought to be naturally skilled is the home and the spiritual education of children and husband.

17. Shulamith Firestone, *The Dialectic of Sex* (New York: William Morrow, 1970), chap. 6.

18. Juliet Mitchell, *Woman's Estate* (New York: Random House, 1971).

19. Socialization into complementary sex roles is responsible not only for job segregation practices' keeping women in low-paid service jobs which are extensions of the supportive work women do in the home as mothers, but also for making it difficult for women to feel confident in their ability to excel at competitive "male-defined" jobs.

20. Thanks to Sam Bowles for this point.

21. Firestone, *op. cit.* The boy and girl both realize that the father has power in the relationship between him and the mother, and that his role, and not the mother's, represents the possibility of achieving economic and social power in the world and over one's life. The mother, in contrast, represents nurturing and emotionality. Both boy and girl, then, in order to get power for themselves, have to reject the mother as a love object—the boy, because he is afraid of the father as rival and potential castrator; and the girl, because the only way as a girl she can attain power is through manipulating the father. So she becomes a rival to her mother for her father's love. The girl comes to identify with her mother and to choose her father and, later, other men for love objects; while the boy identifies with his father, sublimates his sexual attraction to his mother into superego (will power), and chooses mother substitutes, other women, for his love objects.

22. It should be understood here that no claim is being made that bisexuality is more desirable than homo- or heterosexuality. The point is that with the removal of the social mechanisms in the family that

channel children into heterosexuality, there is no reason to suppose that most of them will develop in that direction. It would be more likely that humans with androgynous personalities would be bisexual, the assumption here being that there are no innate biological preferences in people for sexual objects of the same or opposite sex. Rather, this comes to be developed because of emotional connections of certain sorts of personality characteristics with the male and female body, characteristics which develop because of complementary sex-role training, and which would not be present without it.

The other mechanism which influences people to develop a heterosexual identity is the desire to reproduce. As long as the social institution for raising children is the heterosexual nuclear family, and as long as society continues to place social value on biological parenthood, most children will develop a heterosexual identity. Not, perhaps, in early childhood, but certainly after puberty, when the question of reproduction becomes viable. Radical socialization and collectivization of child-rearing would thus have to characterize a society before bisexuality would be the norm not only in early childhood, but in adulthood as well. For the purposes of developing androgynous individuals, however, full social bisexuality of this sort is not necessary. All that is needed is the restructuring of the sex roles of father and mother in the nuclear family so as to eliminate the sexual division of labor there.

23. Charlotte Painter, Afterword to C. Painter and M. J. Moffet, eds., *Revelations: Diaries of Women* (New York: Random House, 1975).

24. It is notable that writers, painters, and other intellectuals, who presumably would need skills of both sorts, have often been misfits in the prevalent complementary sex stereotyping. In fact, thinkers as diverse as Plato (in the *Symposium*) and Virginia Woolf (in *A Room of One's Own*) have suggested that writers and thinkers need to be androgynous to tap all the skills necessary for successful insight.

Lee C. Rice

Homosexuality and the Social Order

I. INTRODUCTION: THE HOMOPHILE MOVEMENT AND CONTEMPORARY SOCIAL PERSPECTIVES

Before the early 1950's the study of homosexuality, from both scientific and socio-cultural perspectives, was almost invariably relegated to rather obscure journals in the social sciences and to more technical sources in the empirical sciences. While scientific studies were most often bent upon the demonstration of rather abstract theories of etiology, more popular and publicly accessible sources were wont to press the subject in an obscure and highly general manner. This is not to dismiss the work of theorists such as Freud, Ellis, Gide, or Adler; but only to insist that the major value of their work was that of turning attention toward the study of homosexuality, rather than of actually proffering any materially adequate theories in their own right. On the crest of this directed scientific interest came Kinsey's 1948 study of male sexual behavior[1], which, for all of its faults, did succeed in strangling the popular myth that homsexuality was an obscure phenomenon affecting a relatively minor segment of the population.

An earlier version of this work was read at the Society for the Philosophy of Sex and Love Meeting of the Pacific Division of the American Philosophical Association at San Diego, March, 1979.

Kinsey's preliminary studies, with their emphasis upon statistical and quantitative elaboration of the very concept of "homosexuality," also succeeded in part in prying loose the concept from the procrustean bed of metaphysical and quasi-theological speculation into which it had been molded by the psychoanalytic school, thus making it fair game for the more scientifically respectable approaches which were in rapid development in sociology and anthropology. This behavioral emphasis even led Kinsey so far as to attempt to define homosexuality in purely behavioral terms—a blind alley which he was not able to pursue consistently himself. Attempting to characterize the homosexual as a person with certain amounts of homosexual experience, while it would be an ideal qualification within a sex-positive environment,[2] is wholly inadequate in a sex-negative environment such as the United States where it is more than likely that social pressure has caused large segments of the homosexual population to encounter greater accession to socially approved heterosexual outlets. Perhaps even more embarassingly, such a taxonomy would also entail a third category of sexuality—neither homosexuality nor heterosexuality, but celibacy. Kinsey later noted that, while taking account of sexual experience, an adequate taxonomy could not overlook "psychosexual reactions"[3]—a euphemism which I shall translate hereafter as "sexual object preference." In somewhat more philosophical jargon, "homosexuality" becomes a disposition term which refers to (possibly unrealized) reactions of a subject under empirically specifiable conditions. This does not entail the reversion of the concept from the quantitative domain to the qualitative ones of psychoanalysis, for it rules out what is perhaps the pivotal concept in the psychiatric obsession with "cause and cure;" the notion of latent homosexuality. If latency meant anything at all, it would be a dispostion toward a condition—in this case a dispositional condition toward sexual object choice, just as "solubilibility" might indicate a disposition toward the disposition of solubility. If we desired to display such a concept in a museum of scientific theories past and justly forgotten, we could call it a second-order disposition, and perhaps display it with the "dormitive power" account in chemistry.

The move toward behaviorally specifiable criteria is, however, only one move in the right direction; for one's bedpartner, we are rightly informed by the social sciences, is only partially a function of specific sexual-object goals, a heavy residue being determined by emotive, cultural, and certainly aesthetic factors operative within the person. The concept of "lifestyle," though a bit vague at this stage of investigation within the social sciences, provides initially what is needed by way of conceptual elaboration. Sexual object choice, rather than a determinant, is now seen as being determined by a set of in-principle specifiable values and attitudes. This is not, incidentally, to beg the probably unanswerable philosophical questions of *free* choice: viewing sexual object choice in terms of lifestyle commits one only to seeing it in causal relationship with other choices and values, and does not immediately raise the question of the casual antecedents of those choices taken collectively. Because determinism is a respectable position within contemporary social science, however, it is safe to say that the homosexual lifestyle is no more (nor less) a free option than is the heterosexual lifestyle; and, if the contemporary psychologist is correct, either option is determined at a fairly early stage in the development of the organism.[4] Having widened the term "homosexual" to cover these dimensions distinct from, but causally related to, sexual object choice, it is also best to follow many writers within the gay movement in revising the term in order to de-emphasize somewhat the purely sexual aspect of it. The term "homophile" provides the desired widening.

In what follows the term "homophile," or "gay" (taken as synonymous), will denote a lifestyle revolving about the love of a person or persons who happen to be of the same sex. This love may, and indeed should, culminate in sexual activity as one of the deeper expressions of that love; but it is certainly not limited to that channel. Indeed the pioneering studies of Masters and Johnson[5] indicate that, in terms of its basic physiological components and degree of intensity, homophile sexuality is little different from its heterosexual counterpart. It can be argued that undue emphasis, especially in the popular press, has been placed on the "what does one do in bed" aspect of homophilia; for the answer is "pretty much the same as anyone else." The Playboy Survey reports that between fifty and eighty-three percent of the male heterosexual population have engaged in oral sexuality; and well over a quarter of married couples under thirty-five now engage regularly in anal sexuality, yesteryear's "unspeakable crime against nature."[6] Favorable attitudes toward these are showing even greater gains in incidence.[7]

With changes in the scientific interpretation of homophilia have come, at an expectedly slower pace, marked changes in social attitude; and, while it would be a mistake to view the homophile lifestyle as socially accepted in the United States, a much greater tolerance is indeed the order of the day. Tolerance, one should note, is an attitude of the superior toward the inferior. The Weinberg and Williams study of male homosexuals[8] reports that just under fifty percent of the American population still finds homosexuality very obscene and vulgar, a marked difference from the readings of 5.4% for the Netherlands and 11.8% for Denmark; and it is safe to say that acceptance rather than toleration has a proportionately smaller incidence in the three societies. Moreover, though social persecution of gays has to some extent decreased, it has not done so in proportion to the increased incidence of toleration. This is probably due to the fact that the police, clergy, and psychiatric professions (the three interest groups most supportive of conventional *status quo* throughout the social order) have been even less supportive of attitudinal change here than in the related areas of black and women's rights. The homophile thus remains, to a great extent legally and to an even greater extent socially, an outcast in his society; though, having discovered his gayness, he or she does have a wider range of options with respect to revealing his stigma than is open to other stigmatized segments of American society. What is distinctive for the homophile—in contrast to the woman, the Black, the Chicano, and members of other stigmatized groups in our society, is his or her possibility of remaining invisible at will. Such an invisibility, for which our society provides tremendous social and economic rewards, is purchased at momentous personal costs: loneliness, depression, anxiety, low self-acceptance, and a high distrust in others. The Weinberg and Williams study[9] shows a remarkable mathematical proportion from the degree of "passing" (as this invisibility is called among gays) to the debilitating socio-psychological correlates which result from it. Some psychiatrists, once the great defenders of repression and invisibility, have gone so far as to conclude that, with a view toward psychological health and adjustment, to risk loss of some economic and social benefits entailed in coming out represents the best option.[10]

The removal of homosexuality in 1974 from its official list of pathologies or diseases by the American Psychiatric Association[11] may eventually remove some of the obstacles to self-declaration or coming out, while more positive assistance is available to the individual gay through the proliferation of homophile organizations throughout the United States. While only a dozen years ago Donald Cantor[12] reported about fifty of these organizations operative within the United States, their number has grown rapidly into the hundreds throughout the country.[13] An even reasonably detailed account of their development would require nothing less than a book, while surveys of the movement are readily available in the existing literature.[14] Their general goals to date have been dual in nature: first, providing assistance (social, psychological, legal, and economic) to the individual gay seeking his own self-identity within a hostile society, and secondly, educational activities aimed outside the gay community at legal and social reform.

Much of the writing within the movement to date has been, quite understandably, negative in tone and immediate in direction; critiques of psychiatry,[15] the existing legal order,[16] and religious oppression[17] have abounded. More positively and internally, writers have reflected on the uniqueness of the gay experience and upon self-discovery and assessment.[18]. The parallel to the earlier black movement and the contemporary feminist movement is fairly close, if somewhat roughhewn: external attention was directed to immediately recognizable forms of oppression and stigmatization, and internal attention was directed to reflection and personal discovery. Just as at the beginning of the black movement, black writers and apologists tended to ape the middle-class white Anglo-Saxon values of their oppressors, desiring only to be integrated into the existing social order, so of late there has been a tendency on the part of these writers to emphasize the need for a change or revolution in the entire social order. The black person and the gay person, being virtually on the outside of American society looking in, are in particularly good intellectual positions for objective assessment of the social order, and for indicating the directions of change, and sometimes even the manner of their implementation. For, let there be no mistake about it, change there will be; and our only choice as social agents (and, it should be added, as philosophers) is whether these ongoing changes should be blind and unforeseen or, within the limits of the possible, under the intelligent control of reflective insight into their causes and directions.

Since the homophile movement is younger than the black movement, it appears natural that integral social criticism and theory has not yet figured heavily as a preoccupation among intellectuals within it. One can discern, however, a cautious tendency in this direction today; and one extensive study, Dennis Altman's *Homosexual: Oppression and Liberation*,[19] does represent a detailed theoretical framework by a competent sociologist operating within the homophile tradition. In what follows, I should like to offer a philosophical analysis and evaluation of Altman's already theoretical account, preceded first by a sketch of the historical framework in which its author claims that it evolved. Then I shall attempt to briefly compare some of Altman's claims with some recent literature which is evolving outside the gay subculture. Finally, I offer a critical but sympathetic assessment of the framework itself.

II. HOMOPHILE LIBERATION AND THE POLYMORPHOUS WHOLE

Intellectuals within any liberation movement usually emphasize the claim that liberation, as opposed to the simple absence of oppression, will require a new morality, a radically altered social order, and perhaps even a revised concept of human nature. The so-called New Left, for instance, found much of the theoretical framework required to support these claims in the writings of Marcuse, especially his *Reason and Revolution*, and to some extent also in his *One-Dimensional Man* and *An Essay on Liberation*. Marcuse's *Eros and Civilization*, subtitled "A Philosophical Inquiry into Freud,"[20] though widely read by social philosophers and psychologists, has received surprisingly little attention to date from writers within the gay tradition, with the exception of Altman, who concedes indebtedness to Marcuse's analysis of sexual repression (p. 70).

Though omnipresent in all western societies, sexual repression is probably nowhere stronger than in the United States. This is partially due to the strong fundamentalist tradition here (which also may account for the current boon in pornography[21]); for the notion of sexuality as secretive, dirty, and guilt-ridden is part and parcel of this tradition. Theological moorings of sexuality to the family and to childbearing constitute another repressive factor, and are illustrative of a general utilitarian view of sexuality which negates all sexual urges other then those which are procreative, genital, and heterosexual. In direct contrast to all of these views of sexuality was Freud's claim that the human infant is "polymorphous perverse" at birth [in Altman's terms, "that the infant enjoys an undifferentiated ability to take sexual pleasure from all parts of the body." (p. 72)]. While Freud posited the general bisexual nature of the sexual drive, he also introduced a linear concept of sexual development: heterosexuality became the mature stage, while homosexuality was interpreted as a condition of arrested development.[22] It is important to note that, unlike the descriptive claim of polymorphous perversity, the second developmental claim is normative in structure and cannot be supported by any empirical evidence offered on behalf of the first. Thinkers within the tradition of sexual libertarianism, who generally accept the first and ignore the second, are guilty of no inconsistency thereby.

To explain the mechanism of sexual repression, Freud advanced an argument partly anthropological in scope. Repression stems from the domination of the father; and the patriarchal family accounts for the inferiority of women as well as the channeling of sexual activity into forms which are socially approved. Freud later[23] tended to associate this patriarchal authority with the rise of religion and the triumph of monotheism. A related account of sexual repression may see the cause of it in religion, thus preserving the basic elements of Freud's account while reversing their causal connectibility.

Since the patriarchal family antedates all but the most primitive of economic systems, only a primitive form of Marxism would attempt to see the development of capitalism as the cause of repression; though one need not be a Marxist to see the rise of capitalism and industrialization, both of which required considerable repression for the sake of economic development, as strongly contributory to it. This is essentially the direction taken by Marcuse:

The organization of sexuality reflects the basic features of the performance principle and its organization of society. Freud emphasizes the aspect of centralization. It is especially operative in the "unification" of the various objects of the partial instincts into one libidinal object of the opposite sex, and in the establishment of genital supremacy. In both cases, the unifying process is repressive—that is to say, the partial instincts do not develop freely into a "higher" stage of gratification which preserves their objectives, but are cut off and reduced to subservient functions. This process achieves the socially necessary desexualization of the body: the libido becomes concentrated in one part of the body, leaving most of the rest free for use as the instrument of labor.[24]

The performance principle is, in Marcuse's jargon, a particular condition of repression required for the rise of capitalism; while the reduction to subservient functions of the sexual drive represents the negation of the principle of polymorphous perversity. One should also note that Marcuse himself never makes it clear whether sexual repression causes economic subordination or vice versa. This is an important ambiguity, since Marcuse's concept of liberation requires a return to polymorphous perversity through the negation of the principles of unification and function-subservience:

> The body in its entirety would become an object of cathexis, a thing to be enjoyed—an instrument of pleasure. This change in the value and scope of libidinal relations would lead to a disintegration of the institutions in which the private interpersonal relations have been organized, particularly the monogamic and partiarchal family.[25]

Liberation will thus enlarge the field and objective of the sexual instinct to become integral to the life of the entire organism. Marcuse refers to this as the "transformation of sexuality into Eros;"[26] though he notes that it constitutes a further departure from Freud, whose tendency was that of viewing Eros as a largely biological instinct.

Altman notes (p. 77) that in this respect the role of the homophile is analogous to that of the critical philosopher: anatomy, having denied him (or her) the navel-to-navel coupling of men/women, has compelled him to explore the realities of erotic experience and its extension beyond the experience of many heterosexuals. Further (p. 78), because homophilia cannot find its justification in religiously sanctioned utilitarian sexuality (procreative), it represents an assertion of human sexuality free of these utilitarian ends; and it is this very freedom which the author intimates may explain the common disgust or horror associated with it.

Repression of polymorphous perversity in society entails both the removal of the erotic from all aspects of life except those which are exclusively sexual and the denial of the inherent bisexuality of the sex drive itself. This second consequence, for Altman, is closely connected to the development of sexual polarization, which includes the concepts of "masculine" and "feminine" which dominate our thought, and the correlative roles which dominate our practice. Just as the entire structure of the social order operates to channel sexual instinct into socially approved norms, so these norms themselves are to be applied within well defined roles. Altman's positive account of the origin of sex roles is thus universalistic in structure, since they are seen as arising out of society's implementation of certain utilitarian social structures. He also suggests a particularistic account (pp. 81–82) in terms of the individual coercion to act the role, as in the socially imbued fear of homosexuality in any of its forms. Other writers within the gay tradition have often linked this fear, homophobia or the fear of homoeroticism, with the violence, repulsion, and irrational public attitudes toward homosexuality which are omnipresent in American life.

Altman's quasi-Marcusian framework is highly general and speculative in nature, making it almost impossible to bring empirical evidence to bear upon it in any direct fashion; though its general conclusions relating to sexual polarization are capable of at least some very indirect empirical testing. In its handling of the patriarchal dominance, the framework would lead us to expect a high correlation, for instance, between homophobia and negative attitudes toward feminism. MacDonald did test two competing explanations for homophobia: a conservative sexual morality, and a need to support a double standard between the sexes. The data received did offer overwhelming statistical support for the latter explanation.[27] Altman's view of the relation between economic functionalism and sexual role is also supported by Smith's 1971 sampling, which indicated that homophobia was directly proportional to authoritarianism, status consciousness, and conceptual rigidity.[28] Many of these results have also been replicated in the more detailed sampling procedures of MacDonald and Games,[29] who conclude that negative attitudes toward homosexuality are causally related to a desire to preserve the dominant-passive roles which are traditional components of the heterosexual relationship. Two further implications of this last-mentioned study also deserve attention. The first, which is relevant to the gay liberation movement itself, is that " . . . increased visibility of 'masculine' male homosexuals may do much to further the success of that movement."[30] Secondly, the rather speculative claim, often asserted in the popular press, that the breakup of sex roles and increased sexual aggressiveness on the part of women will entail an increase in male homosexuality, is not confirmed by these data. The Playboy Survey claimed that in fact the reverse might be the case: decreasing reliance upon sexual roles might be leading to decreased incidence of homosexuality.[31] These results, whose empirical foundation is at this stage open to question, neither confirm nor disconfirm Altman's model, which entails that the homosexual, no less than the exclusive heterosexual, will vanish as an effect of liberation and erotization. I shall return to this consequence of Altman's model at a later stage.

It is basic to the general psychoanalytic conceptualization which Altman takes over from Marcuse that repressed desires and tendencies will find other modes of expressing themselves. Freud himself comes close to deriving his entire theory of civilization from this concept of sublimation, and Marcuse utilizes it at great length in providing a causal account of the trilogy of aggression, depersonalization, and alienation.[32] Despite the popular undercurrent of humor regarding repressed homosexuality which is held to account for a great number of social phenomena, there has been little exploration by social scientists and philosophers of the enormous amount of social energy expended in the repression of homophilia and of homosexual feelings generally. Altman sees as no coincidence the fact that Protestant Anglo-Saxon cultures are notorious both for the repression of homoerotic tendencies and also for the prevalence of overt and exclusive homosexuality: "Men are so concerned to deny any homosexual feelings that they tend to adopt extreme postures of aggression so as to reject feelings of tenderness or love as well as sexual desire for each other" (p.85). In his analysis both the male bonding instinct and the inhibition of tenderness and warmth among men are the results of this repression, especially in American society.

The argument that violence within the present social order is often the effect of sexual repression, frustration, and insecurity has found considerable support in contemporary literature and film. In the first case one thinks of Norman Mailer's novel *Why Are We in Vietnam?*, a book which is obsessed with masculinity; and, though Mailer himself regards homosexuality as the greatest of threats to be mastered by contemporary man, he appears to be no less aware of the price to be paid for this battle.[33] Adopting a form of this argument, Altman gives it a typically dialectical turn. The more men in America are drawn together by social and sexual instinct, the more do they need to repress their feelings. This entails an undercurrent of violence among men (the spirit of competition and amalgamation), which is then turned outwards as an expression of male superiority: toward foreigners (as perhaps in Vietnam), toward women (as in male attitudes toward the feminist movement), and toward other "inferiors" (such as blacks). Thus, Altman writes (p. 89) about this phenomenon:

The argument that men fight each other because they are unable to love each other is a version of Marcuse's formulation that aggression results from a failure to give sexuality free reign. I find this argument persuasive, in part because of my observation of homosexuals. Violence seems on the whole remarkably absent among self-accepting homosexuals, while particularly prevalent among those who have strong homosexual desires that they seek to repress.

This inverse proportionality between violence and self-accepted gayness has been well documented empirically, even in the case of criminal actions within American society.[34] Suzannah Lessard, viewing both the gay and feminist movements in perspective,[35] offers a particularly strong version of the claim:

Much of the physical violence that wracks the country is committed by males between 15 and 25—the period in which traditionally a boy proves his manhood. The masculinity curse also drives the less gory but more common psychological violence, which pervades business meetings, dinner parties, and the home—as people pierce, jab, and scrape to wrest some form of triumph and have it saluted. . . . The masculinity complex lives in our national throne room. The last three presidents have been nearly obsessed with proving their toughness; presidents have bled the nation white to keep from backing down in Vietnam—to keep from looking chicken in backbone warfare.[36]

The thematic connection between masculinity and violence has also been well argued by authors within the feminist movement, particularly by Kate Millett in *Sexual Politics*, a work which chooses to ignore both male and female homophilia.[37]

One fact which must be confronted by the above causal formulations, whether they are made within the feminist or the gay traditions, is the contemporary social move toward sexual libertarianism or permissiveness coupled with no apparent decrease in social violence. Society appears at the same time both more repressive and more tolerant, a fact which Altman, following once again a lead in Marcuse,[38] attempts to explain through the concept of "repressive tolerance" (p. 96). While much of the Western world is in the process of abolishing legal restrictions aimed at gays, the resultant apparent freedom is one that is to be manipulated into acceptable social channels dictated by norms within the present social order: thus tolerance has not been accompanied by acceptance, even in such ostensibly model states as the Netherlands.[39] While sexuality in our own day becomes increasingly a marketable commodity used openly in the advertising media, the stigmas and myths are dislocated from the court of law to Madison Avenue, where they continue to serve utilitarian functionalism. The gap between sexual freedom and repressed eroticism is deepened rather than diminished. "In America," Millett once remarked in an interview, "you can either fuck or shake hands." That about sums up the situation, except that in our own day the former has taken on a marketable advertising appeal. As Altman notes (p. 97):

The ability to feel, to hold, to embrace, to take comfort from the warmth of other human beings is sadly lacking; we look for it in the artificial situations of encounter groups rather than accepting it in our total lives.

From the rock musical *Salvation*: 'If you let me make love to you, Then why can't I touch you . . .' Perhaps there lies the difference between sex and eroticism.

Erotization of the social order, in the areas of both homosexual and heterosexual behavior, would amount to a joyful and spontaneous acceptance of human sexuality; and with it "a withering away of both *Playboy* and the League of Decency" (p. 106).

It should be noted that sexual liberation, as Altman sketches it, is intended as a normative ideal and not as a description of existing sexuality within the so-called gay community itself. Like all minority groups, gays tend to take on the often most undesirable attributes of their oppressors. As a reviewer in Milwaukee's *GPU News* noted, the object change from "chick" to "trick" within the gay subculture in no way augurs for a diminution of sexual exploitation.[40] What is the substance of Altman's programme for sexual liberation is a set of operative ideals from within the gay subculture, and his claim is that these ideals are in many respects superior to those of the dominant culture (which does not entail that they are more often honored in performance). Casual sex, so much present in the gay subculture of bars and baths, can be a good way of getting to know people; though, as Altman notes (p. 100), it is hardly sufficient in and of itself. An additional value, worthy of attention in the gay subculture but absent from Altman's discussion, is the ability to laugh at oneself, a point raised by Suzannah Lessard.[41] Women, gays, and blacks have generally been quite ready to laugh at themselves: the minstrel, the absent-mined idiot, and the mincing drag queen are ready examples. Even worse than being found wrong by a woman, as Lessard notes, is to be joshed by her. The repression of this emotion is one more example of the American heterosexual male's unenviable insecurity: it is second in degree only, I am sad to say, to the American academic's inability to laugh at himself, though perhaps the causal mechanisms differ.

In the remaining pages, I shall take up quite briefly some social criticism from outside the gay subculture, by way of outlining convergence toward common points; and finally a brief critique of Altman's theoretical framework.

III. SEXUALITY AND SOCIAL CRITICISM OUTSIDE THE GAY PERSPECTIVE

Altman's exposition strongly emphasizes the importance of conceiving sexuality as integral to the life of the human being, both as individual organism and in social interaction with others. Analogous framework principles, which tend to converge upon a number of identical themes, are to be found within the so-called humanistic tradition, especially in recent studies by humanists dealing with the sexual revolution, double standard, and American sexophobia. Lester Kirkendall, in the epilogue to his anthology of humanist writings on the sexual revolution, notes that " ... since man is so dependent upon others for his fulfillment and since sex is a part of the nature of each person, no sexual revolution can exist unless it concerns itself with reassessment and reevaluation of human relationships."[42] This parallels well with Altman's insistence upon a new concept of humanity, not simply a revised principle of sexual permissiveness to be grafted onto the existing social order. Additional bibliography from within the humanist tradition is also provided by Kirkendall. While by far the majority of humanists are sympathetic to the vision of homophilia as a valid lifestyle on a level of acceptance equal to that of heterosexual lifestyles as these are presently emerging, a significant deviation from Altman's analysis arises precisely in their conception of homophilia as an emergent alternative: no convergence of the two lifestyles is either predicted or viewed as a positive value. The pluralistic value orientation within contemporary humanism stands in sharp contrast to Altman's monism.

The same point can be made with respect to writings within the comptemporary feminist movement. Gene Marine, for example, concedes as an open possibility that the decline of cultural role "hangups" may indeed lead to the abolition of the hetero/homosexual dichotomy, though he sees no cultural or social significance in this. "What is important," he notes, "is that women's own fear of lesbianism is being overcome, so that even though they may do nothing overtly sexual, they are increasingly less afraid openly to display their affection for one another and their new understanding of each other's sensuality."[43] It is safe to say that, like the present writers within the gay movement with the exception of Altman, feminists have not yet begun to take philosophical stock of the two claims made initially by Altman: that the negative critique of existing sex roles requires a complementary and normative approach programmatic of social evolution, and that both the critique and the programme require a more general theoretical framework by way of justification.

Much the same indecision (or fear?) with respect to the construction of new normative frameworks is present within many writers within the psychiatric tradition who are otherwise most sympathetic to the validity of the gay lifestyle. George Weinberg's *Society and the Healthy Homosexual*[44] constitutes a classic example of this ambiguous stance. Agreeing with Szasz's earlier claim that the medical role of the psychoanalyst is little more than a cloak for that of the moralist and social engineer,[45] Weinberg goes on to offer an eloquent plea for the acceptance of the gay lifestyle, without suggesting that such acceptance on the part of the dominant culture may require normative and social shifts. An even more frontal attack, this time within the psychiatric tradition, upon the tendency in psychiatry to baptize social convention as natural law is made by E. Fuller Torrey, whose analysis follows the general line taken by the humanists:

Homosexuality and other sexual "deviations" are, of course, not real diseases at all. They are ways that people choose to relate to other people sexually. As such, they are merely part of a spectrum of choices open to us. Some are common choices, some uncommon choices, but none are diseases.[46]

Unwilling as I am to shed darkness on all of this sweetness and light, it should be noted that sadism, masochism, and necrophilia are also sexual deviations; which some of us (consistently, one hopes) would like not to rank among an admittedly enlarged canon of valid lifestyles. While many psychiatrists are to be congratulated for abandoning a "sickness" interpretation of homosexuality which was little more than a product of bad science and sloppy experimental techniques, abandonment of the old and inadequate model and its norms only makes more pressing the need for constructing new norms and models. A curious example of this tendency on the part of many within the psychiatric tradition to neglect new models where old ones have proven woefully inadequate is Harvey Kaye's study, *Male Survival: Masculinity Without Myth*.[47] Kaye provides a witty and satirical critique of the myth of the male mystique and its various mechanisms—the dominance drive, the heroic imperative, the neanderthal ideal, and the superman syndrome—but, when the negative aspect of the critique has cleared the sexual air, the reader, seeking a positive vision of the liberated male, is left with little more than a handful of tired clichés.

Final mention should be made of a recent work which deals with a number of the points raised by Altman, though without discussing or even mentioning homosexuality, this by a lawyer, Marc Feigen Fasteau: *The Male Machine*.[48] Though Fasteau concedes that he became interested in the problem of the male mystique through the feminist movement (in which his wife is active), he does not speak for that movement. His account of the male machine in terms of its agressions and defense mechanisms offers little which has not been examined earlier, though he does complement these characterizations with the insistence that the sharing of feelings, emotions, and affections among men constitutes the focal aspect of the move toward liberation from the present confines of the male bonding instincts. His point, Fasteau relates in an interview,[49] is not that men should surrender traditional male virtues, but rather that they should "reclaim the other half of being human." This is hardly the ideal bisexuality offered by Altman, though the blurring of roles intimated by Fasteau would, if provided some theoretical underpinning, surely move him in that direction. Fasteau claims that his own insight into the workings of the male machine arose while he was a member of Senator Mansfield's staff whose duty it was to articulate the underlying premises and rationale of the Vietnam War. After much study, he began to be convinced that U.S. involvement made little sense, and to see this continued involvement as part of the masculinist need never to back down. We saw earlier a parallel theoretical move on Altman's part: the attempt to interpret nonsexual aggression or violence as an extension of sexual repression, specifically of polymorphous perversity.

My point in raising these contrasting positions has been that of indicating the extent to which one may say that Altman's analysis, though constructed within the intellectual perspective of the gay subculture, does represent a genuine synthesis of a number of themes which are slowly evolving within the dominant culture. In contrast to Altman's development, however, these others strike an ultimate discord of incompleteness of ambiguity; which arises at least in part from their inability or refusal to take up more general normative and theoretical questions implied by their proposals. That said, I return to a more critical evaluation of Altman's own more ambitious attempt.

IV. CRITICAL EVALUATION AND CONCLUDING NOTES

I begin by accepting the general framework proposed by Altman, with a view toward underlining three internal weaknesses, the first of which he is not wholly unaware (cf. p. 104). In arguing that much violence is the product of repression, Altman concludes that a disappearance (or at least diminution) of the latter would entail a sharp decrease in social aggression. It is certainly reasonable to argue, however, that aggression, while it may in part be the product of socially repressed polymorphous perversity, also has an existence in the individual independent of sexual characteristics, or that it is even wholly independent of repressive factors of any species whatever. If this is the case, and the author concedes that it would be dishonest to pretend otherwise (p. 104), then his normative model of socialized bisexuality would have to accomodate some principle of socialized aggression. This point, it may be claimed, argues only for the incompleteness of his normative model in its present form; but the situation is somewhat more critical than this, since the account which Altman provides of the present dominance of heterosexuality and the patriarchal family hinges upon a rather univocal interpretation of the mechanisms of repression and aggression. What if one were faced with the counter-claim that, though a residue of violence is due to sexual repression, human nature is basically aggressive or violent in structure? Polymorphous perversity could in principle be postulated as an historical fact of human development; but the reversion to polymorphous perversity, whose normative status depends upon the assumption that such a reversion would be instrumental in eliminating aggression as a social fact, would thereby be called into question. How questionable the norm would become depends upon the extent of the residue of oppression which is produced by sexual repression. This, I should insist, is a problem whose resolution depends upon empirical research rather than upon any *a priori* theory construction, whether sociological or psychological.

A second questionable point arises through the rather general or universal categories which Altman borrows from Marcuse. While he does not take up in detail the question of what social factors are related causally to the production of homosexuality in an homophobic culture, the general thrust of his analysis moves contrary to any attempt to distinguish male from female polymorphous perversity. This entails an analysis of female homophilia from within his elaborated framework which would closely parallel that of its male counterpart; yet present psychological and sociological test data tend to indicate that explanations of female dynamics as mirror images of male dynamics respecting sexual lifestyles are at least inadequate and at most totally wrong. This point could turn once again on a point of simple incompleteness rather than material inadequacy, for at several points (pp. 90, 160, 213–217, 222–234, 235–237) Altman does suggest that the psychodynamics of lesbianism can be explained through the dual factors of homophobia (repression) and the double standard itself (male dominance interpreted in the light of the patriarchal family). The mechanisms of such an explanation, however, are without further explication.

Thirdly, and again perhaps a matter of incompleteness, there is, as I have indicated, both a descriptive and a normative component in Altman's concept of polymorphous perversity. While the latter is connected to a notion of aggression and repression which is also implicitly normative, the descriptive component requires far more support from cross-cultural anthropology than Altman appears willing to provide. Even Churchill's compendious and sympathetic cross-cultural study[50] provides no positive support for the claim that human organisms and primitive social orders can be adequately characterized as polymorphously perverse. The best that can be said, here as in so many areas relating to the gay lifestyle and its evolution, is that the empirical evidence is not available at this stage of our inquiry.

I now turn to three external points relating to the acceptability of the framework itself, the first of which is most easily countered, and would hardly be worth the attention were it not for the fact that discussion of it arises quite frequently in the writings of contemporary social philosophers. It is the generally utopian nature of Altman's framework and normative proposals: the elimination of sexual role seems no less a matter of pie-in-the-sky than does the classless society or any number of other utopian proposals. For the nonphilosopher confronting Altman's study, realization of this point likely leads to a certain malaise; whereas the philosopher, prone to baptize emotive reactions in the waters of pure reason, may offer some form of historical or epistemological scepticism. The malaise in my view is well placed, whereas the scepticism, except in very mitigated form, is not; for utopian differ from more proximate proposals only in the degree to which utilitarian calculations effect their rational expectations, not in kind. Critics of the utopian nature of much that is written regarding sexual liberation have as their proximate parent Karl Popper in his analogous critique of the utopian structure of Marxist social theory. Utilitarian calculation becomes admittedly more hazardous as goals become more remote. This is a matter of decreasing probabilities and increased utilization of the *ceteris paribus* clause, none of which justifies any scepticism other than the piecemeal type which is scientifically justified at each stage of any inquiry. Furthermore, ideals of even the most utopian variety have two functions in human community: they may be (but seldom are) realized, but they may also be acted upon. The latter, even without any historical reflection upon the feasibility of the former, is integral to the moral situation.

A distinct but related claim is less easily answered. Philosophers of a more empirical bent will insist, rightly I believe, that the Marcusian framework in which Altman couches much of his analysis hardly constitutes an adequate tool for either understanding the contemporary social order or for proposing more rational alternatives to it. The murky depths of neo-Freudian metaphysics or neo-Marxist social theory hardly seem promising waters in which to cast one's line in search of the conceptual tools of social analysis and critique; and, though metaphysically sublime or poetically inspiring, a concept like repression has little to commend it by way of experimental confirmation or precision. Again, however, too much may be made of this claim. Though it is true that concepts like aggressive sublimation or repression are empirically underdetermined, there is every reason to believe that the increasingly refined methods in both sociology and anthropology can provide at some stage the necessary conceptual delineations. New wine can often be put into old bottles, with the proviso that these be reshaped and that the packaging be done with a measure of refinement and scientific knowhow. If advances in sociological testing and procedures indicate anything, it is that hitherto suspect concepts can often be handled successfully by an adequate methodology. Like much that goes on in both psychology and philosophy, Altman's analysis can be regarded as a programme for further scientific refinement and theory construction: that it already raises a number of empirical points I have been at pains to point out, and this is more a strength than a weakness.

Finally, and most substantively, I raise a more philosophical point regarding the normative aspect of Altman's proposal. The reversion to polymorphous perversity indicates a certain monistic conception of socialized sexual response as an ideal of human nature. I am personally reminded of those proposals which, rightly spurred by the negative characteristics of nationalism or racism, seek the elimination of all national traits in some polymorphous universal whole—for instance, a universal language to be shared and utilized by all men. Yet it is an historical fact that human cultures have as often been enriched by subcultures as they have been destroyed by them. The rejection of exaggerated sex roles hardly entails the rejection of the concept of sex role itself, provided one remember that roles are made by men and not men for roles. It can be argued rather persuasively that roles are, in our confrontation with an increasingly complex social reality, functionally similar to concepts in our confrontation with a complex intellectual reality—any one of them may be disposed of at the drop of a hat, only to be replaced by a candidate more flexible or more adequate to the task of ordering our experience and expectations. In his study *The Gay Mystique*,[51] Peter Fisher speaks positively and with due optimism of the emergence of a gay identity in contemporary society, coupled with a new pluralism evolving within western culture at however slow a pace. In contrast to Altman's vision of a social order in which the very distinction between homo- and heterosexual will have withered away (p. 236), Fisher appears to view society like a house of cards, supported and nourished at various junctures by a multitude of subcultures and roles. These subcultures would not be characterized, as is so often the case today, by mutual oppression or disgust, but by sympathetic complementation.

I suspect that such a pluralistic vision of the social order could be accommodated within Altman's structure analysis of the development of human sexuality. One need only point out that the concept of polymorphous perversity entails only that human nature, malleable within limits which are as yet to be determined, leaves open to the individual a variety of developmental options the choice among which, in a pluralistic and nonrepressive social order, would be consigned to the individual social agent. Under such a reconstruction of Altman's analysis, the latitude of choice open to the individual would be determined, not entirely by theoretical frameworks constructed to account for the origins of these choices, but rather by a recognition of the extent to which we are prepared as moral agents to accord some measure of autonomy to the individual in constructing a lifestyle in accordance with a maximization of available options. Even with the conceptual shift to this pluralising and constructive view of the social order, Altman's model, whether ultimately determined to be adequate or inadequate, provides a potent source for scientific and philosophical speculation.

NOTES

1. Kinsey, A.C., Pomeroy, W.B., and Martin, C.E. *Sexual Behavior in the Human Male* (Philadelphia: W.B. Saunders, 1948).
2. The terminology is taken from Wainwright Churchill, *Homosexual Behavior Among Males* (New York: Hawthorn, 1967).

3. The summary data and conclusions on homosexuality in the Kinsey Report are reprinted in Joseph A. McCaffrey, ed., *The Homosexual Dialectic* (Englewood Cliffs: Prentice-Hall, 1972), pp. 3–30.

4. See Irving Bieber et al., *Homosexuality: A Psychoanalytic Study of Male Homosexuals* (New York: Basic Books, 1962).

5. W.H. Masters and V.E. Johnson, *Human Sexual Response* (Boston: Little, Brown, and Co., 1966), pp. 378–385. See also the authors' recent *Homosexuality in Perspective* (Boston: Little, Brown, and Co., 1979) for a more detailed clinical discussion of the components of homosexual sexuality, and my own critical review of this book, "Masters and Johnson on Homosexuality—An Overview," *GPU News* VIII, No. 9 (June, 1979), pp. 21–23.

6. Morton Hunt, "Sexual Behavior in the 1970's," *Playboy* (October, 1973–March, 1974): October, 1973, p. 206.

7. *Ibid.*, pp. 199–200.

8. M.S. Weinberg and C.J. Williams, *Male Homosexuals* (New York: Oxford University Press, 1974), p. 84. Reviewed by R.B. Evans in *Journal of Homosexuality* I, No. 1 (Fall, 1974), pp. 127–130, and by Louis Stimac in *GPU News* III, No. 8 (August, 1974), pp. 26–27.

9. *Ibid.*, pp. 190–194.

10. Marcel Saghir and Eli Robins, *Male and Female Homosexuality* (Baltimore: Williams and Wilkins, 1973), pp. 317–318. Reviewed by Violet Franks in *Journal of Homosexuality* I, No. 1 (Fall, 1974), pp. 131–134.

11. See the cover story and statement in *It's Time* (Monthly Newsletter of the National Gay Task Force, May, 1974).

12. Donald J. Cantor, "The Homosexual Revolution—A Status Report," in L.A. Kirkendall and R.N. Whitehurst, eds., *The New Sexual Revolution* (New York: Donald W. Brown, 1971), pp. 85–95.

13. Listings and activity announcements are published regularly in *The Advocate* (Los Angeles: Advocate Publications, Inc.).

14. See Laud Humphreys, *Out of the Closets* (Englewood Cliffs: Prentice-Hall, 1972).

15. Thomas S. Szasz, *The Manufacture of Madness* (New York: Harper and Row, 1970). See also his *Law, Liberty, and Psychiatry* (N.Y.: Collier, 1968).

16. Martin Hoffman, *The Gay World* (New York: Basic Books, 1968).

17. H.M. Hyde, *The Other Love* (London: Mayflower, 1972).

18. Jean LeDerff, *Homosexuel? Et Pourquoi Pas* (Montreal: Ferron, 1973).

19. Dennis Altman, *Homosexual: Oppression and Liberation* (N.Y.: Avon, 1971). To avoid proliferation of footnotes, references to this work will henceforth be given only by parenthesized page citations within the text.

20. Herbert Marcuse, *Eros and Civilization* (Boston: Beacon Press, 1955. Reprinted, N.Y.: Random House, 1962).

21. This connection is made by Edward Sagarin, "On Obscenity and Pornography," in Kirkendall, *op. cit.*, pp. 105–112. See above, note 12.

22. See Charles Berg and Clifford Allen, *The Problem of Homosexuality* (New York: Citadel, 1958), pp. 111–163.

23. Sigmund Freud, *Future of an Illusion* (1927) and *Civilization and Its Discontents* (1930), both in Standard Edition (London: Hogarth Press), Vol. 21. See Marcuse, *op. cit.*, pp. 39–44.

24. Marcuse, *op. cit.*, p. 44.

25. *Ibid.*, p. 184.

26. *Ibid.*, p. 187–190.

27. A.P. MacDonald et al., "Attitudes toward Homosexuality: Preservation of Sex Morality or the Double Standard?", in *Journal of Consulting and Clinical Psychology* XL (1972), p. 161.

28. K.T. Smith, "Homophobia: A Tentative Personality Profile," in *Psychological Reports* XXIX (1971), pp. 1091–1094.

29. A.P. MacDonald and R.G. Games, "Some Characteristics of Those Who Hold Positive and Negative Attitudes toward Homosexuals," in *Journal of Homosexuality* I, No. 1 (Fall, 1974), pp. 9–27.

30. *Ibid.*, p. 26.

31. Morton Hunt, *op. cit.* (March, 1974), pp. 184–185.

32. Marcuse, *op. cit.*, pp. 71–95.

33. Norman Mailer, *Why Are We in Vietnam?* (New York: Putnam, 1967). See also his *An American Dream* (New York: Dial, 1965).

34. P. Gebhard, J. Gagnon, W. Pomeroy, and C. Christenson, *Sex Offenders* (New York: Harper-Hoeber, 1965), pp. 273–336. See also Hoffman, *op. cit.*, pp. 89–92.

35. Suzannah Lessard, "Gay Is Good for Us All," in *Washington Monthly* II (1970): 39–49. Reprinted in *The Homosexual Dialectic*, *op. cit.*, pp. 205–218.

36. *The Homosexual Dialectic, Op. cit.*, p. 217.

37. Kate Millett, *Sexual Politics* (N.Y.: Doubleday, 1970).

38. Marcuse, *op. cit.*, pp. 15–16.

39. See Weinberg and Williams, *op. cit.*, pp. 62–74.

40. Cf. *GPU News* (November, 1974), p. 11.

41. See above note 35.

42. *The Sexual Revolution, op. cit.*, p. 220.

43. Gene Marine, *A Male Guide to Women's Liberation* (New York: Avon, 1974), pp. 234–235. This book contains an excellent bibliography on contemporary feminism.

44. George Weinberg, *Society and the Healthy Homosexual.* (N.Y.: Doubleday, 1973).

45. See above, note 15.

46. E. Fuller Torrey, *The Death of Psychiatry* (Radnor, Pa.: Chilton, 1974), p. 143.

47. Harvey Kaye, *Male Survival: Masculinity Without Myth* (N.Y.: Gros-

set and Dunlap, 1974). Reviewed by Bruce Michael in *GPU News*, June, 1974, pp. 16–17. A more sympathetic review is found in *Milwaukee Journal Magazine* of 9. vi. 74, 32–35.
48. Marc Feigen Fasteau, *The Male Machine* (N.Y.: McGraw-Hill, 1974). Reviewed by Bruce Michael in *GPU News*, November, 1974, pp. 11 and 24. Reviewed in *Chicago Tribune*, 28. xi. 74. Review with interview in *Milwaukee Journal*, 22. xi. 74.
49. *Ibid.*, *Milwaukee Journal*, 22. xi. 74.
50. See above note 2.
51. Peter Fisher, *The Gay Mystique* (N.Y.: Stein and Day, 1972).

Appendix

A major challenge to the philosopher dealing with human sexuality is that of constructing an adequate analytic framework for posing and answering questions concerning the nature of human sexuality. Such a framework, one hopes, would provide some insights necessary to the elaboration of moral models of sexual interaction. It is a presupposition of the preceding study that homosexuality provides a rich testing ground for analysis and model construction of this kind. Fortunately for the philosopher undertaking such a challenge, the area usually dubbed "gay studies" is gradually emerging as a legitimate area of academic, and more particularly philosophical, research. The purpose of this appendix is to cite additional studies which have appeared since the completion of the preceding paper. Since philosophical research is only in its preliminary stages, the philosopher will necessarily draw on interdisciplinary research to the extent that this is relevant to the analytic problems. Sociology and psychology provide a great deal of raw data, as well as the history and literature of gay liberation itself.

An excellent Franch translation of Altman's study [*Homosexuel (-le): Oppression et Liberation*, transl. Claude Elsen., (Paris: Fayard, 1977)] will provide the reader with an updated bibliography of works (French and English) specifically relevant to Altman's themes. Harvey and Jean Gochros' anthology, *The Sexually Oppressed* (New York: Association Press, 1977) provides a unifying set of data on oppression and the internalization of stereotypes in blacks, Asians, the poor, gays, and women in American society. Notions bearing a family resemblance to Altman's concept of the polymorphous social whole produced by liberation emerge in Charles Stember's *Sexual Racism* (New York: El Sevier, 1976), which also develops the analogy between sexism and racism further than did Altman.

An historical approach to the concept of oppression is taken by Vern and Bonnie Bullough in *Sin, Sickness, and Sanity* (New York: New American Library, 1977). While agreeing with the general critique of Thomas Szasz, the Bulloughs' approach is more documentary than analytical. A comprehensive survey of the effects of stereotyping upon the American legal system is to be found in D. MacNamara and Edward Sagarin, *Sex, Crime, and the Law* (New York: Free Press, 1977). Sociological surveys of internal and external oppression are presented by Mirra Komarovsky [*Dilemmas of Masculinity* (New York: W.W. Norton, 1977)] and James McCary and Donna Copeland in *Modern Views of Sexual Behavior.* (Palo Alto: Science Research Associates, 1976.): the former is a case-study survey of sexual attitudes in college students, the latter is an anthology of general studies of the relation between behavioral and attitudinal change in American society. Programmatic studies aimed at educators seeking to undo sexual stereotyping in the classroom are found in Marcia Guttentag and Helen Bray, *Undoing Sex Stereotypes* (New York: McGraw-Hill, 1977) and A.P. Nilsen *et al.*, *Sexism and Language* (Urbana: National Council of Teachers of English, 1977.).

Historical perspectives on the gay liberation movement which are more comprehensive than Altman's survey of America in the 1960's are presented in A.L. Rowse's *Homosexual in History* (New York: Thomas Crowell, 1976, paperback reissue, Avon Books, 1978), and Georges-Michel Sarotte's *Comme un Frere, comme un amant* (Paris: Flammarion, 1977). Sarotte's study, which is devoted to gay and gay liberation themes in American theatre and literature from Melville through Mailer, is probably the best thematic study of gay literature currently available. An English translation is forthcoming from Doubleday in 1979. A leading novelist and playwright in contemporary gay literature is Daniel Curzon, author of dozens of plays, short stories, essays in literature criticism, and three novels (*Something You Do in the Dark* (New York: G.P. Putnam's Sons, 1971; revised edition, Port Washington, New York: Ashley Books, 1979), *The Misadventures of Tim McPick* (Los Angeles: John Parke Curtis Press, 1975), and *Among the Carnivores* (Port Washington, New York: Ashley Books, 1978). Additional materials and documentation on the contemporary growth of gay literature are omnipresent in the small-press periodicals of the movement itself, and in the newsletters of the Lamda Book Club (Box 248, Belvidere, NJ 07823).

As Altman notes, bisexuality is a serious concept both from empirical and analytic perspectives on sexuality; and the literature still remains rather dismal. Charlotte Wolff's *Bisexuality: A Study* (New York: Horizon Press, 1977) offers a biographical and clinical approach. Janet Bode's *View From Another Closet* (New York: Hawthorn, 1977) also takes a descriptive and clinical approach. No analytic hypotheses are developed by either of these studies.

Lesbianism also remains rather neglected from empirical and philosophical perspectives. Mary Vetterling-Braggin *et al.*, *Feminism and Philosophy* (Totowa, N.J.: Littlefield, Adams, & Co., 1977) probably offers the best collection of essays dealing with the application of many of Altman's analytic concepts to both feminism and lesbianism. One study of considerable importance is Barbara Ponse's *Identities in the Lesbian World: The Social Construction of the Self* (Westport, Conn.: Greenwood Press, 1978). Ponse develops the outline of a social-learning model, similar to those developed by John Gagnon's school, alongside a dynamical theory of stereotyping, the latter analogous to Altman's account of counter-stereotyping and internal stereotyping.

Two theoretical works, both from a Jungian perspective, also deserve attention. June Singer's *Androgyny: Toward a New Theory of Sexuality* (New York: Doubleday, 1976) promises more than it can deliver given the conceptual ambiguities and vagaries of psychoanalytic models generally. The philosopher reading the literature of androgyny may well conclude that the concept is more slogan than substance. Ruth Barnhouse's *Homosexuality: A Symbolic Confusion* (New York: Seabury Press, 1977) uses the same Jungian framework to conclude that homosexuality is a form of intellectual "stunted growth"—all of which leads one to conclude that it is the psychological framework, and not homosexuality, which is rife with conceptual confusion.

Religious attempts to erect a more adequate framework for understanding human sexuality also merit brief mention. Derrick Bailey's *Homosexuality and the Western Religious Tradition* (London: Longmans, Green, 1955) is the now-classic attempt to accomodate liberationist themes within a framework of Christian humanism. Developments of Bailey's themes are found in Malcolm Macourt's anthology, *Toward a Theology of Gay Liberation* (London: SCM Press, 1978). Thomas Horner's *Jonathan Loved David* (Philadelphia: Westminster Press, 1978) is one of many fine studies demonstrating the inadequacy of traditional moral assessments of homosexuality based on a misreading of scriptural passages. Marc Oraison's *The Homosexual Question*, translated from the French by Jane Flinn (New York: Harper & Row, 1977) tries to develop a new Catholic perspective on sexuality which can accommodate liberation themes, and a similar attempt is made within the Protestant perspective in *Human Sexuality: A Preliminary Study* (Philadelphia: United Church of Christ Press, 1977). In general it is fair to say that Christian thinkers have yet to succeed in liberating themselves from the conceptual muddles so well entrenched in their past. For Catholic thinkers, tied to a functional view of human sexuality, homosexuality and masturbation offer similar and virtually insurmountable conceptual barriers. For Protestant thinkers, the concept of monogamy seems still to reign supreme. Gay lifestyles in this rather clouded perspective derive moral legitimacy by being mirror images of nongay couplings, and the one-night stand remains the archetype of cosmic evil.

Three studies particularly noteworthy for their ingression into philosophical analysis deserve special mention in closing. Donald J. West's *Homosexuality Re-Examined* (Minneapolis: University of Minnesota Press, 1977), though it presents a sometimes tedious compilation of data from a quasi-psychiatric perspective, has a good deal to say about homophobia, stereotyping, and oppression. Martin L. Gross' *The Psychological Society* (New York: Random House, 1978), while directed to a popular audience, offers a sustained and pointed critique of most of the contemporary psychological frameworks. Human sexuality occupies a major portion of the critique, homosexuality only a small portion of that; but its philosophical lessons lie close to the surface. The philosopher seeking to develop a general framework for dealing with human sexuality will find the beginnings of more mature and well reasoned frameworks in sociology rather than in psychology. Finally, Alan Bell and Martin S. Weinberg, *Homosexualities: A Study of Human Diversity* (New York: Simon & Schuster, 1978) is a monumentally important study from Indiana University's Institute for Sex Research which succeeds in putting to rest many psychological myths about the gay personality, and in making many tentative suggestions for the development and sharpening of new concepts to deal with human sexuality generally.

The best source and guide to the ongoing journal literature remains *The Journal of Homosexuality*. *JH* has expanded its format to include studies in literature and philosophy; and its cumulative annotated bibliography, appearing in each issue and including current journal literature, provides a major source of additional bibliographical information.

Bernard Gendron

Sexual Alienation

...We should first get a clearer sense of the meaning, or meanings, of the word "alienation." Much has been said about alienation recently, most of it confusing and unhelpful. One gets the impression from the mystifying claims made by scholars and theoreticians that questions concerning the nature of alienation are very difficult and require a deep answer. This seems wrong to me. As I see it, "alienation" is simply a code word for a number of easily defined forms of individual frustration and social dysfunction. Obsurity and mystery enter when investigators attempt to specify the distinguishing characteristics common to all instances of alienation. The truth is, the word "alienation" has a number of different but overlapping meanings; there is no common meaning underyling all its uses. Once this is appreciated, the mystery surrounding its use disappears.

As I see it, there are three types of alienation referred to, or three broad meanings of alienation operating, in Countercultural critiques of technology. They are the alienation from self, the alienation from others, and the alienation from nature. Let me say something briefly about each of these.

I. ALIENATION FROM SELF

The alienation from one's self is exemplified either in the alienation from one's activity or the alienation from the product of

Gendron, Bernard. "Sexual Alienation," in his *Technology and the Human Condition* (New York, N.Y.: St. Martin's Press, 1977), pp. 114–133. Reprinted by permission.

one's activity. Consider a particular activity, and suppose that humans generally do not enjoy doing it, and avoid doing it whenever possible, though they may be compelled on a regular basis; that they have no control over the way they are to do it, and are serving someone else's interest rather than their own; that they are bored and perform the activity mechanically; that it is unchallenging and without social significance; and that they do not at present have the opportunity or capacity to do this activity in a fulfilling manner. If most of the above conditions are met, then humans would be "alienated" from this activity. If true human satisfaction is impossible or incomplete without the performance of this particular activity, then humans can be emancipated from their alienation only by learning, and being allowed, to perform it in a truly fulfilling manner. If this activity is always incompatible with complete satisfaction, then humans will be emancipated only when the conditions which make this activity necessary are eliminated.

Taking their cue from Sigmund Freud and Karl Marx, the Countercultural Dystopians have focused on work and sex as the two major forms of alienated activity. Humans are forced to perform exhausting, insignificant, and boring labor; they are socialized to abstain from exactly those forms of sensuous experience which are truly fulfilling, leaving as alternatives the performance either of actions devoid of sensuous content or of sexual actions which are mechanical and unsatisfying. The sexual alienation will be overcome presumably when humans "recover their bodies and their senses," that is, when they learn to infuse everything that they do with real sensuous consciousness. However, on the question of the emancipation from the alienation of labor, the Countercultural humanists side with Freud against Marx. According to them, there will be alienation as long as humans continue to labor, presumably because of the inherent tension between work and sexual liberation. In the unalienated state, it will be all play and no work. What systematically differentiates the Counterculture further from Marx and Freud is its tendency to impute the alienation of labor and sex to the imperatives of institutionalized technology, rather than to class exploitation or to civilization as such.

The alienation from self also finds expression in the alienation from the product of one's activity. Humans are alienated from their own product if it is used by others to exploit or manipulate them, or if it acquires a life of its own and in turn comes to dominate its producers. Such, according to Karl Marx, is the condition of the worker who is exploited through the commodity which he produces. According to the nineteenth-century atheist philosopher Ludwig Feuerbach, it is also the condition of the religious persons dominated by their own artifacts (namely, God and religion) and who have imputed to those artifacts their own potentialities. In this spirit, Countercultural Dystopians have maintained that we are alienated from our own technology as an object of our activity. We have lost control over institutionalized technology; the development of organization and machinery, according to them, is now autonomous and unimpedable. Technology has a life of its own, and we serve it rather than direct it.

II. ALIENATION FROM OTHERS

If humans are continually in conflict with one another; if they manipulate one another, or exhibit little care for the needs and feelings of others; if individuals are isolated from others, lonely, and lost; if societies are massified or homogenized—if any or all of these conditions hold, then humans are alienated from one another. According to the Counterculture, contemporary technology and its institutionalized values are the causes of a large number of types of social alienation, such as personal detachment, disrespect for the privacy of others, the experimental manipulation of others, conformism, consumerism (orientation toward things rather than people), the subordination of the individual to the organization, the decreasing social importance of the individual, the increasing role of machines in mediating between people and things, anonymity and isolation, the deemphasis of permanent relationships between persons, the demise of traditional communities (such as the family), mass society and cultural homogenation, and the rise of the warfare state.

III. ALIENATION FROM NATURE

This concept is somewhat metaphorical and it is constructed on the model of the alienation from others. To the extent that it makes sense to say that people are oppressing, exploiting, or dominating nature, or that they have lost all feel for, or intimacy with nature, or that they disrespectfully disrupt natural processes, or that they are no longer at home in nature, or that they are no longer properly integrated with nature or within natural systems, then it makes sense to say that people are alienated from nature.

Countercultural thinkers have claimed that there are at least two kinds of alienation from nature caused or reinforced by technology, its growth, and its values. First, modern technological growth has led to the growth of cities, increasingly surrounding people with artifacts and cutting them off from untouched, or barely modified, natural environments. The Countercultural response to this is a new kind of primitivism advocating a return to rural living, self-sufficiency, and a minimal dependence on artifacts. Second, the pursuit of modern technological values (technological rationality) has created increasing ecological disruption in the form of pollution, population growth, and the depletion of nonrenewable resources. The only answer to this, according to Countercultural Dystopians, is to eliminate all forms of growth—population growth, economic growth, and even technological growth. . . .

IV. THE PLAYBOY SYNDROME

Among the many problems which it has attacked, the Countercultural youth movement has directed most of its energy at sexual alienation, which it assumes to be widespread and deep. Its call has been primarily for sexual liberation. Its adherents have continually exhorted us to overcome our repressions, "uptightness," desensitization, and alienation from our bodies. In opposition to Marxist radicals, Countercultural radicals stress the primacy of sexual alienation over social alienation. While Marxists claim that alienation from oneself (including sexual alienation) is rooted in social alienation (such as exploitation, oppression, and objectification of others), Countercultural Dystopians claim that social alienation is rooted in alienation from oneself, and especially, in sexual alienation. According to the former, we must be emancipated socioeconomically before we can be emancipated sexually; according to the latter, we must be emancipated sexually before we can be emancipated socioeconomically.

On this theme, the Countercultural youth movement has been greatly influenced by the work of Wilhelm Reich, Paul Goodman, Norman O. Brown, and Herbert Marcuse, all of whom have given sexuality a central place in their analysis of the illnesses of modern societies. The movement, however, claims to have added new dimensions to this analysis, which theorists like Theodore Roszak, Charles Reich, and Philip Slater have attempted to capture (though not always successfully).

It is not clear what Countercultural Dystopians take sexual liberation to be. To find out, we must first determine what they mean by "sexual alienation." This is no easy matter, for their conception of sexual alienation is somewhat complicated and unusual.

Clearly this much is true. Anyone who is not capable of enjoying sex in its socially harmless forms, or who is not willing or allowed to do so, is alienated from sex. This kind of sexual alienation exists when there are social taboos against premarital sex, or against nonstandard sexual practices (such as oral sex); it exists where people feel deeply guilty about sex, or treat it merely as a means for procreation. In the past one hundred years, but especially since the appearance of Sigmund Freud's work, a number of groups have propagandized for the elimination of sexual taboos and sexual guilt, and for the liberation of sex from its purely procreative function. Countercultural Dystopians clearly are not the first to struggle against sexual alienation, nor are they the only ones doing so today. We are presently undergoing a major sexual revolution of which the Countercultural youth movement is only a part.

But it would be wrong to see the Countercultural movement simply as repetition of past movements for sexual liberation, or to submerge it undifferentially in the present sexual revolution. It would be especially wrong to interpret the Countercultural movement merely as a response to the recalcitrant remnants of puritanical taboos and guilt obsessions in our society. This interpretation would force us to group together in the same movement people whose sexual attitudes are radically different. For example, imagine bracketing jet-setters and playboys (or playgirls) with hippies, or mate-swapping clubs with communes. To ensure accuracy, it is better to speak of two ongoing sexual revolutions, the first embodied in life-styles exemplified by such magazines as *Playboy* and *Playgirl*, and the second embodied in Countercultural life-styles; the first arising in opposition to the old restrictive moralities, and the second in oppostion to the new sexual permissiveness of playboy and playgirl sex as well as to the old restrictive moralities. For Countercultural Dystopians, both the sexual restraints of the middle American and the sexual promiscuities of the playboy and playgirl are symptoms of sexual alienation. Indeed, for them the playboy and playgirl life-styles constitute the more serious danger, since they arise out of the new technocratic order rather than some dying moral order, and since they appear as sexual liberation and fulfillment rather than as just another version of desensitization and repression.

At this point I should mention that most theorists of the Counterculture had completed their work before the emergence of such publications as *Playgirl* and *Viva* magazines. They therefore tend to focus on the inadequacies of playboy sex, making little or no mention of its female counterpart. But I am sure that all the evils they impute to playboy sex they would also impute to playgirl sex.

The Countercultural movement's castigation of playboy sex is confronted immediately with the following objection. Since playboys are encouraged to engage in whatever sexual activity they please, and since they seem to have no inhibitions about any kind of sexual activity, then in what sense can they be called "repressed" or "unfree" or "alienated" from their bodies? And on what basis can it be claimed that the current forms of sexual promiscuity exemplified by playboy sex are generated by the institutionalization of technological rationality?

Countercultural Dystopians, and especially Herbert Marcuse and Theodore Rozsak, have been quick to point out the undesirable features of the current forms of sexual permissiveness. For example, playboy sex is the prerogative of the wealthy and the privileged and thus symptomizes the unjust stratifications and distributions of our socioeconomic system.

In the affluent society, we have sex and sex galore—or so we are led to believe. But when we look more closely we see that this sybaritic promiscuity wears a special social coloring. It has been assimilated to an income level and social status available only to our well-heeled junior executives and the jet set. After all, what does it cost to rent these yachts full of nymphomaniacal young things in which our playboys sail off for orgiastic swimming parties in the Bahamas? *Real* sex, we are led to believe, is something that goes with the best scotch, twenty-seven dollar sun glasses, and platinum-tipped shoelaces. Anything less is a shabby substitute. Yes, there is permissiveness in the technocratic society; but it is only for the swingers and the big spenders.[1]

Playboy sex is obviously male chauvinist.

The ideal of the swinging life we find in *Playboy* gives us a conception of femininity which is indistinguishable from social idiocy. The woman becomes a mere playmate, a submissive bunny, a mindless decoration. At a stroke, half the population is reduced to being the inconsequential entertainment of the technocracy's pampered elite.[2]

Though made more plentiful, sex is integrated into the system of production and exchange of commodities, thus becoming an important instrument for social control and manipulation.

It has often been noted that advanced industrial civilization operates with a greater degree of sexual freedom—"operates" in the sense that the latter becomes a market value and a factor of social mores. Without ceasing to be an instrument of labor, the body is allowed to exhibit its sexual features in the everyday work world and in work relations. This is one of the unique achievements of industrial society—rendered possible by the reduction of dirty and heavy physical labor; by the availability of cheap, attractive clothing, beauty culture, and physical hygiene. . . . The sexy office and salesgirls, the handsome, virile junior executive and floorwalker are highly marketable commodities. . . . Shops and offices open themselves through huge glass windows and expose their personnel; inside, high counters and nontransparent partitions are coming down. . . . Technical progress and more comfortable living permit the systematic inclusion of libidinal components into the realm of the commodity production and exchange.[3]

The officially sanctioned promiscuous sex is impersonal and detached.

Moreover, *Playboy* sexuality is, ideally, casual, frolicsome, and vastly promiscuous. It is the anonymous sex of the harem. It creates no binding loyalties, no personal attachments, no distractions from one's primary responsibilities. . . . The perfect playboy practices a career enveloped by noncommittal trivialities: there is no home, no family, no romance that divides the heart painfully. Life off the job exhausts itself in a constant run of imbecile affluence and impersonal orgasms.[4]

The increase in the availability of sex has been accompanied by a constriction of the bodily and environmental zones of pleasure Whole sectors of the human environment and the human body have been deeroticized.

The environment from which the individual could obtain pleasure . . . has been rigidly reduced. . . . The effect is a localization and contraction of the libido, the reduction of erotic to sexual experience and satisfaction. For example, compare lovemaking in a meadow and in an automobile, on a lovers' walk outside the town walls and on a Manhattan street. In the former case, the environment partakes of and invites libidinal cathexis and tends to be eroticized. In contrast, a mechanized environment seems to block such self-transcendence of the libido.[5]

These observations, though apparently correct, are not altogether helpful. They may show that the playboy or his equivalent is immoral or asocial, but they do not necessarily establish that he is sexually repressed. If playboy sex is the preserve of the rich, if it is male chauvinist, and if it is used as an instrument for manipulation in commodity production and exchange, then it is obviously exploitative and unjust; and insofar as it reinforces detachment and uninvolvement, it is anticommunal. For these reasons and others, one can conclude that the playboy or any other beneficiary of the official sexual permissiveness is socially alienated. But it does not follow that he is sexually alienated. Is someone to be termed "sexually repressed" or "unsensuous" simply because he or she treats others as things or looks upon sex as a commodity? If so, then how can sexual alienation be distinguished from social alienation? In this context, isn't the expression "sexual alienation" totally superfluous?

It makes sense to say that the playboy is sexually repressed or alienated only if one is willing to claim that he misses out on some important types of sexual enjoyment. Of the five criticisms of his lifestyle quoted above, only the last explicitly makes this charge. Herbert Marcuse claims here that for the playboy much of the human body and much of the environment has been deeroticized. The playboy is not sensitive to the beauty of the natural environment or of the parts of the body which are not relevant to genital pleasure. Marcuse seems to assume that certain kinds of environment are intrinsically erotic (for example, a woodland setting) and some are intrinsically unerotic (such a playboy bachelor "pad"), and that the playboy is oblivious to these differences. But this seems wrong. Whether or not one's environment is erotic depends on one's taste and one's response to that environment. Even a parked car may be erotic for one who has a fetish for, say, the Cadillac Eldorado. And there is no doubt that the exemplary playboy will provide an environment suitable for his brand of lovemaking, and hence an environment which is in his eyes erotic. No doubt someone like Marcuse, or any other representative of the Counterculture, would be offended by *Playboy* publisher Hugh Hefner's mansion in Chicago. We may agree that Hefner has philistine taste, but still, perhaps like beauty, the erotic is in the eye of the beholder. What is for a participant of the Counterculture a desensitized environment may for the playboy be an erotically stimulating environment.

There is no doubt that playboy sex fixates in an exaggerated way on genital pleasure. This obviously does not mean that for the playboy the other parts of the human body and the environment are not erotic. It means that the other parts of the body and the environment are sources of sexual pleasure for the playboy only to the extent that they contribute to or pave the way for genital pleasure, and especially genital orgasm. If true, this is an inadequacy. It seems that other parts or contours of the body, other movements of the body, as well as many features of the environment, ought to be intrinsic sources of sensual pleasure, independent of their contribution to genital pleasure. And if the playboy fails to derive pleasure from sensory contact with these parts or contours or movements, in the absence of present or future genital stimulation, then he can be said to be missing some important kinds of sensuous enjoyment. He can thus be termed "sensuously alienated" or "desensitized;" one can say that he is "out of harmony" with his body. It is presumably this sort of sensuous enjoyment which sensitivity programs try to reawaken or recreate. Participants are encouraged to increase their tactile concentration on their bodily parts and movements by touching, slapping, and lifting them. And they are drawn into a number of tactile rituals with other persons, involving anything from toe touching and back rubbing to blind walking, head washing, palm dancing, and body lifting. No doubt, much of what is prescribed in these sessions is quackery. Still, the large demand for these programs is evidence of a need felt by many to acquire the capacity for sensuously enjoying, in a manner independent of genital sexuality, theirs and other persons' bodies. Insofar as the playboy is in need of such therapy, then he can be deemed sensuously repressed. This Countercultural critique of playboy sexuality, though persuasive and on the right track, is as it stands too weak and ill-defined. For the argument faults the playboy not for the sensuous activity which he does exhibit (genital sex), but for the sensuous activity which he does not exhibit. The playboy is criticized not for what he gets but for what he misses. But why couldn't the playboy be trained to add to his repertoire of pleasures those nongenital sensuous pleasures prescribed by the Countercultural humanist? Why couldn't he broaden his sensuous horizons by taking part in sensitivity sessions while keeping the remainder of his life-style intact? The Countercultural argument would be effective only if it established either that playboy genital sex is a distorted form of sensuality which inhibits the development of a capacity for nongenital sensuous enjoyment, or that the interpersonal lifestyles associated with playboy sex (such as casualness, uninvolvement, and male chauvinism) are incompatible with true sensuous fulfillment, whether of the genital or nongenital type. But the argument as it stands fails to establish either of these points. Thus, it fails to show that the playboy cannot remain a playboy and still participate fully in the nongenital sensuous enjoyments prescribed by the Counterculture.

The Countercultural critique of playboy sex, in its present form, is also vague and ill-defined. It shifts in focus from the idea of sexual repression, which is only a particular kind of sensuous repression, to the idea of sensuous repression as such, or desensitization. That is, it shifts from the narrow and fairly clear notion of genital sex to the much broader and more vague notion of sensuousness. The playboy is accused of missing nonsexual forms of sensuousness. But while the demarcation between sexual and nonsexual pleasure is fairly clear, the demarcation between sensuous and nonsenuous pleasure or activity is not so clear. What is to count as sensuous pleasure and what as nonsensuous pleasure? What is to count as the sensuous component in pleasure and what as the nonsensuous component? Sensuous enjoyment simply cannot be identified with tactile enjoyment. However sensuality is defined, it obviously involves gustatory, olfactory, visual, and auditory components. Are the pleasures generated by the discovery of a new theorem, the study of philosophy, the discovery of oil deposits, the making of an important sale, or the reading of a good book sensuous or not? If not sensuous, then what precisely do they lack?

According to spokespersons for the Counterculture, all or most of us brought up in a technocratic society are sensuously alienated or desensitized. This being the case, they cannot easily teach us the meaning of the term "sensuous" demonstratively by pointing to those of our experiences which are unqualifiedly sensuous; we probably have few undistorted sensuous experiences. "Sensuous" then is a theoretical term, which can only be defined indirectly, negatively, and analogically.

What then can the Counterculture mean by "sensuous alienation," "desensitization," "sensuous uptightness?" Perhaps we will get a clue if we find out what connection there is, according to spokespersons for the Counterculture, between the growing institutionalization of technological values (technological rationality) and the growth of the new forms of sensuous alienation associated with playboy sex.

V. SENSUOUS REPRESSION: THE COMPLETE TECHNICIAN

In what way does the institutionalization of technological rationality lead to desensitization? If the principles of technological rationality govern the processes of production, then they are most probably internalized by the population involved in production. This internalization may be so effective that it carries over into the leisure life of the working population. Desensitization may thus be a consequence of the fact that all the experience and activity of this population, either at or away from work, is interpreted exclusively in terms of, and governed exclusively by, the principles of technological rationality.

It is a common complaint against scientists and technicians that they allow the attitudes and mentalities which prevail in the laboratory or office to govern their personal and social lives. This is the point behind castigations of scientists and technicians for being "robots" or "computers." It is assumed that a scientist or technician, when acting in his or her capacity as scientist or technician, is not experiencing or performing in a sensuous manner. Thus a person who always experiences or performs as scientist or technician, even in contexts which are not appropriately scientific or technological, is deemed to be desensitized or sensuously repressed. For the Countercultural Dystopian, the paradigm case of the sensuously repressed individual is that of a person who behaves as a technician in wholly inappropriate contexts, such as sexual interaction, dance, music performance and composition, informal conversation, gymnastics, and interaction with wildlife.

This provides us with at least the basis for a negative elucidation of the Countercultural notion of the sensuous. Those forms of cognition, activities, and attitudes which are sensuous are most perspicuously describable in terms of their contrasts with forms of cognition, activities, and attitudes which are scientific and technological. Consider the following examples. For science and technology, sensory perception is simply a means or a starting point; it is essential that the functions of science and technology go beyond sensory perception, or what is given in sensory perception. Scientists use perception to aid in the discovery or confirmation of nonperceptual truths about the universe; they make theoretical claims which, among other things, explain away what is given in perception. Technologists use perceptual experience mainly in order to increase their manipulative power over nature, and particularly over the objects of sensory perception. In sensuous cognition, on the other hand, the sensory experience is an end in itself. It requires one's undivided attention. One simply savors the sensory experience without reference to any ulterior motives. Whether submitting oneself to psychedelic drugs or listening to music or participating in sensitivity sessions, the sensuous person is in a wholly receptive, rather than interpretative or manipulative, frame of mind.

Scientific and technological activity is reflective; sensuous activity is not. The technician typically subjects future projects to elaborate planning and careful deliberation and subjects past projects to detailed scrutiny. Sensuous experience or activity, on the other hand, is presumably "spontaneous," that is, it is not preceded by specific expectations and preparations, and cannot after its occurrence be subject to dissection and analysis. Thus, the playboy, in virtue of the fact that he involves himself in elaborate schemes for future seductions and elaborate reviews of past seductions, can be described as desensitized.

Science and technology are open-ended disciplines. There is always more to be learned about nature and more power over nature to be acquired; there are always more tasks to be done and more objectives to be reached. Therefore, scientists or technicians are essentially future oriented and are willing to engage constantly in routine or frustrating or exhausting work in order to achieve some future good. They are thus willing to forego present enjoyment for future enjoyment. In contrast, people involved in sensuous activity are completely absorbed in the pleasures of the moment, and are minimally inclined to postpone present gratification in order to achieve some future good.

One in a scientific or technical state of mind tends to atomize cognitions and behavior; one in a sensuous state of mind treats them as wholes which are irreducible to their component parts. A well-conceived research project or experiment is broken down into basic steps and stages, and into subtasks and subroutines. Scientific conjectures are similarly broken down into component claims which can be discretely and differentially tested. It is well known that the maximization of efficiency demands a continued microfractionalization of technical occupations. The Countercultural Dystopian assumes that it would be desensitizing to atomize in this way one's sexual experiences and activities, one's intimate interpersonal relations, one's dancing, and one's sensory enjoyment of nature.

One distinction continually made between science and technology, on the one hand, and true sensuousness, on the other, is that the former is dominated by "technique" (formal rules specifying the most efficient means for achieving given ends) in a way in which the latter is not. A major Dystopian complaint against modern "liberated" sex is that it has been completely "technized;" Dystopians point to the proliferation of "how to do it" books on sex which promise automatic success if certain techniques are followed or certain exercises are carried out. Our sensuous capacities presumably are blunted by this excessive preoccupation with technique. Of course, the successful performance of any sensuous activity, be it sex or dancing, requires some artfulness, and artfulness presupposes the implemenation of some techniques. And it is also true that most scientific and technological activities are not completely circumscribed by technical rules. Technical rules provide a complete decision precedure for arithmetical calculation and for the validation of mathematical proofs, but they fail to provide a complete decision procedure for the making of mathematical, scientific, or technological discoveries, or for the confirmation or disconfirmation of scientific hypotheses. Nevertheless, it could be claimed for the following reasons that technique has a much greater impact on scientific and technological consciousness than it does on sensuous consciousness. One learns science by being explicitly and systematically taught to follow technical rules. And the practicing scientist not only acts in accordance with technical rules, but is always in the process of formulating old and new rules and procedures, of consciously bringing these rules to bear in plans and deliberations, and of consciously assessing by reference to these rules. On the other hand, it is often claimed that the capacity for sensuous enjoyment is a natural rather than a learned capacity, and that, like the capacity to walk, it is developed and molded through the processes of physical maturation rather than through technical inculcation. The stress on the learning of techniques, it is assumed, would merely distract from these natural capacities and stunt their growth. Furthermore, though mature sensuous activity may conform with some technical rules, it is not preceded and accompanied by the continuous formulation and consideration of these rules and it is not assessed after the fact by the application of these rules. Presumably, the heavy emphasis on the consciousness of techniques, typical of science and technology, inhibits or distorts sensuous enjoyment.

The attitude of science and technology relative to its object of study is one of personal detachment and uninvolvement. In contrast, the attitude of sensuous cognition is essentially one of empathy for the object of knowledge; in sensuous awareness, cognition entails conation. This is not to say, however, that the scientist as scientist is dispassionate in the pursuit of professional goals. The ideal scientist surely has a strong passion for truth and beauty, and certainly is emotionally involved in the work at hand. Still, it is irrelevant to this work that there be a strong personal attachment on the part of the scientist to the coparticipants or the objects of the inquiries. Indeed, as is well known, such personal involvements, though allowed, jeopardize objectivity.

All scientific and technological knowledge is verbally expressible and when communicated is communicated verbally. According to Countercultural spokespersons, this is not true of many forms of sensuous cognition, such as psychedelic experience or intimate interpersonal experience. For example, one's intimate knowlege of a given person's face, it is assumed, cannot be fully expressed verbally. Furthermore, it is emphasized that sensuous communication is more effectively carried out through body movement, facial expression, touch, and music than it is through linguistic interchange. Finally, science is directed mainly at the knowledge of classes or types, whereas sensuous experience is directed at the knowledge of individuals.

The above, I think, is a fairly accurate reconstruction of the Counterculture's understanding of the contrasts between the way of life of the pure technician and that of the wholly sensuous person. From these contrasts the following conclusion can be drawn. Any person can be deemed wholly desensitized or sensuously repressed who, during all of both leisure and work time consistently experiences things or persons in a theoretical, manipulative, and detached state of mind, consistently subjects every action to careful planning and detailed atomization, is consistently inclined to postpone present gratification, consistently brings techniques to bear in everything learned or done, and consistently accentuates verbal (at the expense of nonverbal) cognition and communication. Consequently, anyone is desensitized who has internalized the principles of technological rationality in both leisure life and work life.

It is obvious that in any technologically advanced society, and especially in a technocracy, work activities and experiences will be imbued with the principles of technological rationality. But why should we expect the leisure experiences and activities of these same employees also to be dominated by the principles of technological rationality? Why couldn't the scientist or technician who behaves nonsensuously while on the job behave in a wildly sensuous manner while off the job (as many try to do)? The Dystopian's response to this objection would be straightforward and reasonable. In any full-employment economy, leisure is institutionally subordinated to work. Most of the workers' most precious hours and much of their concentration and energy are mobilized for their work. Most of their socialization, education, and training are directed toward the preparation for future employment; an important function of school is to inculcate work disciplines as well as to teach work skills. Only those forms of leisure life which are compatible with, or contribute to, maximum work productivity are tolerated or reinforced; and apparently, according to Countercultural Dystopians, persons who enjoyed a completely sensuous life would hardly be inclined to spend their most important waking hours at work. Hence, it is not surprising that, in a full-employment economy, the values internalized in one's work experience and activity should also be internalized in one's leisure experience and activity.

But why should we expect that in technocratic America, in an America dominated by modern technology, the economy will continue to be a full-employment economy? Shouldn't the emergence of a postindustrial era, involving as it does the spread of computer technology and automation, entail a constant reduction in the size of the work force and in the length of the work-year? In the long run, would it not entail the virtual elimination of human productive labor? Can Dystopians rationally deny this? Let us see on what basis they would.

VI. SENSUOUS REPRESSION: THE IMPERATIVES OF WORK

Countercultural Dystopians seem to agree on this point: postindustrial technocracies, as well as the industrial capitalist societies of old, are and will continue to be compulsively committed to maximal economic growth. They think that continued economic growth is one of the most important values embodied in technological rationality: the "good" of technology, they think, requires economic growth. There appear to be two reasons for this. Economic growth is necessary for the continued expansion of human collective power over nature and for the continued development of scientific and technological knowledge. But control over nature and growth in technology are the two most basic goals of institutionalized technology and of the decision-making technicians overseeing its development.

Wealth obviously is a form of power; one's wealth is measured by one's command over resources, goods, and services. It is reasonable to believe that continued growth in our collective power over nature presupposes continued growth in our collective wealth, this in turn being made possible by continued growth in the gross national product (GNP).

Furthermore, it could be argued with some plausibility that continued technological growth will require increasing demands for research and development funds, and that these demands on the community pool of investment funds can be met more easily in the face of competing demands from other interests by continually enlarging the available pool.

Thus a Dystopian might argue that for the foreseeable future economic growth will be required to meet the needs of modern technology. . . . [L]et us follow the Dystopian argument to its natural conclusion.

Even in an age of automation, the pursuit of economic growth is in conflict with the pursuit of leisure. Suppose that in a given year the modernization of machinery raises the hourly productivity of each worker by 5 percent. One option in response to this is to decrease the working time of each worker by 5 percent while providing the same income. This, however, disallows any increase in total production. Another option is to increase total production by 5 percent by adding to the stock of machinery, but then any increase in leisure is disallowed.

Any growth economy presupposes the existence of scarcity, whether natural or contrived. Without scarcity, the worker will not ask for more work and the consumer for more goods. It has been argued by Dystopians (and most perceptively by Philip Slater) that sex, as the object of a primary human need and as the only source of gratification which is plentiful in the "hypothetical state of nature," must be made artificially scarce in societies committed to sustained economic growth. How this is accomplished depends on the relative wealth of the society in question. In poor countries with a shortage of savings and capital, the emphasis is on frugality and self-denial; sexual scarcity is generated by the imposition of restrictions or taboos on sex with respect to time, place, manner, and person. In more opulent countries where savings tend to be overabundant, the emphasis is rather on self-indulgence and consumption. Sexual scarcity is bred in these permissive societies, not by imposing restrictions, but by so integrating sex in the system of compulsive commodity consumption that no finite amount of sexual indulgence can ever satisfy one's sexual needs. Inanimate commodities (such as soaps and cars) and animate "commodities" (such as Playmates and fashion models and stripteasers), as well as certain forms of dress and communicative behavior, are imbued with a sexual significance they cannot possibly fulfill. Philip Slater makes this point fairly nicely.

> Thus, while increases in the number, variety, and severity of sexual restrictions may intensify the subjective experiences of sexual scarcity, a subsequent trend toward sexual "permissiveness" need not produce a corresponding decrease in scarcity. . . . The fundamental mechanism for generating sexual scarcity is to attach sexual interest to inaccessible, nonexistent, or irrelevant objects. . . . Today this basic technique has become the dominant one. By the time an American boy or girl reaches maturity he or she has so much symbolic baggage attached to the sexual impulse that the mere mutual stimulation of two human bodies seems almost meaningless. Through the mass media everything sexless has become sexualized: automobiles, cigarettes, detergents, clothing.[6]

In conclusion, it would seem that the imperatives of technology require maximal economic growth. This in turn entails full employment and compulsive consumption. Full employment presupposes that work is at the center of each person's life; it presupposes that each person internalizes the perspectives of work and is willing to postpone gratification. In an advanced technological full-employment economy, the worker will internalize the technical point of view (the principles of technological rationality) in leisure life as well as work life. For all these reasons, workers in advanced technological societies will tend to be desensitized. Desensitization is further instilled by the requirements of compulsive consumption. Compulsive consumption exists when the wants of consumers grow faster than the stock of goods and services or when existing wants cannot be satisfied by any amount of goods and services. Compulsive consumerism requires contrived scarcity within a context of abundance, and this in sexual matters as well as others. Insofar as playboy sex is "technical sex," fashioned by the experiences of technical work, and insofar as it presupposes or instills sexual scarcity within a context of abundant sex, then it is by the standards of the Counterculture a form of desensitized or repressed sex.

So goes the Dystopian argument. It purports to show that playboy sex is a natural concomitant of advanced technological societies and that it is a form of desensitized sex. This argument, I think, is stimulating and interesting. Whether it works depends on some key assumptions which have to be investigated later (like the assumption that advanced technological societies are necessarily committed to maximum growth). . . .

NOTES

1. Theodore Roszak, *The Making of a Counter-Culture* (Garden City: Doubleday, 1969), pp. 14–15.
2. *Ibid.*, p. 15.
3. Herbert Marcuse, *One Dimensional Man* (Boston: Beacon, 1964).
4. Roszak, *The Making of a Counter-Culture, op. cit.,* p. 15.
5. Marcuse, *op. cit., One Dimensional Man,* p. 73.
6. Philip Slater, *The Pursuit of Loneliness* (Boston: Beacon, 1970), p. 85 .

Richard Sennett

Destructive Gemeinschaft

Every generation engages in a life-long struggle with what it first believed. Sometimes people repudiate early ideals, but their temperament remains unchanged, as, for example, those rigid Stalinists who have become fiercely anti-Marxist. In other generations, like our own, the first truths are not challenged explicitly, rather they are affirmed with a voice that grows ever more tired, weak, and resigned.

The truth to which our generation assents is that psychological self-exposure is a moral good. In this view it is better to show your feelings to another person, no matter how wounding the feelings are, than to suppress or disguise what you feel. A person is not being authentic with you unless he or she is willing to share his or her secrets. This compulsion to expose the self shows up in many different ways: it is the rationale of the feeling-industry, from Esalen to rolfing to encounter weekends at hotels in the Catskills. It is the rationale of the modern biography or autobiography, in which exposure of the subject's intimate affairs is presumed to have an important bearing on how he painted or wrote. It is the rationale also of our political imagination: a politician's "credibility" is measured not so much in terms of his past performance as through a reading of what sort of personality he "projects."

But it is in an increasingly passive spirit that we take self-disclo-

Reprinted by permission from *Partisan Review* 43, No. 3 (1976), pp. 341–361.

sure to be a moral good; this passivity is forced upon us by the very nature of our belief. An existence of unrelieved confession, openness, and revelation of inner secrets would be absolute hell. It is by no accident that encounter groups are pleasurable only as weekend affairs at hotels, nor that in marriages sustained confrontation leads so often to divorce, nor that the political imagination searches only for glimpses of the man behind the legislator to measure the credibility of the legislator at work. If in general people can bear only so much truth, it would seem that they have an especially limited tolerance when it comes to sustained awareness of the maelstrom of envy, kindness, rapacious desire, and gentleness of which the human psyche is composed. Most societies confine this chaos in public forms like religious rituals or acts of obedience to secular ideology, which offer alternative modes of expression to the display of raw psychic energy. When a culture moralizes the very existence of this energy, it ensures that its experience of the moral life will occur only in fits and starts. The weight of circumstance, of getting from day to day, will make the moments of self-exposure sudden upheavals beneath the surface of everyday order. The upheaval people do not so much greet with demonic glee as humbly accept, for when you are under the whip of primal passion you are forced into heresy for real.

It is true that a life of constant psychic disguise would be as intolerable as a life of constant self-revelation. All cultures arrange some rhythm of alternation between the two; the question is how people feel the rhythm: do they believe there is equal value in moments of disguise and revelation, or are people unmoved by the virtues of conventional, ritual behavior and aroused only when self-display occurs? This question of the value placed on self-revelation is a social and historical question; the seriousness with which people take their psyches depends on the culture in which they live. It is important to keep these dimensions of the question in mind, for all too often the critics of authenticity, after paying lip service to the conditions of advanced capitalism and of secularism which have led people to be so concerned with their private feelings, cast aside the social considerations and criticize authenticity as an abstract psychological condition. Instead of being regarded as a product of a deformed culture, the desire for authenticity comes to be seen as a sign of the innate sinfulness of human nature. This is the failing of Theodor Adorno's *The Language of Authenticity*, for example. His critique of authenticity soon puts the reader on familiar conservative terrain; the impulse life of man comes to be equated per se with the destructiveness of self-revelation; therefore social repression per se becomes a moral good. One of the great virtues of Lionel Trilling's *Sincerity and Authenticity*, which is conservatism of an altogether different and more noble kind, is to show how the morality of authenticity is ineluctably the product of historical changes in modern culture. Moreover, Trilling has shown how the emphasis on self-revelation which erupted in the last decade is not a freak condition whose origins lie simply in the war between the generations in the late 1960s; this self-absorption is the result of hidden changes in modern culture in the making since the French Revolution.

Self-revelation is also social, rather than an abstract psychological, preoccupation, for the attitudes people have about their own emotions they tend to project on others. People feel close, and their relationship seems real, if they show themselves to each other; by contrast, it is hard for us to imagine that people determined to hold things back in each other's presence can have much of a relationship. An authentic social relationship must thus progress through mutual self-revelation; inauthenticity in social relationships is identified with what used to be called discretion. The ideal, authentic social bond is today alluded to in many familiar code words that posit a society in which people are "open" to each other, "responsive to each other's needs," ready to "interact freely." All of these code words convert social relationships into psychological transactions; the model underlying all of them is a bizarre form of canasta in which each of the players competes to show the others the cards of identity he holds.

There is a technical sociological word whose changing meaning captures this conversion of social relations into psychological terms: it is *Gemeinschaft*. The sociologist Ferdinand Tönnies at the end of the nineteenth century used the word to mean full and open emotional relations with others. In opposing *Gemeinschaft* to *Gesellschaft* he wanted to create an historical, rather than a purely analytic contrast. *Gemeinschaft* relations existed in the precapitalist, preurbanized world of the *ancien régime*; *gesellschaft* relations, in which people split up their emotions according to the principle of the division of labor, Tönnies depicted as characteristic of the modern world. Much as he mourned the loss of *gemeinschaft* relations, he never thought they could be revived, for that would mean reviving the hierarchic, personalistic world of the *ancien régime*. The longing for *Gemeinschaft* he in fact criticized as "displaced pastoralism."

Today, *Gemeinschaft* has been redefined, shorn of the historical meaning Tönnies gave it, and converted into a moral absolute—a condition of authenticity, of good faith. The celebration of *Gemeinschaft* as a pure state is captured in the ordinary English translation of the word: community. When people are open with each other and expose their feelings to each other, they create a community. An encounter group is the most obvious example of a community conducted on psychological principles of openness, but these principles enter into ideas about other kinds of communities as well. In the debates about centralization and decentralization in urban planning, for instance, the proponents of decentralization often argue that local communities should take precedence over the needs of the city as a whole, because in the local community people have real human relationships, in which they can be open with each other, get to know each other, and share their feelings, while strangers in the city at large don't. And this notion of community is connected with disclosure: thus, in the literature on the family as a community, full interaction is often presented as an optimum condition, and the insistence on one's right to keep things back from those one loves is seen as a form of bad faith which threatens the family as a whole.

Needless to say, the authentic interchange, the authenticity event, is only infrequently experienced. Local communities do have occasional flashes of this feeling of people really sharing with each other—usually during periods of crisis when the community is threatened from outside. But microcommunities (and these would include the family) can bear moments of mutual self-disclosure only as periodic upheavals below the surface of day-to-day order. Yet no matter how infrequently we can actually experience *Gemeinschaft*, we persistently seek it out, measuring real social relations by this ideal which can be sustained only in imagination. What I want to show here is why the very idea of self-disclosure, the authenticity event, the open community, is destructive. This ideal makes our real social relations seem sterile, and often poisons human relationships by creating a sense of crisis which can be resolved only if the persons involved abandon each other. My critique does not assert that *Gemeinschaft* is destructive per se, but attempts to indicate why changes in modern society have made it so. These changes involve the redefinition of nineteenth-century eroticism into twentieth-century sexuality, and the transformation of privacy as it was understood in the last century into a new idea of intimacy.

I. EROTICISM TRANSFORMED INTO SEXUALITY

When we think of our great-grandparents' experiences of physical love, we are most like to think about the inhibitions and repressions. Victorian bourgeois prudery was so extreme it occasionally acquired an almost surreal quality; a common practice, for instance, was to cover the legs of grand pianos with leggings, because a bare leg as such was thought "provocative." This prudery lay at the root of a number of psychopathologies especially acute at the time—not only hysterias, but also what the Victorians called "complaints," which among women were manifested by such symptoms as uncontrollable vomiting at the sight of menstrual blood and among men by such symptoms as acute attacks of anxiety after the discovery of an ejaculation occurring during sleep. Certainly no one today could possibly hope for a return to such repression. Yet it is important to see the rationale behind this sexual repression and even to comprehend a certain dignity among bourgeois men and women in these Puritanical struggles with themselves. A code of eroticism ruled nineteenth-century bourgeois consciousness, an eroticism composed of three elements.

The first of these elements was the belief that states of feeling and signs of character manifest themselves involuntarily. Hence, what is deeply felt or deeply rooted in character is beyond the power of the will to shape or hide: emotion appears unbidden, and at moments of vulnerability emotion is a betrayal. The involuntary expression of emotion received its greatest theoretical elaboration in Charles Darwin's *The Expression of Emotion in Animals and Man*. Darwin connected the involuntary betrayal of emotion with the necessities of biology which ruled the human organism. But the same idea had more popular expressions which sought to indicate ways of detecting transitory states of feeling. Thus, depression was supposed to reveal itself by involuntary tension in the cheeks, an episode of masturbation by the sudden growth of a spot of hair on the palms.

Similarly, character traits were to be read through details of appearance. The involuntary expression of character involved a particular system of cognition, as in the practice of phrenology and Bertillion measurement: the shape of the skull, hand, or foot supposedly revealing the presence of certain characterological traits which the criminal, defective, or salacious person could do nothing to disguise. The Bertillion measures of criminality concern

millimeters of difference between the cranial shape of the criminal
and the law-abider. Because these involuntary clues of personality
were like cameos, personality itself was felt to be so difficult to
control; one might control most of one's behavior and still some
little thing would give one away.

In such a culture, anxiety about sexual matters formed part of a
larger belief that the expression of all feeling escaped control by
the ego. One's only defenses were either to shield oneself as completely as possible, to neutralize one's appearance, as the Victorians did through their clothing, or to attempt to repress feeling
itself. For if a transitory emotion is uncontrollably manifest
through the most minute clues, one can be secure only if one tries
to stop feeling in the first place. Shielding and denial, then, are
logical consequences of believing in the *immanence* of the personality; the line between inside and outside is dissolved.

This Victorian belief led to a fetishism of appearances. I use this
term more in a Marxian than a Freudian sense, to indicate how
the trivia of appearance could be believed to be signs of a whole
human being. If the self speaks through minutiae of appearance,
then every appearance must be a guide to some characterological
state. Thus, it becomes logical to cover the legs of a piano with
skirts, because an exposed leg is the sign of lewdness. In the clothing of the Victorian era, this fetishism of appearances was especially strong. A gentleman wearing a drab black broadcloth coat
could be distinguished from an ordinary bourgeois wearing a similar garment because the buttons on the gentleman's sleeve could
actually button and unbutton. For men this fetishism centered
around questions of class; for women it centered around sexual
propriety. The differences between the dress of "loose" women
and the proper ladies who appeared in *Le Moniteur de la Mode*
lay in minor distinctions in the use of color for shawls and hoods,
or the length or shortness of gloves. Minute differences between
objects speak of vast differences in feeling between those who
wear them.

In the sections of the first volume of *Das Capital* where Marx
takes up the subject of fetishized objects, he explains them as a
veil modern capitalism draws over production relations, so that
the inequities of production, which might be visible if goods were
conceived of simply in terms of use, are obscured; these objects
seem instead to contain mysterious and enticing psychological
qualities. Missing in his analysis, however, is a consideration of
the psychological consequences of becoming mystified, of believ-

ing in the minutiae of man-made things as personality omens, for the person so mystified. The Victorian bourgeoisie was more than a class laboring under an illusion; it was also a class trying to make sense of its daily experience on the basis of this illusion. People scanned the public world for signs of the private life of others at the same time that each attempted to shield himself from being so read. This double process of searching and shielding was hardly a simple state of equilibrium or a matter of balance between public and private.

Sexual relations in a world conceived in such terms had of necessity to be social relations. Today, having an affair with another person would not be likely to cause someone to call into question his or her capacities as a parent, or—if it were someone sufficiently "liberated"—his or her capacities as husband or wife. For the Victorian bourgeoisie, those connections had to be made. If every act, every feeling, counts in terms of defining the whole person, then emotional experience in one domain carries unavoidable implications about the character of the person acting in another. A violation of morality in one sphere signifies a moral violation in every other; an adulteress cannot be a loving mother, she has betrayed her children in taking a lover, and so on. Again, I wish to call attention not so much to how brutal this repressive code could be as to the premise which produced the repression. The immanence of character in all appearances forced the Victorian to weigh each experience in relation to other experiences to us seemingly quite dissociated. For all the desire to flee the world at large and hide in privatized, isolated places, the Victorians had to measure the acts of the private sphere on the basis of their public implications. This is how a system of social relations was produced.

People so concerned with the involuntary expression of feelings, with fetishized objects, each of which contains clues to the personality of its wearer or owner, people who conceived of their sexual relations as having repercussions beyond the bedroom door; these people inhabited an erotic world. It was a sensual world, but overwhelmingly, uncontrollably so, and as a consequence it prompted attempts at repression and self-discipline which were in fact of the most destructive sort. Eroticism and repression: these two psychological phenomena dominated the capitalist bourgeoisie in its first epoch of domination in Western society.

What has occurred in the present century is that we have overturned the eroticism of that world, hoping to escape from its repressiveness, in such a way that we have substituted a new slavery for the old. We have desocialized physical love, turning eroticism into the more isolated and inward terms of sexuality. But this change is not so much a contrast as it is a form of continuity with the Victorian situation. The desocializing of physical love which has taken place in the present century is a result of carrying to an extreme the Victorian's first principle, the principle of personality immanent in appearances.

Now it is a truism that Americans and American culture tend to be personalistic in their view of social relations. Aspects of class, race, and history are easily abandoned in favor of explanations of events which center on the character and motivation of the participants involved. But the American viewpoint represents a psychological vision of society which is taking hold in Western Europe in the present century as well. Think, for instance, of how Left leaders in England, France, and West Germany are spoken of as "legitimate" or "credible." Such judgments are based not so much on the leader's ideological purity or coherence as on his ability to appeal personally and so to command the votes of those who do not share his left-wing ideas. Or think of the increasing tendency of people in the upper working classes and the new *classes moyennes* to view their positions in society as simply the result (or failure) of their personal abilities. This personalizing of class occurs even though people may understand in the abstract that their positions result from the blind workings of advanced capitalism.

To view one's experience in the world as a consequence or mirror of one's personality is narcissism. By this is not meant love of self, but more precisely the tendency to regard the world as a mirror of self. When personality is believed to be causally at work in all human experiences, the world will soon seem to be only a mirror of the self. At this point, the idea of *Gemeinschaft* acquires its absolutist, moralistic form: if people are not revealing their inner feelings to others, they are not being "for real." As the principle of immanent personality appearing in the nineteenth century has expanded its hold upon people's minds to such an extent that all appearances in society seem real only as manifestations of personality and personal feelings, narcissism has been mobilized as a cultural condition. Narcissism has become the norm, the code of meaning.

As we know, the psychological disorders which psychotherapists treated most often eighty years ago were hysterias. But today hysteria is a relatively rare complaint. Instead, what appears most commonly in clinics for treatment are "character disorders." The patient feels empty, dead, or dissociated from the people around him, but has no objectified neurotic signs such as an hysteria or a phobia. One has this feeling of deadness, of an inability to feel or to relate to other people, precisely because one has begun to conceive of that outside world as a peculiar mirror of self. It exists to fulfill the self; there are no "human objects" or object relations with a reality all their own. The peculiarity and the destructiveness of this narcissistic vision is that the environment of the human being becomes less fulfilling the more it is judged in terms of its congruence with or subservience to self needs. Expectations of the outside grow enormous. It is a sea in which the self floats without differentiation; and for the very reason that expectation of fulfillment becomes at once so vast, and so amorphous, the possibilities of fulfillment are diminished. Because there are no boundaries between self and other, experiences lose their form; they never seem to have an end or a definition of completion. Concrete experience with other people therefore never seems "enough." And because gratification from this oceanic, boundaryless outside never seems enough, the self feels empty and dead. The obvious content of a character disorder is, "I am not feeling;" the hidden narcissistic content is, "the world is failing me, and so I am not feeling."

This shift in clinical data from Freud's generation to the present has occurred because the society has changed. It is a society which has orchestrated the energies of narcissism around the theme of emotional "liberation." This new music drowns out the very idea of society itself. By "society" I mean a situation in which people weigh different domains of experience against one another so that choices are made, and people sacrifice one set of gratifications for the sake of another. Moreover, "society" involves the operation of external, believable constraints upon the self (like class consciousness, religious commitment, manners or rituals of kindness) having a reality of their own.

Let me give an example of how this mobilization of narcissism operates in one of the popular ideologies of sexual liberation. In Germaine Greer's *The Female Eunuch* one is presented with a clear and incontestable picture of the domination of men over women in jobs, education, homelife, etc. Then one is told that this situation obtains because a social "system" operates in society: men aren't tyrants, modern life simply makes them play that role. Well and good. The next step in the argument is the assertion that

a woman has to rebel against this system by being able to do anything a man does; she "deserves" whatever men have. The author
argues that women should try to get "total gratification," that
they deserve whatever they desire. As the book unfolds, the idea
recedes that a system of bad social relations created female oppression in the first place. A woman who gets what she "deserves"
in the system simply changes positions in the game of musical
chairs. Thus, in the course of making an argument for the equality
of the sexes, Greer winds up forgetting about society. Total gratification of the self becomes the alternative to systematic discrimination against females. The world, at first seen as socially unjust,
becomes a mirror or resource for the self. This is the unfolding of
narcissism at work in an ideology of liberation, and it defeats
goals of that ideology by gradually blotting out the reality which
caused the problem. The conversion of the desire for social liberation into the desire for personal liberation maintains the system as
a whole; the social network of inequalities is not challenged, although the sex of a few of the players may be changed.

But what is truly perverse about narcissistic projections is that
they are seldom self-evident; nor are they simple demands for
pleasure. For example, one attempts to explain to himself why he
has failed to be upwardly mobile, and arrives at the conclusion—
despite all his abstract knowledge that social organization controls his chances—that some personal failing is the cause. In this
he is mirroring the self onto the world. This is as much a narcissistic formulation as is the credo that in the end liberation from a
subdominant role involves free gratification of the self through use
of the "resources" of society.

Elsewhere I have argued that there is a correlation between the
increasing bureaucratization of modern capitalism and the mobilization of narcissism in society. Large-scale bureaucratic structures function according to a system of promised rewards based
on the supposed talent, personal affability, and moral character of
the employee at work. Reward thus becomes tied to the exercise
of personal ability, and the failure to receive reward—in fact a
systematic necessity since large bureaucracies are sharp pyra-
mids—is increasingly interpreted by those in the lower middle positions as a failure on their own parts to be rewardable, by virture
of their personalities. Thus, it is also for functional reasons, and
not only as a consequence of the intensified belief in personality
manifest in all social relations, that narcissism has come increasingly to be mobilized.

When bureaucracy and the collective consciousness of personality join forces, it becomes possible to believe, as the Victorian bourgeoisie could not, in a protean self. The American psychiatrist Robert J. Lifton defines a protean self as a conception of identity involving the belief that one's personality is always undergoing fundamental changes, or is capable of doing so. There is consequently no core of "innate" human nature or of fixed social conditions which define it: it is a self so totally immanent in the world that it is a product of immediate appearances and of sensations. This notion of selfhood puts an immense premium on "direct" experiences with other people; it detests reserve or masks behind which other people are felt to lurk, because in being distant they seem to be inauthentic, failing to take the immediate moment of human contact as an absolute. About this protean self, Lifton is highly ambivalent. He sees its value, as a pure analytic construct, because the vision of an infinitely malleable human nature does away with the whole problem of ahistorical, innate personality factors; but he fears this protean man somewhat as a cultural phenomenon. For if one dedicates oneself so thoroughly to a life of direct sensate experience, one cannot make long-term commitments, and resistance to immediate moments which are malign or unjust becomes difficult. A protean man may live a rich immediate life, but only at the cost of accommodation to his environment. By contrast, the person who feels his selfhood to be constant has acquired the will to resist his environment.

Belief in a protean self follows logically from a loss of boundaries around the self. If the world of impersonal necessity is erased, and reality becomes a matter of feeling, then changes in feeling, transitory impressions and sensations come to seem like fundamental changes in character. The self-concept as a whole is thus fetishized, just as individual objects were a century ago.

This totally phenomenological view of the self achieved one of its most dramatic expressions in the commune movements of North America and Western Europe during the last decade. These communes were seen less as arrangements valuable or pleasurable in themselves than as models of how the larger society ought to reform itself. Indeed, the millenarian commune involves a conviction that changes in one's immediate life space are so important and changes in the quality of feelings between people who become intimate are of such value, that these changes somehow become emblems of what the whole of society ought to be like. Thus, there is no vision of the operation of society as something different from intimate transactions. But it is possible to believe that changes in one's immediate feelings are political in character only if one assumes that the whole of society is made up of creatures defined essentially by their immediate feelings. And if one accepts such an assumption, then it is logical to believe that this society of protean selves is waiting for a "model" of changes in feeling to guide the transformation of the whole.

But the "counter culture" here is only an expression of the larger ordinary culture as is evident in the realm of sexuality. In this area, belief in a protean self suggests to people that "who" they are depends on who their lovers are: love thus becomes another mirror of the self. In the last century, Lamartine could put forward as a poetic conceit the notion that "who I am depends on whom I love today," but that conceit has been transformed in this century into a commonplace. And as a result of the acceptance of this notion, sexuality has been burdened with tasks of self-definition and self-summary which are inappropriate to the physical act of making love with another person.

There are many studies of the anxiety with which people approach the matter of sexual selection of a partner, and some evidence that this anxiety has replaced the rather different anxieties of two generations ago about the experience in bed the partners might later have. If the act of lovemaking itself has lost its terror, the prior selection of partners seems to have absorbed that same terror. For all the talk in the popular media about promiscuity, there is little evidence that free-floating sexuality is on the rise. Rather the reverse; "mate-selection" (as the sociologists call it) seems to be becoming a tense process because the choosing of someone to sleep with is a reflexive act: it tells who you are. Thus, in the Van Burgh researches, for example, there appears a consistent worry about whether "this person is right for me," a worry which crowds out such questions as "is he or she attractive?" or "do I like him or her?" Once the self becomes a protean phenomenon, the reality of the other person is erased as an Other; he or she becomes another "resource" for inner development, and loving the other person for his or her differences recedes before a desire to find in that person a definition of oneself.

The belief in protean selfhood treats intimate interchanges like a market of self-revelations. You interact with others according to how much you tell them about yourself; the more confessions you have made, the more "intimate" you have become. When the partners are out of self-revelations, the relationship all too often comes to an end: there is nothing more to say. Making human contact by marketing confessions in this way easily results in boredom, or it forces people to start all over again in a relationship once they have shown themselves to each other. Thus, psychologists, for instance, usually have to start over when training as diagnostic interviewers. The tyro interviewer is convinced that to treat another human being with respect, he must match whatever is revealed to him with a similar experience of his own. This shows that he "understands," that he "sympathizes." In fact, this card game leads neither to understanding nor sympathy; if he is any good, the trainee starts over with the knowledge that real respect for other human beings involves a respect for human differences. Such a therapist is increasingly in a minority, however, as the marketing of self-revelation appears in encounter groups, "T" groups, and the like. The marketing of confession has also become one of the main modes of interaction through which married people experience short-term extramarital affairs, which are initiated by that classic complaint, "my spouse doesn't understand me." The market exchange of confession has a particular logic in a society ruled by the fear that one has no self until one tells another person about it: and this is the protean man's dilemma.

These are the three conditions of modern personality: it is narcissistic, protean, and marketable. Together these conditions color our imagination of social relations which are real, authentic, and moral: there is an insistence that these relations also be open—people must show themselves to each other; they must tell the truth, about themselves, and about the strengths and weaknesses they perceive in others, no matter what. Such psychological imagination of authentic social life represents a notion of *Gemeinschaft* stripped of all the historical associations Tönnies first gave the word, and converted into a moral absolute. This notion of *Gemeinschaft* is not only crude and uncivilized, but also, as a moral interpretation of human relations, as an expectation of what reality ought to be, it has enormous destructive power.

One of the destructive aspects of modern *Gemeinschaft* lies in the way it perverts the experience of conflict. It makes people see conflict as an all-or-nothing contest for personal legitimacy. If you are different from someone else, and he reacts negatively when you reveal yourself to him, the conflict appears to you to challenge the very worth of yourself. Once conflict is escalated to the point at which it becomes a question whether it is legitimate to have your own feelings, only two endings are possible: one can either try to overwhelm the other person so that he is no longer different, or one can abandon him. Either way, an ongoing human relationship is destroyed. An unavoidable difference challenges the narcissistic modality of seeing the self mirrored in the world. This mode depends on projection and the sharing of similarity. In conflict, people are faced with a problem which will not mirror each in the other, which cannot be marketed to the other. The experience of interpersonal conflict then escalates to the more all-encompassing question of which person, which side of the difference, should legitimately exist at all.

Just as individuals involved in such a conflict struggle over who they are rather than specifically what they want, larger groups view conflict as a form of struggle for legitimacy between collective personality types. Instead of a neighborhood, class, or ethnic group pressing for specific gains, it tries to find an "identity." It then uses this identity as a moral weapon: because the group has a collective self, it therefore deserves fulfillment; because the members of the group feel close, feel as one, their claims upon society are legitimate, no matter what the substance of the claims, or the means of their realization. An extreme example of this pattern is to be found in ethnic-terrorist groups. The fact of having discovered a common self legitimates the means of terror to preserve that end; and this is equally true at the opposite end of the political spectrum in Falangist or other modern Fascist groups. If one moves from these political extremes to more ordinary forms of conflict, the same process is at work. The locality asserts the integrity of its demands against a central planning organization not on the grounds that the actual practices of the central bureaucracy are unjust but rather on the grounds that the solidarity of the neighborhood will be destroyed. It is no accident that local politics conducted on this basis of identity-as-legitimacy so often becomes self-defeating. At the same time as the neighborhood fights the outside world for threatening its solidarity, within itself it conducts continual tests of who really belongs, who really expresses the sense and the interests of the collective whole, and this testing leads to fragmentation, intramural struggles over who is an authentic member of the group, and so on. Powerlessness comes from the very attempts to define a collective identity instead of defining the common interests of a diverse group of people. This latter idea was I believe what Marx meant by a class out for itself, an idea *Gemeinschaft* obliterates.

What makes *Gemeinschaft* pernicious is that this desire to share one's feelings with others like oneself feels so close to the ideal of fraternity. It would be unreal to deny the general human need for fraternity, but what has happened today is that the concrete experience of fraternity has become perverted by the assumptions about personality which rule our culture. Fraternity should be a condition of common action, and its psychological rewards ought to come from pursuing action together. Today, fraternity is regarded instead as a state of being—one in which finding out who we are becomes of overwhelming concern. And the very process of defining who we are, like the process of defining a single me, is troubled because conflict, diversity, and complexity are not part of the process of self-definition. When conditions of external or internal conflict face the group, unity of impulse becomes more important than concrete common interests. If there is not unity of impulse (and, given the richness of human impulses this is rare), then the struggle centers on the question of whose impulses are legitimate. Marriages or long-term affairs become testing grounds of personalities, rather than relationships with constraints and interests of their own. Larger communities break apart along the same lines: no matter what the scale of modern *Gemeinschaft*, the logic of sharing feelings is that the self is made powerless when feelings cannot be shared. This is why there exists the conviction, now so prevalent, that one's real problems are those of the arousal of feeling in the presence of others. Sometimes this problem is overtly presented as self-failure; but covertly, in collective as well as individual cases, the desire for *Gemeinschaft* with others is really an accusation against the world for not mirroring back to one the resources for completing an identity.

I have spoken of a crisis of legitimation produced in ordinary life by our very belief in being open and psychologically "liberated." Jürgen Habermas takes up this theme in more abstract terms in his influential book, *Legitimationsprobleme in Spatkapitalismus* (The Problems of Legitimation in Late Capitalism). In this work, Habermas calls for a better society in which human communication is freed of all the constraints of arbitrary power which operate in advanced capitalism. He advances a theory of cognition *(Erkenntnisleitenden)* in which "distortion-free" communication between people is possible. I think his view is psychologically naive but also instructive. For Habermas, the psychological world is deformed by the social realities of power and control; while Habermas seems to be talking about the pressures of capitalism, his real worry, I think, is about the intrusion of society itself upon psychological openness, for in any society power of an unjust and dominating sort will exist. The problem of modern culture lies in its assumption that human beings must somehow get away from the issue of domination in order to be communicative and open. To dream of a world in which psychological processes of open communication, processes which are taken to be morally good, are free from social questions, is to dream of a collective escape from social relations themselves. The elevation of a psychology of openness above the dirt and compromise of power politics is precisely the dynamics of modern *Gemeinschaft*. Habermas's work is not so much a critique of the problem of legitimation now faced by the culture as the very embodiment of this problem.

In sum, the repressive eroticism of the nineteenth-century bourgeoisie was the product of three beliefs. The first and most important was that individual personality was immanent in appearances in the public world. The second was that all the details of appearance had a personalistic meaning, so that appearances became fetishized. And the third was that, for all the desire to retreat and make private the realm of feeling, intimate emotions like those involved in sex remained exposed and judged in societal terms. There are also three beliefs underlying modern *Gemeinschaft*. The first is the intensification of the idea of immanent personality to such an extent that the world becomes a narcissistic mirror of the self. The second is the belief that the self is a protean phenomenon. The third is that this immanent, protean self interacts with others and creates the conviction of its own existence by engaging in market transactions of self-revelation. In part, then, twentieth-century personality is clearly a consequence of nineteenth-century assumptions, but it is also significant that modern terms of personality coincide with the increasing bureaucratization of industrial society. And the result of modern *Gemeinschaft* is that people unable to "find themselves" become all-too-willing to abandon each other.

II. PRIVACY TRANSFORMED INTO INTIMACY

Today the phrase "the private family" seems to connote a single idea, but until the eighteenth century privacy was not associated with family or intimate life, but rather with secrecy and governmental privilege. There have been numerous attempts to explain the union of privacy and family life in the modern period, the most notable and direct being that of Engels. Because of the sterility of human relations in the productive system of capitalism,

Engels argued, people concentrated their desires for full emotional relations in a single sphere, the home, and tried to make this sphere privileged, exempt from the emptiness which pervaded office or factory. Engels's idea of privatization supplements the movement which Tönnes perceived in the larger society from *Gemeinschaft* to *Gesellshaft* relations; in sum, the family becomes a miniature *Gemeinschaft* in a largely alien world.

The term privatization has become a cliché today among those who study and write about the family, and has taken on two overtones which obscure its meaning. All too often writings on the private family (an isolated nuclear family in form) assume that privatization can actually work: people who want to go and hide can really do so. This is the assumption of the historian Phillippe Ariès and those of his school when they talk about the family withdrawing from the world in modern times. Missing in this account is a recognition that the social forces which divide work from family also invade the family itself. If we do recognize the pervasive power of capitalism, then we must think of the experience of privatization in the nineteenth-century family as an attempt to make the family warm and snug against the outside, but an attempt which constantly failed because the alien world organized personal relations within the house as much as impersonal relations without.

Secondly, the cliché of privatization misleads by suggesting a static condition that of a permanently privatized family. But what happens once the family becomes privatized? After all, this process of privatization has been at work for 200 years, and yet many of those who study it use terms to describe it which apply to fixed emotional states: "isolation," "emotional overinvolvement with kin," and the like. Surely the families of *Emma Bovary, Buddenbrooks*, and *Herzog*, all ostensibly privatized, are not the same.

Let us return for a moment to Engels's view of the pressures creating privitization in the nineteenth century. These are pressures of displacement in one direction: from a work experience more and more empty to family experience forced to provide a full range of emotional relationships, including those which properly belong to, but have been shifted from, the public world of production. What then would generate a contrary pressure, so that the family ultimately failed in its efforts to provide a refuge, failed to become securely privatized? Critical in producing this contrary motion was the idea of personality revealed in external appearances which had crystallized by the 1860s and early 1870s.

In the child-rearing manuals published in the 1860s in both

France and England, a common, almost monotonous theme occurs: for children to grow up with stable characters, they must
maintain orderly appearances in the family circle. Not only must
the child, whether boy or girl, act consistently through "good
habits" and "beneficent rules," but the parents must display good
habits and act consistently in front of their children. The reason
this advice about family dynamics was given is that the Victorian
bourgeoisie feared that if appearances were not routinized in the
home, and if spontaneity were not effectively suppressed, then the
personality would never crystallize and the child would never
grow emotionally strong. This fear is linked to a series of assumptions which we have already examined: since basic personality
traits are linked even to the minutiae of external appearances, in
order for basic personality traits to be formed appearances must
be rigidly controlled.

For all the desire family members had to withdraw from the
terrors of the world into a relaxed warm zone, the codes of personality in the last century pushed family relations back into the
welter of contradictory impulses of order and immanence which
troubled the public world. Between husbands and wives the same
pressure for stabilization of behavior existed as governed the relations of parents and children. Love between man and woman de-
pended on the ability of the partners to conform to the rules of
what a husband and wife should be. But if adherence to rules of
propriety was necessary at home, the realms of work and home
were not therefore identical. In the home, changed appearances
would threaten the partners' trust in each other, threaten their
sense that each knew who the other was. A repressive, rigid routine became the means of certifying that the marriage itself was
real—just as the child was thought to grow in a healthy way only
if he experienced others in terms he could trust. For the Victorians, trust meant trust to remain the same.

Thus, the privatization the family experienced in the nineteenth
century was a consequence of its search for an order in which stable personality could flourish; and yet it involved a belief in immanent personality which thrust the family back out into the very
anxieties about order and immanent meaning which ruled public
life. *Both* the desire to retreat and the reconstruction of the outer
society are elements of privatization. The first would soon have
exhausted itself as a desire had not the second so insistently thrust
family dynamics back into the public contradiction, so that the
family's mission of orderly retreat never seemed accomplished.

For families of the present generation, privatization on these terms has ceased to exist. There is no longer a world alien to the self to which the self refers. For example, to preserve a marriage as a social contract, people today are not willing to observe proprieties of the rigid sort which characterized the last century; if one is obliged to make great sacrifices of immediate feeling and perception about the other partner in the marriage, then the marriage itself soon seems sour. Because so many nineteenth-century people were imprisoned in respectable but loveless marriages, the breaking of rigid codes of correct behavior may well seem all to the good. The problem is that this change in the terms of privatization has not liberated individuals within the family, but paradoxically, has made the family bond more important and more destructive. The reason for this is that when family relations become withdrawals from the world the person has no experiences outside the family which can be used to judge experiences within it. The family comes to seem the terrain on which all emotions are displayed: emotions which are not familial have no reality because the world outside is only instrumental. The movement from privacy to intimacy is a movement from the family as an unsuccessful private institution to the family as a tyrannical, psychologically pure universe.

What is the rationale for conceiving of the family as socially withdrawn and emotionally complete? It is that of the narcissistic mirror. If the family is not a work unit as in the *ancien régime*, if it is not an arrangement involving an arbitrarily rigid set of roles, as in the nineteenth century, then what appears in this "free" psychic network has a reality and purity unsullied by alien contingencies. Once freed from the world, the family will appear to be a disclosure of pure psychological experience. The lessons of such experience will then be taken out beyond the family circle, and psychological transactions in the world will be judged in terms of familial categories, which seem like pure types.

Let me give some concrete examples. Patterns of friendship among adults at work today follow a course unlike those which obtained four generations ago. The more a friendship between adults at work grows, the more attempts are made to integrate the adults into the respective family circles, and to form friendships between the families. American middle-class workers open the gates to the home rather readily to their friends, the French bourgeoisie rather reluctantly, but the path of friendship is the same. One of my students has done a comparative study of friendships between middle-class adults in London and Paris in the 1870s, as these are portrayed in the pulp fiction of the time, and found something entirely different from this modern pattern. Among males, a friend became someone with whom you could engage in escape from the rigors of the family; a friend was someone to take out rather than invite in. Among females, friendship also involved progressive dissociation from family relations; a friend was someone who could become a confidante for grievances against both one's children and one's spouse. Because women were incarcerated in the house, female relationships appeared familial, but in fact friends in the house provided a chance to rail against the tyrannies of the home. A century ago, then, friendship for both sexes meant escape from family ties; today it involves a reinforcement of them.

Take even something so apparently opposed to the mores of the bourgeois family as the hippie commune. A study of communes in the 1960s found them to be insistently concerned with reliving old family issues and relationships in order to create a higher kind of family. A common problem for the collective family arose whenever psychological needs were asserted against the whole, such as the need for psychological experience outside the commune. When these needs could not be made consonant with the commune's life, then the commune was threatened. For example, if you are sleeping with someone not part of the commune, why is it you don't ask him or her to come live in the commune? The refusal to familize these relations was taken as a betrayal.

The most profound indicator of the family as an image of a purely psychological and morally dominant condition comes from the realm of ideology. Today our concept of psychological emancipation involves liberation of the self rather than liberation from the self. In ordinary speech we idealize being able to express our feelings openly or feeling free to do so. Habermas's model of open communication has its vulgar counterpart in the belief that social institutions are bad at the moment when they get in the way of human expression. One example of that vulgar belief is Germaine Greer's *Female Eunuch*. Liberation of one's feelings is basically a familistic ideal. Liberation from one's feelings is a nonfamilistic ideal. The first refers to the possibility of experience in which anything one wants, any sensation one has, can be received by others; that is, liberation of one's feelings presupposes an accepting environment, one in which interest in whatever one does feel, and appreciation for it, will be shown by others. The model for such an accepting environment is the child displaying himself to an audience of adoring parents. Liberation from one's feelings, on the other hand, refers to the possibility of experience which is impersonal, experience in which the person observes a convention, plays a role, participates in a form; the classic locus of such liberation is the city, its classic name cosmopolitanism.

But the contrast cuts further. The self-conscious display of newly discovered feelings to an accepting environment is usually a post-Oedipal phenomenon—that is, it follows upon the child's first consistent declarations of his own independence. The display of behavior in which the child participates in a social form with impersonal conventions is usually a pre-Oedipal experience—it follows upon the child's discovery that he can engage in games. Game-play involves pleasure in the observance of a form, a convention not dependent upon individualized, momentary impulse. Conservative critics of the modern culture of a boundaryless self usually base their attacks on the notion that this culture is regressive and childish. The real problem is that the terms of modern bourgeois personality are not regressive enough; these terms do not permit the adult to call upon the most fundamental and earliest of the social impulses, the impulse to play. The reproach one ought to make to the notion of liberation of the self is that these energies of play remain dormant as the adult regresses only to that point where the self-conscious declaration of his own feelings was an event his protector-parents accepted, even cherished. It is this most fragile, withdrawn moment of family history which becomes enshrined as a cultural ideal when we dream of free self-expression.

A society in which liberation of self replaces liberation from the self as an ideal has obliterated any possibilities of self-transcendence from its moral life. Instead of transcending the self, one makes it into a comprehensive standard of reality. One does not balance public against private; instead, one assumes that one *is*, that life is authentic, when one focuses inward, taking moments of self-disclosure in the family to be the reality in which the self is nourished. The outside is vaguely threatening but also simply vague, a reality of necessities, constraints upon the self, bonds to be broken. It is this intimate imagination which destroys the idea of self-transcendence; and when that idea is destroyed, the moral life of a society has become fully secularized.

Transcendence of the self is so deeply a part of the Catholic and Protestant traditions that it is easy to imagine that this ideal is possible only in an overtly and strongly religious culture. But that need not be so; any society believes in transcendence when people imagine that their impulse life may be destructive as well as constructive, and therefore create social rituals of conventions which served to control the impulsive destructiveness of the people in the society. Two of the least religious thinkers of modern times, Rousseau and Freud, believed in their very different ways in a society where such transcendence becomes a moral goal. It is true that ideals of transcendence do involve a certain kind of faith, if not in collective progress or the moral regeneration of man, at least in the possibility of people collectively lifting some of their own psychological burdens.

It is this faith which a society destroys when it sees only personality immanent in any genuine human relationship. The immanent is opposed to the transcendent, the intimate to the social; an anxious expectation of self-gratification is opposed to a faith in mankind despite itself. I believe that this secular vision of ours is a blindness. If a society believes in the unqualified liberation of the self, how can it take into account the simple fact that human beings have destructive impulses which should be hidden from others? This is why a society like ours, celebrating the sheer existence of human feeling, cannot be called privatized. There is no understanding of what it means to harbor an impulse in private. Disguise is taken to be only a further proof of the authoritarian injustices of present social arrangements; we are prone to convert discretion and tact into signs of domination. Surely the word liberation is itself misleading as a description of the present situation if it connotes a state of progress. A hundred years ago, personality was socialized only by ideas of repression; today it is not socialized at all. These are opposite and equal evils.

Today there is community without society: this pure *Gemeinschaft* is a self-destructive ideal which reifies the family and makes us blind to the evil in ourselves. We might try to end this destructive *Gemeinschaft* from within or from without. The best element of the women's movement has tried the first course; people start with their own immediate feelings and through group transactions and common action try to socialize these feelings, to move from a language of intimate injuries to a shared political commitment. When this process works, men as such cease to be the enemy and the set of conditions which lead men to play oppressive roles comes into focus; a social reality comes alive. One of the great failures of the antiwar movement of the last decades, by contrast, was its inability to organize discontent among soldiers because many people in the antiwar movement so personalized the war that every soldier was treated as responsible for the war unless he somehow could prove himself innocent. The idea of the woman's movement that intimate relations can be transformed into social relations is based on the notion that the destructive features of *Gemeinschaft* can be eliminated if people resolve truly to understand the origins of their feelings.

Destruction of *Gemeinschaft* from within is obviously a difficult business: chancy in its outcome, perhaps too idealistic in its assumptions, certainly dependent on considerable character strengths for the people involved. The other strategy against this modern *Gemeinschaft* is no less difficult. To weaken *Gemeinschaft* from without would mean renovating an impersonal social world in which people could escape their families or the burdens of their own feelings. The classic terrain of such a social world is the cosmopolitan city. Yet how can one revive crowd life, a social existence passed among relative strangers at bars, theaters, and cafes, when all the pressures of the culture are oriented to restoring human scale, creating environments in which people get to know each other as individuals and other forms of oppressive localism? Or when the city itself is fled as a place of danger, dirt, Negroes; when the logic of capital development follows the cultural logic of withdrawal? No one could argue that the city in its present state is very attractive, nor that the *flâneurs* of Baudelaire's Paris or the sense of the *monde* of Marivaux's can be recreated as though city planning were an essay in nostalgia. Yet the only concrete strategy against the psychological morality of modern capitalism, the only countervailing power from without against destructive *Gemeinschaft*, lies in renovating the city as a human settlement. The word crisis is abused but it has a meaning: there is a moral crisis in advanced capitalism and there is an urban crisis in it; these two have a real relationship, for until we learn how to create a living, impersonal environment in which people can wear the masks of sociability, and so disguise themselves, the pursuit of a true, essential, and authentic self will continue to be our moral compulsion.

Fred R. Berger

Pornography, Sex and Censorship

An observer of American attitudes toward pornography faces a
bewildering duality: on the one hand, we buy and read and view
more of it than just about anyone else, while, on the other hand,
we seek to suppress it as hard as anybody else. I presume that
these facts do not merely reflect a judgment of social utilities,
namely, that the best balance of goods is achieved by having it
available, but under conditions of prohibition![1] I believe, in fact,
that this state of things reflects aspects of our attitudes toward
sex, and much of the current controversy has tended to obscure
this fact, and to ignore important issues concerning sex and freedom to which the pornography issue points.

There is an important reason why the pornography controversy
in the American context has tended to be narrowly focused. Our
First Amendment prohibits government from abridging freedom
of speech and press. Whatever interpretation is to be given that

Reprinted by permission from *Social Theory and Practice* 4, No. 2 (1977), pp.
183–209. A somewhat shorter version of this paper was presented at the meeting of
the Society for Philosophy and Public Affairs, held in conjunction with the Pacific
Division meetings of the American Philosophical Association, March 28, 1975, in
San Diego. Professor Ann Garry delivered a commentary on the paper, for which
I am grateful; in several places I have utilized points she made. I also wish to
thank Susan Denning for her extremely diligent and helpful research assistance.

amendment, it is, in fact, stated in absolutist terms, and carries no mention or definition of obscenity or pornography. This difficulty is exacerbated by the fact that in the common-law background of our legal system, there is very little litigation which established clear legal definitions and doctrines. Obscenity convictions in the form we know them seem very much an invention of the 1800s, and the late 1800s at that.[2] Moreover, in our experience with obscenity litigation, we have discovered that an enormous array of serious, even important, literature and art has fallen to the censor's axe. Thus, liberals and conservatives alike have feared that the removal of pornography from the protections of the First Amendment can endanger materials the Constitution surely ought to protect. This has given the constitutional issue great urgency.

The upshot has been that much of the debate has centered on the question of definition, and, moreover, that question has been pursued with legal needs in mind.

In this paper, I want to put aside the First Amendment to ask if there are any justifiable grounds for rejecting the arguments offered for the censorship of pornography independent of First Amendment considerations. Moreover, I shall be concerned with the *censorship* of pornography, not its *regulation*. The regulation of speech often has the same effect as censorship, and that is an important danger; nevertheless, censorship and regulation differ radically in intention, and that is an important difference.[3] I should also indicate that I shall suppose that those who favor censorship (I shall refer to them as "the censors") are not *generally* in favor of censorship, and would not prohibit what they regard as "true" art or literature.

Moreover, to lend further clarity to my discussion I shall propose a definition which is useful for the purposes of this paper, and which picks out most of what is usually regarded as pornographic, and that is all I claim for it. I define pornography as art or literature which explicitly depicts sexual activity or arousal in a manner having little or no artistic or literary value.[4] (I am assuming that scientific and medical texts are a kind of literature, with appropriate criteria of acceptability.)

The definition does, I believe, make pornography a relatively objective classification, insofar as there are clear cases on both sides of the divide, and there are relatively standard literary and artistic criteria by which to judge disputed cases.[5] In this respect, I am somewhat sympathetic to the conservatives who chide those liberals who claim they are not able to recognize standard cases of pornography as such.[6]

I. OBJECTIONS TO PORNOGRAPHY: CONFLICTING VIEWS ON SEX

Generally speaking, there are three forms of argument employed by the conservatives in favor of censorship. First, they simply hold that pornography itself is immoral or evil, irrespective of ill-consequences which may flow from it.[7] Second, they sometimes assert that, irrespective of its morality, a practice which most people in a community find abhorrent and disgusting may be rightfully suppressed. Finally, they sometimes contend that pornography promotes or leads to certain kinds of socially harmful attitudes and/or behavior.

In this paper, I wish to concentrate on this last form of argument. The proponents of the first kind of claim cannot, for the most part, meet Ronald Dworkin's challenge to specify some recognizable sense of morality according to which their claims are true.[8] Though I am aware of one form of this argument which I think *can* meet that challenge, it is dealt with obliquely in my responses to the other claims. The second form of argument has been widely debated in the literature, and I have little to add to that debate.[9] The arguments do not turn on the nature of pornography as such, and, moreover, it is fairly clear that in contemporary America there is not an overwhelming abhorrence of pornography as such.[10] The last form of argument has been given new life, however, by claims based on analyses of pornographic materials as such. These new conservative arguments differ in important ways from the traditional views of the censors, and their arguments have been extremely influential. Each of the articles I shall discuss has been widely referred to; each has been reprinted a number of times, and all but one are cited in support of recent decisions in the courts.[11]

The traditional form of the claim can be labeled the "incitement to rape" theory. It holds that pornography arouses sexual desire, which seeks an outlet, often in antisocial forms such as rape. It is this version of the claim we are most familiar with, and the evidence which is available tends to refute it.[12] I shall have more to say about it later.

The conservative views I want to take up hold that the harms from pornography are somewhat long-range. These commentators maintain that the modes of sex depicted in pornography, and the manner of depiction, will result in altering our basic attitudes toward sex and to one another, so that in the end a climate of antisocial behavior will result. I have isolated four instances of such arguments in the literature of pornography.

The first claim I shall take up is put forth in an essay by George Steiner, entitled "Night Words," which has provoked considerable comment.[13] Though Steiner expressed disapproval of censorship because it is "stupid" and cannot work, his views have been taken as an argument supporting censorship. Steiner holds that pornography constitutes an invasion of privacy:

Sexual relations are, or should be, one of the citadels of privacy, the night place where we must be allowed to gather the splintered, harried elements of our consciousness to some kind of inviolate order and repose. It is in sexual experience that a human being alone, and two human beings in that attempt at total communication which is also communion, can discover the unique bent of their identity. There we may find ourselves through imperfect striving and repeated failure, the words, the gestures, the mental images which set the blood to racing. In that dark and wonder ever renewed both the fumblings and the light must be our own.

The new pornographers subvert this last, vital privacy; they do our imagining for us. They take away the words that were of the night and shout them over the rooftops, making them hollow. The images of our love-making, the stammerings we resort to in intimacy come prepackaged. . . . Natural selection tells of limbs and functions which atrophy through lack of use; the power to feel, to experience and realize the precarious uniqueness of each other's being, can also wither in a society.[14]

The second claim against pornography is made by Irving Kristol, in an article arguing for censorship. Kristol claims that pornography depersonalizes sex, reducing it to animal activity and thus debases it; that it essentially involves only the readers' or viewers' sexual arousal, and thus promotes an infantile sexuality which is dangerous to society:

The basic psychological fact about pornography and obscenity is that it appeals to and provokes a kind of sexual regression. The sexual pleasure one gets from pornography and obscenity is autoerotic and infantile; put bluntly, it is a masturbatory exercise of the imagination, when it is not masturbation pure and simple. . . . Infantile sexuality is not only a permanent temptation for the adolescent or even the adult—it can quite easily become a permanent, self-reinforcing neurosis. It is because of an awareness of this possibility of regression toward the infantile condition, a regression which is always open to us, that all the codes of sexual conduct ever devised by the human race take such a dim view of autoerotic activities and try to discourage autoerotic fantasies. Masturbation is indeed a perfectly natural autoerotic activity.... And it is precisely because it is so perfectly natural that it can be so dangerous to the mature or maturing person, if it is not controlled or sublimated in some way.[15]

The danger is borne out, he thinks, in *Portnoy's Complaint*. Portnoy's sexuality is fixed in an infantile mode (he is a prolific and inventive masturbator), and he is incapable of an adult sexual relationship with a woman. The final consequences are quite dire, as Kristol concludes: "What is at stake is civilization and humanity, nothing less. The idea that 'everything is permitted,' as Nietzsche put it, rests on the premise of nihilism and has nihilistic implications."[16]

Professor Walter Berns, writing in the magazine *The Public Interest*, maintains that pornography breaks down the feelings of shame we associate with sex. This shame, he holds, is not merely a dictate of our society, it is natural in that it protects love, and promotes the self-restraint which is requisite for a democratic polity:

Whereas sexual attraction brings man and woman together seeking a unity that culminates in the living being they together create, the voyeur maintains a distance; and because he maintains a distance he looks at, he does not communicate; and because he looks at he objectifies, he makes an object of that which it is natural to join; objectifying, he is incapable of uniting and is therefore incapable of love. The need to conceal voyeurism—the concealing shame—is corollary of the protective shame, the shame that impels lovers to search for privacy and for an experience protected from the profane and the eyes of the stranger.... Shame, both concealing and protective, protects lovers and therefore love.[17]

The upshot, as we might have suspected, is catastrophic. Under the banner of "the forgotten argument," Berns writes:

To live together requires rules and a governing of the passions, and those who are without shame will be unruly and unreliable; having lost the ability to restrain themselves by observing the rules they collectively give themselves, they will have to be ruled by others. Tyranny is the natural and inevitable mode of government for the shameless and the self-indulgent who have carried liberty beyond any restraint, natural and conventional.[18]

Finally, Professor Ernest van den Haag, in a series of articles, has argued for censorship on the grounds that pornography encourages "the pure libidinal principle," which leads to loss of empathy with others, and encourages violence and antisocial acts:

By de-individualizing and dehumanizing sexual acts, which thus become impersonal, pornography reduces or removes the empathy and the mutual identification which restrain us from treating each other merely as objects or means. This empathy is an individual barrier to nonconsensual acts, such as rape, torture, and assaultive crimes in general. . . .

By reducing life to varieties of sex, pornography invites us to regress to a premoral world, to return to, and to spin out, preadolescent fantasies—fantasies which reject reality and the burdens of individuation, of restraint, of tension, of conflict, of regarding others as more than objects of commitment, of thought, of consideration, and of love. These are the burdens which become heavy and hard to avoid in adolescence. By rejecting them, as least in fantasy, a return to the pure libidinal pleasure principle is achieved. And once launched by pornography, fantasy may regress to every more infantile fears and wishes: people, altogether dehumanized, may be tortured, mutilated, and literally devoured.[19]

My response to these claims has two parts. First, I shall try to show that they reflect certain attitudes toward sex that are rejected by many, and that pornography will be judged differently by people with different attitudes toward sex. Second, I shall try to show why the gruesome results these writers foresee as the consequences of the state's failure to suppress dirty books and art are *not* likely consequences. Pornographic materials, *by their nature*, I shall contend, are an unlikely source or means of altering and influencing our basic attitudes toward one another.

Let us begin by noting certain features of pornography on which the conservative claims seem to hinge. First of all, by virtue of its lack of finesse, pornography is stark; it tends to remove those nuances of warmth and feeling which a more delicate approach is more apt to preserve. Second, there is some tendency of much pornography to assult our sensibilities and sense of the private, to estrange us somewhat. This is not difficult to understand, and it is not simply a result of our culture's attitudes toward sex. Sex, quite naturally, is associated with the notion of privacy because in sex we are in a vulnerable state, both emotionally and physically—we are very much in the control of our feelings and sensations, less aware of environmental factors, very much involved in and attending to our state of feeling and present activity.[20] Such vulnerability is the mark of private states—states on which we do not want others to intrude. This is reflected also in our attitudes toward grief and dying. Moreover, because we *want* to be totally taken with the activity itself, we do not usually want others present. So, we can concede that there is some truth to the conservative analyses of the nature of pornography.

These conservative arguments, however, involve and presuppose views on sex that many people reject. I think it is important to make these more explicit. Steiner, as we have seen, regards sex as a source of "inviolate order and repose," in which a sense of our identity is achieved by virtue of the private words, gestures, mental images which are shared with loved ones. (I envisage a hushed atmosphere.) For Van den Haag, sex, or mature sex, properly involves the burdens of "conflict, commitment, thought, consideration and love." And Kristol has distinguished mere "animal coupling" from making love, labeling the former "debased." Professor Berns's views about the nature of sex are, perhaps, clarified in a footnote:

It is easy to prove that shamefulness is not the only principle governing the question of what may properly be presented on the stage; shamefulness would not, for example, govern the case of a scene showing the copulating of a married couple who love each other very much. That is not intrinsically shameful—on the contrary—yet it ought not to be shown. The principle here is, I think, an aesthetic one; such a scene is dramatically weak because the response of the audience would be characterized by prurience and not by a sympathy with what the scene is intended to portray, a beautiful love.[21]

The trouble with these views is that they see sex as normal or proper only within the context of deep commitment, shared responsibility, loving concern, and as involving restraint and repression of pure pleasure. Indeed, Professor Berns's footnote not only carries the suggestion that anything but married love is shameful, but also could be uncharitably interpreted as holding that "a beautiful love" is something which holds between disembodied souls, and in no way involves sexual communion, or the sharing of physical joy and pleasure. It seems to him that if we got some sense of the pleasure the couple take in one another physically, some hint of the physical forms of their communication and sense of mutuality, that this would somehow detract from our sympathy with their "beautiful love."

Now, many in our society reject these analyses of sex, either totally or partially. I want to sketch two possible views so that we might have a sense of the wider context of attitudes within which the pornography problem should be discussed. As many liberals share the conservative attitudes toward sex and many political conservatives do not, I shall label the views I discuss as "radical" and "radical-liberal," with no further political significance to be attached to them.

The radical maintains that the entire facade of sexual attitudes in contemporary society represent sham, hypocrisy, and unnecessary forms of social control. Sexual relations are governed by the notions of duty, shame, guilt. As such, there can be no honest sexuality, since mediating all sexual relations are feelings and associations which have nothing to do with our feelings *for* one another, and, often, little to do really with our sexual natures. The conservative picture of shared communication, in an aura of intimate connection, expressive of tender love, concern, commitment which are involved in mature (preferably married) sex, is an idealized, romanticized, unreal (perhaps even infantile) depiction of what really happens in sex. The fact is that most sex is routinized, dull, unfulfilling, source of neurosis, precisely because its practice is governed by the restraints the conservatives insist on. Those constraints dictate with *whom* one has sex, *when* one has sex, how *often* one has sex, *where* one has sex, and so on. Moreover, the web of shame and guilt which is spun around sex tends to destroy its enjoyment, and thus to stunt our sexual natures—our capacity of joy and pleasure through sex. The result is a society which is highly neurotic in its attitudes toward and practice of sex—all of which interferes with honest communication and self-realization.

The radical solution to this perceived situation is to treat sex *as* a physical act, unencumbered with romanticized notions of love. Human sex just *is* a form of animal coupling, and to make more of it is to invite dishonesty and neurosis.

It seems to me that it is *this* sort of attitude which the conservative most fears. Though the conservative claims that such an attitude will result in devaluing humans, it is not clear why. He seems to infer that because the radical is willing to treat others as sources of pleasure, without the necessity of emotional commitment, he therefore perceives them as mere *instruments* of pleasure. This, of course, does not follow, either logically or as a matter of probability. Nor have I ever met a conservative who thought that correspondingly, if people are permitted to make profits from others in business dealings, they will come to view them as mere sources of profits. The point is that it is absurd to suppose that one who no longer thinks of *sex* in terms of shame and guilt must lose the sense of shame and guilt at harming others, either through sex, or in other ways.

I do not wish to dwell on the radical position, however, because there is a more widespread view which I have labeled the "radical-liberal" view which I wish to consider. This conception accepts a large part of the radical critique, in particular the notion that guilt and shame, duty and commitment, are not necessary to fully human sex. The radical-liberal agrees that much of our ordinary sexual relations are marred by the inhibitions these impose. He or she need not, however, reject sex as an element in loving relationships, and he or she may well insist that love does engender special commitments and concern with which sex is properly entangled. But, the radical-liberal does not reject physical sex for its own sake as something debased or wicked, or shorn of human qualities. Indeed, he or she may insist that greater concern with the physical aspects of sexuality is needed to break down those emotional connections with sex which stand as barriers to its enjoyment, and as barriers to free open communication with others, and to one's development of a sense of one's sexual identity—a development in terms of one's own needs, desires, and life-style.

The intensity of such needs on the part of many people is, I believe, well-depicted in Erica Jong's contemporary novel, *Fear of Flying*. In the book, her heroine expresses her reaction to the attitude that a woman's identity is to be found in her relationship with a man. Female solitude is perceived as un-American and selfish. Thus, women live waiting to be half of something else, rather than being simply themselves. These American attitudes are perceived as inhibitions to the woman's self-discovery. The heroine describes her reaction:

My response to all this was not (not yet) to have an affair and not (not yet) to hit the open road, but to evolve my fantasy of the Zipless Fuck. The zipless fuck was more than a fuck. It was a platonic ideal. Zipless because when you came together zippers fell away like rose petals, underwear blew off in one breath like dandelion fluff. Tongues intertwined and turned liquid. Your whole soul flowed out through your tongue and into the mouth of your lover.

For the true, ultimate zipless A-1 fuck, it was necessary that you never get to know the man very well. I had noticed, for example, how all my infatuations dissolved as soon as I really became friends with a man, became sympathetic to his problems, listened to him *kvetch* about his wife, or ex-wives, his mother, his children. After that I would like him, perhaps even love him—but without passion. And it was passion that I wanted.[22]

She thus concludes that brevity and anonymity are requisite to the perfect zipless fuck. Finally, after describing a sample fantasy, she says:

The incident has all the swift compression of a dream and is seemingly free of all remorse and guilt; because there is no talk of her late husband or of his fiancee; because there is no rationalizing; because there is no talk at *all*. The zipless fuck is absolutely pure. It is free of ulterior motives.

There is no power game. The man is not "taking" and the woman is not "giving." No one is attempting to cuckold a husband or humiliate a wife. No one is trying to prove anything or get anything out of anyone. The zipless fuck is the purest thing there is. And it is rarer than the unicorn.[23]

Whatever one may interpret as the book's final evaluation of the Zipless Fuck, it is clear that the fantasy is a response to the need for a different attitude toward sex.

The point is that to many people, the conservative's picture of sex, and the sorts of social relations in which he imbeds it, has served to starve them of the unique development of their personalities, or an aspect of it. The antidote they see is a freer, more open attitude toward sex, removed from what they regard as a mystique of duty and guilt and shame.

People with the attitudes of the radical-liberal or who see themselves as impeded in their full self-realization by the traditional views on sex, may well find pornography something of no consequence, or may even find it beneficial—a means of removing from their own psyches the associations which inhibit their sexual natures. The plain fact is that pornography is used for this effect by various therapists, who have thereby aided people to more fulfilled lives for themselves, and happier, healthier relations with loved ones.[24]

Will such a concern with physical pleasure result in nonattachment, in antihuman feelings, in the loss of loving relationships? It is at least as plausible that just the opposite is the probable result, that by virtue of lessened anxiety and guilt over sex, an important source of human communion will be enhanced. In a Kinsey-type sex survey sponsored by *Playboy*, there was demonstrated a greatly heightened freedom in sex in America, and a greater emphasis on physical enjoyment, but this has not resulted in a significant lessening of the importance accorded to emotional ties.[25] Greater concern with pleasure has been used to *enhance* those relationships. Thus, it is no accident that among the millions who have lined up to see *Deep Throat*, *Behind the Green Door*, and *The Devil in Miss Jones*, have been a great many loving, married couples. Indeed, that there has come to be a body of "popular pornography"—porno for the millions—holds out some small hope that our culture will eventually develop a truly erotic artistic tradition, as explicitness becomes more natural, and tastes demand more of the productions.

We have seen that the conservative position presupposes attitudes toward sex which many reject, and that the alternative attiudes are consistent both with the acceptance of pornography and the values of care and concern for others. Let us turn now to the specific points the conservatives make concerning alleged harms.

II. THE RESPONSE TO CONSERVATIVE OBJECTIONS

I want to consider first the argument concerning privacy. It was Steiner's claim that pornography takes the "words of the night," and "by shouting them over the rooftops," robs us of the ability to use them or find them in private—sex becomes a matter in the public domain. Moreover, by dehumanizing the individual, people are treated as in concentration camps. As Steiner expressed it subsequent to the original publication of his essay: "Both pornography and totalitarianism seem to me to set up power relations which must necessarily violate privacy."[26]

If there is any plausibility to the first part of these claims, it must derive entirely from the metaphor of shouting the sacred night words over the rooftops. Were anyone to do such a thing with night words, day words, winter words, and so on, we would have a legitimate gripe concerning our privacy. But in what *way* is the voluntary perusal or viewing of pornography an invasion of privacy? His point *seems* to be that the constant consumption by the public of explicit sexual materials will come to make sex something "pre-packaged" for us, so that we will not discover how to do it ourselves, in our own ways. This is extraordinarily implausible, and if it were true, would constitute a reason for banning all literature dealing with human feelings and emotions, and ways of relating to one another. The evidence is that greater sexual explicitness is utilized as a means for people to have greater awareness of their sexuality and its possibilities, and to assimilate the experiences of others into their own lifestyles. The capacity to do this is *part* of what is involved in our being the unique invididuals we are. At any rate, people who *want* the stimulation of erotic materials, who feel freer in expressing themselves through the influence of sexy art, who do not *want* an environment in which sex cannot be appreciated through explicit literature and art, will hardly be impressed with the manner in which the censor protects *their* privacy.

I want now to turn to Kristol's view that pornography is auto-erotic, hence, infantile, and thus promotes a sexual regression which is a danger to civilization itself. The danger which this supposed form of infantilism poses is that it would destroy the capacity for an integral feature of mature relations (and ultimately civilized relations) if "not controlled or sublimated in some way."

Now the ultimate ground for censorship which the argument poses really has only secondary connections with the charges of autoeroticism and infantilism. Lots of things are "self-pleasuring" without being thought infantile or dangerous on that account. Consider the pleasures of the gourmet, or wine afficionado, or devotees of Turkish baths.

Kristol believes that masturbation, and pornography which is its mental form, has an appeal to us as adults, and this is dangerous. Because it *is so* attractive, it is liable to draw us away from real love, and this is why it must be headed off at the pass. The charge of infantilism, then, is only Kristol's way of making us feel bad about masturbating. By virtue of his claiming to know the rationale underlying "all the codes of sexual conduct ever devised by the human race," we are made to feel beyond the pale of civilized adult society. The argument turns, really, on the supposed dangers of an *overly* autoeroticized society, which he thinks the legalization of pornography will help produce.

In criticizing pornography on these grounds, Kristol has surely overshot his mark; for, there is nothing more masturbatory than masturbation itself. If Kristol is right, then his concern with pornography is too tepid a treatment of the danger. What the argument would show is that we must stamp out masturbation itself!

Moreover, Kristol is mistaken if he thinks that censorship of pornography will make one whit of difference to the incidence of masturbation. This is because the masturbatory imagination is perfectly limitless; it does not *need* explicit sexual stimuli. Deprived of that, it can make do with virtually anything—the impassioned kisses of film lovers, a well-filled female's sweater, or male's crotch,[27] even, we are told, a neatly displayed ankle or bare shoulder. The enormity of the problem Kristol faces is shown in the revelation of the *Playboy* survey that: "a large majority of men and women in every age group say that while they masturbate, they fantasize about having intercourse with persons they love."[28] The implications for the censor are staggering!

There are two further reasons why reasonable people will not take Kristol's view seriously. First, he underestimates the human capacity to assimilate varieties of sexual experience. People can enjoy pornography and intercourse without giving up one or the other.[29] Second, his entire argument grossly undervalues the appeal and attraction to us of the very thing he wants to preserve—

mature sexual love which is fulfilling, rewarding, and integrated into the course of a loving relationship. Pornography may be in some sense autoerotic; it can be pleasant to be sexually stimulated. But it is rarely its own source of ultimate satisfaction; it usually stimulates to acquire further satisfactions. Indeed, this is presupposed by some of the conservative arguments. But there is no reason to assume that such satisfaction will be sought exclusively through masturbation, when a healthy sex relation is available with a loved one. I have *never* heard anyone, male or female, complain that their love life had been ruined by their partner's turn to masturbation as a result of an excess of pornography. On the other hand, I have heard couples rave about sex had after viewing pornographic films.

Still, there does seem to be a lingering problem which the conservatives will regard as not adequately dealt with in anything said thus far. They think that literature and art *can* influence people's attitudes and beliefs, and also their behavior, and they cannot understand why the liberal, who believes this to be true in other cases, is unwilling to admit this with respect to pornography. Now, I believe the liberal *can* admit the possibility of a causal role for pornography with respect to people's attitudes and behavior. Such an admission does not, however, establish a case for censorship.

It would be quite extraordinary if literary and visual materials which are capable of arousing normal men and women did not also have some tendency to arouse people already predisposed to harmful conduct, and especially people with an unstable psychological makeup. It is believable, even apart from any evidence, that such people might act from the fantasies such stimuli generate.

When the conservative is reasonable, however, he recognizes that the stimulation and consequent influence of pornography is a function not merely of the nature of the stimulus, but also of the person's background, upbringing, cultural environment, and his own genetic and personality structure and predispositions.[30] Put *this* way, the conservative has a somewhat plausible claim that pornography can sometimes be implicated as having some causal role in the etiology of social harms.

Put in its most reasonable form, however, the claim makes quite *un*reasonable the censorship of pornography. There are two primary reasons for this: (1) Pornography is not distinguishable from other materials in producing *direct* harms of this kind; it may, in fact, exert a counter-influence to other materials which are more likely to have these effects. (2) The *indirect* harms—those produced through the influence of altered attitudes and beliefs, are highly unlikely, and not of a kind a society which values freedom will allow to become the basis of suppression without strong evidence of probable causal connections. It will seek to counter such remote influences with noncoercive means.

Let us turn to the first point—that other materials which no one would dream of suppressing are as likely to produce harms. Earl Finbar Murphy, writing in the *Wayne Law Review*, has given some graphic illustrations. He begins by pointing out that "everything, every idea, is capable of being obscene if the personality perceiving it so apprehends it." He continues:

It is for this reason that books, pictures, charades, ritual, the spoken word, *can* and *do* lead directly to conduct harmful to the self indulging in it and to others. Heinrich Pommerenke, who was a rapist, abuser, and mass slayer of women in Germany, was prompted to his series of ghastly deeds by Cecil B. DeMille's *The Ten Commandments*. During the scene of the Jewish women dancing about the Golden Calf, all the doubts of his life came clear: women were the source of the world's trouble and it was his mission to both punish them for this and to execute them. Leaving the theater, he slew his first victim in a park nearby. John George Haigh, the British vampire who sucked his victims' blood through soda straws and dissolved their drained bodies in acid baths, first had his murder-inciting dreams and vampire-longings from watching the "voluptuous" procedure of—an Anglican High Church Service!

The prohibition and effective suppression of what the average consensus would regard as pornographic would not have reached these two. Haigh, who drank his own urine as well as others' blood, was educated to regard "all forms of pleasure as sinful, and the reading of newspapers undesirable." Pommerenke found any reference to sex in a film, however oblique, made him feel so tense inside that, "I had to do something to a woman." Albert Fish, who has been called the most perverse case known to psychiatry, decided he had a mission to castrate small boys and offer them as human sacrifices to God as a result of reading the Old Testament. Each of these had the common quality of being beyond the reach of the conventionally pornographic. They had altered the range of the erotically stimulating, and each illustrates how impossible it is to predict what will precipitate or form psycho-neurotic conduct. . . . The scope of pornography, so far from being in any way uniform, is as wide as the peculiarities of the human psyche.[31]

These are extreme cases, but they do represent a pattern on the part of people disposed to deviant behavior as is borne out by studies of the personalities and backgrounds of sex offenders. In

their book, *Pornography and Sexual Deviance*, Michael J. Goldstein and Harold S. Kant report:

A problem that arises in studying reactions to pornography among sex
offenders is that they appear to generate their own pornography from
nonsexual stimuli. . . . The sex offenders deduced a significantly greater
number of sexual activities from the drawings (children playing near a
tree, figure petting a dog, and three people standing unrelated to each
other) than did the nonsex offenders. They also were more prone to incorporate recently viewed sexual pictures into a series of gradually more
explicit drawings. These results imply that the sex offender is highly receptive to sexual stimuli, and reads sexual meanings into images that
would be devoid of erotic connotations for the normal person. Certainly,
this finding was borne out by our study of institutionalized pedophiles
(child molesters), who found the familiar suntan lotion ad showing a
young child, with buttocks exposed to reveal his sunburn as a dog pulls at
his bathing suit, to be one of the most erotic stimuli they had encountered.[32]

Indeed, their studies seem to yield the conclusion that pornography itself does not tend to produce antisocial behavior, and that,
at least in the case of rapists, other materials are more likely to do
so:

We must consider that sex offenders are highly receptive to suggestions of
sexual behavior congruent with their previously formed desires and will
interpret the material at hand to fit their needs. It is true, however, that
while few, if any, sex offenders suggest that erotica played a role in the
commission of sex crimes, stimuli expressing brutality, with or without
concomitant sexual behavior, were often mentioned as disturbing, by rapists in particular. This raises the question of whether the stimulus most
likely to release antisocial sexual behavior is one representing sexuality,
or one representing aggression.[33]

In summarizing the evidence they gathered, and which is supported by other studies, they conclude that pornography does not
seem to be a significant factor in the behavior of sex offenders.
Moreover, there is some evidence that "for rapists, exposure to
erotica portraying 'normal' heterosexual relations can serve to
ward off antisocial sexual impulses."[34]

The point is that if we take the conservative's "harm" claim in
its most plausible form, we must conclude that while pornography
can play a causal role of this type, the evidence is that many other
ordinary visual and literary depictions are more likely to do so. If
we take seriously the claim that having this kind of causal role is
sufficient for a case for censorship, then we must do a much great-

er housecleaning of our media offerings than we had imagined. The problem is that while we know where to begin—with unalloyed portrayals of violence, we can hardly know where to end.

A further serious difficulty for the conservative "harm" argument arises when we ask just what *kinds* of backgrounds and attitudes *do* predispose to the unwanted behavior. The studies of Kant and Goldstein are of help here, especially with respect to rapists:

The rapists, who found it very difficult to talk about sex, said there was little nudity in their homes while they were growing up and that sex was never discussed. Only 18 percent of the rapists said their parents had caught them with erotic materials; in those instances the parents had become angry and had punished them. (In the control group, 37 percent reported that their parents know they read erotic materials, but only 7 percent reported being punished. Most said their parents had been indifferent, and some said their parents had explained the materials to them—an occurrence not reported by any other group.)[35]

For the *rapists*, the data suggest very repressive family backgrounds regarding sexuality.[36]

Moreover: "It appears that all our noncontrol groups, no matter what their ages, education, or occupations, share one common characteristic: they had little exposure to erotica when they were adolescents."[37]

These results at the very least carry the suggestion that the very attitudes toward sex which motivate the censor are part of the background and psychological formation of the personality patterns of sex offenders—backgrounds which include the repression of sexual feelings, repression of exposure to explicit sexual stimuli, an overly developed sense of shame and guilt related to sex. As we have seen, some of the censors advocate *just* this sort of model for all of society, wherein suppression of pornography is just *one* way of safeguarding society. It may well be that they are in the paradoxical position of isolating a possible evil of great extent, and then recommending and fostering a response which will help produce that very evil.[38]

There is, however, a more profound reason why the admission of a possible causal role for pornography in affecting attitudes and behavior need not support the conservative view, and why the traditional liberal may well have been right in not taking pornography seriously.

To begin with, I believe we have granted the conservatives too much in admitting that pornography depersonalizes sex. While there is a measure of truth in this claim, it is not literally true. By concentrating on physical aspects of sex, pornography does, somewhat, abstract from the web of feelings, emotions, and needs which are usually attendant on sexual experience in ordinary life. Nonetheless, people are not depicted as mere machines or animals. Indeed, where there is explicit pornographic purpose—the arousal of the reader or viewer—the end could not be accomplished were it not real fleshy people depicted. In addition, pornography almost always does have *some* human context within which sex takes place—a meeting in a bar, the bridegroom carrying his bride over the threshold, the window washer observing the inhabitant of an apartment. A study of pornography will reveal certain set patterns of such contexts; there is, indeed, a sort of orthodoxy among pornographers. And, there is an obvious reason: pornography springs from and caters to sexual fantasies. This also explains why so little context is needed; the observer quickly identifies with the scene, and is able to elaborate it in his or her own mind to whatever extent he or she wishes or feels the need. That pornography is intimately tied to fantasy—*peopled* fantasy—also accounts for one of its worst features—its tendency to treat women in conventional male chauvinist ways. Pornography, as a matter of sociological fact, has been produced by and for men with such sexual attitudes.

There are further grounds for holding that pornography does not, by its nature, dehumanize sex in the feared ways. It usually depicts people as enjoying physical activity, that is, as mutually experiencing *pleasure*. Typical pornography displays sex as something people take fun in and enjoy. There is usually little doubt the persons involved are *liking* it. All of the censors we have discussed treat *Fanny Hill* as pornographic, but it is obvious to anyone who has read the book that it absolutely resists the claim that the characters are not portrayed as real people with the usual hopes and fears, who desire not to be harmed, and desire a measure of respect as persons. The book concentrates on sex and sexual enjoyment, and *that* is why it is taken as pornographic.[39] Even sadistic pornography, it should be noted, depicts people as having enjoyment; and, it is usually sado-*masochistic* pleasures which are portrayed, with a resultant equalizing of the distribution of pleasure (if not of pain). In this respect, most pornography does not portray humans as *mere* instruments of whatever ends we have. And, in this respect, pornography does not express or evoke the genuinely immoral attitudes which a great deal of our movie, television, and literary materials cater to and reinforce.[40]

Indeed, much of what is found in the media *is* immoral in that it is expressive of, caters to, and fosters attitudes which *are* morally objectionable. People are treated as expendable units by international spies for whom *anything* is permitted in the name of national security; the typical laundry soap commercial treats women as idiotic house slaves; situation comedy typically portrays fathers as moronic bunglers who, nonetheless, rightfully rule their homes as dictators (albeit, benevolent ones); the various detective programs cater to the aggressive, dominating, *macho* image of male sexuality which is endemic within large portions of American society. Pornography cannot get off the hook merely by pointing out that it depicts *people*. On the other hand, most of it does not reflect or cater to attitudes as objectionable as one now finds dominating the output of television alone. And, where it does, it is not a result of the fact it is pornographic, but, rather, that it reflects conventional views widely expressed in other forms.[41]

There remains a final point to be made about the influence of pornography on attitudes. Pornography, when it does attract us, affect us, appeal to us, has a limited, narrowly focused appeal—to our sexual appetite. Such appeal tends toward short-lived enjoyments, rather than any far-reaching effects on the personality.[42] This is why pornography has essentially entertainment and recreational use and attraction; it is taken seriously by almost no one but the censors. It shows us people having sex, and that is it; we must do the rest. Serious literature and art, however, appeal to the whole person—to the entire range of his sensibilities, desires, needs, attitude patterns and beliefs and is thus far more likely to affect our ultimate behavior patterns. Even the limited reaction of sexual arousal is often better achieved through artistic technique. The conservatives deny this, but it is difficult to see on what grounds. Both in the essays of Van den Haag and of Walter Berns, there is the claim that aesthetic value would detract from the purely sexual appeal of a work.[43] I can only suppose that they think all people are possessed with, and exercise, the aesthetic sensibilities of literary and art critics, and thus readily separate out and analyze devices of technique in the experiencing of a work. This assuredly is not the case. Moreover, it is hardly plausible that artistic technique should enhance and further every *other* objective of an artist, and *not* be an accessory to the end of evoking sexual arousal. Real artistic value is unobtrusive in this respect.

Of course, television pap may well influence attitudes without having significant artistic value, merely by its sheer preponderance on the airwaves. But it is not *this* sort of role we need envisage for pornography liberated from censorship. Moreover, it is not clear its influence would be worse than that of other materials which now hog the channels.

It seems to me, however, that we have yet to make the most important response to the conservative's claims. For, up to now, we have treated the issue as if it were merely a matter of weighing up possible harms from pornography against possible benefits, and the likelihood of the occurrence of the harms. Unfortunately, this is the form the debate usually takes, when it is not strictly concerned with the First Amendment. But, something important is lost if we think the issue resolves into these questions. The more important issue turns on the fact that a great many people *like* and *enjoy* pornography, and *want* it as part of their lives, either for its enjoyment, or for more serious psychological purposes. This fact means that censorship is an interference with the freedom and self-determination of a great many people, and it is on this ground that the conservative harm argument must ultimately be rejected. For a society which accepts freedom and self-determination as centrally significant values cannot allow interferences with freedom on such grounds as these.

To give a satisfactory argument for these claims would require another paper. Moreover, I believe (with certain reservations) this has been adequately done in Mill's *On Liberty*. As the conservatives do not regard *that* as enunciating a clear, defensible body of doctrine,[44] I cannot hope to present an entirely convincing argument here. I want at the very least, however, to outline a minimal set of claims which I think bear on the issue, and which can provide ground for further debate.

The idea of a self-determining individual involves a person developing his or her own mode of life according to the person's own needs, desires, personality, and perceptions of reality. This conception has at least three features: (1) the person's desires are (so far are possible) expressions of his or her own nature—not imposed from without; (2) the manner of the development of his or her character and the pattern of the person's life, are, in large measure, a resultant of his or her own judgment, choice, and personal experience; and (3) the person's unique capacities and potentialities have been developed, or at least tried out.[45] Now, *if* one regards this as a valuable manner of living, and freedom as of value, *both* because it is intrinsic to treating others *as* self-determining agents, *and* because it is requisite for the realization of self-determination, then I think one will accept the following propositions concerning freedom:

1. The burden of producing convincing reasons and evidence is always on the person who would interfere with people's freedom and life-styles.
2. The person who would interfere with freedom must show that the activity interfered with is likely to harm others or interfere with their rights as individuals.[46]
3. Those who would deny freedom must show that the harm or interference threatened is one from which others have a superior right to protection.

Though these propositions are subject to considerable interpretation, it seems to me that one who accepts them will, at the least, recognize that the burden of proof is not symmetric either in structure or degree. The person who would deny freedom shoulders the burden, and, moreover, he or she does not succeed merely by showing *some* harms are likely to result. Accepting freedom and self-determination as central values entails accepting some risks, in order to *be* free. We do *not* presuppose that freedom will always produce good. And, insofar as the alleged harms are indirect and remote, we are committed to employing noncoercive means to combat them. Of course, we need not interpret this in a suicidal way—allowing interference only when the harm is inevitably upon us. But, at the least, we should require a strong showing of likely harms which are far from remote, and this is a burden which the censors of pornography *cannot* meet. Indeed, on this score, the conservative arguments are *many* times weaker than ones which can be made concerning many other kinds of communications, and such activities as hunting for sport, automobile racing, boxing, and so on.[47] If anyone wants a display of the extent to which our society allows recreation to instigate socially harmful attitudes and feelings, all he or she need do is sit in the stands during a hotly contested high school football or basketball game. And, of course these feelings quite often spill over into antisocial behavior.

Though I have defended pornography from criticisms based on its content or nature, I have certainly not shown that it is always unobjectionable. Insofar as it arises in a social context entirely infused with male sexism, much of it reflects the worst aspects of our society's approved conceptions of sexual relations. Too often, the scenes depicted involve male violence and aggression toward women, male dominance over women, and females as sexual servants. Moreover, there are aspects of the commercial institutions which purvey it in the market which are quite objectionable. My argument has been that this is not necessary to pornography as such; where it is true, this reflects social and sexual attitudes already fostered by other social forces. Moreover, I have maintained that by virtue of a feature which does seem to characterize pornography—its break with certain inhibiting conceptions of sexuality, pornography may well play a role in people determining for themselves the life-style which most suits them. A society which values self-determination will interfere with it only under circumstances which the censors of pornography cannot show to hold.

Of course, I have said almost nothing about the nature of the specific freedoms we incorporate in our notion of freedom of speech. It may well be that that set of rights imposes even stricter obligations on those who would suppress forms of its exercise.

NOTES

1. This proposition is argued for by one advocate of censorship. See Irving Kristol, "Pornography, Obscenity, and the Case for Censorship," *New York Times Magazine* (March 28, 1971), p. 23.
2. There are a number of brief summaries available of the development of the common-law approach to obscenity. See *The Report of the Commission on Obscenity and Pornography* (New York: Bantam, 1970), pp. 348–54; Michael J. Goldstein and Harold S. Kant, *Pornography and Sexual Deviance* (Berkeley: University of California Press, 1973), pp. 154–56; and an untitled essay by Charles Rembar in *Censorship: For and Against*, ed. Harold H. Hart (New York: Hart Publishing Co., 1971), pp. 198–227. Apparently, the leading case prior to the 18th century involved Sir Charles Sedley, who, with some friends, had become drunk in a tavern, appeared naked on a balcony overlooking Covent Garden, and shouted profanities at the crowd which gathered below; then he urinated upon, and threw bottles of urine on, the bystanders.
3. Regulation of speech is one of the most pressing problems for free speech in our contemporary, mass society, in which the control of the media is in relatively few hands, primarily concerned with the use of that media to produce profits. Moreover, the spectre of nonlegal controls, which Mill feared, is very much with us. It is surprising that so little attention has been given to the issue of the principles properly governing regulation. An indication of various forms of control utilized by government for the suppression of pornography is found by studying the development of censorship in the United States. See

James C. N. Paul and Murray L. Schwartz, *Federal Censorship: Obscenity in the Mail* (New York: The Free Press, 1961).

4. I regard it as a serious drawback of the definition that it rules out by *fiat*, the claim that pornography *can* be, in and of itself, significant literature. This claim is convincingly argued for by Susan Sontag in her essay "The Pornographic Imagination," reprinted in *Perspectives on Pornography*, ed. Douglas A. Hughes (New York: St. Martin's Press, 1970), pp. 131–169; also in her book *Styles of Radical Will* (New York: Farrar, Straus & Giroux, 1966). The argument for a broader, more inclusive definition is made convincingly by Morse Peckham in *Art and Pornography* (New York: Basic Books, 1969), chapter 1. Anyone with a serious interest in the subject of pornography will find this a most important work.

5. It is also clear that the definition would be a disaster in the legal context, since there is so great an area of *disagreement*. Moreover, there is a tremendous danger of a secondary form of censorship, in which literary critics come to watch closely how they criticize a work lest the critique be used by the censors. That this in fact has happened is testified to in an eye-opening note by the English critic Horace Judson, in *Encounter* 30 (March 1968), pp. 57–60. To his dismay, a critical review he wrote of Selby's *Last Exit to Brooklyn* was read into the record and used in banning that book in England.

6. See, for example, Ernest van den Haag, writing in *Censorship: For and Against*, p. 158. Also, in "Is Pornography a Cause of Crime?" *Encounter* 29 (December 1967), p. 54.

7. I believe that the minority report of the Presidential Commission on Obscenity and Pornography reduces to such a view, when it is not concerned specifically with possible harms. See, for example, the rationale given on pp. 498–500 of the report, for their legislative recommendations. Sense can be made of these passages *only* on the assumption the commissioners believe pornography is itself immoral. I might also note that if one looks up "pornography" in the *Readers' Guide*, he is advised "See immoral literature and pictures."

8. Ronald Dworkin, "Lord Devlin and the Enforcement of Morals," *Yale Law Journal* 75 (1966), pp. 986–1005; reprinted in *Morality and the Law*, ed. Richard Wasserstrom (Belmont, Calif.: Wadsworth, 1971), pp. 55–72.

9. For starters, one might review the essays in Wasserstrom, *Morality and the Law*.

10. In surveys done for the Presidential Commission, it was found that a (slim) majority of adults would not object to the availability of pornography if it could be shown it is not harmful. While hardly a declaration of adoration for pornography, this is not a demonstration of utter, overwhelming intolerance for it, either.

11. See, for example, Paris Adult Theatre I v. Slaton, 431 U.S. 49 (1973).

12. Report of the Commission on Obscenity, pp. 26–32, in which the ef-

fects are summarized. Also, Goldstein and Kant, *Pornography and Sexual Deviance*, pp. 139–153.

13. George Steiner, "Night Words: High Pornography and Human Privacy," in *Perspectives on Pornography*, pp. 96–108.
14. *Ibid.*, pp. 106–107.
15. Kristol, "Pornography, Obscenity and the Case for Censorship," p. 113.
16. *Ibid.*
17. Walter Berns, "Pornography vs. Democracy: The Case for Censorship," *The Public Interest* 22 (Winter 1971), p. 12.
18. *Ibid.*, p. 13. Berns cites Washington, Jefferson, and Lincoln as holding that democracy requires citizens of good character and self-restraint, and he seems to think that somehow this is a "forgotten argument" against pornography.
19. Van den Haag, in *Censorship: For and Against*, pp. 146–148.
20. The extent to which feelings of vulnerability can be involved in sex is testified to by the kinds of fears which can inhibit orgasmic response. In her book reporting on techniques she has used with non- or preorgasmic women, Dr. Lonnie Garfield Barbach reports that among the factors which inhibit these women from having orgasms is the fear of appearing ugly, of their partners being repulsed by them, of losing control, fainting, or screaming. See Lonnie Garfield Barbach, *For Yourself: The Fulfillment of Female Sexuality* (Garden City, N.J.: Doubleday, 1975), pp. 11–12.
21. Berns, "Pornography vs. Democracy," p. 12.
22. Erica Jong, *Fear of Flying* (New York: Signet, 1973), p. 11.
23. *Ibid.*, p. 14.
24. In *For Yourself*, Dr. Lonnie Garfield Barbach recommends the use of pornography for preorgasmic women seeking increased sexual responsiveness and fulfillment. See *For Yourself*, pp. 75, 77, 85, 86. Dr. Wardell B. Pomeroy, one of Kinsey's collaborators, wrote *Playboy*, in reaction to a 1973 Supreme Court ruling on pornography:

    As a psychotherapist and marriage counselor, I sometimes recommend various erotic films, books and pictures to my patients. Many of them report that erotica helps them to free them of their inhibitions and, thus, helps them function better with their spouses. Now they will have more difficulty in seeing and reading such seriously valuable material, and I am afraid I must enlarge my own library for their perusal. *Playboy* 20 (October 1973), p. 57.

25. This point is made at length in the report. One example: "Despite the extensive changes that the liberation has made in the feelings that most Americans have about their own bodies, about the legitimacy of maximizing sexual pleasure and about the acceptability and normality of a wide variety of techniques of foreplay and coitus, sexual liberation has not replaced the liberal-romantic concept of sex with the

recreational one. The latter attitude toward sex now coexists with the former in our society, and in many a person's feeling, but the former remains the dominant ideal." *Playboy* 20 (October 1973), p. 204.

26. Steiner, "Night Words," in *Perspectives*, p. 97.

27. That women look at, and are excited by, the bulges in men's trousers is given ample testimony in Nancy Friday's book on women's sexual fantasies. See *My Secret Garden* (New York: Pocket Book, 1974), the section entitled "Women Do Look," pp. 214–222.

28. *Playboy*, p. 202.

29. See, for example, *Report of the Commission on Obscenity*, pp. 28–29; also, Goldstein and Kant, *Pornography and Sexual Deviance*, p. 30.

30. Van den Haag seems to recognize this point. See "Is Pornography a Cause of Crime?" in *Encounter*, p. 53.

31. Earl Finbar Murphy, "The Value of Pornography," *Wayne Law Review* (1964), pp. 668–669.

32. Goldstein and Kant, *Pornography and Sexual Deviance*, p. 31.

33. *Ibid.*, p. 108–109.

34. *Ibid.*, p. 152.

35. *Ibid.*, p. 143.

36. *Ibid.*, p. 145.

37. *Ibid.*, p. 147.

38. To compound the paradox, if being a remote cause of harms is a prima facie ground for censoring literature, then we have some evidence that the conservative arguments ought to be censored. This is *not* a view I advocate.

39. I do not appeal to its conventional format—girl meets boy, girl loses boy, girl reunites with boy in marriage.

40. Professor Van den Haag holds that pornography "nearly always leads to sadistic pornography." It is not clear what this means; moreover, his argument is that this results *because* pornography dehumanizes sex. Since we have grounds for doubting this, we have grounds for doubting the alleged result. Also, since I am denying that pornography significantly dehumanizes sex, I am implicitly rejecting a further conservative argument I have not taken up, namely, that pornography is itself expressive of immoral attitudes irrespective of any further harmful effects. Since some liberals seem to be willing to silence Nazis or racists on such grounds, some conservatives think this argument will appeal to such liberals. I believe that both Kristol and Van den Haag maintain this view. See also Richard Kuh, *Foolish Figleaves?* (New York: Macmillan, 1967), p. 280ff. A position of this sort is maintained by Susan Brownmiller in her book *Against Our Will: Men, Women and Rape* (New York: Simon and Schuster, 1975), p. 201. Brownmiller regards pornography as an invention designed to humiliate women. I have not responded to her arguments as she gives none. Moreover, she employs a curious "double standard." She gives great weight to law enforcement officials' opinions

about pornography, but would hardly be willing to take these same persons' views on rape at face value.

41. In this paragraph I have attempted to bring to bear on the argument some points made by Professor Ann Garry, in her commentary on the paper at the meeting of the Society for Philosophy and Public Affairs in San Diego, March 18, 1975.

42. *Report of the Commission on Obscenity*, p. 28; and Goldstein and Kant, *Pornography and Sexual Deviance*, p. 151.

43. Berns, in *The Public Interest*, p. 12 footnote, and Van den Haag, in *Perspectives*, p. 129.

44. See, for example, Gertrude Himmelfarb's recent critical account of Mill, *On Liberty and Liberalism: The Case of John Stuart Mill* (New York: Alfred A. Knopf, 1974). It appears to me that she has not really understood Mill. Ronald Dworkin has picked out some of the most glaring of her errors in his review in *The New York Review of Books* 21 (October 31, 1974), p. 21.

45. I believe this is Mill's conception. See also Sharon Hill's essay, "Self-Determination and Autonomy," in *Today's Moral Problems*, ed. Richard Wasserstrom (New York: Macmillan, 1975), pp. 171–186.

46. I want to note three points here. First, this view of freedom permits interferences for *moral* reasons; it does *not* insist on the moral neutrality of the law. It does, however, focus on the *kinds* of moral reasons allowed to count as grounds for the denial of freedom. Second, it does not rule out special legal recognition of modes of living which are central to the culture, for example, monogamous marriage. This will have indirect effects on freedom which a liberal theory would have to recognize and deal with, but it need not rule out such recognition out of hand. In addition, the notion of "harm" could be taken to include conduct or practices which are both intrusive on public consciousness, and offensive. This could provide a basis for *regulating* the sale and distribution of pornography, even if *prohibition* is not justified. Important discussion of the principles underlying the treatment of offensiveness in the law is to be found in an article by Joel Feinberg, "Harmless Immoralities and Offensive Nuisances," in *Issues in Law and Morality*, ed. Norman Care and Thomas Trelogan (Cleveland: Case Western Reserve University, 1973). Michael Bayles's commentary on that paper, also found in the same volume, is very useful. Third, valuing self-determination may entail a limited paternalism in circumstances where noninterference cannot possibly further autonomy. That it is at least possible for noninterference to promote self-determination seems to have been conceived by Mill as a presupposition for applications of his principle of liberty. This helps explain some of his "applications" at the end of the essay. Just how to incorporate limited paternalism in a liberal theory is a thorny issue. The pornography issue, however, does not appear to significantly involve that issue. A useful treatment of paternalism is in Gerald

Dworkin, "Paternalism," in *Morality and the Law*, pp. 107–126.

47. So far as I can judge, the most telling "evidence" the conservatives have thus far come up with is: (a) *some* reasonable criticisms of the studies which have been done, and the interpretations which have been given them; and (b) a few, isolated, contrary studies (which are, coincidentally, open to similar or stronger objections). See especially the criticisms of Victor B. Cline in the minority report of the Presidential Commission on Obscenity and Pornography, pp. 463–489. While I do not think the conservatives need produce ironclad scientific data demonstrating their claims, we surely cannot allow the suppression of freedom when the reasons offered are poor, and the weight of available evidence is heavily *against* those claims. The minority report (it may be Dr. Cline writing in this instance—it is unclear) asserts that the "burden of proof" is on the one who would change current law. This is an indefensible imprimatur of existing law as such; and it is absolutely inconsistent with the recognition of freedom and self-determination as important moral values. The mere *existence* of law cannot be allowed as a ground for its continued existence, if freedom is to have anything but secondary importance.

Alison M. Jaggar

Prostitution

Prostitution has long been referred to as "the social evil."[1] "Whore" or "tart" has long been the ultimate epithet to be hurled against women. Social reformers, feminists and government agencies have long sought, in their various ways, to put an end to the sale of sexual services. But there are signs that this centuries old taboo is about to be reversed. Prostitutes themselves have organized unions calling for the decriminalization of prostitution. A recent survey showed that 59% of Republican voters favored its legalization in the United States.[2] And her supposedly autobiographical series detailing the life of "the happy hooker" have made Xaviera Hollander a best-selling author.

Is there any reason to oppose the decriminalization of prostitution or even the western European innovation of publicly raising capital to finance prostitution hostels?[3] The conditions of modern society appear to have undermined many traditional arguments against prostitution. Venereal disease can be detected quickly and

© 1980 by Alison M. Jaggar. A draft of this paper was read to the Society for Women in Philosophy at the Pacific Division meetings of the American Philosophical Association in March 1976, and also to the Canadian Philosophical Association in June 1970. The commentators were Christine Pierce, Susan Sherwin, and Winnie Villeneuve; to all of them I am indebted for their helpful suggestions. Since 1976, the paper has been read on a number of campuses both in the U.S. and the U.K. I am grateful to all those who helped me clarify my views in discussion and especially to the following people who were kind enough to send me written comments: Sara Ann Ketchum, Sara Ruddick, Michael Fox, Alan Soble, and Rollin Workman. Penelope Smith helped me with resources.

treated effectively. Illegitimacy can be prevented by modern contraceptive techniques; indeed, prostitutes now have a lower fertility rate than other women. And changing sexual mores mean that
sexual activity outside the marriage bed is increasingly taken for
granted. To decide how to respond to these developments, we
need a philosophical theory of prostitution. Such a theory should
state exactly what prostitution is, should tell us what, if anything,
is wrong with it and should help us determine what, if anything,
should be done about it. In this paper, unfortunately, I am not
able to offer a full-fledged theory of prostitution. Instead, I compare the relative merits of three attempts to provide such a theory
and identify the philosophical basis on which a comprehensive
theory of prostitution must rest. Thus I view my paper as a prole-
gomenon to a theory of prostitution.

The three approaches to prostitution that I shall discuss are the
liberal, the classical Marxist, and the radical feminist approaches.
Obviously, these do not comprise all possible views on prostitution. I choose them in part because they are all current views and
in part because I find them all, to some extent, plausible. In addition, they provide interesting contrasts not only in moral and political theory but in their accounts of just what they take
prostitution to be. Each begins from the paradigm case of the
prostitute as a woman selling her sexual services, but each picks
out very different features as essential to that situation. Thus, a
comparison of these theories of prostitution illustrates an important general point about the appropriate philosophical methodology for approaching not only the issue of prostitution but also a
number of other normative social issues.

I. LIBERALISM

The standard liberal position on prostitution is that it should be
decriminalized. This was the conclusion of the 1963 British *Wolfenden Report of the Committee on Homosexual Offences and
Prostitution* and it is the view of the American Civil Liberties
Union. The Wolfenden Committee argued that "private immorality should not be the concern of the criminal law."[4] They believed
that the function of the law was not "to punish prostitution *per
se*," but rather to regulate "those activities which offend against
public order and decency or expose the ordinary citizen to what is
offensive or injurious."[5] Hence, they argued that prostitutes might
be arrested for "importuning" but neither they nor their custom-

ers should be subject to any penalties for actually engaging in prostitution.

The American Civil Liberties Union argues that laws prohibiting prostitution are unconstitutional on several grounds.[6] For one thing, they deny equal protection of the law to women. In some states, prostitution statutes apply only to females. Indeed, according to traditional case law, a prostitute is by definition female; thus by legal definition a man cannot be a prostitute. The male customer of a female prostitute, moreover, is rarely subject to legal penalty while the female prostitute invariably is. In these and other ways, prostitution laws discriminate against women. Another argument for the unconstitutionality of prostitution laws is that they often treat the mere status of being a prostitute as an offence, thereby inflicting "cruel and unusual punishment". And the use of loitering as a criterion for prostitution is said to violate a woman's right to due process. Finally, the ACLU argues that prohibitions on prostitution are an invasion of the individual's right to control his or her body without unreasonable interference from the state. This last argument is the most important, for it entails that prohibition laws cannot simply be "tidied up" by such reforms as writing them in gender neutral language or by insisting on strict standards of evidence before convicting someone of prostitution. Instead, it argues that there should be no law prohibiting prostitution.

The private sexual act involved in prostitution is no less a personal right for being commercial. Therefore, the government should not be able to prohibit it unless the state can meet the very heavy burden of proof that banning it is beneficial to society.[7]

This author even goes beyond the Wolfenden Report by arguing that solicitation for prostitution should be decriminalized. She doubts that it is genuinely offensive to men and claims that "to legalize prostitution while prohibiting solicitation makes as much sense as encouraging free elections but prohibiting campaigning."[8]

Their agreement on the decriminalization of prostitution does not mean that liberals share a common view about its moral status. Liberal feminists have always seen prostitution as degrading to women and conclude that it should receive no encouragement even though it should be decriminalized. This attitude is implicit in the report of the NOW Task Force on prostitution which supports full prosecution of any acts of coercion to any person, public agency or group to influence women to become prostitutes.[9]

Others, however, claim to see nothing wrong with prostitution. Some prostitutes view themselves as entrepeneurs, choosing to go into business for themselves rather than to work for someone else.[10] One prostitute remarked that the work was really not tiring, that it was often less humiliating than dating.[11] The prostitute may see herself as the boss because she can say "No" to the deal;[12] as someone, therefore, who is less exploited than exploiting. Thus it may be argued that decriminalization will finally allow "the oldest profession" to take its place among the other professions so that prostitutes will be respected as offering a skilled service.

These liberal reflections on the moral status of prostitution, however, are generally taken as mere side comments. The central liberal line of argument is to stress the need for decriminalization by appeal to classical liberal ideals. Thus, liberal arguments emphasize the importance of equality before the law and of individual rights. They attempt to minimize government interference in the lives of individuals and they assume that there is a "private" sphere of human existence

comprehending all that portion of a person's life and conduct which affects only himself (sic) or if it also affects others, only with their free, voluntary and undeceived consent and participation.[13]

Prostitution, they believe, falls obviously within that sphere.

The usual liberal recommendation on prostitution, then, is that it should be treated as an ordinary business transaction, the sale of a service; in this case, of a sexual service. Because the prostitute engages in it out of economic motivation, liberals view prostitution as quite different from a sexual act commited by physical force or under threat of force; they view prostitution as quite different, for instance, from rape. Instead, they see it as a contract like other contracts, entered into by each individual for her or his own benefit, each striking the best bargain that she or he is able. The state has exactly the same interest in the prostitution contract as in all other contracts and may therefore regulate certain aspects by law. For instance, the law may concern itself with such matters as hygiene, control of disease, minimum standards of service and of working conditions, misleading advertising, payment of taxes and social security, etc. It should also ensure equal opportunity by redrawing the legal definition of prostitution so that an individual of either sex may be a prostitute. In these sorts of ways, the state would fulfill its traditional liberal function of ensuring fair trading practices. It should assure consumers of "a clean lay at a fair price."[14]

At first sight, the liberal approach to prostitution seems refreshingly straightforward and uncomplicated. As so often happens, however, this appearance is deceptive. One problem concerns the normative assumption that prostitution is a contract whose legitimacy is equal to that of other business contracts.[15] Although liberals view the paradigmatic social relation as contractual, they do not believe that all contracts are legitimate. Mill, for instance, denied the legitimacy of contracts by which individuals permanently abdicated or alienated their freedom to decide on future courses of action, and on this ground he argued that the state should not enforce either lifelong marriage contracts or contracts where an individual sold her- or himself into slavery.[16] Similarly, Joel Feinberg offers a number of different arguments which suggest why voluntary slavery contracts may be illegitimate. For instance, he suggests that it is inherently immoral to own another person and that such immorality ought to be forbidden by law; and he also suggests, on what he calls Kantian grounds, that we may not dispose of our "humanity" and that attempts to do so should not be recognized by law.[17] Without examining all the liberal arguments in detail, it is clear that the early liberal conviction that the primary purpose of the state was to uphold the sanctity of contracts has been weakened in contemporary times and liberals now also expect the state

to provide against those contracts being made which, from the helplessness of one of the parties to them, instead of being a security for freedom, become an instrument of disguised oppression.[18]

These restrictions on legitimate contracts might be strong enough to exclude prostitution. It may well be that prostitution constitutes the sort of selling of oneself that a liberal would refuse to countenance. And it is surely not implausible to consider many prostitution contracts as instruments of not very well disguised oppression. Those liberals, therefore, are being too hasty who simply assume the legitimacy of prostitution contracts. In order to establish that prostitution is simply an ordinary business contract, they need a clear theory of what kinds of contracts are legitimate. (Robert Nozick, for instance, believes that the law should recognize and enforce people's right to sell themselves even into slavery.)[19] And they need a clear analysis of prostitution together with a normative theory of sexuality.

Liberal writers have not devoted much attention to the latter question at least. Since they ordinarily assume that sexual relations fall within the "private" realm and hence are outside the sphere of legal regulation, the development of a normative theory of sexuality has not seemed important for their political philosophy.[20] Their main contribution to the analysis of prostitution has been to insist that a prostitute may be either male or female. Thus, liberals would rewrite laws regarding prostitution in gender-neutral language and would also, presumably, wish to revise the first part of the definition of "prostitution" in *Webster's New Twentieth Century Dictionary* which currently reads:

prostitute, n. 1, a woman who engages in promiscuous sexual intercourse for pay; whore; harlot.

Here, liberals would presumably substitute "person" for "woman" and would construe "sexual intercourse" broadly enough to cover sexual encounters between individuals of either sex. Such an interpretation would also allow so-called massage parlors within the definition of "prostitution." This liberal revision of the concept of prostitution may seem at first sight to be in line with common usage, with common sense and with common justice. As we shall see, however, there are other accounts of prostitution which draw the boundaries quite differently.

A final problem with the liberal position on prostitution concerns its assumption that the prostitute enters into the transaction voluntarily. It has often been pointed out in other contexts that the liberal concept of coercion is very weak. It may well turn out that the sorts of economic considerations that impel some persons into prostitution do indeed constitute a sort of coercion and that the prostitution contract may therefore be invalidated on those grounds. This is one of the objections made by the Marxist theory of prostitution, to which I now turn.

II. MARXISM

The Marxist approach to prostitution is considerably wider-ranging than the liberal approach, both because it attempts to understand prostitution in its social context and because it construes prostitution much more broadly. For instance, Marxists view prostitution as including not only the sale of an individual's sexual services; they see it also as the exchange of all those tangible and intangible services that a married woman provides to her husband in return for economic support. Sometimes they believe that prostitution may cover even the exchange of the services that a man provides when he marries a rich woman.

Whether or not marriage is a form of prostitution is determined, for the Marxist, by the economic class of the marriage partners. It is only where property is involved that marriage degenerates into prostitution; where no property is involved, for instance among the proletariat, marriage is based solely on mutual inclination. Thus Engels writes that, within the bourgeoisie,

the marriage is conditioned by the class position of the parties and is to that extent always a marriage of convenience. . . . this marriage of convenience turns often enough into the crassest prostitution—sometimes of both partners, but far more commonly of the woman, who only differs from the ordinary courtesan in that she does not let out her body on piecework as a wageworker, but sells it once and for all into slavery. And of all marriages of convenience Fourier's words hold true: 'As in grammar two negatives make an affirmative, so in matrimonial morality two prostitutions pass for a virtue'.[21]

In describing bourgeois marriage as a form of prostitution, Marx and Engels assume not only that men as well as women may prostitute themselves; they assume also that what is sold may not be restricted to sexual services. From this, it is but a short step to describing the sale of a number of other services as types of prostitution. Indeed, in the *Economic and Philosophical Manuscripts*, Marx asserts that all wage labor is a form of prostitution. He writes, "Prostitution (in the ordinary sense) is only a *specific* expression of the *general* prostitution of the *labourer*."[22]

Someone might object that this usage of Marx's is merely metaphorical, that he is simply utilising the pejorative connotations of "prostitution" in order to condemn wage labor. But the following entry in *Webster's New Twentieth Century Dictionary* supports the claim that Marx's broader usage is not metaphorical:

prostitute, *n*. 2. a person, as a writer, artist, etc., who sells his services for low or unworthy purposes.

If *Webster's* too is mistaken, and if there is indeed a philosophically significant distinction to be made between the woman who sells sexual services and the individual who sells services of any kind, then that distinction must be given a philosophical rationale.

Does the Marxist corpus contain such a rationale or does it, on the other hand, provide a reason for assimilating wage labor to prostitution? I think that it contains traces of both but that the tendency to assimilate prostitution to wage labor is probably stronger. Some of Engel's objections to prostitution in the narrower sense seem to depend on two specific normative beliefs about sexuality, that sex should be linked with love and that "sexual love is by its nature exclusive."[23] It is because of the latter belief that he worries, since he views both monogamy and prostitution as results of the same state of affairs (namely, male ownership of the means of production), whether "prostitution [can] disappear without dragging monogamy with it into the abyss?"[24] He is anxious to make monogamy, or at any rate sexual fidelity, "a reality—also for men."[25] Similarly, he wants to make the "paper"[26] description of bourgeois marriage into a reality by turning an economic transaction into a free agreement based on mutual sex-love. He writes:

Full freedom of marriage can therefore only be generally established when the abolition of capitalist production and of the property relations created by it has removed all the accompanying economic considerations which still exert such a powerful influence on the choice of a marriage partner. For then there is no other motive left except mutual inclination.[27]

Unfortunately, the theory of sexuality on which these objections to prostitution are based is left undeveloped. We are given no reason to believe that Engels's notion of "modern individual sex-love," which he describes as "the greatest moral advance we owe to [monogamy],"[28] is in fact anything more than a romantic Victorian prejudice.

Even if our intuitions about sexual relations do not agree with Engels's, however, I do not think that we are necessarily thrown back to the liberal view about prostitution. Instead I believe that it is possible to draw from the Marxist corpus another, more searching, more plausible, and more specifically Marxist critique of prostitution. This critique, however, is very similar to the critique of wage labor and thus leads us in the direction of assimilating female prostitution to the wage labor of either sex.

There are a number of different ways of explaining Marx's critique of the system of wage labor. In his earlier works, Marx stresses the concept of alienation, the estrangement of wage laborers from the process and the product of their work, from their co-workers and from their humanity itself. In his later works, Marx drops the terminology of alienation; there is considerable controversy over whether he retained the central ideas or whether there is an "epistemological break" between his earlier and his later work. Certainly in his later work Marx seems concerned to detail in a more concrete way the devastating consequences to the worker of the capitalist system. He shows how the bodies of wage laborers are distorted by industrial diseases and how their minds are damaged by the boredom of repetitive tasks. Under capitalism, he argues, workers become mere appendages to their machines, no longer human beings but merely factors in the capitalist production process. Their human capacity to work becomes reduced to the commodity of labor power and the value of this is measured not in terms of its ability to provide useful products but merely in terms of its price on the labor market. In both his earlier and his later work, Marx stresses the lack of genuine freedom that exists under capitalism. In particular, he argues that so-called free wage labor is free only in the sense that it is no longer limited by the medieval laws restricting entry into the labor market. But although individuals are free to decide for which capitalist enterprise they want to work, they are not free to refuse wage labor entirely. In order to survive, they are forced to become wage laborers.

The Marxist analysis of the position of women under capitalism is notoriously sketchy; in fact, the classic analysis was left to Engels after Marx's death. Engels's explanation of the special oppression faced by women under capitalism appeals to women's exclusion from wage labor and argues that women's liberation requires that they should be drawn into "public production." Nevertheless, in spite of the importance that they place on the distinction between those who are engaged in captalist production and those who are not, there are a number of places where Marx and Engels seem to draw parallels between the situation of women under capitalism and the situation of wage-laborers. For instance, in *The Communist Manifesto* Marx and Engels claim that the bourgeois fear that the communists will introduce "community of women" stems from the fact that

the bourgeois sees in his wife a mere instrument of production. He hears that the instruments of production are to be exploited in common, and, naturally, can come to no other conclusions than that the lot of being common to all will likewise fall to women.[29]

Both the bourgeois wife and the wage laborer, therefore, can be seen as "instruments of production," the latter of commodities, the former of babies. Prostitutes in the narrower, more conventional sense cannot be viewed in this way, of course. They perform a service rather than create a product.[30] Nevertheless, Marx presents prostitution as a paradigm case of the sort of alienated relationships that are created by capitalism, where money substitutes for concrete human characteristics. He writes that, under capitalism,

What I am and can do is, therefore, not at all determined by my individuality. I am ugly, but I can buy the most beautiful woman for myself. Consequently, I am not ugly, for the effect of ugliness, its power to repel, is annulled by money.[31]

Just as the capacity to labor become a commodity under capitalism, so does sexuality, especially the sexuality of women. Thus prostitutes, like wage laborers, have an essential human capacity alienated. Like wage laborers, they become dehumanized and their value as persons is measured by their market price. And like wage laborers, they are compelled to work by economic pressure; prostitution, if not marriage, may well be the best option available to them.

On the Marxist view, prostitution and wage labor (in so far as they are still separable) degrade not only the prostitute and the wage laborer. They dehumanize also the prostitute's client and the laborer's employer. Marx writes:

in the approach to *woman* as the spoil and handmaid of communal lust is expressed the infinite degradation in which man exists for himself.[32]

Engels goes further. He writes that prostitution

demoralizes men far more than women. Among women, prostitution degrades only the unfortunate ones who become its victims, and even these by means to the extent commonly believed. But it degrades the whole male world.[33]

(The last sentence provides an interesting comment on the extent of prostitution in Victorian England.) Marx describes the capitalist in a similar way:

Prostitution is only a *specific* expression of the *general* prostitution of the *labourer*, and since it is a relationship in which falls not the prostitute alone, but also the one who prostitutes—and the latter's abomination is still greater—the capitalist, etc., also comes under this head.[34]

Given this critique, it is hardly surprising to find in *The Communist Manifesto* the explicit statement that it is necessary to abolish "prostitution both public and private."[35] But Marx and Engels certainly do not suggest that this end may be achieved by legal prohibition. Since all forms of prostitution result from inequality of wealth, such inequality must be eliminated. And in our time this means that capitalism must be abolished. For it is capitalism that gives men control over the means of production, thus forcing women to sell their bodies and allowing men to maintain a sexual double standard in marriage. And of course it is capitalism, by definition, that maintains the wage system and so forces the majority of the population to prostitute themselves by selling whatever capacities to labor that they may possess. Thus Marxists believe that the elimination of prostitution demands a full communist revolution. Until then, in one way or another, "capital screws us all."

The Marxist discussion of prostitution is illuminating in many respects. It brings out the real economic coercion underlying the apparently free market contract and the parallels between prostitution and wage labor must still raise questions for some people, as no doubt they did for a Victorian audience, about the moral status of the system of wage labor. (It is perhaps a measure of how far contemporary populations have internalized bourgeois values that it is possible for liberals nowadays to use the comparison not to discredit wage labor but rather to rehabilitate prostitution.) Certainly, the philosophical assimilation of prostitution to wage labor is supported by the two entries in *Webster's Dictionary*. But this assimilation may not only be illuminating. It may also obscure certain important differences between prostitution and wage labor. It may not be a matter of indifference whether the prostitute is male or female or whether it is an individual's sexuality that is sold rather than her or his capacity to labor. Radical feminism argues that an adequate account of prostitution requires an emphasis on the feminine gender of the prostitute and the sexual nature of her service.

III. RADICAL FEMINISM

For contemporary radical feminists, prostitution is the archetypal relationship of women to men. Karen Lindsey sums it up this way:

We have long held that all women sell themselves: that the only available roles of a woman—wife, secretary, girlfriend—all demand the selling of herself to one or more men.[36]

Even a century ago, some feminists saw marriage as a form of prostitution and as long ago as 1909 Cicely Hamilton wrote that, although a woman cannot predict before marriage which of an infinite variety of possible tasks her husband may expect her to perform, the only thing she can be fairly certain of is that he will require her to fulfill his idea of personal attractiveness. As a matter of business, then, and not purely from vanity, she specialises in personal attractiveness.[37]

Contemporary radical feminists have extended this insight and now perceive most social interaction between women and men as some form of prostitution. Thus, they believe that almost every man/woman encounter has sexual overtones and typically is designed to reinforce the sexual dominance of men. Correspondingly, men reward this sexual service in a variety of ways: the payment may range from a very tangible dinner to the intangible but nonetheless essential provision of male approval and patronage. Paradoxically, radical feminists argue, some women are even forced to prostitute themselves by selling their celibacy. They may retain their alimony or their social security payments only by remaining "chaste."[38]

This radical feminist view contrasts both with liberalism and with Marxism in its insistence that prostitutes must be defined as women. It differs from liberalism in its broad construal of what constitutes sexual services and from Marxism in its refusal to assimilate prostitution to other types of wage labor. It sees the social function of prostitution primarily as a means neither for sexual enjoyment nor for profit. Instead, radical feminists see prostitution as an institution to assert the dominance and power of men over women.

With respect to prostitution in the narrow conventional sense, radical feminists admit that it may indeed satisfy the physical desires of men, but they see this as being only a subsidiary function. Primarily, they believe,

Prostitution exists to meet the desire of men to degrade women. Studies made by men reveal that very few even pretend they frequent prostitutes primarily for sexual gratification. Young boys admit they go to achieve a sense of male camaraderie and freedom. They usually go in groups and gossip about it at length afterward in a way that is good for their egos. Other men have expressed the prime motive as the desire to reaffirm the basic 'filth' of all women; or to clearly separate 'good' from 'bad' women in their minds, or for the opportunity to treat another person completely according to personal whim.[39]

In addition, conventional prostitution is seen as a way of controlling other women who are not culturally defined as prostitutes.

The existence of a category of women defined by this function of sex object, plus the fact that every woman must guard against 'slipping' into this category or being assigned to it (and the absence of a comparable group of men), is sufficient to understanding prostitution as oppressive to all women. By the ubiquitous 'threat' of being treated like a 'common prostitute' we are kept in our places and our freedom is further contracted.[40]

Thus,

The [prostitution] laws are fundamental to the male protection racket—to maintaining most women as private rather than public property.[41]

From this account of prostitution, it is clear that the radical feminist does not regard it as a morally neutral institution, either in the narrow or in the broad form. The radical feminist denies the liberal contention that conventional prostitution is a victimless crime. The victims are all women, but particularly the prostitutes themselves, outcast, degraded and exploited by all the men who, directly or indirectly, enjoy the benefits of prostitution.[42] Prostitution in its broad form is, of course, no more acceptable to the radical feminist. But,

Unlike religious reforms of the past, feminists do not base opposition to prostitution on anti-sex values. Just as with marriage, our opposition is to the economics of the situation. Sex is a fine thing when it is the free choice of the individuals involved—free of economic coercion. No one should be dependant on selling herself for support; all love should be free love.[43]

So it is the economic coercion underlying prostitution, which requires that a woman's sexuality can be expressed only in a manner pleasing to men, that provides the basic feminist objection to prostitution. This economic coercion means that ultimately the moral status of prostitution is identical with that of rape. Like rape, prostitution perpetuates the oppression of women by encouraging the view that women are mere sexual objects, hence reinforcing male dominance and female inferiority.

Needless to say, radical feminists want to eliminate prostitution in all its forms. For this, they see two preconditions. One is that the male demand for prostitutes should be eliminated. This requires a total transformation of men's attitudes towards women and it also requires the abandoment of such conventional myths about male sexuality as that men have a much stronger biological appetite for sex than women.[44] When masculinity is no longer so inseparably tied to heterosexual performance, feminists hypothesize that men will no longer demand prostitutes.

Recognition that the demand for prostitutes is not a biological inevitability is a comparatively recent insight in our culture. But feminists have always recognized that the *supply* of prostitutes is a function of women's inferior social status. Over fifty years ago, Emma Goldman remarked:

Nowhere is woman treated according to the merit of her work but rather as a sex. It is therefore almost inevitable that she should pay for her right to exist, to keep a position in whatever line, with sex favors. Thus it is merely a question of degree whether she sells herself to one man, in or out of marriage, or to many men. Whether our reformers admit it or not, the economic and social inferiority of woman is responsible for prostitution.[45]

Radical feminists believe, therefore, that the eradication of prostitution requires the abolition of the male monopoly of economic power together with an abandoment of the view that women are primarily sexual objects. So long as these two interdependent conditions exist, almost any significant transaction between a woman and a man must be a form of prostitution. Susan Brownmiller sums it up:

Prostitution will not end in this country until men see women as equals. And men will never see women as equals until there's an end to prostitution. So it seems that we will have to work for the full equality of women and the end to prostitution side by side.[46]

These two tasks are indistinguishable. And, until they are achieved, radical feminists believe that, contrary to what conventional morality may indicate, women are confronted by a choice which is morally indistinguishable: it is the choice between "sucking cock and kissing ass."[47]

To many people and especially to many men, the radical feminist account of prostitution seems startling and offensive. A number of objections to it spring immediately to mind. In order to try to make the radical feminist account more plausible, I shall outline some of these objections and probable radical feminist answers to them.

One common objection to the radical feminist view of prostitution argues that it is preposterous to suppose that, when a man brings gifts to a woman he loves or takes her out to dinner, he is treating her as a prostitute.[48] Such gestures are intended and should be received simply as tokens of affection. The radical feminist answer to this objection is that individuals' intentions do not necessarily indicate the true nature of what is going on. Both man and woman might be outraged at the description of their candlelit dinner as prostitution, but the radical feminist argues this outrage is due simply to the participants' failure or refusal to perceive the social context in which their dinner date occurs. This context is deeply sexist: the chances are that the man has more economic power than the woman; and it is certain that much of woman's social status depends on her attractiveness as defined by men. For women in our society are defined culturally as sexual objects so that "every day in a woman's life is a walking Miss America contest."[49] In these circumstances, it is almost inevitable that the man is buying "his idea of personal attractiveness."

But "almost inevitable" is not inevitable. It may be true that many more dinner dates are forms of prostitution than would appear at first sight. But surely it is not logically necessary that a man is prostituting a woman when he takes her out to dinner. What about the occasions when she pays for herself? Or even when she pays for him? Surely it is logically possible for a woman to treat a man as a prostitute? Some men even define themselves as prostitutes.

Here again the radical feminists point to the social context. They point out that the customers of so-called male prostitutes are invariably men and they argue that much of the indignity of being a so-called prostitute, for a man, is that he is being forced to assume what is paradigmatically a woman's role, that he is being feminized. Radical feminists argue that there is an asymmetry in social attitudes towards man's and women's sexuality. The portly, grey-haired man with the young blonde woman on his arm is viewed with nudges, envy and even admiration. But the portly, grey-haired woman, if she were ever able to induce a young blonde man to lend her his arm, would be viewed with scorn, ridicule or pity. She is viewed as being "used" by her young gigolo in a way that even a "golddigging" young woman is not able to use her older lover. For, given the different social status of women and men in our society, it is always true that, in sexual encounters between women and men, a man "has" and a woman "is had." And when a man "has" another man, he is depriving him of his masculine status. Young dependent males in prison are even referred to as "women."

In arguing that prostitution is paradigmatically a relation of women to men, radical feminists are remembering the sexism that has structured our history and that continues to pervade every aspect of contemporary life. They are remembering that women appear to have been defined always as "sexual objects" and that the "traffic in women" appears to have been the earliest form of exchange.[50] They are remembering that people's personal identity is grounded on their gender-identity so firmly that, while they may "pass" for black or white or be upwardly or downwardly mobile from their class, any attempt to change their gender is met inevitably with extreme anxiety, confusion and even hostility. They are remembering that a defining feature of gender is the way in which sexuality is expressed so that homosexuals, for instance, are commonly viewed as failing to be appropriately masculine or feminine. And finally, radical feminists are remembering that not only is gender in general tied up inextricably with sexuality but also that femininity in particular is defined in large part by the ability to be attractive sexually to men. Most women have internalized the need to be "attractive" in this way and even those who have not done so usually cannot afford to be indifferent to men's opinions. Whether housewife or wage-earner, therefore, and whether or not she allows genital contact, a woman must sell her sexuality. And since, unlike a man, she is defined largely in sexual terms, when she sells her sexuality she sells herself.

IV. TOWARDS A PHILOSOPHICAL THEORY OF PROSTITUTION

Although these arguments may not establish conclusively the correctness of the radical feminist approach to prostitution, they do make it much more plausible. And the questions raised by radical feminism help to determine what is required for a philosophical account of prostitution that is adequate.

First of all, an adequate account of prostitution requires a philosophical theory of sexuality. Such a theory must be in part conceptual, in part normative. It must help us to draw the conceptual boundaries of sexual activity, enabling us to answer both how non-genital activity can still be sexual and even how genital activity may not be sexual. Given our ordinary ways of thinking, this latter suggestion may sound paradoxical but it is becoming a commonplace for feminists to define rape as a form of physical assault rather than as a form of sexual expression. Similarly, some feminists are now insisting that prostitution raises no issues of *sexual* privacy: "Prostitution is a professional or economic option, unrelated to sexual/emotional needs."[51] And we have seen other feminists deny that the main purpose of prostitution is sexual, even for men. Not only must the needed philosophical theory of sexuality help us to identify just what sexual activity is; it must also help us to make the conceptual connections and distinctions between forms of sexual expression on the one hand and gender and personal identity on the other hand. It must clarify the relationship, if any, between sexual expression and love. And it must compare the human capacity for sexual activity to the human capacity to labor. Thus it must tell us, for instance, whether there is anything especially degrading about the sale of sexual services.

An adequate account of prostitution also rests, obviously, on a philosophical account of coercion. In particular, we need to know whether economic inducements are coercive and, if so, in what circumstances. Only from this philosophical basis can we work out the conceptual relationships between prostitution, rape and "free enterprise."

In addition to these conceptual and normative presuppositions, a useful account of prostitution also requires an investigation of the way in which the institution functions in contemporary society. We need to know why women engage in prostitution and why men do so. We need to understand the relationship between "the traffic in women" and other forms of exchange in our society; in other words, we need to understand the political economy of prostitution. Without such knowledge, our account of prostitution will remain at a very high level of abstraction; we will not be able to understand the specific phenomenon of prostitution in contemporary society, we shall not be able to determine what, if anything, is wrong with it and what, if anything, ought to be done about it.

But how can we ever arrive at these decisions when the various theorists, liberal, Marxist and radical feminist, all hold such widely different concepts of prostitution? Not only do the theorists disagree on what is wrong with prostitution and on what ought to be done about it; they even disagree on what it is. They each accept the paradigm case of a woman selling sexual services, but each presents a very different analysis of that paradigm case. For example, the radical feminist argues that the gender of the seller is essential to determining whether a situation is a case of prostitution, the liberal insists that it is the sale of a sexual service that is the central feature, while the Marxist focusses on the sale of an important human capacity by an individual of either sex.

How is this disagreement to be resolved? Is there a single correct analysis of prostitution on which we must agree before we can construct a normative moral and political theory about it? And is such a correct analysis to be found by looking up dictionary definitions or paying closer attention to ordinary usage?

I do not think so. I think that the issue of prostitution presents a clear example of the futility of that conventional wisdom which recommends that we begin by defining our terms. For the divergence in the competing definitions of prostitution does not result from failing to consult the dictionary or from paying insufficient attention to ordinary usage. It results from normative disagreements on what constitutes freedom, on the moral status of certain activities and, ultimately, on a certain view of what it means to be human. Thus, the disagreement on what constitutes prostitution is merely a surface manifestation of a disagreement over the fundamental categories to be used in describing social activities and over what are the important features of social life which need to be picked out. The inability of moral theorists to agree on what constitutes prostitution is an instance of the interdependence of principles and intuitions, of theory and data, even of fact and value.

The only conclusion that I draw from all this is perhaps the obvious one that prostitution is far from being a self-contained moral or political issue. What prostitution is, what is wrong with it and what should be done about it can be determined only within the context of a comprehensive social philosophy. This philosophy must explain what it is to be human, what it is to be a man or a woman, what kind of relationships should exist between individuals of the same and different sexes, what kind of social relationships will permit the institution of such relationships and what is the proper role of sexuality and work in human life. Reflections on the issues raised by prostitution shows the need for such a philosophy, but prostitution will be only one of the areas where it helps us determine what is to be done.

NOTES

1. Leo Kanowitz, *Woman and the Law: The Unfinished Revolution* (Albuquerque: University of New Mexico Press, 1969), p. 15.
2. Linda Thurston, "Prostitution and the Law," *The Second Wave* 1, No. 4 (1972), pp. 7–8, refers to an AP report, " 'Bawdy House Baron' Objects to Political Role," *Boston Globe* (September 1, 1970).
3. Marilyn G. Haft, "Hustling for Rights," *The Civil Liberties Review* 1, Issue 2 (Winter/Spring 1974), p. 23.
4. *The Wolfenden Report: Report of the Committee on Homosexual Offences and Prostitution*, Authorized American edition (New York: Stein and Day, 1963), p. 132. Another argument commonly given for the decriminalization of prostitution is that it would lessen the opportunities for blackmail, police pay-offs and protection rackets and hence break the current connection between prostitution and such crimes as blackmail, theft, rape, assault, drunkenness, drug abuse and bribery. Some prostitutes are in favor of this in the hope that it will legitimize their work.

5. *Ibid.*, p. 163.
6. The ACLU position on prostitution is summarized in their handbook by Susan C. Ross, *The Rights of Women* (New York: Discus Books, 1973), pp. 176–179.
7. Haft, *op. cit.*, p. 16.
8. *Ibid.*, p. 20.
9. NOW Resolution 141, passed at the sixth national conference of the National Organization for Women in Washington, D.C., in February, 1973.
10. Kate Millett, "Prostitution: A Quartet for Female Voices," in Vivian Gornick and Barbara K. Moran, eds., *Woman in Sexist Society* (New York: Basic Books, 1971) p. 52. It should be noted, however, that the woman who makes this claim also condemns prostitution as "slavery, psychologically."
11. *Ibid.*, p. 59.
12. *Ibid.*, p. 48.
13. John Stuart Mill, *On Liberty*, reprinted in *The Utilitarians* (New York: Anchor Books, 1973), p. 486.
14. Susan Brownmiller, "Speaking Out on Prostitution," in Anne Koedt and Shulamith Firestone, eds., *Notes From the Third Year* (New York: Notes From the Second Year, Inc., 1971), p. 38.
15. I owe this, together with a number of other important points, to Professor Christine Pierce who commented on an earlier draft of this paper when it was read to the Pacific Division of the American Philosophical Association in March, 1976.
16. Mill, *op. cit.*, p. 583.
17. Joel Feinberg, "Legal Paternalism," *Canadian Journal of Philosophy*, No. 1 (1971), pp. 105–124.
18. T. H. Green, *Liberal Legislation and Freedom of Contract* III, p. 388, quoted in D. J. Manning, *Liberalism* (New York: St. Martin's Press, 1976), p. 20.
19. Robert Nozick, *Anarchy, State and Utopia* (New York: Basic Books, 1974), p. 331.
20. Robert Solomon identifies liberal views on sexuality as a "mythology [which] appears to stand upon a tripod of mutually supporting platitudes: (1) and foremost, that the essential aim (and even the sole aim) of sex is enjoyment; (2) that sexual activity is and ought to be essentially private activity, and (3) that any sexual activity is as valid as any other." R. Solomon, "Sexual Paradigms," in this volume, pp. 89–99; p. 92.
21. Frederick Engels, *The Origin of the Family, Private and the State*, (New York: International Publishers, 1942), p. 63.
22. Karl Marx, *The Economic and Philosophical Manuscripts of 1844*, edited with an introduction by Dirk J. Struik, (New York: International Publishers, 1964), p. 133, footnote.
23. Engels, *op. cit.*, p. 42. I do not know how far Marx shared this belief, but it is certainly echoed in Lenin's rejection of "the glass-of-water"

theory of sex in communist society. "To be sure, thirst has to be quenched. But would a normal person normally lie down in the gutter and drink from a puddle? Or even from a glass whose edge has been greased by many lips?" V. I. Lenin, *The Emancipation of Women* (New York: International Publishers, 1934) p. 106.

24. Engels, *op. cit.*, p. 67.
25. *Ibid.*
26. *Ibid.*, p. 72.
27. *Ibid.*
28. *Ibid.*, p. 61.
29. Karl Marx and Frederick Engels, "Manifesto of the Communist Party," reprinted in *Selected Works of Marx and Engels* (Moscow and New York: New World Paperbacks, 1968), p. 50.
30. Professor Sara Ketchum pointed this out to me in a letter which discussed prostitution and Marxist theory in a very illuminating and helpful way.
31. Marx, *op. cit.*, p. 167.
32. *Ibid.*, p. 134.
33. Engels, *op. cit.*, p. 66.
34. Marx, *op. cit.*, p. 133, footnote.
35. Marx and Engels, *op. cit.*, p. 51.
36. Karen Lindsey, "Prostitution and the Law," *The Second Wave 1*, No. 4 (1972), p. 6.
37. Cicely Hamilton, *Marriage as a Trade* (London: Chapman & Hall, Ltd., 1909); selections reprinted in Nancy Reeves, *Womankind* (Chicago: Aldine-Atherton, 1971), p. 209. Some authors go so far as to charge that, contrary to public belief, marriage is less of an "honourable estate" than prostitution. "The wife who married for money, compared with the prostitute," says Havelock Ellis, "is the true scab. She is paid less, gives much more in return in labor and care, and is absolutely bound to her master. The prostitute never signs away the right over her own person, she retains her freedom and personal rights, nor is she always compelled to submit to man's embrace." Quoted by Emma Goldman, *The Traffic in Women* (New York: Times Change Press, 1970), p. 26. Contemporary radical feminists voice a similar point of view. "Wifehood is slavery with a measure of status and security; prostitution is a bit of freedom coupled with the stigma of outcast." Barbara Mehrhof and Pamela Kearon, "Prostitution," *Notes from the Third Year, op. cit.*, p. 72.
38. Mary Lathan, "Selling Celibacy," *Women: A Journal of Liberation 3*, No. 1 (1972), pp. 24–25.
39. Mehrhof and Kearon, *op. cit.*, p. 72. A similar claim is made by one of the prostitutes interviewed by Kate Millett: "There's a special indignity in prostitution, as if sex were dirty and men can only enjoy it with someone low. It involves a type of contempt, a kind of disdain, and a kind of triumph over another human being." Kate Millett, *op. cit.*, p. 54.

40. Mehrhof and Kearon, *op. cit.*, p. 74.
41. Jackie MacMillan, "Prostitution as Sexual Politics," *Quest: A Feminist Quarterly* IV, No. 1 (Summer, 1977), p. 43.
42. The men who profit from prostitution, according to the radical feminist, are not merely the customer and the pimp, but also the policemen, the prostitution lawyer, the judge, organized crime and ultimately, because of the "class significance" of prostitution, every man in this society.
43. Linda Thurston, "Prostitution and the Law," *op. cit.*, p. 8.
44. Recent findings by such researchers as Masters and Johnson suggest that the traditional belief in the lower sexuality of women is totally unfounded. Researchers are now questioning "the unproven assumption that powerful psycho-sexual drives are fixed biological attributes." Cathy Nossa, ("Prostitution: Who's Hustling Whom?," *Women: A Journal of Liberation, op. cit.*, pp. 26–27) quotes this from an article called "Psychosexual Development," *Transaction* (March, 1969), pp. 10–12.
45. Emma Goldman, *op. cit.*, p. 20.
46. Susan Brownmiller, *op cit.*, p. 39.
47. Cathy Nossa, *op. cit.*, p. 29.
48. This objection was expressed persuasively to me by Michael Fox. I don't know if he still would wish to press it.
49. Carol Hanisch, "A Critique of the Miss American Protest" in Shulamith Firestone and Anne Koedt, eds. *Notes from the Second Year: Women's Liberation* (New York: Radical Feminism, 1970), p. 88.
50. Gayle Rubin, "The Traffic in Women," in Ranya Reiter, ed., *Towards An Anthropology of Women* (New York: Monthly Review Press, 1975), pp. 157–210.
51. Jackie MacMillan, *op. cit.*, p. 47.

Elizabeth Rapaport

On the Future of Love: Rousseau and the Radical Feminists

I. INTRODUCTION

Love can make people happy or miserable. It can be mutual or one-sided. It can be symmetrical, two people loving each other in the same way, or asymmetrical. Love can express itself in the sharing and fusing of lives or in pathological dependence one upon another. Radical feminists tend to portray love as we know it as a one-sided pathological dependency of women on men. Can there be, could there be, mutual, symmetrical, nonpathological love between men and women?

Feminism, even a moderate feminism, is a doctrine with very radical implications. It is all the more surprising that radical feminist ideas have gained very large numbers of more and less unreserved adherents. It seems that virtually everyone now understands and agrees with the feminist slogan that "The personal is political." Nowhere is the political more personal than in sexual love between men and women. I have been surprised to find therefore that radical feminists tend to have temperate, even conserva-

Reprinted by permission from *The Philosophical Forum* 5, Nos. 1–2 (1973–74), pp. 185–205. My thanks to Joseph Agassi and Alice Jacobs for discussions we had about love; and to the editors, Carol Gould and Marx Warofsky.

tive views, on the possibility of love between men and women. Radical feminists for the most part present variants of a common analysis and critique of love. The analysis supports the conclusion that love between men and women is extremely difficult if not impossible in the present. But it also supports the conclusion that in a future in which women's liberation has been effected through radical economic and social reorganization, especially of our sexual, familial and childrearing institutions, love between men and women will be possible. Not only will it be possible but it will be one of the principal, if not *the* principal, supports and expressions of human happiness. It is striking that while feminists stigmatize love as we know it as a central cultural mechanism through which women's oppression operates and by which it is mystified and legitimated, love retains in the society of the future that same place at the pinnacle of valuable human experience that our culture ascribes to it.

The analysis of love as we now know it, which I'm calling the radical feminist analysis, pictures love as a destructive dependency relationship. Or rather women's love is pictured as a destructive dependency upon men; men are pictured as neither harmed by nor dependent upon the women they love, if they love at all. Love is not seen as a structurally symmetrical relationship which men and women love each other in the same way and have a similar or identical experience of love. Why don't radical feminists make their quietus with love present and future? There seem to be features of the experience of love which would incite a flat denial that love could lead to anything but heartbreak or suffocation.

My aim in writing this paper is to vindicate radical feminist optimism about the future of love. I want to compare three theories: that of Rousseau with that of two radical feminist writers, Ti-Grace Atkinson and Shulamith Firestone. Atkinson presents a rare truly denunciatory radical feminist rejection of love now and forever. Firestone is perhaps the most influential contemporary American radical feminist to have written on love. Her views are representative of that combination of optimism for the future and condemnation of the present possibility of love which I attributed to most radical feminists above.

Rousseau, that arch-wallower in sentimentality, author of two best-selling blockbuster love stories, *La Nouvelle Héloïse* and *Emile*, in which the love of Emile and Sophie is chronicled, had despite these credentials a theory of love which vividly elaborates the negative features of love. He depicts love as an inherently pathetic or perhaps tragic loss of personality and destructive dependency relationship for both men and women. Yet love has for him precisely that feature of mutuality, of symmetry of quality or character for men and women the lack of which the radical feminists claim is a chief flaw of love as we know it. Mutuality is apparently not enough for the rehabilitation of love, unless landing men and women in the same soup is sufficient for its reclamation.

The sort of radical feminist theory which Firestone presents puts forward two theses as to the conditions which must be satisfied if benign and humanly rewarding love between the sexes is to be possible:

Thesis I. What is wrong with love as we know it can be traced to differences in male and female personality constellations which give rise to characteristically different male and female love-pathologies. These pathologies are the product of the social and economic inequalities that obtain between the sexes and can be eliminated with the rectification of sexual inequality.

Thesis II. Love as we know it is a destructive dependency relationship. But dependency relationships need not be destructive. Constructive and mutually rewarding dependency relationships are possible.

The full meaning of Thesis II can only emerge upon reading what I have to say below. To the extent that I can rely upon it being initially understood, it may appear to be a trivial claim. Who indeed would deny it? Atkinson and Rousseau deny it. They deny it because they subscribe to the Counter-Thesis that all human dependency relationships are destructive. Both Atkinson and Rousseau are wedded to the very far from trivial psychological thesis that the human individual can only hope for happiness if he or she is emotionally and otherwise autonomous. Without autonomy the social condition of human life can only bring misery to the human subject.

If the feminist thesis, Thesis I, is detached from the social psychological thesis, Thesis II, and Thesis II is denied, the result is the extreme radical feminist view of Atkinson, in which love is banished from even a utopian conception of the future. Atkinson simply assumes dependency relations are always destructive. Firestone similarly assumes Thesis II is true. Its importance for the vindication of the future of love is easy to miss in her account. Rousseau was no feminist. His interest in love was not motivated by any concern with revealing the oppression of women. His views on love are explicitly developed within his social psychology. Rousseau's psychology therefore provides a useful framework in which to raise and study the social psychological aspects of love which are neglected by the radical feminists. It also provides a useful correction to the tendency in radical feminism to picture women as the sole victims of love as we now know it.

II. ATKINSON ON LOVE

It is not easy to imagine a more extreme view of sexual love than Atkinson's.[1] Yet she argues from some premises which are the common ground of radical feminists. Allow me to present a reconstruction of her argument in schematic form:

(1) There is no basis in essential or essentially different biological or psychological traits for the differences in social role and personality between men and women save one: women can bear children and men cannot. Otherwise, male and female roles and traits are cultural, not natural.

(2) Culturally acquired sexual roles and traits have a political origin. Very early in human history "men" took advantage of the one biologically different aspect of "women," childbearing, and the relative weakness and vulnerability that pregnancy entails to impose a differentiation of social function on "women." "Women" were forced to accept confinement and social definition in the ramified role of reproducing the species—childbearing, child-tending and familial service. This political imposition created men and women.

(3) Since male and female roles and traits are wholly the product of political oppression they can and should be eliminated in favor of a sexually undifferentiated human personality, culture and social system. "Men" and "women" must be destroyed.

(4) The politics and culture of sexual oppression is made possible by the sexual reproduction of the human species. A necessary step in extricating men and women from their present conditions of oppressor and oppressed is to eliminate sexual reproduction in favor of extra-uterine conception and incubation, now technically feasible. Sexual intercourse is not a human need but a social institution. Allegedly natural or biological sexual drives or needs would disappear with the elimination of their reproductive and political functions. "Sexual 'drives' and 'needs' would disappear with their functions."[2]

(5) Sexual love is wholly and inextricably bound up with the pathological deformations of human personality and its potentialities for realization associated with the humanly deplorable conditions of being a man or a woman. When sex goes, sexuality and sexual love go with it, and good riddance.

Atkinson says of sexual love, which for her has no human future:

The most common female escape (from their imprisonment in the female role and the denial of their humanity) is the psychopathological condition of love. It is a euphoric state of fantasy in which the victim transforms her oppressor into her redeemer: she turns her natural hostility towards the aggressor against the remnants of herself—her Consciousness—and sees her counterpart in contrast to herself as all powerful (as he is by now at her expense). The combination of his power, her self-hatred, and the hope for a life that is self-justifying—the goal of all living creatures—results in a yearning for her stolen life—her Self—that is the delusion and poignancy of love. 'Love' is the natural response of the victim to the rapist.[3]

What gives Atkinson's argument an air of the incredible is her attack on sexual intercourse itself.[4] She speculates that in a human future there may be some human value in "cooperative sensual experience" whose function and value would be a social and public expression of approval of the sensually gratified subject. She says that "the outside participant expresses by its presence an identification with the recipient's feelings for itself. This could serve as a reinforcement to the ego and to a generalization from the attitude of the agent towards the recipient to the attitude of the public as a whole toward the recipient."[5] Note that she is speculating not about the sexual future but the sensual future and that the kind of experience she envisions is not reciprocal but the gratification of one subject by another who represents the social community. Although Atkinson does not banish sensuality, this cannot be construed as a rehabilitation of love.

(1)–(3) are common ground for many feminists. Atkinson's uniqueness is her insistence that all aspects of sexuality including sexual intercourse itself are humanly eliminable, destructive cultural constructs. The question arises, why do not all feminists who share the view that maleness and femaleness are oppressive social constructs share the view that with the elimination of these constructs must come the elimination of if not human sexual contact then at least sexual intercourse between "men" and "women?" Can sexuality and sexual love be separated from "maleness" and "femaleness" as they have been socially constructed?

Atkinson's remarks about "cooperative sensual experiences" suggest the following theory about that complex emotional and sexual relationship we call romantic or sexual love. Sexual love is a destructive dependency relationship. It is incompatible with human autonomy, with the recognition by the self and others of the independent worth of the individual, for that human individual to be dependent upon any other particular individual or individuals for the fulfillment of its needs or the affirmation or conferral of its value. A human individual may need, however, or be enhanced in its sense of worth by, the generalized social recognition of its worth and the legitimacy of its needs. Therefore in an androgynous human future it would be wrong to expect what would formerly have been identified as "men" and "women" to want or have experiences of sexual love for people of the same or the opposite "sex." There is something wrong with love in addition to sexual oppression. It is a dependency relation which robs the lover of its autonomy, something that will be no more desirable when we are freed from the pathology of sexuality than it is now. Fortunately we will have no inclination for love once freed of the political and cultural compulsion to act out the roles of male and female, oppressor and oppressed.

This seems to me to be a not implausible theory for anyone who holds that love is a destructive dependency relationship and that "men" and "women" should be superceded. It certainly does induce shudders in anticipation of a world even more bereft of intimate contact than the isolation we presently endure and before which the contemporary spirit already quails.

I now want to turn to the kind of view of love which has more preponderant radical feminine support. We will see that it is Firestone's willingness to see dependency relationships rehabilitated that permits her to be both a good feminist and a partisan of a future for love.

III. FIRESTONE ON LOVE

I said in my introduction that for the radical feminist love is now impossible, but will be possible in a liberated human future. This is not quite accurate. The radical feminist thesis is that love as we now know it is a culturally pathological dependency relationship but that love can be a healthy and enriching dependency relation in the revolutionary future. The distinction is really between healthy and destructive love, not between love and no love. In the section on Rousseau below, we shall see a challenge to the claim that dependency relationships can be rehabilitated. Rousseau, like Atkinson, holds that all dependency relationships are destructive. Let us examine both the bad love of the present and the good love of the future as portrayed by Firestone.[6] I will begin by setting forth what I take to be Firestone's requirements for healthy love and then show why and how she thinks love as we know it differs from healthy love.

Mutuality

"Love between two equals would be an enrichment . . ."[7] The love relationship must be symmetrical in that both man and woman love each other in a similar or identical fashion. But another sort of mutuality is required if this is to be possible. Both man and woman must be and recognize themselves and each other as free-standing independent beings possessing equal and unqualified human worth as persons. Love has a precondition of self-respect and respect for the beloved's status as a free and equal human being.

Vulnerability, Openness, Interdependency

"Love is being psychically wide-open to another. It is a situation of total emotional vulnerability. "[8] An individual cannot be open, not to say wide-open, to another unless he or she respects himself. To be vulnerable is to recognize our need and desire for the other person. It is also caring for or prizing the other as much as ourselves because of his or her unique value for ourself. Love is thus both selfish and unselfish,[9] a feature of love founded in the recognition of our vulnerability. In healthy love dependency is not merely tolerable. It is essential.

Idealization

". . . the beauty/character of the beloved, perhaps hidden to others under layers of defenses is revealed."[10] Firestone emphasizes that the vulnerability of love makes it possible for lovers to reveal the best of themselves to each other, permitting an idealization more in the sense of a prizing of what is really there for each other rather than an over-estimation of the qualities of the beloved. Others have noticed another possible aspect of a not unrealistic or falsifying idealization of the beloved. Love may provide an opportunity for the recognition by the self of qualities he or she did not know he or she possessed before the lover discovered them and revealed them. Love may also occasion the growth and positive development of personality.[11]

The Fusion of Egos, the Exchange of Selves

Love between two equals would be an enrichment, each enlarging himself through the other: instead of being one, locked in the cell of himself with only his own experience and view, he could participate in the existence of another—an extra window on the world. This accounts for the bliss that successful lovers experience: Lovers are temporarily freed from the burden of isolation that every individual bears.[12]

Firestone argues that love as we know it does not satisfy any of these conditions. She claims that women love pathologically and men don't love at all. Firestone is in essential agreement with points (1)–(3) set forth in my reconstruction of Atkinson's argument above. We may therefore take (1)–(3) as the first installment of Firestone's analysis of love as we know it. The remaining crucial stages of the argument which provides the context for Firestone's critique of love are these:

(4') The political origins of the oppression of women by men have long been forgotten by both sexes. It is generally believed that the politically conditioned sexually differentiated social roles and statuses of men and women are essential or natural features of the two sexes. This is expressed as the ideology of male supremacy. Men are seen as powerful, active, self-sufficient and fully human; women as weak, passive, and dependent—support players in the essentially male human drama. Male nature is human nature, female nature is to be helpmeet of man.

(5') The ideology of male supremacy corresponds to the real economic, social and political condition of men and women in the present and through most of human history. Women *are* dependent on men. For the most part whatever women may achieve socially and economically in the real world of oppression in which we live is through their acceptance by and associations with men.

(6) Many of the changes introduced by modern industrial society have tended to undermine the power of men over women as well as the ideology of male supremacy—e.g. birth control technology, the possibility and the desirability of women having fewer children, women entering the paid labor force in massive numbers. "Romanticism develops in proportion to the liberation of women from their biology."[13] The love of women for men has the function of mystifying and reinforcing patriarchal hegemony. The function of romantic love is therefore the reinforcement of an otherwise weakened male hegemony.

(7) In the modern industrial world it is possible for women, by acting in concert politically and to a much lesser extent through

individual action, to establish lives for themselves as independent, active social and economic beings. Love induces them to try to live for and through men instead. Love robs them of the will, strength and insight into political realities and human possibilities necessary to attempt to overthrow male hegemony.

Firestone argues that under such conditions the love of woman for man can only be pathological and that men cannot love women at all. The mutual and self-respect which is necessary for healthy love is impossible where neither men nor woman regard women as genuine and autonomous persons. They cannot, therefore, be mutually wide open to each other. Men do not see a person worthy of the effort. Women's self-contempt precludes seeing themselves as having any personal substance and worth to reveal. They hope to gain substance and worth through the love of men.

Firestone claims that it is not generally the case that women idealize the men they love, although men tend to idealize the women they fall in love with. ("Falling in love" is very different from "loving" for Firestone, as I shall momentarily explain.) "...idealization occurs much less frequently on the part of women.... A man must idealize one woman over the rest in order to justify his descent to a lower caste. Women have no such reason to idealize...."[14] They regard themselves as defective and men as full human beings. All men are in a sense idealized in female eyes. They all possess the value of being self-sufficient, authentic, human subjects which women concur in believing is not true of themselves. However, it is not true that any woman can love any man. Social and economic status make some men more lovable than others.

Men, Firestone claims, don't love, they fall in love. They see special virtues in one woman, which she for her part knows are not there and so lives in terror of his disillusionment, which comes often enough. Firestone accepts the Freudian thesis that men at least are seeking an ego-ideal and substitute for the forbidden mother in the women they fall in love with. Freud himself seems to support Firestone. He holds that the satisfaction of love's desire lessens or leads to the cessation of love. Firestone and Freud find men fickle and prone to disillusionment. Firestone claims men fall in love rather than love both because they undervalue all women and unrealistically idealize the woman they fall in love with. Both prevent the intimate and open interaction with women that love requires. Women on their side prevent real contact by desperately trying to shore up men's illusions about them in order to hold their love.

Firestone has another reason for claiming men do not love and why when they fall in love they are wont to fall out of love soon after: Men fear dependency. Their model for vulnerability is not the openness of genuine love but the dependency-love of women as they know them. They associate dependency with weakness and insufficiency. They have good cause to fear the love women offer them as well. Women are after all seeking to devour men's independent substance. Without openness or respect on either side there can of course be no fusion of egos. In no way is love as we know it the genuine article.

I find Firestone's stigmatization of love as we know it as serving the function of legitimating and reinforcing male hegemony convincing. I also believe that there is much to be said for her distinctions between destructive and healthy love. Her account does not however deal adequately with the social psychological issue of the possibility of non-destructive dependency relationships. Rousseau's account of destructive love locates the pathology of love precisely in the destructive character of all dependency relationships. It is a critique of this sort of psychology which partisans of love's future must provide. Rousseau's account of destructive love also supplies a needed corrective to the radical feminist claim that men do not love. The pathology of destructive love engulfs both men and women.

IV. ROUSSEAU ON LOVE

Rousseau's theory of love might be captured by the traditional adage of husbands, "I can't live with her and I can't live without her," were the adage not so wry. The climate of love for Rousseau is bathed in intense feeling. Sexual love is portrayed by Rousseau as mutually destructive to men and women. Sexual love is at the center of Rousseau's account of social relations. It is the first other-regarding emotion that the developing human individual experiences and the paradigm of social relations with others. Sexual love is an inescapable human need. But the pursuit of love inevitably leads to frustration and unhappiness. The way we love inevitably defeats the end of love. Defeat in love engulfs our whole personality. It destroys not only love but the lovers as well. For Rousseau man's love is like his sociality. Man is naturally social. But social living, the condition of human development and self-realization, is the irredeemable cause of human misery. To be happy we must be self-sufficient. But because we are human we need others. We are therefore happy neither in isolation nor in company.

Love, according to Rousseau's psychology, is a natural but not an original human need or desire. The distinction between original and nonoriginal elements in the human constitution is crucial in Rousseau's psychology. For Rousseau ontogeny recapitulates phylogeny. The nature of the human species and the human individual can only be understood in terms of their identical developmental courses. Savage man is not natural man but natural man at the beginning stages of human development. He has the potential to develop intellectual and moral capacities which will carry the human race from the savage to the civilized state. The development of these capacities is necessary for the full realization of human possibilities. Savage man is an isolate, a self-sufficient creature, with minimal, peaceful and uneventful interactions with others of his kind. He develops the characteristic and essential human capacities of reason and conscience as his world becomes social. As human life becomes social, he comes to need and depend upon others. He gains his humanity but loses his self-sufficiency. The quality of his life depends on the quality of his society. The human personality requires social living for its development. Its contours and contents vary with different sorts of society, some of which suit the inborn features of human personality very much more comfortably than others. A bad fit produces much avoidable misery. But societies cannot be torn off and replaced like ill-fitting suits of clothes. Tragically the best fit is not nearly good enough to prevent human misery. Why this is so can be seen by tracing out the parallel ontogenetic developmental course.[15]

The human child like the human savage is an essentially asocial creature. Rousseau sees the human adult as ruled and motivated by two "sentiments" which organize and color his affective structure, *amour de soi*—rendered in English as "self-preservation," "self-love" or "proper self love" and *amour propre*, rendered in English as "pride," "selfishness" or "egotism." *Amour propre* is not yet an active principle in the infant and child. He is wholly a creature of self-love. *Amour de soi*, in savage and child, Rousseau regards as a benign principle. *Amour propre* is regarded as a pernicious principle that always leads to personal unhappiness and interpersonal conflict. The whole strategy of childhood education that Rousseau sets out in his *Emile* revolves around allowing the child to develop the powers to satisfy the desires of self-love in such fashion as to be as far as possible autonomous and self-sufficient. Both the powers and desires are naturally given and naturally develop commensurately so that the powers are adequate for the satisfaction of desire. Of course the child will need adult help and guidance. But adult help and guidance should be aimed at increasing his autonomy as well as perhaps the illusion of a greater autonomy than he really has. "True happiness consists in decreasing the distance between our desires and our powers, in establishing a perfect equilibrium between power and will."[16] Happiness will therefore be possible for the well-educated child as it never will be for the man in any possible human society.

If the child is made to feel dependent on the will of others, whether they are generous with him, over-generous, or whether they deny him, he will develop hostile feelings towards those around him. Worse, his personality structure will be adversely affected. He will be by turns servile and domineering in his attempts to gain his will through those on whom he is forced to depend. Rousseau's doctrine is that both tyranny and servility stem from impotence and breed hatred for those with the power to satisfy and withhold satisfaction of our desires. Tyrannical or servile, the frustrated child is equally miserable.[17]

Amour propre, sexual desire and the capacity for sexual love, all develop at the same time, at puberty, and bring in their train the development of genuinely other-regarding emotions and social interactions which go beyond an awareness of others as simply helps or obstacles to the child's own ends.

As soon as man needs a companion he is no longer an isolated creature, his heart is no longer alone. All his relations with his species, all the affections of his heart, came into being along with this. His first passion soon arouses the rest.[18]

Sexual love is a natural but not an original desire. The sexual desire is original but can be satisfied indifferently by any one of the opposite sex. Savages meet and couple in passing. They form no sexual relationships which endure beyond the desires of the moment. Sexual love involves choice of a lover. This choice involves comparison and preference. These preferences require standards of beauty and virtue. These standards of beauty and virtue are products of social living and culture.

All women would be alike to a man who had no idea of virtue and beauty, and the first comer would always be the most charming. Love does not spring from Nature, far from it; it is the curb and law of her desires; it is love that makes one sex indifferent to the other, the loved one alone excepted.[19]

But the lover desires to be loved in turn. And here is where *amour propre* enters, like the snake into the Garden of Eden.

We wish to inspire the preference we feel; love must be mutual. To be loved we must be worthy of love; to be preferred we must be more worthy than the rest, at least in the eyes of our beloved. Hence we begin to look around among our fellows; we begin to compare ourselves with them, there is emulation, rivalry and jealousy.[20]

The lover wants his love to be reciprocated. She must see him as preeminent in virtue and beauty, if he is to succeed. This necessarily activates the human capacity for *amour propre*, for jealousy, rivalry and the desire to gain an invidious esteem. He must strive to be or at least appear to be in her eyes the pre-eminent possessor of the qualities she prizes most. His child's autonomy, were he lucky enough to have achieved it, falls away. It is perilous to human autonomy to need another. But love, were it possible, would more than fully compensate. The lover loses his autonomy in a deeper sense. He must give up a life guided by *amour de soi*, by the pursuit of the natural desires that his heart has and which would realize the potentialities of his personality, and assume the straightjacket of being or appearing to be the man of her heart's desire. So it is with love and so it is in all other human relations in which the affections and esteem of others are courted. They necessarily make rivals of men, force us to give up independent standards of self-esteem for socially imposed standards of our worth. We lose touch with our natural feelings, forfeit the chance for self-actualization. We lose ourselves and present a false self in the lists of social competition. While it does not prevent feelings of affection or continual growth of sympathy for others, it does neutralize or prevents affection and concern for others whenever one's own desire for the affection and esteem of others are active. *Amour propre* haunts and destroys all our attempts to reach out and make genuine contact with others.

With these psychological doctrines as necessary background, let us look at Rousseau's theory of love, at what a benign and happy love would be like and of what love must become in the irremediable circumstances of human social living.

Natural Attraction, the Fusion of Egos

Rousseau emphasizes the affective aspects of love. The goal of love is the fusion of two personalities. For this union to occur there must first be an initial attraction founded in like sensibility.

This initial recognition of one's male or female counterpart provides the sentimental basis and the pull which draws us into union. Julie writes to her lover, Saint-Preux,

> Our souls touch, so to speak at all points, and we feel an entire coherence ... hence forward we shall have only mutual pleasures and pains; and like those magnets of which you were telling me that have, it is said, the same movements at different places, we shall have the same sensations though we were at the two poles of the earth.[21]

Dependency

Love begins with the recognition of a need for another, with the discovery of the radical insufficiency of the self and one's own powers for self-realization. The lover recognizes and feels his lack of or loss of autonomy. Saint-Preux writes to Julie, "I am no longer master of myself, I confess, my estranged soul is wholly absorbed in yours."[22]

Mutuality

Love would be mutual. Saint-Preux wants to possess as well as be possessed by Julie. If love is to be returned both man and woman must regard each other as worthy of love. Rousseau is certainly a male supremicist. He holds male and female nature are essentially different. Woman was made for man. The essence of womanhood is to serve, to please and to nurture man. Yet men value and respect the complementary and alien submissive virtues of women despite the defectiveness of female nature when judged by the standard of male nature. All the intellectual and moral inequalities of the sexes are neutralized by the mutual recognition of the need for love. Men do not respect women as full persons in the male sense. But they respect the terrible power women have to give or withold the love they need. Men and women are equal in love. They are equally vulnerable and equally powerful.

Idealization

Love begins with the attraction and recognition of a like sensibility which seems to hold out the possibility of fusion of personalities. But love also requires that we see in the other and continue to see features of personality radically different from our own. The lover must find the perfections of the other and alien sex in the beloved, the perfections he or she necessarily lacks. Since love involves choice and standards of compassion between members of a sex, love's choice is for the man or woman pre-eminent of their sex. The standard of perfection will be a mixture of the personal and the public. It will be public insofar as canons of male and female beauty and virtue are cultural norms. It will be personal insofar as it involves placing a high value on the possession of certain qualities which may be found in either sex and which the lover finds in both himself and the beloved. These make possible the natural affinity of particular men and women for each other.

Exclusivity

If one man or woman is found perfect and finding perfection is a requirement for loving, there must be exclusive, complete fusion with and absorption in another. A multiplicity of love relations is precluded.

Rousseau holds that the achievement of love is illusional or delusional. To see why we must look at one more feature of love.

The Logic of Dependence

The lover is dependent, entirely, terribly dependent on his beloved for something he needs, the reciprocity of his love. Therefore loving falls under the domain of *amour propre* not *amour de soi*. The lover cannot achieve love's desire, reciprocity, by the exercise of his own powers. He will only be loved if she finds him pre-eminent. He must present himself in the guise in which she would see her beloved. This leads to a false presentation of the self and the chronic fear of exposure and loss of love. Along the way the lover loses himself and necessarily the opportunity to gain love for this lost self.

But what of the fortunate possibility that a pair of lovers actually possess the very virtues that they seek and find in each other? Might not fortunate couples each rich in personal merit not escape the predicament of self-falsification and self-loss in love. The answer, I think, must be no. Love operates in the domain of *amour propre* not *amour de soi*. The reciprocity of need and dependence cannot prevent the disastrous working out of the effects of dependence in the human personality. To be happy we must be autonomous. But we are not autonomous in love. Therefore we cannot be happy in love. Love operates in the domain of *amour propre*. Human beings can only act in a fashion not self- and mutually destructive when they are motivated by desires whose satisfaction is within their own powers. If we need another, the terrible possibility remains that their gratification of our need will be withdrawn. Even if love has been met with complete responsiveness, there is the future to dread. It is not within our power to secure the future love of our beloved against surfeit, disillusionment, or a rival found more worthy. Therefore, the lover is in a position of weakness, of impotence. Impotence forces him to employ tyrannical or servile means in futile attempts to secure what cannot be secured. The lover becomes a tyrant or a slave because of his impotence. In so doing he must both become and reveal a personality lacking in the perfections the lover sought and that he or she had found. In his weakness he confirms or creates the very doubts about his worthiness he feared his beloved was entertaining. Even if the doubts and fears that consume lovers and the jealous and craven responses they make do not result in the withdrawal of love, these feelings themselves, together with the sense of impotence they spring from, make the lover miserable. Such is certainly the case with Saint-Preux who is given to depressive fits of jealous rage against his friend and protector, Lord Edward. Love is an illusion or a delusion. Or if you prefer, love is a genuine enough human experience, but a miserable one. Lovers may possess each other and consume each other, but they lose themselves.

I believe that Rousseau's two great fictional accounts of love, the story of Emile and Sophie and of Saint-Preux and Julie, support my interpretation of Rousseau's theory of love if properly read. Despite the undeniable aspects of the sentimental celebration of romantic love characteristic of these works and which largely account for their tremendous popular success, love is portrayed as a tragic disappointment in both. Rousseau had what has been called a bourgeois conception of love.[23] The ideal is married love. In one of his two great love stories the hero marries the girl and loses her. In the other he simply loses her. Both losses propel the male lovers, whose side of the story Rousseau identifies with and treats more fully, into massive depressions and sends them off on years-long travels to try to forget and heal their wounds. Both Emile and Saint-Preux are depicted as men of unusual pasts and merits. Emile is unusual in that he has been carefully educated for the attainment of happiness and virtue despite, and in the midst of, what Rousseau regarded as a deplorable social environment. Saint-Preux is portrayed as a man of unusual talents and qualities. Both, as a result of loving, succeed in doing nothing of any note in the world, more significant in Saint-Preux's case, and feeling nothing but intense misery, more significant in Emile's case.

Julie writes to her lover Saint-Preux:

Love is accompanied by a continual uneasiness over jealousy or privation, little suited to marriage, which is a state of enjoyment and peace. People do not marry in order to think exclusively of each other, but in order to fulfill the duties of civil society jointly, to govern the house prudently, to rear their children well. Lovers never see anyone but themselves, they incessantly attend only to themselves, and the only thing they are able to do is love each other.[24]

Despite his bourgeois ideal of love, it seems to be Rousseau's opinion that even the slight requirements for the fulfillment of women's social role are incompatible with love, while potentially great and virtuous men have their capacity to act in the world as well as their happiness destroyed by love. In the little read and as far as I know untranslated sequel to *Emile, Emile et Sophie*, the tragic dissolution of Emile's marriage is portrayed. Emile's marriage falters because that paragon of virtue is distracted by Parisian pleasures and neglects his wife. It seems that when a social evil is not introduced as an obstacle to love's desire (Saint-Preux's low birth prevents his marriage to Julie), and even when the best of men and women have the best of chances for success love fails. His desire realized, Emile loses interest in his wife until her unfaithfulness revives the fires and torments of love.

V. THE FUTURE OF LOVE: SEXUAL LOVE AND SOCIAL PSYCHOLOGY

I have been writing about love as if there were one kind of experience of love that was uniform for all people or among all people of the same sex. This is almost certainly not the case. No doubt there are very different sorts of sexual love. But the theories I have been considering focus on certain core features of sexual love that reflect either psychological invariance or the differential impact on men and women of social conditions and cultural norms. These features permit considerable latitude for talking about the experience of men and women in love in a univocal way without inadmissible abstraction or distortion.

There is something to be learned from both Firestone's and Rousseau's accounts of love. We can make at least a beginning to identifying the causes of the pathologies that disfigure sexual love and point the way to its rehabilitation. Radical feminism need not lead to the excesses of Atkinson or to the denial that men as well as women are the victims of love as we now know it.

It seems to me that Firestone's account of the pathology of

women's love is essentially accurate. Without self-respect and the respect of men grounded in the social and economic equality of the sexes, men and women cannot meet on the terrain of mutual openness and appreciation which love requires. Although Firestone claims that men can't love, her account of man's sexual and romantic encounters with women and Rousseau's are in fact much closer than this startling claim would seem to suggest. Firestone traces male inability to love to the fear of dependency. Rather than inability to love, we should follow Rousseau in identifying the distinctive pathology of male love as precisely that fear of dependency which he claims is the explanation for the dysfunctional character of love for *both* men and women. We should retain however a Firestonean prospective on the distinctiveness of male and female experience of love and their roots in the social inequality of the sexes.

If love is to be rehabilitated, something must be very wrong with the Rousseauvian thesis that dependency relationships are always self- and mutually destructive. Something *is* very wrong with this thesis. The radical feminist Thesis I, which explains the pathology of love as we know it as the product of sexual inequality, must be supplemented by an elaboration and substantiation of Thesis II. Dependency relations need not be destructive if our social psychological natures and the social conditions which they reflect are transformed.

There is a paradox at the heart of Rousseau's account of social relations. To be humanly happy we need others. But if we need others we are lost. Rousseau wanted to repudiate the kind of psychological egoism which regarded human beings as wholly selfish and as having purely instrumental interactions with each other. Interactions whose goal was the satisfaction of the self, a self which was only in peripheral ways effected by or a product of its society and culture. But he was too deeply mired in individualism to make more than a very partial break with its social and psychological theory. He was able to project the essential effects of social living on the individual's personality structure only as threats to the integrity and happiness of the self. The result is a theory which posits the insufficiency of the human individual to achieve his or her self-realization in society. But what is really wanted is a theoretical critique of the insufficiency of individualism. This is a very large and a very difficult theoretical task which it goes without saying I cannot undertake here. But a few remarks will show the relevance of this critical task to the rehabilitation of love.

If autonomy from the need for others is posited as a necessary condition for human happiness, all dependency relations are necessarily pernicious. Add that they are unavoidable and you have the plight of Rousseauvian love. But suppose that the just fear of dependency of men on women and women on men that now obtains is the product of dysfunctional economic and social relations not just between the sexes but throughout social life, not the product of some deficiency in human nature. Suppose that the fear of dependency is a variable feature of human personality attributable to social conditions which drive them into invidious competition for the social status and esteem which could be accorded everyone in a society where cooperative institutions supported fruitful and healthy interdependency. Suppose that the thesis is false, that love, respect, and esteem are only given to him who is so pre-eminent in the eyes of others as to scarcely seem to require the further perfection of being loved by others. Suppose we could grant our love on some basis other than the supposed absolute pre-eminence of the beloved. Under conditions in which lovers did not seek pre-eminence according to social norms of attainment in those whom they loved, dependency would not have the terrible aspect of courting almost certain exposure and failure. Love's eye could still seek and find the special qualities that lead to preferment, draw affection and nourish the growth of personality in lovers. Human differences and variety in sensibility and qualities would still guide and motivate love-choices. Such encounters would still be fraught with the perils of rejection and failure but not hopelessly and inevitably so. What I am proposing is a socialist theory of social psychology, of which we have now only the barest sketch. Love may be rehabilitated if the just fear of dependency relations we learn from love as we know it turns out to be grounded not in fear of ourselves but the pathological distortions of human personality produced by an unjust, destructive and successfully alterable social order.

Radical feminists have forced an admission on the part of many socialists that traditional socialist programs are insufficient for achieving women's liberation. The insufficiency of a feminist program alone to give love a future shows that this most personal of political problems requires more than sexual equality for its solution.

NOTES

1. Ti-Grace Atkinson, "Radical Feminism" and "The Institution of Sexual Intercourse," both in *Notes From the Second Year: Women's Liberation*, Boston, 1969.

2. Atkinson, "The Institution of Sexual Intercourse," p. 45.
3. Atkinson, "Radical Feminism," *Notes from the Second Year: Women's Liberation*, pp. 36–37.
4. Atkinson's attack on sexual intercourse is part of her contribution to the debate about female sexuality and in particular, the vaginal orgasm. She writes, "The theory of vaginal orgasm was created quite recently to shore up that part of the foundation of a social institution that was being threatened by the increasing demand by women for freedom for women. The political institution I am referring to is the institution of sexual intercourse. The purpose, i.e., the social function, of the institution is to maintain the human species." (*Ibid.*, p. 42.)
5. Atkinson, "The Institution of Sexual Intercourse," *Notes From The Second Year: Women's Liberation*, p. 47.
6. Cf. *The Dialectic of Sex*, New York, 1970; especially Chapters 5 and 6, "Love" and "The Culture of Romance."
7. Firestone, *ibid.*, p. 128.
8. *Ibid.*,
9. Cf. J. O. Wisdom, on the paradoxically selfish and unselfish quality of love, "Freud and Melanie Klein: Psychology, Ontology and Weltanschauung" in *Psychoanalysis and Philosophy*, ed. by C. Hanley and M. Lazerowitz (New York: 1970), pp. 349–354.
10. *Ibid.*, p. 132 .
11. Cf. Wisdom, *ibid.*, p. 383. Also Simone de Beauvoir, *The Second Sex*, Bantam Books, New York, 1953.
12. Firestone, *ibid.*, p. 128.
13. Firestone, *ibid.*, p. 146.
14. Firestone, *ibid.*, p. 131.
15. Cf. Rousseau's *A Discourse on the Origin of Inequality*, for his phylogenetic account.
16. *Emile*, Everyman Library, p. 44.
17. Cf. *Emile*, Part II.
18. *Ibid.*, p. 175.
19. *Emile, ibid.*, p. 175.
20. *Ibid.*, p. 176.
21. *La Nouvelle Héloïse*, Pennsylvania State Press, 1968, p. 47.
22. *La Nouvelle Héloïse*, p. 83.
23. Denis de Rougemont, *Love in the Western World*, New York, 1956.
24. *La Nouvelle Héloïse*, p. 261–262.

Jacqueline Fortunata

Masturbation and Women's Sexuality

The following paper is a contribution to a future, more inclusive theory of sexuality in our culture. This theory is not biased against masturbation as are the traditional male-authored theories with which it is contrasted. It offers at least a partial explanation of the inequalities suffered by women in sexual encounters with men. Further, it provides a reasonable framework in which to understand some facets of a woman's sexual experience with both female and male partners. Briefly, I argue that an ideal sexual act is, at least in part, an act of inquiry and of coming to know.

Our culture provides us solely with male-authored theories of sexuality, which reflect male values, needs and experiences, and which virtually ignore the values, needs and experiences of women. These theories are biased in favor of heterosexuality, intercourse and sex with a partner, which are seen as the most desirable and normal kinds of sexual behavior. They are teleological, ascribing a purpose to sex, be it reproduction, orgasm or communication. These theories suggest that sex is, ideally, one kind of experience, uniform for all people in our culture. On each of these theories, masturbation falls short of the ideal sexual act in some

This paper is an expanded version of a paper read at a meeting of The Society for the Philosophy of Sex and Love, Eastern Division of the American Philosophical Association, Washington, D.C., December, 1978. I read the paper under my former name, Jacqueline Kinderlehrer.

way and, therefore, is seen as perverse, immoral, incomplete, narcissistic or minimal sex.

In devaluing masturbation, these theories implicitly devalue women's sexuality. The well-known investigations of Masters and Johnson have significantly challenged the traditional Freudian notion that a mature woman's orgasmic center must be transferred from the clitoris to the vagina, thus making her dependent on intercourse for mature sexual satisfaction. The clitoris, and not the vagina, is the primary locus of a woman's sexual pleasure; therefore, direct stimulation of the clitoral area by any part of the body is perhaps the most effective method of arousing a woman to orgasm. For both men and women, self-stimulation and stimulation by a lover can be similar acts. A woman can achieve sexual satisfaction by herself, with a man or with another woman, and the path to satisfaction is similar in each case. If masturbation is devalued, it would seem as if a woman's needs for sexual satisfaction are in general devalued. In hypervaluing heterosexuality and/or intercourse, traditional theories reinforce the unquestioned and naive assumption that a woman's sexual satisfaction is dependent upon a man. In hypervaluing two-person sex, traditional theories reinforce the unquestioned and naive assumption that a woman's sexual satisfaction is dependent upon another person. Two-person sex, possibly with conditions to be met by the interpersonal attitudes and responses of the partners, is seen as real sex by every theory I discuss; masturbation is an imitation of the real thing.

That self-stimulation and manual stimulation by a lover are seen to be similar acts in some circumstances is reflected in some common uses of the term "masturbation." The following statements exemplify two such uses: "he masturbated his partner to orgasm," "he masturbated himself with her vagina." In another use, a person using his or her own hand to achieve arousal or orgasm, in the presence of a lover, is described as masturbating. These uses appear to be inconsistent with the common definition of masturbation as a solitary sexual activity.

For the purpose of this paper, "masturbation" is defined as a sexual activity in which there is only one participant. It is contrasted with sexual activity with more than one participant. The focus of the definition is on how many participants there are. What the activity consists in, and what the attitudes and beliefs of the participant(s) are towards each other, themselves, and the sexual activity they are engaged in are not relevant.

The main reason for adopting this definition is to avoid ambiguity. The ambiguity present in "masturbation" allows the term to be used as an insult to women, as can be seen in the following example.

The following question appeared on the Hite Questionnaire: "Do most men masturbate you?"[1] Women expressed anger at this question, one responding, "To call vaginal stimulation of the penis intercourse, and to call manual stimulation of the clitoris masturbation, insults me and makes me angry."[2]

The ambiguity of "masturbation" also allows masturbation to be conflated with intercourse, as in the following example. R. D. Laing states:

If masturbation counterfeits intercourse, intercourse can be a counterfeit of masturbation. Intercourse may merely mask the essentially masturbatory nature of the act.[3]

Laing does not clarify the sense of his statements here, but given Laing's stipulated definition of masturbation as an act of "self-induced bodily excitement in relation to an imagined other(s),"[4] it would seem that intercourse could be a counterfeit of masturbation if some or all of the following conditions were met: (1) The other person has the ontological status of a thing, not a person; (2) The act of sexual excitement was self-induced rather than other-induced; (3) The so-called masturbating partner was excited in relation to imagined others rather than to her (his) partner. If some purpose is served by distinguishing (1), (2) and (3) from ordinary intercourse, it is clearly in our interest to distinguish them unambiguously, especially as (1), (2) and (3) have negative moral connotations.

For the purposes of this paper, then, masturbation is any sexual activity in which there is only one participant. Masturbation is not contrasted with sexual activity in which orgasm is reached by sexual intercourse, nor is it contrasted with sexual activity with another person in which one's own bodily movements account for part (all) of one's sexual pleasure.

If a person employs fantasy while masturbating, s(he) does not typically believe s(he) is not alone. If s(he) confuses reality and fantasy and believes that s(he) is in the presence of another person when in fact s(he) is not, it seems to me that this person is masturbating but does not realize s(he) is doing so.

Proposed theories of sexuality provide many things. It is possible to view several of them as expressing ideals or describing paradigmatic sex. A theory of sexuality might also try to explain the contingent facts of our sexual development (hand-in-hand with psychology). But it seems to me that a theory of sexuality can have another task: it may help us organize, interpret and evaluate the experience of sex. This is a legitimate task for philosophy and one that I will carry out in this paper.

I would like to illustrate this point with two folk theories of sexuality with which I grew up. One theory closely resembles Aristotle's theory of tragedy. This is not, however, an imitation theory; sexual activity with another person is a real sexual activity. The theory entails an imitation theory of masturbation. Under this theory there is a plot to sex with a beginning, a middle and an end: foreplay, intercourse and orgasm. Orgasm is a kind of catharsis: one enjoys a diminution of a strong feeling, an emotional release and relief. There is the spectacle of sex: this ranged from the back seat of an automobile to a romantic setting in bed, with soft lights and soft music. In actual heterosexual practice, the plot of sex was tied to the male's needs: sex began with his arousal, continued for his pleasure, and ended when his needs were met. The plot describes his sexual response. In general, orgasm follows intercourse for the male; as performer, he acted upon the woman and enjoyed his solitary orgasm. As audience, she observed him.

One of the myths attached to this theory of sexual activity was that simultaneous orgasm was achievable in the missionary position. According to the myth, it would be impossible in the ideal orgasm, which was the *sine qua non* of the ideal sexual act, to distinguish my orgasm from my partner's. This seems incoherent to me; on a par with sharing the same toothache with another.

The theory more closely fits heterosexual sex with a partner than it fits either masturbation or sex between two women. It fits fairly well sex between two men, who can achieve intercourse. It provides a way of evaluating sex; sex missing any of the key nodal points, foreplay, intercourse and especially orgasm, is to be devalued accordingly.

Under this theory of sexuality, masturbation is viewed as "imitation" sex. Instead of a real partner, one employs a fantasy partner (or partners). One uses fantasy through each of the steps: foreplay, intercourse, orgasm. This seems to more closely fit the male experience of masturbation than the female experience of masturbation. Women do not, generally, counterfeit intercourse while masturbating.[5]

The second folk theory which I will consider is one based on a semi-combative situation: a baseball game. Sexual partners are on opposite teams. Baseball game stages have, roughly, the following sex stage equivalents:

Getting to first base: holding hands
Getting to second base: kissing, hugging
Getting to third base: petting, leading perhaps to orgasm
Home run: intercourse leading to orgasm (scoring).

As in the first theory, the final stage of the ideal sexual act is seen as intercourse/orgasm. The stages of mutual arousal are seen as preparatory to, and incomplete without, the final step, which marks the end of sexual desire. Each of the bases is seen as a stage of increased intimacy. These bases the male attempts to achieve; the female resists. For females to yield any particular base, we were told, was to decrease their ability to resist yielding to the next base. We were told this to strike fear into our hearts, for to yield to the last step was to risk pregnancy and the loss of respect of the male aggressor, indeed of all males. The achievement of each step marked better sex for the male, the achievement of the last step marked the best sex for the male.

These theories, which have a male-bias implicit in their emphasis on intercourse, are common and probably thought by many to be commonsensical ways of organizing and evaluating sexual behavior. They illustrate what I see is one purpose served by theories of sexuality: they may help us to understand and evaluate a sexual experience. As theories, they provide a point of view which can help to organize the experience with its accompanying chaotic emotions. The theories can help us to find a design, form or pattern in our sexual experience, or suggest a purpose it may serve.

Is sex then a tragedy or game? This question might be answered, "it depends upon one's point of view" or "it may be viewed in either way, or even in both."

It seems to me that we may tolerate more than one theory of what sex is because each theory may clarify various sexual experiences for us,[6] or provide us with a new way of viewing the experience.

Under the following theory, an ideal sexual act, at least in part, is an act of inquiry and of coming to know. This is an act of artistic inquiry rather than scientific inquiry. In masturbation, one's subject of inquiry is one's own body and its response to touch, environment and fantasy. In the case of sex-with-a-partner, the subject of inquiry is one's own body in relationship to another's, and also the body of one's lover. In sex-with-a-partner, one is, in turn, a subject of inquiry for one's partner. There is a relationship between the self-knowledge gained in masturbation and successful sex with oneself or with another person. There is also a relationship between the knowledge gained in sex-with-a-partner and successful sex with that partner and perhaps other partners as well. Successful sex is seen as mutually satisfying sex where the rights and desires of each person involved in a particular sexual act are acknowledged and respected by each person. This involves acknowledgment of and respect for one's own rights and desires as well as acknowledgment of and respect for one's partner's rights and desires.[7] Self-sacrifice in a sexual encounter has the negative moral consequences that it has in other situations.[8] I will not detail the rights and desires of sexual partners, nor what constitutes acknowledgment and respect for such rights and desires.

After presenting my contribution to a theory of sexuality in our culture, I will briefly discuss several male-authored theories of sexuality, exhibiting their implicit male bias and consequent devaluation of masturbation and by extension, female sexual response.

The artistic inquirer values a sexual act not for its outcome but for its structure in the present. The structure is valued as coherent, interesting and pleasing. The structure of the activity is the result of my actions and possibly the actions of another person. Lovers are seen in this structure as individuals with unique responses to the changes we make in our environment, to the things I do with them.

If sexual behavior is seen as a scientific inquiry, the qualitative differences between lovers is ignored. Rather than consider this lover in terms of his or her unique qualities, desires and responses (especially his or her attractive qualities, desires and responses), the scientific inquirer concentrates only on what every lover has in common: breasts, mouth, genitals. Being seen as an interchangeable body involves an extreme loss of individuality. The scientific inquirer is out to be "good in bed" as if this were an independent skill, like being a good swimmer. The artistic inquirer is out to be "good for this person, my lover, in bed." This lover is not indistinguishable from all others.

The scientific lover may suffer from what I call the "kinflicks syndrome."[9] Rather than coming to know and accepting who his (her) partner is, s(he) sees her (him) as material to be acted upon so as to transform her (him) into a new person who better answers his (her) needs. The person is seen as something to be molded, rather than something to be accepted.

I choose to call the type of lover I have been advocating an "artistic inquirer." The artistic inquirer sees a partner as a particular individualized human being. This lover is fragrant, attractive, responsive, has a particular shape, color, texture, taste, and inspires in me various emotions such as fear, hope, joy, sorrow, aversion and desire. This particular lover responds and reacts to me in his or her unique way. I have a relationship to this person that I have with no other. I respond to this person in a way I respond to no other. Time is taken to attend to the minute details of the experience with the other.

In the case of masturbation, a similar process is noticed. My own body responds to my fantasies, my touch, my chosen environment. I can be an attentive, inventive lover of myself.

Masturbation is not then seen as a stop-gap sexual activity to be used to fill up the lag-time between sexual relationships. It is, rather, a legitimate learning activity which requires that one have solitude. The desire to be alone contrasts with the frustrated desire to be with friends and/or lovers.

The nature of the inquiry with respect to self is very thoroughly described by the women quoted in the *Hite Report*. Women who responded to Shere Hite's question, "What is the importance of masturbation?" with the answer, "Masturbation is a learning experience," have elaborated on this answer with great scope. As one woman stated, "Through masturbation I learn how my body can feel and how it wants and likes to feel."[10] To systematize their responses, these women learned:

(1) That they could achieve orgasm.
(2) How to achieve orgasm.
(3) What happens during arousal and orgasm.
(4) What is pleasurable to their bodies.

They also learned to have orgasms and to accept their having them, which reflects an attitudinal change about their sexuality. All this self-knowledge seems to me to be contributory to successful sex with another person, which is not to say that women will not gain more self-knowledge in a sexual experience with a partner.

I am not arguing that the sole purpose of sexual self-knowledge is its possible effect on enhancing sexual experiences with a partner.

With sex-with-a-partner, we modify our knowledge of another person and we modify their knowledge of ourselves. We are taught and we are teachers. Sexual behavior is an overt doing: we make definite changes in our environment and in our relation to it. The outcome of sexual behavior is, under my theory, a coming to know more about one's self in relationship to another person and a coming to know another person. As such, one is free to experiment with sex. Making love tests my beliefs about who my lover is, how she or he will respond to me, and how I will respond to him or her. Making love modifies my knowledge of my lover and myself. I initiate actions which elicit some previously unperceived qualities and responses of my partner. Together, we are both subject and objects of this experience. With a long-time partner, I initiate actions which elicit qualities and responses which are not usually perceived; our sexual response to each other is generally private to us.

In making love with another person, it is clear that I am learning about my body in response to another particular person's body. Contrast my lover's touch and a stranger's touch. If someone puts his/her hand between my legs on a crowded bus, I feel harmed, degraded, used and angry. If my lover puts his/her hand between my legs it may feel warm, inviting, comforting, pleasing, soothing, loving and sexually exciting.

If the other person is an open question, not a closed one, there is no closure after an act of love.[11] Orgasm does not automatically signal the end of sexual feeling. There is, also, a part deferred for another occasion, no final definition of who I am and who my lover is. There is always the uncertainty of the future, with each particular act of sex hopefully establishing conditions favorable to subsequent acts. I have a tendency to modify indeterminate and ambiguous conditions in the direction of a preferred and favored outcome: what I want. That is, usually, a continuation of a relationship in which my needs and my lover's needs are met. The same can be said in regard to masturbation where I and my lover are one and the same. Each particular act of masturbation hopefully establishes conditions favorable to subsequent acts. It is possible to be alienated from myself. For example, I may use fantasies which arouse self-disgust or self-pity and thereafter hesitate to continue a sexual relationship with myself.

What I have learned from past experiences with other people is data which may serve as an indication or clue as to how to love a particular person, but it is an indicator or clue of something still to be reached. It is an intermediate step, not a finality. What I have known in the past is not a standard which my present lover must live up to. Various pornographic publications, such as *Penthouse*, imply standards of sexual behavior and response. For example, they imply that many women achieve orgasm via anal and oral intercourse. They are more radical than was Freud, in this respect. This is a performance standard which many women do not live up to. It can be used by a male partner to treat his woman as abnormal, not sexy and so on. I argue that it is incoherent to inflict pseudo-moral condemnations on a partner's sexual performance, as a sexual relation to another starts with that other as the unique individual he or she is, with the right to have his or her sexual preferences and desires respected.

My theory of sexuality yields one more definition of sex object, and explains why it is offensive to be treated as such. I am a sex object if I am with a scientific lover who treats me as if I were interchangable with any other woman. Such a lover loves me "by the book," pushing buttons and waiting for the desired response. It is offensive because it involves, among other things, an extreme loss of individuality.

According to my theory, minimal sex includes one-night stands and sex with prostitutes because there is, generally, no importance in these situations attached to coming to know the other person, who is likely to be treated as a sex object. Other persons are not valued for who they are in themselves and the possibility of intimacy is shunned or ignored. These minimal sexual experiences increase self-knowledge very little, if at all. I am not in relationship to another person who is acting as an anonymous body. I am avoiding the other and, therefore, avoiding myself.

What kind of self-knowledge does one gain from sex with prostitutes and one-night stands? It seems to me that if these practices made up the bulk of one's sexual experience, it would indicate a lack of self-knowledge and knowledge of others, just as it would indicate a lack of self-knowledge and knowledge of art if one chose paintings and prints by the cubic foot to cover a wall, or a lack of self-knowledge and knowledge of literature if one bought books by the yard to fill shelves.

It seems to me that sex with prostitutes and one-night stands are employed to gain sexual satisfaction by eliminating the problems of coping with other real persons. It does so only by disregarding or having little concern for one's sexual partner in a situation fraught with potential for regarding this person. In coupled sexual behavior one can satisfy a general desire to be recognized as a particular real person who positively affects another particular real person. To ignore this, it seems to me, is to ignore a large part of what makes coupled sexual behavior rewarding.

Have I been arguing that sex is immoral in the absence of intimacy? An analysis of the concept of intimacy is beyond the scope of the present paper. It seems to be a concept at least as complex as sex. The concepts of self-knowledge, knowledge of partners and (probably) intimacy, are related to the concept of vulnerability. Many women feel vulnerable in sexual relations with others. The following analogy may illustrate the desirability, from the point of view of the vulnerable, of knowledge of self and of partners.

Suppose friendly fights were seen in our society as a "natural" way of expressing that side of our human nature. It would seem that we'd want to control various parameters of encounters in which interpersonal violence would be likely to occur. We probably would like to know our potential sparring partners at least well enough to trust them not to use brass knuckles or other unfair tactics, or to take advantage of our revealed weaknesses. We would probably like to know them well enough to support the belief that we are like them in strength, proficiency, stamina and the other variables relevant to fighting. On a meta-level, we'd probably like to know them well enough to believe that they have been honest in revealing to us what we have come to learn about them as potential sparring partners and actual sparring partners. We, on our part, have had to be honest with them about our own fighting strengths, weaknesses, abilities, patterns and trustworthiness. We could have fights with people that we didn't have negative feelings towards, but might feel that fights where such feelings mutually existed were indeed more satisfying. It seems clear, however, that trust in and knowledge of the other person would be significantly more important prerequisites to satisfying fight encounters than mutual enmity. The strongest reason for this is that in the fight we are vulnerable: we are liable to be wounded or hurt. Knowledge of our potential sparring partner enables us to gauge how vulnerable we are likely to be and to decide where, when, how and with whom to fight. Exactly how vulnerable do we wish to allow ourselves to be, relative to what we judge to be the benefits and desirability of fighting? The weakest of us will be the least likely to pick fights with complete strangers, especially those who appear to be much stronger than ourselves. I conclude it would be mutually desirable to be intimate , knowledgeable fighters if we didn't want to take unfair advantage of or be unfairly taken advantage of, in fight encounters.

Sexual encounters are distinct from the imaginary fighting encounters I have described above in that the desire is *not* to minimize being hurt and/or hurting but to maximize being pleasured and/or pleasuring. Perhaps it is easier to hurt someone than to pleasure them. The following are some of the reasons why women feel vulnerable, open to wounding, in sexual encounters. Women have "performance anxiety," they feel they are inadequate in their ability to pleasure. Is it assumed in our culture that you'll be an excellent lover, advanced in the technique of love making? In the "fight metaphor" it seemed unlikely that the assumption that each and every potential sparring partner would be an excellent, highly experienced fighter would be made.

In being honest about our sexual needs, in being simply naked with our imperfect bodies, we are open to ridicule. Women in our culture fear that male sexual partners are interested only in self-gratification. Women are afraid they will become subjects of "locker room" discourse and be on display as a prime trophy, a sexual conquest. There are probably other reasons for feeling vulnerable as well. All the fear, low esteem, and lack of confidence which gather about the thought of ourselves cluster also about the thought of actions in which we are sexual partners.

Am I arguing that, ideally, fantasy is not a part of sex with oneself or sex with other people? In masturbation, it seems clear to me that self-knowledge can arise out of the reflective use of fantasies. It is clear also that fantasies can be employed in a similar way in two-person sex. It is only when I use the other person as an anonymous body upon which to project my sexual fantasies that I am avoiding the person I am presumably being intimate with.

The following male-authored theories of sexuality ignore women's experience of sex, especially as it is described in the *Hite Report*. These theories all describe masturbation as less than ideal sex when masturbation is compared to sex with a partner. They do not attempt to coherently describe the experience of masturbation, and they distort the experience in order to fit the particular theory. As such, they simply reflect common prejudices about masturbation.

The traditional puritanical view of sex is that sex is strictly for an ulterior purpose—producing babies. Pleasure is a by-product if it is there at all. The most stunning condemnation of masturbation, from this traditional point of view, was probably written by Immanual Kant, who wrote that it "transcends in magnitude the guilt of self-murder."[12] This he concluded because it shows an admirable valour to commit suicide, while masturbation is the "effeminate surrender to sensitive excitement."[13] Kant believes it is a moral failing even to use the word "masturbation"[14] and it is possible to know what he is talking about only from the context of his words. Kant offers the following argument by analogy to prove that the purpose of sex is reproduction: "As the love of life is bestowed upon us for the preservation of our person . . . so the love of sex is bestowed upon us for the continuance of our kind."[15] It therefore subverts the end of nature to masturbate. However, Kant also argues that masturbation is unnatural because a man is impelled to do it not by a real sexual situation but by the productive power of his imagination.[16] This is an objection to masturbation which he shares with Sartre and Laing. Furthermore, he goes on to state that "man meanly abdicates his personality, when he attempts to employ himself as a mere means to satisfy a brutal lust."[17] Why is masturbation not seen as a purely pleasurable activity, important in its own right? This is certainly a common view of masturbation, as indicated by respondents to the Hite questionnaire.

Kant's second objection to masturbation has an epistemological foundation. Sartre writes, ". . . Solitude, impotence, the unreal, evil, have produced, without recourse to being, *an event in the world*."[18] R. D. Laing writes, "the body-in-relation-to the actual others is in some senses an instrument for dealing with others. But the body as used in the act of masturbation is employed with the express intention of gaining satisfaction by eliminating the problems of coping with other real bodies."[19] Laing, Sartre and Kant all object to masturbation on the grounds that a fantasy and not a real person produces real bodily excitement, real orgasm and real relaxation. A food fantasy when you are hungry will not produce a real feeling of having feasted. Notice also that all three view sexual feelings as reactive in nature. Bodily excitement is a feeling produced by the other, either real or imagined. It seems to me that the responsibility for my arousal and my orgasm lie with me.

All three conceive of masturbation as a counterfeit of sex-with-a-partner. Laing confuses the issue even more by stating that sex-with-a-partner may be a counterfeit for masturbation.[20]

Laing states that sexual fantasies may become a substitute for reality or even become confused with reality. He details how confused this reality may become:

The habitual masturbator often feels awkward, gauche, self-conscious, fearful that he will get inappropriately worked up in the real presence of others. He is afraid that his body will be out of his control if his masturbatory images 'come into his mind' when he is with others—he is afraid that his body will start reacting as he has trained it to do 'in' imagination. In this, there may be a wide difference between how his body feels to him and how it appears to another. But the physical fusion of imagination and reality in masturbation may lead him to fear that he will confuse them in a public situation. Such intrusion from the private masturbation situation in the public realm entail the possibility that the real others fail to be adequately and veridically perceived in their otherness.[21]

It is not necessary to employ fantasy in masturbating, and it may be sufficient. It is very baffling to philosophers that persons may respond to a sexual fantasy by having all of the emotions that they would have if the fantasy were true, that is, an actual happening. It seems to me that only in pathological instances does a masturbator believe that he or she had a sexual experience with a real partner. Further confusion is contributed by Sartre, who calls "honest" the masturbator who resorts to masturbation for want of anything more actual (as if anything were more actual), and "dishonest" the masturbator who prefers it.[22]

Why is truth or reality such an important value in sexual activity? How can a person be sexually moved by—or even actually seek—fantasies? Since fantasies are not true, the effect is inappropriate and, were some common masochistic and sadistic fantasies true, the effect would be guilt-producing or nonexistent. Are not fantasies of inflicting pain, being raped, or having pain inflicted panderings to human baseness? I do not have the answer to these questions.

What fascinates me is that this condemnation of masturbation, which is an objection to a fantasy creating a real sexual response, exactly parallels Plato's condemnation of the arts. Plato objected to the fact that people viewed tragedies, fictional in nature, and experienced real tears.

Plato believed that the dramatic might become a substitute for reality. Laing worries that masturbation might become a substitute for sex-with-a-partner. The parallel breaks down at this point. Masturbation is not a dramatic fiction, a representation of a sexual experience while not itself a sexual experience. Masturbating is not acting, or method acting; it is an actual sexual act.

Is there a substantial basis for Laing's fear? Aristotle attempted to justify "catharsis," or the real emotional relief achieved by viewing a tragedy. He felt there was a reality behind a dramatic fantasy, that there was a truth to the realization and presentation of specific experiences. It seems necessary to answer the question: what is the reality behind fantasy in sex? I cannot answer it.

Freudians, in addition to Sartre, argue that habitual masturbators suffer a pesonality split. The masturbator becomes both lover and loved. Since Freudian theory yields this conclusion which is so contrary to common sense and the experience of women, I feel the theory should be rejected. It is surely absurd to claim that all habitual masturbators are by definition schizophrenic!

Robert C. Solomon is a modern philosopher who has offered the novel theory that sexuality is a body language, at least in our society. His view leads to two paradoxical conclusions: (1) sex is not, purely and primarily, a matter of enjoyment; (2) masturbation is like talking to one's self.[23] His view also leads to the factually false conclusion that masturbation is practiced after the body language is learned from another person.[24] While it may be true that one can employ the English language alone only after one has learned it from others, it is simply false that the so-called language of sex is employed alone only after one has learned it from others. George Groddeck's comments from *The Book of The It*, while exemplifying the seemingly inevitable male bias (by restricting masturbation to onanism, he is talking about spilling one's seed), make this point very well:

... I should like to call attention to a strange distortion of the facts of which even men otherwise sensible are found guilty. They call masturbation a substitute for the normal sex act. Ah, what might not be written about that word "normal" sexual act!

... In one form or another onanism accompanies man throughout his life, while normal sex activity only begins at a particular age, and often ceases at a time when onanism takes on again the childish form of a conscious playing with the sexual organs. How can the one process be regarded as a substitute for another which only starts fifteen to twenty years later?[25]

Solomon argues that sex is not, primarily, a matter of enjoyment. He states that there are three platitudes constituting the liberal attitude towards sexuality: (1) sexuality aims at pleasure; (2) sexual activity is and ought to be essentially private; (3) any sexual activity is as valid as any other. Solomon denies (1) in favor of the communication model: (4) sexuality aims at communicating feelings. Note that he does not have to deny (1) in order to affirm (4). He reasons that if sexuality is aimed at pleasure, then masturbation would be preferred to sexual activity between persons, because according to tests made by Masters and Johnson, the intensity of orgasm is stronger during masturbation than during intercourse. This proof that sexuality does not aim at pleasure is

only a proof that it does not necessarily aim at maximizing orgasmic intensity. It ignores the fact that in two-person sex it is very
possible to achieve the intensity of orgasm reached in masturbation merely by achieving it in a way that doesn't require intercourse. It ignores the fact that some people may prefer sex-with-a-
partner even though the intensity of orgasm may be diminished.
In fact, some women prefer sex with a partner even though they
do not "achieve" orgasm when having sex with a partner, as was
indicated by some of the women in the *Hite Report.*[26]

If sex is a language, Solomon argues, masturbation is like talking to one's self. He writes:

Masturbation is not 'self-abuse,' as we were once taught, but it is, in an
important sense, self-denial. It represents an inability or a refusal to say
what one wants to say, going through the effort of expression without an
audience, like writing to someone and then putting the letter in a draw-
er.[27]

There are people who keep journals, and those who sit and
think to themselves. It does not seem necessary to have a continual audience. Since language is an independent skill, which is conventional in nature, Solomon appears to be advocating a type of
sexuality exhibited by what I called the "scientific lover."

Alan H. Goldman's analysis of sexuality is both over- and un-
der-inclusive, although he attempts to eliminate obvious counter-
examples to it. He defines sexual desire/activity as follows:

Sexual desire is desire for contact with another person's body and for the
pleasure such contact produces; sexual activity is activity which tends to
fulfill such desire of the agent.[28]

Goldman considers several apparent counter-examples to show
it is over-inclusive. It seems over-inclusive, according to Goldman, because it would lead us to ". . . interpret physical contact as
sexual desire in activities such as football and other contact
sports"[29] and to interpret as sexual desire ". . . a baby's desire to
be cuddled and our natural response in wanting to cuddle it."
Goldman feels that he has eliminated these two apparent counter-
examples and/or reinterpreted them as examples of sexual desire
in the following way. The first apparent counter-example he eliminates on the grounds that the desire for contact ". . . is not directed toward a particular person for that purpose, and it is not the
goal of the activity—the goal is winning or exercising or knocking
someone down or displaying one's prowess."[30] He also reinter-

prets this counter-example in order to show that it might be seen as an example of sexual desire. He states, "If the desire is purely for contact with another specific person's body, then to interpret it as sexual does not seem an exaggeration."[31] This is Goldman's supplement to his original definition. He manipulates very similarly the apparent counter-example about the baby. If ours or the baby's actions are intended to show affection or seek a sign of affection, it is not the desire for "pure physical contact" and, therefore, it is not "clearly sexual." Again, Goldman adds that it is possible to view the baby's desire for cuddling and our response to it as sexual. He also considers signs of affection among men or women and eliminates them for the same reasons. He states: ". . . these certainly need not be homosexual when the intent is only to show friendship, something extrinsic to plain sex although valuable."[32]

The counter-examples are very interesting to me in their selectivity rather than their inclusivity. Contact sports. A baby's desire to be cuddled. Signs of affection among members of the same gender-identity group. Contact sports have been, almost exclusively, a male's domain. Babies are not singular in their desire to be cuddled; this is a trait they share with adults. It would seem that members of different gender-identity groups could show signs of non-sexual affection towards each other. Goldman's definition clearly must find some way of eliminating a lot of touching, in fact most touching between human beings that intuitively seems non-sexual. Do the criteria that he uses in eliminating the above counter-examples work? It seems to me that there are quite obvious counter-examples to Goldman's supplement to his original definition. Assuming that pure desire is desire untainted by any other desires, I rewrite Goldman's original definition as: Sexual desire is pure desire for contact with another specific person's body and for the pleasure which such contact produces; sexual activity is activity which tends to fulfill such desire of the agent. This revised definition will exclude much ordinary sex. Many desires and actions that appeared sexual in pre-Goldman-analysis days, are not sexual on the basis of this definition. It is a brute fact that people desire contact with another person's body without directing that desire towards another specific person's body. Men sometimes desire to have sex with a prostitute, and any prostitute will do. Men and women pick up others in bars, and any person will do. Men commit rape and any woman will do. Goldman's definition revised so as not to include too many desires/acts as sexual now excludes many desires/acts surely sexual in nature.

It is also a brute fact that many sexual desires/acts are included in other intentional acts that the participant(s) hope to achieve. Sex may be "used" to comfort, and/or to be comforted, to love and/or be loved, to dominate and/or to be dominated, and so on. Again, on the revised definition, they are not sexual desires/acts.

Both his original definition and the amended definition have a significant poignant counter-example. Consider a woman who is facing her first sexual experience which will include intercourse with a male. She knows that the experience is likely to be very painful. Does she, by Goldman's definition, experience a sexual desire/act? If so, do we conclude she is a masochist? If not, the definition is inadequate.

Goldman eliminates obvious counter-examples to the effect that his definition is too narrow, such as "looking or conversing in a sexual way without body contact, voyeurism and masturbation," by making all three "parasitic" on the real thing.[33] The first is seen as a fore-fore play, at least in intention. Goldman writes: "while looking at or conversing with someone can be interpreted as sexual in given contexts it is so when intended as preliminary to, and hence parasitic upon, elemental sexual interest."[34] Voyeurism and masturbation are imaginative substitutes for the real thing. Therefore, these three apparent sexual activities are not in fact sexual activities.

The difficulties inherent in Goldman's attempts to define sexual desire/act become apparent in the following construction of a similarly simplistic definition. *Plain violence*: The desire for violence is the desire to inflict pain on another person's body and for the pleasure such contact produces; violent activity is activity which tends to fulfill such desire of the agent.

Again we'd have to worry about contact sports, spanking children, friendly fights and, if we revised the definition to eliminate these counter-examples, we'd have to worry about randomly violent actions and fights in which other intentions are present. Nonphysical violence, voyeuristic violence that comes in watching T.V., and self-inflicted violence would be reinterpreted as imaginative substitutes for the real thing. They would be deviant violent behavior, parasitic upon real (plain) violence.

Masturbation is sinful, states Kant. According to Solomon, it's done for the sake of autoeroticism, which he sees as childish behavior, or it's done out of narcissism, which he sees as potentially pathetic or selfish and self-indulgent. According to Sartre it's "honest" if one does it for want of anything better and "dishonest" if one prefers it. Goldman finds it a substitute for the real thing. If we examine women's experience, as revealed by the *Hite Report*, there are far more reasons given for masturbation:

A. Masturbation as a substitute for sex (or orgasm) with a partner.
B. Masturbation as a learning experience.
C. Masturbation as an aid to having better sex with another person.
D. Masturbation as a means of independence and self-reliance.
E. Masturbation as pure pleasure, important in its own right.

In closing, I would like to make some comments about A, C and D.

The most common response to "What is the importance of masturbation" was A. Masturbation as a substitute for sex (or orgasm) with a partner. This answer bears a resemblance to the characterization of masturbation given by male-oriented theories of sexuality. It substitutes for sex with a partner, either by choice or necessity. There is an important difference in the response of the women to Hite's questionnaire. Women who are engaging in sex with a partner sometimes masturbate because they fail to achieve orgasm while doing so.[35] The addendum "either by choice or necessity" seems to me to be a *non sequitur* in this latter instance. One can choose not to be with other people, although one has the possibility of being so; one may feel that "by necessity" one masturbates, because there is no possibility of being with another person. It stands in need of a great deal of qualification to speak of choosing not to orgasm with a partner or not orgasming with a partner "by necessity" because one cannot choose to. The former smacks of masochism and the latter of physical infirmity. Speaking in this way, it lays the burden of responsibility for choosing to or having to masturbate in order to achieve sexual satisfaction after sex with a partner on the woman and not on her partner. The possibility that her partner is partially responsible for the fact that she failed to achieve orgasm is at least a real one.

Masturbation helped some women to have better sex with another person. This answer raises some interesting points about sex. In our society, it is still generally momentous to engage in sex with another person. This has made it imperative to most of us that we control as much as possible what happens in a sexual encounter. The self-knowledge gained from masturbating helps us to control the situation. In other societies "breaking bread" with another has the effect of substantially changing one's relationship with another—in our society sex has a privileged position of significance. Saving another person's life is perhaps the only other act of similar significance.

Perhaps few men can appreciate the fact that masturbation is an important means of independence and self-reliance for women. Solomon asks why we bother with two-person sex given the enormous amounts of effort and the continuous threats to our egos and our health. But women risk far more in our society than their egos and their health if they do not or cannot engage in sexual activity with the socially defined "right" person at the socially defined "right" time. In being sexually intimate with a man, they risk loss of virginity, still a gift to bring to marriage, unwanted pregnancy and/or unwanted complications from dangerous birth control devices, a loss of status, esteem and power. In being sexually intimate with another woman they risk the love of friends and family, jobs and even occupations, the loss of children in child-custody suits, and the loss of credibility and power. I'm sure I've just scratched the surface as to what women have to lose by engaging in sexual activity not validated by cultural norms. A woman has, also, something to lose in engaging in sexual activity validated by cultural norms—the loss of her freedom. For many women, the question may well be, is sex worth all of that?

NOTES

1. Shere Hite, *The Hite Report: A Nationwide Study of Female Sexuality* (New York: Dell, 1976), p. 61.
2. *Ibid.*,
3. R. D. Laing, *The Self and Others: Further Studies in Sanity and Madness* (Chicago: Quadrangle Books, 1962), p. 47.
4. *Ibid.*, p. 39.
5. Hite, *op. cit.*, p. 123. "Of all the women who described how they masturbated, only 1.5 percent masturbated only by the vaginal insertion, plus another .4 percent who used this method sometimes. Over half of these women stimulated their clitoral areas first manually."
6. For an explanation of a related phenomenon in aesthetics, see Joseph Margolis, "The Logic of Interpretation," *Philosophy Looks at the Arts: Contemporary Readings in Aesthetics*, ed. Margolis (New York: Charles Scribner's Sons, 1962), pp. 108–117.
7. This is properly the subject of another paper.
8. For a discussion of self-sacrifice in general see Judith Tormey, "Exploitation, Oppression and Self-Sacrifice," in Carol C. Gould and Marx W. Wartofsky, eds., *Women and Philosophy: Toward a Theory of Liberation* (New York: Putnam's, 1976), pp. 206–221.

408   **THE PHILOSOPHY OF SEX**

9. Ginny, heroine of Lisa Alther's *Kinflicks* (New York: New American Library, 1977) is a paradigm victim of the Kinflicks syndrome.
10. Hite, *op. cit.*, p. 74.
11. A stranger, to continue the metaphor, is not an open question because s(he) is not a question at all.
12. Immanuel Kant, *The Metaphysic of Ethics*, trans. by J. W. Semple (Edinburgh: Thomas Clark, 1836), p. 265.
13. *Ibid.*,
14. *Ibid.*, p. 264.
15. *Ibid.*, p. 262.
16. *Ibid.*, p. 263.
17. *Ibid.*, p. 264.
18. Laing, *op. cit.*, p. 43.
19. *Ibid.*, p. 40.
20. This is discussed earlier in the present paper.
21. Laing, *op. cit.*, pp. 40–41.
22. *Ibid.*, p. 42.
23. Robert Solomon, "Sex and Perversion," in Robert Baker and Frederick Elliston, eds., *Philosophy and Sex* (Buffalo, N.Y.: Prometheus, 1975), p. 281.
24. Robert Solomon, "Sexual Paradigms," in this volume, pp. 89–98; p. 96.
25. George Groddeck, *The Book of The It* (New York: Vintage, 1961), p. 45.
26. Hite, *op. cit.*, pp. 135–137.
27. Solomon, "Sex and Perversion," *op. cit.*, p. 283.
28. Alan H. Goldman, "Plain Sex," in this volume, pp. 119–138; p. 120.
29. *Ibid.*, p. 121.
30. *Ibid.*, p. 121.
31. *Ibid.*, p. 121.
32. *Ibid.*, p. 122.
33. *Ibid.*, p. 122.
34. *Ibid.*, p. 122.
35. Hite, *op. cit.*, pp. 72–78.

Notes on Contributors

FRED R. BERGER, Associate Professor of Philosophy at The University of California at Davis, is the author of *Studying Deductive Logic*, the editor of *Freedom of Expression*, and is currently writing a book *Happiness, Justice and Freedom: Central Themes in the Moral and Political Philosophy of John Stuart Mill*. He has also published articles on ethics and contemporary social and political philosophy in *American Philosophical Quarterly, Ethics, Philosophical Review,* and *Interpretation*.

ANN FERGUSON teaches philosophy at the University of Massachusetts in Amherst. Active in the Marxist Activist Philosophers group, her interests include social thought, ethics, aesthetics, and feminist studies.

JACQUELINE FORTUNATA, formerly a philosophy teacher at the College of St. Catherine, has begun a new career in educational technology. At the Control Data Corporation in Minneapolis, she has been developing management courses using computer-assisted instruction.

BERNARD GENDRON is Associate Professor of Philosophy at The University of Wisconsin (Milwaukee). He has published mainly in the areas of philosophy of science, philosophy of technology, and Marxism. The author of *Technology and the Human Condition,* he is currently working on a book, *Exploitation,* which will include a discussion of sexual exploitation.

ALAN GOLDMAN is Associate Professor of Philosophy at The University of Miami. He is the author of *Justice and Reverse Dis-*

crimination, Moral Foundations of Professional Ethics, and articles on epistemology and metaphysics.

ROBERT GRAY has been Assistant Professor of Philosophy at both McMaster University and The University of Richmond. He is currently studying computer science. His articles on Hume, Hobbes and Berkeley have appeared in *Hume Studies, Journal of the History of Ideas* and *Journal of the History of Philosophy.*

ALISON M. JAGGAR is Associate Professor of Philosophy at The University of Cincinnati. She is the author of a number of papers on feminism and other topics within ethical, social and political philosophy. The co-editor of *Feminist Frameworks,* she is currently working on a new book, *The Philosophical Foundations of Feminism.*

SARA ANN KETCHUM teaches ethics, political philosophy, and philosophical feminism at The State University of New York College at Oswego. She has published articles in these fields, and is currently working on theoretical problems related to the inclusion of reproduction and of labor on persons in Marxist political theory.

DONALD LEVY teaches philosophy at Brooklyn College (City University of New York) and The New School for Social Research. His "The Definition of Love in Plato's *Symposium*" appeared in *The Journal of the History of Ideas* in April, 1979. He is currently editing *Philosophy and Psychology of Love,* to be published by the Free Press.

JANICE MOULTON has taught philosophy at the University of North Carolina, Temple University and the University of Maryland, and is currently at the University of Kentucky. She is author of the *Guidebook for Publishing Philosophy,* coauthor (with G. M. Robinson) of *The Organization of Language,* and has written in the fields of the philosophy of language, philosophy of mind, philosophy of feminism and philosophical methodology.

THOMAS NAGEL, Professor of Philosophy at Princeton University and associate editor of the journal *Philosophy and Public Affairs,* is the author of *The Possibility of Altruism* and *Mortal Questions.*

L. NATHAN OAKLANDER studied with Gustav Bergmann at The University of Iowa and is presently Associate Professor of Philosophy at The University of Michigan—Flint. He has published articles in *Mind, Nous, Philosophical Studies,* and *Philosophy of Science* on various topics, including univerals and particulars, the emotions, Berkeley's philosophy, and time. He is currently working on a book on the Russellian theory of time.

ELIZABETH RAPAPORT is Associate Professor of Philosophy at Boston University. She has written articles on ethics, politics and feminism. She is currently writing a book on Marxist political theory.

LEE C. RICE did his graduate work as a Fulbright fellow at the University of Paris and as a Kent and Woodrow Wilson fellow at St. Louis University. He is now Associate Professor of Philosophy at Marquette University. His published works include articles on Spinoza, reviews and discussion articles in the philosophy and history of science, and a large number of critical reviews in gay liberation periodicals.

RICHARD SENNETT is University Professor of the Humanities at New York University. Among his books are *Families Against the City, The Uses of Disorder,* and *The Fall of Public Man* . He is a regular contributor to *The New York Review of Books, The New Yorker,* and *Partisan Review,* and is currently working on a book, *The Sadness of the Eye,* about the psychology of authority.

IRVING SINGER is Professor of Philosophy at the Massachusetts Institute of Technology. He is the author of several essays on myths of love in the Western world and of three books related to the philosophy of love and sexuality: *The Nature of Love: Plato to Luther, The Goals of Human Sexuality,* and *Mozart and Beethoven: The Concept of Love in Their Operas.* Professor Singer has also published articles on art theory and a book on aesthetics. He is currently at work on a book, the sequel to *The Nature of Love,* which studies courtly, romantic, and naturalistic concepts of sexual love from the 12th through the 19th century.

ALAN SOBLE has taught philosophy at the State University of New York at Buffalo, The University of Texas at Austin, Southern Methodist University, and The University of New Orleans. In 1977 he founded *The Society for the Philosophy of Sex and Love.*

ROBERT SOLOMON is Professor of Philosophy at The University of Texas at Austin. Among his books are *From Rationalism to Existentialism, The Passions,* and *History and Human Nature.* He is currently writing a book on romantic love.

ROGER TAYLOR is Lecturer in Philosophy at Sussex University in England. He is the author of *Art an Enemy of the People* and the forthcoming *Beyond Art.* He is currently working on the construction of a new theory of anarchism.

HUGH T. WILDER is Associate Professor of Philosophy at Miami University in Ohio. He has written in the philosophy of language, including transformational grammar and French "post-structuralist" critical theory. He is now working on theories of psychoanalysis, especially as it relates to sexuality and language.